Postsuburban California

Orange County: cities and major unincorporated communities

Postsuburban California

The Transformation of Orange County since World War II

EDITED BY

Rob Kling,
Spencer Olin,
and
Mark Poster

UNIVERSITY OF CALIFORNIA PRESS
Berkeley   Los Angeles   Oxford

University of California Press
Berkeley and Los Angeles, California

University of California Press, Ltd.
Oxford, England

© 1991 by
The Regents of the University of California

Library of Congress Cataloging-in-Publication Data

Postsuburban California : the transformation of Orange County
since World War II / edited by Rob Kling, Spencer Olin, and Mark
Poster.
    p. cm.
Includes bibliographical references.
ISBN 0-520-06716-9 (alk. paper)
    1. Orange County (Calif.)—Social conditions.   I. Kling, Rob.
II. Olin, Spencer.   III. Poster, Mark.
HN79.C220726   1991
306'.09794'96—dc20   90-10703
                                                                      CIP

Printed in the United States of America
1   2   3   4   5   6   7   8   9

CONTENTS

ONE

The Emergence of Postsuburbia: An Introduction

Rob Kling,
Spencer Olin, and Mark Poster

THE GROWTH OF ORANGE COUNTY

On March 8, 1889, the California Senate voted to carve a new political entity out of the southern portion of Los Angeles County. Two months later the voters of this proposed County of Orange overwhelmingly approved its formation. At that time the editorial writer of the Los Angeles *Express,* a leading newspaper of the day, proclaimed: "Wayward sister, depart in peace."

Now, a century later, that wayward sister, Orange County, has matured into an increasingly important component of a larger southern California region comprising Los Angeles, Ventura, San Bernardino, Riverside, and Orange counties. For several decades this region has been one of the major industrial metropolises in the world.[1] Within it Orange County has developed its own powerful subregional economy, which exceeded $60 billion in 1989 (compared with $13.5 billion in 1975), making it the nation's tenth largest county economy. That economy has not only surpassed the neighboring state of Arizona's but now ranks among the top thirty in the world, along with the economies of Argentina, Austria, Denmark, and Egypt.

After World War II Orange County evolved from a rural county into an industrial region and bedroom adjunct to Los Angeles and finally into a complex metropolitan region, consisting of twenty-eight separate municipalities, with its own economy and cultural life.[2] In 1940 Orange County's population was less than one-tenth that of Los Angeles, which had about 1.5 million people. World War II accelerated Los Angeles's growth. It became a major aircraft manufacturing center with firms like Douglas Aircraft and Lockheed. And it became a major military center to help protect the West Coast and to transport troops to the Pacific war theaters.[3] Los Angeles's postwar economy also mushroomed around the wartime defense firms; and many soldiers and sailors were drawn to the region after experiencing the temperate winters, seductive sandy beaches, and majestic nearby mountain ranges, which tower to ten thousand feet. Long Beach, a city south of Los Angeles, was jokingly called "Iowa's seaport" in recognition of a major migration from the Midwest to southern California. Starting in the 1950s, as Los Angeles grew and its open space became scarce and expensive, some residents and major aircraft firms sought cheaper land to the south in Orange County.

Orange County's postwar population has multiplied ten times, from two hundred thousand in 1950 to more than two million by 1987. Commercial firms that owned massive parcels of land developed whole planned communities in Irvine, Laguna Niguel, and Mission Viejo. Their utopian images of a trouble-free, healthy life for families included modern housing, rural open space, high-quality schools, superb amenities, and a temperate climate that permitted an easy-going outdoor life year-round. This utopian promise was a powerful magnet, drawing many people to Orange County communities (not just the new towns), even though those communities better fit the pastoral ideals of the British garden-city movement of the late nineteenth century than the advertised utopia.[4] Orange County's immigrants included people who had previously lived and worked in Los Angeles and who were seeking more space and less expensive housing, as well as people from elsewhere in the nation who were drawn to the county's mix of temperate climate and open space.

Since the arrival in the 1970s and 1980s of nonaerospace firms that operate internationally, Orange County's regional economy has become increasingly integrated into a worldwide capitalist market system. The executives of these enterprises are eager to create a new center of world trade in the county—a desire expressed in such organizations as the International Trade League of Orange County and the World Trade Center Association of Orange County. By 1988 Orange County's growing high-tech export business had led to the opening of an export licensing office in Newport Beach, the first such branch outside of Washington, D.C.[5] This impressive growth of the economy increased employment opportunities for the county's residents, and accordingly the amount of personal income earned outside of Orange County dropped from 21 percent in 1971 to less than 10 percent in 1981.[6] Furthermore, by 1985 more than 80 percent of Orange County's residential work force of approximately 1.1 million commuted to a job within the county.[7]

Like much of Los Angeles County, Orange County has been rapidly transformed from a predominantly agricultural area into an important industrial and postindustrial society. A social transformation that has taken place over the course of a century or more in most nation-states and many major cities occurred in Orange County during a mere forty years. Between 1945 and 1965 Orange County developed from a network of small distinct towns and villages within a rural region into a sprawling suburban area. By the mid-1980s the region had further evolved into a complex and decentralized mixture of urban, suburban, and rural spaces. Unlike the traditional suburb, Orange County of the 1970s mixed large poor neighborhoods, including several Mexican barrios, with middle- and upper-class neighborhoods.[8] This new postsuburban spatial form, which we characterize later in this chapter, was pioneered in Los Angeles in the 1920s and 1930s and developed in other metropolitan areas after World War II. It is a key part of Orange County's character today.

ORANGE COUNTY AS A SUBJECT OF INQUIRY

Given the growing importance and complexity of the region, it is surprising that Orange County has thus far received so little serious scholarly attention. Although it has been the subject of numerous, often celebratory, newspaper and popular magazine articles, there are few critically probing analyses of the region's historical and contemporary developments. Many urbanists and journalists outside of Orange County are ignorant of its recent transformation. They hold the anachronistic view that Orange County is too isolated from the mainstream, too embryonic in its emergence as an advanced industrial area, too aberrant in its major characteristics to offer much opportunity for significant generalizable findings. Orange County's national image as a bastion of conservatism and a hotbed of right-wing activism has long substituted for deeper analyses of the complexities of the region.[9]

We bring a different perspective to bear. We believe that Orange County is far from being a static, kooky backwater area. Since the 1960s, new businesses and their owners, managers, and workers have transformed it into a dynamic postindustrial society. In the 1940s, Orange County was a rural region distinct from Los Angeles. During the 1950s and 1960s, it developed as an almost indistinguishable part of Los Angeles's suburban fringe. In the late 1970s, it began to develop a self-sustaining, complex economy and cultural life, which is sufficiently interesting and significant to make Orange County a distinct object of study.

Although every metropolitan area has unique characteristics, Orange County's transformation parallels the development of about twenty other metropolitan areas in the United States. Although we are attentive in this book to Orange County's unique features (climate, topography, location, large Spanish land grants) and their influence on the region's socio-economic and cultural development, we are particularly interested in the ways in which key themes of Orange County's development shed light on important social changes elsewhere in the nation. Most of the chapters in this book examine how developments in Orange County increase our insight into important social changes taking place throughout the United States.

We believe that Orange County's emerging social order should be presented through its spatial organization, its economy, its technologies, its cultural orientations, and its political life—and through the interplay of these factors. This book differs from many regional studies that focus exclusively on one slice of the social order. Through nine multifaceted case studies of a region that exemplifies and even exaggerates some key themes in the postwar United States, the book describes and evaluates a paradigmatic example of a larger social transformation. These case studies cannot begin to capture fully the richness and diversity of such a large and socially complex area. Many important areas of inquiry—such as Orange County's economic infrastructure, the roles of ethnic and racial minorities and women, and the nature and impact of religious fundamentalism—await further studies, and we hope that this book helps to stimulate them.

The authors of these studies do not share a single theoretical or disciplinary frame of reference. In a few cases they use somewhat different terms for similar concepts. And they do not always agree on key issues, such as the role of defense funding in Orange County's social development. But they do share many key perceptions about Orange County, and they use similar elements of social analysis. They are especially sensitive to questions of spatial organization, economic change, social meaning, culture and ideology, social stratification and structure, and political power. These are not the only themes that can inform a study of a metropolitan region, but we believe they are essential ones. This book maintains a delicate balance between the specific and the general. It focuses on Orange County's development with sufficient detail to interest readers who want to learn about recent social developments in southern California. At the same time, it illustrates general patterns of social change in the United States that will interest urban historians and sociologists.

We have identified four concepts to help us interpret Orange County's remarkable transformation from a minor agricultural region into a substantial metropolitan area in less than forty years: postsuburban spatial organization, information capitalism, consumerism, and cosmopolitanism. These concepts help sharpen our understanding of economic, social, cultural, and political life in Orange County, as we assume they will for other similar regions. Indeed, while developments in Orange County parallel those in other areas of the country, Orange County is also an anticipatory region that may exaggerate some trends but that also foreshadows the future. Its residents both enjoy and suffer the prospects of tomorrow.

POSTSUBURBAN SPATIAL ORGANIZATION:
THE MULTICENTERED METROPOLITAN REGION

The traditional urban region is characterized by relatively high population and by a wide variety of commercial and industrial development concentrated in a small area. The primary conceptual alternatives to urban are rural and suburban. As sociologist Mark Baldassare has noted, "Suburbia from the 1920s through World War II tended to be white, middle class, family oriented, and socially homogeneous. Land-use patterns were low density, nonindustrial, and primarily residential."[10] Since World War II, North American suburbs have become socially varied because they increasingly house the working class as well as the middle class, racial minorities as well as whites, and single people as well as traditional families. But they are still characterized by a land-use pattern that is dominantly residential and a transportation pattern that is dominantly one in which people commute to work outside the area.

Traditional suburbs thus function as peripheral bedroom communities from which commuters travel to workplaces in an urban core. As such, they are in large measure economically inert and have not been centers of high culture. They are sleepy places with little of the nightlife that characterizes cities. A small literature devoted to suburb bashing portrays suburbs as second-class, standardized components of the urban environment and as objects of scorn and derision. However, Herbert Gans's pioneering study of Levittown, New Jersey, showed that suburban life is no less lively than urban life, although it focuses much more on family activities and private institutions, such as clubs. Furthermore, it is not organized around high-density housing, with its substantially more active street life. Suburbs are also much less likely than cities to be the homes of higher-class cultural institutions such as major museums and performing arts centers that can attract world-class orchestras. Suburban cultural life is more provincial than cosmopolitan (if we ignore the fact that people throughout the country can to some extent share cosmopolitan culture through access to the same mass media).

In the 1960s Orange County was changing from a rural region based on a network of small towns into a large suburban complex. Its bedroom communities developed in the North County because southern Los Angeles had become fully developed. But Orange County today does not fit the suburban pattern, and it is also neither primarily urban nor primarily rural. Instead, it mixes these forms. Robert Fishman describes the social and spatial development of regions such as Orange County in these terms:

Postwar American development has been characterized by the almost simultaneous decentralization of housing, industry, specialized services, and office jobs; the consequent breakaway of the urban periphery from the city it no longer needs; and the creation of a decentralized environment that nevertheless possesses all the economic and technological dynamism of the city. . . . This *new city* is . . . a peripheral zone, perhaps as large as a county, that has emerged as a viable social and economic unit. Spread out along its highway growth corridors are shopping malls, industrial parks, campuslike office complexes, hospitals, schools, and a full range of housing types. Its residents look to their immediate surroundings rather than to the city for their jobs and other needs; and its industries find not only the employees they need, but also specialized services.[11]

We label this "new city" a *postsuburban* spatial formation because it evolves from the spatial organization of a low-density suburban region.[12] Strongly influenced by the path-breaking works of our cocontributor M. Gottdiener, we note that Orange County is not simply decentralized, but, as Gottdiener and George Kephart observe in Chapter 2, it is multicentered as well.[13] It is organized around many distinct, specialized centers rather than a traditional city center surrounded by industrial and residential areas. A visitor who is used to traditional cities with central downtowns to house city halls, museums, churches, and major businesses may be bewildered by Orange County's spatial layout. As of 1988 Orange County had twenty-eight separate municipalities, ranging in population from roughly 10,000 to nearly 250,000. The downtowns of some of the older cities still function as regional centers; in addition, developers have promoted and built new centers outside the old downtowns around shopping centers, industrial parks, and large amusement parks.

Starting in the late 1960s, several large land developers who dominated building activity in the southern portion of the county were able to sell a vision of the "great life" in relatively homogeneous planned communities and large housing tracts. These residential tracts were a key element of the multicentered spatial form because they excluded substantial stores or workplaces through strict zoning regulations. Such structures were restricted to other specialized land parcels.

Today the cities appear to sprawl and merge into one another because they do not have distinctive architectural features or clear separation zones at their peripheries. City boundaries are commonly marked only with a sign along a street or a boulevard. Moreover, only a few architectural genres are represented because much of Orange County was built up in a short period. Consequently visitors and residents see less variety in many neighborhoods than in older urban areas—or even in suburban areas in which homes are custom built. (Today tract homes in Orange

County sell for $150,000 to $750,000, while custom-built homes often cost upwards of $1,000,000. The economics of housing does much to shape the visual landscape.)

Another reason for the homogeneous architecture is that the specialized zones of Orange County are more functionally differentiated than are traditional urban areas, where combinations of land use—residential, commercial, and public—predominate. Orange County's residential neighborhoods, like those in many other urban regions developed after World War II, are often devoted exclusively to tract houses.[14] In most parts of Orange County one is likely to see a homogeneous landscape block after block, with occasional transitions to different, but also internally homogeneous, areas. These areas are not only residential; they are also commercial and industrial. Their architecture can even be quite attractive. But large areas of attractive buildings of similar design deprive the county of the highly localized visual variety that is common in older cities. Long stretches of flat acreage bounded by mountain ranges support a predominantly low-rise landscape that spreads for miles. The tallest buildings are now about twenty stories high and are clustered in several diverse locations.

These specialized residential, commercial, and industrial zones, difficult for pedestrians to navigate, were designed to accommodate the automobile driver. The various shopping, civic, recreational, religious, and cultural centers are usually miles apart. Eight-, ten-, even twelve-lane freeways guide hundreds of thousands of motorists between these places without beginning or terminating at any of them. The beaches, themselves major recreational centers, stretch some thirty-five miles from the north to the south end of the county, with a series of beach towns five to ten miles from the nearest freeway. Shopping areas are concentrated in regional centers or neighborhood centers that are too far to be a convenient walk for most residents. Although there is a substantial bus system, it is not widely used, and the private automobile is essential.

Further, many of the residential and commercial structures are implicitly designed to emphasize private domesticity and material consumption. As in many suburbs, the single-family homes open onto private patios rather than onto the streets. Porches, which were common in prewar American architecture, are exceptional in modern California designs. Many of the more affluent neighborhoods are designed so that individual homes are walled off from the street with enclosed front courtyards and limited entryways. Orange County's temperate climate enables homes to have large glass windows, but these usually face private patios. Such residential designs turn people inward toward the private spaces of their homes.[15] Residents who walk through their neighborhoods may see some of their neighbors out doing yard work by day. But such neighborhoods do not provide much support for casual interaction and thereby dilute the possible richness of public social life.

The newer shops, built in the 1970s and 1980s, are designed for efficient shopping. In addition to neighborhood shopping centers built around a supermarket, there are regional centers anchored by several large department stores. Efficient shopping is pushed to a further extreme in specialized shopping centers: auto malls, which gather five to twenty car dealerships, auto-parts shops, and auto-repair shops in one mammoth complex; household complexes, which combine furniture stores and department stores that sell household goods. One cannot buy clothes in the auto mall or a car muffler in the household complex. These shopping complexes do not provide many areas to relax and linger. Some even discourage teenagers from loitering, except in video arcades, where they are confined as consumers. Like their counterparts elsewhere in the country, the regional shopping malls are designed to maximize sales and minimize the opportunities for those who wish to idle away time without participating in shopping and buying. Although enclosed shopping malls were not invented in Orange County, they dominate the region's retail life. The multicentered spatial elements of Orange County function synergistically to highlight the core cultural value of consumerism, which we discuss later in this chapter. In the prophetic terms of Paul and Percival Goodman, Orange County's spatial specialization creates a place of efficient production and consumption.[16]

This multicentered region can appear as a hodgepodge of specialized centers built miles apart and separated by large suburban-style housing tracts. But this postsuburban spatial formation differs from the traditional suburb by having lively commercial and cultural centers for residents. It differs markedly from more distinctly suburban regions, like Marin County in California or Westchester County in New York, which are more demographically homogeneous and where the major nearby cities are the primary sources of high culture, lively street life, and ethnic diversity.

Studies such as those by Fishman, Peter Muller, Carl Abbott, Kenneth Jackson, and Gottdiener present a picture of postsuburban regions such as Orange County that sharply differentiates them from both cities and suburbs.[17] In fact, the operating logic of these postsuburban regions would appear to be the exact opposite of that of the conventional suburb. They are not sleepy provincial regions, although they have their quiet suburban neighborhoods. Their most important aspects, to repeat, are their origins in the suburban periphery of another urban core (in this case, Los Angeles) from which they have broken away, and the emergence within them of a new decentralized environment possessing the economic vitality and cultural diversity formerly associated with the traditional central city. Through decentralization, the parochial and primarily residential suburb becomes a vital metropolitan region. This pattern occurred in Orange County and is also found on eastern Long Island, as well as in a new metropolitan area developing in a northeast corridor outside of Atlanta and in more than a dozen other areas (see Chapter 2).

It is traditional to discuss suburban regions as located on a continuum that ranges from rural to urban in housing density, distance from major economic and cultural centers, and so forth. We do not locate postsuburban regions along such a continuum. They are not simply more urban than suburbs. In fact, some urban developments have been influenced by postsuburban developments, particularly the enclosed urban shopping mall. The suburban shopping mall is often a strip of small stores and medium-sized chain stores such as K-Marts. The postsuburban mall differs from the suburban mall in that it is usually enclosed and houses several major department stores as well as many smaller shops. The enclosed urban mall, like the Beverly Center in Los Angeles, is patterned on the postsuburban mall. But it contains shops that sell goods and services that appeal more to urban tastes. For example, the urban movie theaters may be fourplexes or sixplexes, but they are more likely than suburban movie-theater complexes to show foreign films.

Los Angeles County and Orange County are the most developed examples in the United States of postsuburban regions. They thereby provide the most promising places to study this important, emergent social formation. According to *New York Times* architectural critic Paul Goldberger, "There is no better place to think about the American landscape and what it is turning into than in Orange County, where brand-new suburbs sprawl across the land with such intensity that Los Angeles, by comparison, seems almost an old-fashioned, traditional city."[18] One Orange County regional center, for example—the Costa Mesa–Newport Beach–Irvine complex—is California's third largest "downtown," as measured by office and business space. Office space in that complex now surpasses 21.1 million square feet. Although still well behind Los Angeles's 36.6 million square feet, it is not far from San Francisco's 26.8 million and is rapidly gaining on both. In addition its leading shopping mall, South Coast Plaza, has more sales than any other such center in the United States, perhaps the world.[19] Other malls, such as those in the cities of Orange, Westminster, and Mission Viejo, also have a huge volume of sales. Thus Orange County residents, like residents of similar postsuburban regions elsewhere, seek their employment and their primary consumer and cultural satisfactions in their own area, not in a distant city.

"Orange County, with Irvine at its heart," argues Goldberger, "has become a new kind of place—not a conventional city, not a conventional suburb, but possessing the attributes of both." He goes on to identify high-rise office towers, luxury hotels, a jet airport, a performing arts center, and museums designed by internationally renowned architects as new features of Orange County. That county, he goes on to claim, symbolizes "the end of the traditional, dense, street-oriented city as a necessary element in American cultural life—and . . . [it] now shows us, more clearly than anywhere else, exactly what kind of city builders consider the ideal for middle-class Americans at the end of the 1980s."[20]

Postsuburban regions have become the most common form of metropolitan development in this country. And this emergence has undeniably transformed our lives, for better and for worse. Orange County resembles at least twenty other regions in the United States. Chapter 2 places Orange County in this larger framework. These new outer cities are large conglomerates of technologically advanced industry, services, and information processing. They are sharply differentiated by class, income, and life-styles. In addition demographers have noted that by the 1970s they contained the bulk of the population of the United States, thus reversing a five-thousand-year trend of urbanization. Gottdiener and Kephart, in Chapter 2, call this new historical stage "deconcentration," arguing that it requires a reconceptualization of spatial organization.

Postsuburban spatial organization is no accident. It is the result of complex and weakly coordinated sets of conscious decisions by private entrepreneurs and many politicians who reflect their interests. A specific example of how this spatial form evolved is provided by Orange County's largest private landholder, the Irvine Company. This company implemented its corporate vision of growth in the city of Irvine, which it developed from a large ranch into a city of some 100,000 residents within twenty years. By design Irvine has no downtown but is a deconcentrated mosaic of residential villages, small shopping centers, and industrial parks. Irvine's city hall is not a routine walk from any of the city's villages.

In Chapter 3 Martin Schiesl describes the Irvine Company's role in transforming a rural agricultural region into a dynamic postsuburban complex. Its activities were a bold departure in community planning and building and have been emulated by other development companies in the county that are building whole cities, such as the Mission Viejo Company and the Rancho Santa Margarita Company. Schiesl shows how the Irvine Company's vision of the future of Orange County often clashed with those of city and county planning officials. These professional planners were particularly concerned with an overdependence on automobile transportation and with what they regarded as insufficient attention to the problem of housing for low-income and moderate-income workers and their families. Popular resistance to the Irvine Company's plans for a city of 300,000 prompted the new owners of the firm in the early 1980s to reevaluate some of their cherished development policies and to work more cooperatively than they had in the past with different segments of the community who sought a less congested and socially more varied community than they proposed. The Irvine Company also owns the major shopping and financial centers in Newport Beach—Fashion Island and Newport Center. Its plans for expanding Newport Center have also aroused considerable opposition and have resulted in compromises.

Despite these periodic clashes, the development firms have won most of their major battles. Sometimes they have compromised with regulatory boards, such as city councils or the California Coastal Commission. For example, the Irvine Company owns a several-mile strip of land between Newport Beach and Laguna Beach. It offers spectacular hillside and ocean views, and it is one of the few large undeveloped parcels between Los Angeles and San Diego. Irvine Company officials had long wished to build thousands of homes, hotels, and resort complexes along the hillside. After considerable negotiation with environmental groups and the California Coastal Commission, the Irvine Company agreed to donate about 75 percent of the land for parks and open space in exchange for being able to build a few thousand homes and a few hotels. Although the Irvine Company's developments will not be as intensive as its officials had hoped, they will be able to transform the last remaining long rural stretch of Orange County coastline into another developed area. In 1988 environmental groups attempted to slow development in the rural southern areas of Orange County by sponsoring a public referendum to limit developments to the capacity of the roads that would be available. This referendum was the most serious growth-limiting effort yet by local people who had grown tired of watching hillsides turn to tracts and open roads become clogged with commuter traffic. Developers lobbied hard in the media and through private channels to defeat the measure. They argued that growth restrictions would cost jobs, weaken the local economy, and substantially raise the cost of housing, thereby disenfranchising poorer people who might someday wish to buy a home. The referendum was defeated by a substantial margin, and the dense development of the South County continues unabated.[21]

THE TRANSFORMATION OF THE ECONOMY
TO INFORMATION CAPITALISM

Although the sheer growth of Orange County's regional economy has been significant and striking, the kind of economy that emerged there after World War II is also important. Orange County's economy is best examined within the broad national and international context. Not only has production in the United States become increasingly international with the rise of multinational corporations since the late 1940s, but the internal character of American capitalism has also changed dramatically. These large changes are clearly reflected in Orange County.

Until recently historians and social scientists conceived of broad historical change in the economic organization of societies as a progression from agricultural, preindustrial society to industrial, "advanced" society. Since the 1960s a vigorous debate has emerged about the transition to yet a third main stage beyond industrial society. This third stage has been variously labeled the *postindustrial society,* the *service society,* and, the term we prefer, the *information society* (although we differ among ourselves about the relative emphasis to give to its various aspects).[22]

Occupations in the information sector are those in which the processing and distribution of information are central and time-consuming activities. These occupations are diverse; they include managers, lawyers, accountants, realtors, stockbrokers, and clerks of all kinds. As Rob Kling and Clark Turner report in Chapter 4, the information sector in the United States accounted for more employment than either manufacturing or services as early as 1950. Furthermore, information activities produced more than 46 percent of United States national income by the late 1960s, a figure that rose dramatically during the 1970s and 1980s.[23]

The information work force differs significantly from the high-tech work force that Gottdiener and Kephart examine in Chapter 2. The high-tech sector includes a variety of technical jobs within manufacturing. The approximately 100,000 high-tech workers in Orange County in 1988 constituted about 40 percent of the manufacturing work force and less than 10 percent of the county's total work force.[24] Manufacturing firms, even high-tech firms, employ many low-tech workers such as equipment handlers, salespersons, bookkeepers, and clerks. In contrast, information-sector jobs are found in services such as finance, insurance, real estate, and travel, as well as in manufacturing. Kling and Turner calculate that about 58 percent of Orange County's work force is in the information sector. Thus, a minority of Orange County's work force is composed of high-tech workers, while a majority of the work force is in the information sector. In fact, Orange County's information work force is about six times the size of its high-tech work force. Although the county's work force has been rapidly growing, manufacturing has been slowly declining in relative size since the late 1960s.

The term *information society* is often invoked reverentially on the assumption that it constitutes an advanced stage of social evolution. We do not accept many of the conservative premises of such evolutionary views. We see societies as changing through collective action stimulated by a small number of intentional agents rather than as evolving naturally like flowers. In Western societies, business interests and the state are major, but not exclusive, activists pressing for and shaping important social changes. In Orange County the Irvine Company and other large-scale developers, the major national corporations, and grass-roots social movements are some of the key actors.

We do not believe that these lead actors always get their way. There are often conflicts of interest within various business and governmental coalitions, as several authors in this book demonstrate. Moreover, particular interest groups act on a social canvas that is shaped by local environments and resources, as well as by large-scale national and international actions, such as wars, inflation, or new tax structures, which they do not directly influence. However, we see social changes as emerging from the interplay of interest-driven behavior.

We have found the concept of information capitalism especially useful in analyzing the economic changes that led from an industrial economy to an information economy because it anchors new strategies of managing information in the practical activities of businesses and governments. Information capitalism refers to forms of organization in which data-intensive techniques and computerization are key strategic resources; these forms of organization occur in all sectors of the economy—agriculture, manufacturing, and services.[25] The owners and managers of agricultural, manufacturing, and service firms are relying increasingly on imaginative strategies for basing production on information. Computerized information systems have joined factory smokestacks as major signifiers of economic power.

Information usually does not replace other products or services. But the management of information through cost accounting, production monitoring, and market surveys becomes a key resource in advancing a firm's competitive edge and also in devising new ways to manage and to provide services. Point-of-sale terminals, automated teller machines, credit cards, and the widespread use of desktop computing are some of the visible by-products of information capitalism. Platoons of specialized information workers—from clerks to professionals—are hidden behind these information technologies, which have become critical elements for many businesses and public agencies.

Fast-food chain restaurants provide a good example of information capitalism in action. Viewed as a service, fast-food restaurants simply sell rapidly prepared food for relatively low prices and stimulate a high rate of customer turnover. They are simply furnished, provide no table service, and are staffed by low-paid workers (often teenagers). It is a traditional business managed in traditional ways to provide a low-cost service. Fast-food chain restaurants differ from other low-cost restaurants by buying in immense volume, standardizing menus, using drive-up windows and walk-up counters, and franchising their outlets in special ways.

Fast-food restaurant chains are especially competitive and successful when they have an infrastructure of information professionals and technologies. The information component helps them to select restaurant sites, to alter their menus to match the changing tastes of their clientele, to audit the services of each establishment, and carefully to monitor costs, cash flow, inventory, and sales. Their operational efficiencies thus hinge on information technologies as much as on economies of scale—from the microphones and audio systems that make it easy for drive-through customers to order food to the simplified electronic cash registers that automatically calculate costs and change so that less-skilled teenage workers can be relied on as labor. The skills of backstage professional analysts consuming bytes of data expedite the large-scale sale of bites of food.

Fast-food restaurant chains, it should be stressed, have not shifted from selling food to selling information, but their operations have become intensively based on information.[26] The major fast-food restaurant chains operate in Orange County as they do in other areas of the United States. Their operational style simply illustrates what we mean by information capitalism, an economic stage that, while hardly unique to Orange County, is nonetheless more highly developed there than in most other urban and suburban areas.

Kling and Turner indicate in Chapter 4 how different analysts posit the relationship between an information economy and other formations, such as an industrial economy and a postindustrial economy. The size of an information economy is based on the number of people who work in information-handling jobs across all economic sectors—agriculture, manufacturing, and services. In our view, the transformation to an information economy does not necessarily require a corresponding decline in the number or size of traditional agricultural and manufacturing organizations, even though it does require a reduction in the proportion of workers who directly farm or manufacture goods. In fact, the United States had moved from a manufacturing (industrial) economy to a service (postindustrial) economy by 1960 and had become the first society in history in which less than half the labor force was engaged in the production of food or goods. In the late 1960s and 1970s, this economy became based increasingly on information. Today such information-producing activities are of great economic and political importance.

Behind all these changes are a variety of information workers, who have become especially important to Orange County's economic growth. Orange County epitomizes the leading occupational trends in the national economy, where most new jobs created since 1950 have been in the service and information sectors.[27] With one of the nation's largest per capita incomes and one of the lowest unemployment rates, the county has for years paced much of the nation in the growth of the service sector, electronics, high-tech manufacturing, and medical technology. Firms in these industries employ a disproportionate number of information workers. The city of Irvine, for example, is a major center for high-tech activity. The Irvine Industrial Complex, established in the mid-1960s, had attracted more than thirty-seven hundred firms by the early 1980s. These firms manufacture and distribute a variety of high-tech products from artificial heart valves to computers, and others provide business services for such firms. Combined employment countywide in three industries critical to the future—trade, electronics, and service—was 56 percent of the work force in 1986, compared with 48 percent nationwide. Information capitalism gives these industries greater leverage than their less technologically sophisticated precursors had.[28]

The region's growing ethnic and racial diversity complicates the structure of its labor markets so that occupational counts alone cannot clearly reveal who does which work. In this regard, Orange County has been profoundly affected by the massive immigration (most of it from Asia and Latin America) that has transformed the entire southern California area. From 1970 to 1980, for example, the number of Hispanics, who have constituted the county's largest racial minority since 1910, increased 147 percent (to 14.8 percent of the total population of the county), while the Asian population grew 371 percent (to 4.8 percent of the total), and the black population increased 140 percent (to approximately 1 percent of the total). Since the mid-1970s, Orange County's expanding service economy and its need for inexpensive blue-collar manual workers have combined to attract the nation's fourth-largest permanent settlement of undocumented Mexican immigrants.[29] Although they have customarily been perceived primarily as agricultural labor, a significant number of Latinos and especially Asians are in fact employed in the industrial and high-tech sectors, where they often form the core of an army of assembly-line workers who construct computer and biomedical equipment and other products in the electronics and instruments industries.

GROWTH OF A CONSUMER CULTURE

One of the salient changes in this century concerns the relation between production and consumption, and the shift in importance from one to the other. The concept of consumerism serves, after postsuburban spatial arrangements and information capitalism, as a third organizing theme for this book. During the first century of the industrial revolution, the major economic issue was increasing productivity. The reorganization of labor and the application of science and technology to the production process were the chief concerns of industrialists. The ability of the new industrial sector to mass-produce inexpensive commodities was the most striking achievement of the period from roughly 1820 to 1920. Enormous increases in gross national product were realized. These commodities were distributed to a population with a low level of consumption that eagerly absorbed whatever the industrial base could supply.

Starting in the 1920s, however, most consumers' basic needs for shelter, clothing, food, and furnishings were satisfied, and their demand for goods and services began to diminish. Production began to outstrip the nation's capacity to consume, given the relatively simple needs of most of the population.

Industrialists thus faced a crisis. The solution lay in transforming the living patterns and consumption behavior of the masses. Starting in the 1920s, producers began to slant their advertisements toward the symbolic value of products as well as toward their functional utility.[30] The mass media enabled advertisers to broadcast their messages throughout the nation, while local markets gave way to nationwide retail chains. Commodities became indices of success, and the masses became consumers in the sense that they adopted the task of maintaining life-styles designed and advocated by advertisers. The work ethic that had informed the moral life of the early industrial revolution made room for a new consumerist ethic. Henri Lefebvre accurately characterized this shift when he wrote, "It is the transition from a culture based on the curbing of desires, thriftiness, and the necessity of eking out goods in short supply to a new culture resulting from production and consumption at their highest ebb."[31]

These changes took place over decades, as producers, their marketing agents, and the media refined their techniques. Many of the key strategies of symbolic marketing were well established by the early 1960s, a decade before Orange County became a major national market. However, in the 1970s, marketing became increasingly information intensive as computer systems became less expensive, mailing-list brokers became more established, and advertisers learned how to segment their potential audiences and target demographically identified groups with customized advertising. Consumerism became linked, in short, with information capitalism, and this linkage was especially evident in Orange County, as we will see later in this chapter.

In Chapter 5, Alladi Venkatesh shows how Orange County has perfected a new brand of consumerism. Examining specific developments that are shaping the region into a modern consumer society, he argues that the convergence of some extraordinary forces has given the county its special consumer-oriented character. These forces include the amount and distribution of discretionary income and the general level of education.

Between the mid-1960s and the mid-1970s, six huge regional shopping centers opened in Orange County, each anchored by several department stores, and dozens of smaller neighborhood centers were built around supermarkets and diversified drugstores. In the 1970s and early 1980s, these regional shopping centers boomed. By the fall of 1987, Orange Countians spent more per capita at retail stores than the residents of any other county in California ($2,680 per resident, or 25 percent higher than the statewide average of $2,139).[32]

Orange County's housing is another aspect of consumerism. In the late 1980s the county had one of the most expensive housing markets in the United States. The median home price of about $250,000, the third highest in the country in mid-1989, required first-time buyers to have family incomes over $80,000 per year. Only 13 percent of Orange County's households could afford to buy a home for the first time, although about 29 percent of households could qualify to purchase a condominium. And because homes can be most easily afforded by families with two incomes, Orange County families are usually dependent on two or more cars. A new home and two late-model cars can easily cost a family 40 to 50 percent of its post-tax income.

Since the 1960s, Orange County's consumer culture has become increasingly cosmopolitan. South Coast Plaza, a major regional center with eight large department stores and about three hundred shops, houses clothing stores with an international flavor, such as Courrèges and Gucci, and cafés such as Amato's and Caffe Pasquini. About five miles away, Newport Beach's Fashion Island hosts comparable boutiques, such as Pariscope and Salvaggio, and a small array of eateries serving international cuisines. These stores cater to Orange County's largely white middle and upper-middle class. Venkatesh argues that this economic elite sets taste trends for others in Orange County. The wealthiest residents own homes, in exceptional cases with ocean views. But many residents fantasize about owning a home, even if they can afford only to buy a small condominium or to rent an apartment. Similarly, the economic elite sets cosmopolitan tastes in car ownership, clothing, and food that many others emulate on a less opulent scale. For the affluent residents of the South County, cosmopolitan consumption may be marked by driving a German car, wearing Italian shoes, and dining in a French restaurant with other affluent whites. For the poorer residents of the Central County and North County, cosmopolitan consumption may be marked by having dinner in a Thai café that has a predominantly Thai clientele. A Mercedes automobile brings little German culture into the car owner's life; and eating dinner among Thais does not make that complex culture immediately accessible to a white diner. Orange County's new cosmopolitan consumerism—like its counterpart in major North American metropolitan areas—is characterized primarily by the purchase of novel and often expensive foreign products rather than by immersion in the arts, politics, and languages of other cultures.

However, the poorer residents of Orange County have a more indigenous, and somewhat more genuine, form of cosmopolitan consumption. North County cities such as Garden Grove and Westminster have large Asian populations; Santa Ana, in the center of Orange County, has a large Mexican population. These ethnic groups have their own specialty shops and restaurants. Unlike the affluent whites of the South County, Orange County's ethnic populations do not go out for Vietnamese or Mexican food as a change of pace; it is their indigenous cuisine. Lower-middle-class and working-class whites in the Central and North County cities also patronize these relatively inexpensive ethnic cafés and restaurants.

In addition to its links with cosmopolitanism, consumerism is also connected with information capitalism, as we mentioned previously. To return to the example of fast-food restaurants, these businesses use information technologies, advertising in particular, to define the experience of frequenting their establishments in a positive light. This aspect of the information society allows cultural experiences—in this case, consumerism—to be shaped by electronically mediated communications, constituting entirely new levels of language interactions. These communications thus further encourage the shift from a rational, work-oriented culture to a postrational, consumer-oriented culture. Several aspects of this culture are addressed in other chapters in this book.

Businesses and marketing experts have also refined analytical techniques to identify and target specialized markets. Disneyland, in northeast Orange County, was one of the first facilities anywhere in the nation to be located with the help of demographic surveys. In addition, Orange County's shopping-center owners, especially the Irvine Company, are particularly sensitive to the mix and potential profitability of shops in a particular mall. Although shopping-center owners nationwide seek to profit from their investments, the Irvine Company pioneered information-intensive sales forecasting and accounting systems because their leases require shop owners to pay them a fraction of their gross revenues as well as a fixed monthly rent. Beyond a demonstrated ability to turn a profit and pay the rent, the shop owner must also fit a profile determined by market studies and accounting reports. Information capitalism thus quietly but persistently shapes the environment in which Orange County's residents play their roles as consumers.

Information capitalism and consumerism have also become linked with politics in Orange County. In the late 1970s, a political consulting firm that used advanced marketing techniques opened its doors in Irvine. This firm, Butcher-Ford, employed standard marketing techniques of information capitalism such as sophisticated polling and customized direct-mail campaigns to identify different audiences and send them selected materials promoting the usually conservative candidates who were the firm's clients. Thus, instead of marketing services or commodities to the public, Butcher-Ford marketed political products—their candidates—in a way that was foreshadowed in Eugene Burdick's *The 480*.[34] Butcher-Ford was criticized by some for running dirty-tricks campaigns in which they faked endorsements for their candidates and designed their unofficial mailings to make them appear as though they came from government agencies. But they were seldom criticized for transforming political elections into mundane marketing campaigns.

A key link between political life and consumerism in Orange County is political campaigns designed to limit public spending and thereby allow the public to retain funds for private consumption. In the late 1970s California was rocked by a series of tax-reform initiatives that aimed to limit taxes and to cap public spending. The most famous of these—Proposition 13—placed such a cap on property taxes. In Chapter 10 William Gayk analyzes how homeownership and income, among other factors, influenced support for these propositions.

Consumerism also has far-reaching effects on other parts of the culture. Orange County differs from other urbanized and suburbanized regions in the rapidity with which certain traditional institutions and practices are being displaced by others. In particular, the specific, localized neighborhood has given way to geographically dispersed shopping malls and controlled recreational environments as the new neighborhoods for a highly mobile and fragmented population. For some residents, furthermore, especially the more affluent and recent immigrants without strong family ties in southern California, consumption has replaced the family as an important basis of human interaction.

In the earlier part of this century elsewhere in the United States, the change from work to consumption as the central feature of life in industrial society accompanied the shift from urban neighborhoods to suburban provincialism, from community to domesticity. A relatively public local life slowly disintegrated as the streetcar and automobile enabled wide distances to separate work and home and as new media (telephone, radio, television, and, most recently, videotapes) encouraged the withdrawal of the family from the community.

Debra Hansen and Mary Ryan trace these developments in Orange County. In Chapter 6, they show how local public celebrations, such as the Fourth of July, became part of mass leisure and, in such amusement parks as Disneyland and Knott's Berry Farm, came under the control of large corporations, thereby losing their community roots. Leisure in Orange County discloses the anonymous face of the new social forms, in which *community* is largely a term of real estate advertising, not social reality.

These broad social changes in work, consumption, and community life have had devastating effects on the traditional nuclear family that characterized industrial society from about 1820 to 1920. Mark Poster in Chapter 7 defines the characteristics of an emerging postnuclear family type. His examination of family life in the wealthier areas of Orange County indicates that much experimentation is taking place. Adult spouses and partners are exploring new styles of living together, with male-dominated households giving way to equitable arrangements. New styles of child rearing emphasize self-development over imposed goals and self-regulation over obedience, practices that are highly controversial yet afford children a degree of freedom not dreamed of in early industrial society. This new, segmented family type is much less unified and concentrated than its predecessor. Each individual within it has a particular cultural sphere of reference and pursues that significant relation by means of new communication technologies.

THE SHIFT FROM PROVINCIALISM TO COSMOPOLITANISM

Orange County's transformation from an agricultural region with two dozen small towns and cities and an economy dominated by small firms serving regional markets into a vigorous and ethnically diverse metropolitan region with a strong information economy of international dimensions and a pronounced consumer culture was accompanied by another key shift: from provincial orientations to cosmopolitan ones. Aerospace-defense firms such as Northrop Corporation's Nortronics Division and Hughes Aircraft Company's Ground Systems Division initiated the change by creating huge facilities in Orange County in the 1950s.[35] Other aerospace, electronics, and computer firms followed them in the 1960s. These firms began to link Orange County businesses with the international economy. Simultaneously, the Irvine Company began marketing its new Irvine Industrial Complex and attracted thousands of businesses, large and small. By the early 1970s, many other medium-sized and large-scale firms, which operated nationally and internationally, also relocated in Orange County or established subsidiaries there. In addition, some local firms that emerged in the 1970s were soon operating in national and international markets.[36] To serve all these businesses, major American computer and office-equipment firms and several Japanese, Canadian, and European banks opened Orange County branch offices.[37]

These organizations recruited key professionals and managers from national and international as well as local labor markets. According to a

1988 survey, 43 percent of new residents have college or graduate degrees compared with 35 percent of longer-term residents.[38] Many of these highly educated employees had developed cosmopolitan tastes in other urban areas before emigrating to Orange County. They created a ready clientele for ethnic restaurants, European and Japanese cars, a wide variety of imported goods, and cultural events such as modern theater, foreign films, and classical music. Not satisfied with mainstream goods and services that were available in their neighborhood shopping centers, these residents were willing to patronize establishments virtually anywhere in the county that catered to their tastes. They were able to support a sufficient number of businesses and arts organizations with world-class aspirations so that, by the 1980s, a cosmopolitan culture was well developed in the county.

In Chapter 8, Spencer Olin examines changing forms of city government in relationship to economic shifts within a politically fragmented metropolis. By looking at local versus cosmopolitan political agendas and the battles between growth networks and slow-growth forces, he offers a variation on the well-studied theme of neighborhood/ward interests against downtown/corporate interests. Focusing almost exclusively on the business, or owning, class of Orange County, he argues that a contest between provincial (or regional) and cosmopolitan (or global) entrepreneurs has dominated the region's political life. The intense controversies over the county's rate of growth are one by-product of that contest.

Chapter 9 continues to explore the theme of urban and postsuburban politics and is especially relevant to another aspect of Orange County's cosmopolitanism—its impressive mingling of diverse cultures. Unlike Olin's inquiry into intraclass politics at the upper levels, Lisbeth Haas's focus is on grass-roots movements that have contested redevelopment and planning schemes since 1976 in Santa Ana, the county's former urban center. In the course of examining these movements, Haas illustrates an exception to the general trend in Orange County: namely, the continued existence in Santa Ana of geographically contained neighborhoods. She argues that well-established community networks within these neighborhoods provided the early foundation for grass-roots urban protest. The movement developed at a time when Santa Ana was becoming the most important Hispanic urban area within the multicentered metropolitan region. By 1984 large numbers of the undocumented immigrants among the city's predominantly Hispanic population began to organize to fight threatened displacement resulting from urban policy. Two years later Hispanic and Anglo residents joined to form a larger grass-roots coalition intent on changing the structure of city government and democratizing urban planning. They have not succeeded. Instead, the political and fiscal importance of the redevelopment agency has grown, and urban designs mod-

eled on the new outer cities and favoring middle-class residents continue
to be the norm in Santa Ana.

AN EMERGING UTOPIA?

Utopias are model societies, sources of inspiration and of guidance for
improvement, visions that have not yet materialized. A utopia is a possible
end, suggesting a future that can derive from conditions in the present.
For more than a hundred years, California, a region especially conducive
to new beginnings and to experimentation, has served as a hospitable site
for utopian communities of all kinds.[39] Santa Ana, in fact, was the final
destination for some thirty-five former "Bible Communists" from the
utopian Oneida Community in northern New York, which disbanded in
the early 1880s.[40]

This utopian quest continues today in Orange County, but in a camou-
flaged and conservative form. For example, as Schiesl indicates in Chapter 3, the Irvine Company has explicitly marketed Irvine as a carefully
planned, middle-class, suburban utopia. Its advertisements project images of neatly landscaped communities, convivial village life, freedom
from crime and congestion, upscale consumer conveniences, and other
pleasant amenities. Land developers who built several other cities in the
vast open areas of southern Orange County and numerous subdivisions
throughout the region adopted the Irvine Company's utopian images in
their own marketing strategies.

Ironically, however, some of Orange County's virtues derive from its
complex postsuburban character rather than from the development of
"white-bread" suburban tracts. It is more culturally and visually diverse,
as well as more ethnically mixed, than the suburban images suggest. The
city of Santa Ana is a large Hispanic center, and other areas in the county
have distinct concentrations of Asian and Hispanic populations. In Westminster and Garden Grove, long boulevards post store signs almost exclusively in Korean and Vietnamese. The street signs in Garden Grove are
bilingual, in English and Vietnamese. Laguna Beach, a small city with a
large arts community, is also the center of a large gay community and has
had gay mayors and city council members. Orange County's vast size
allows a degree of anonymity and freedom of life-style that would be
much more difficult to achieve in tightly knit suburban villages.

Social scientists such as Baldassare, however, have observed that Orange County citizens have become distraught over congested roads and
high housing prices.[41] Chapter 8 examines the intense political battles
that have occurred around the issue of growth. A new pessimism mars the
pastoral calm of the Orange County utopia. A slight majority of Baldassare's *Orange County Annual Survey* respondents believe their quality of life

is likely to decline in the future.[42] These problems emerge from the very success of the developers because congestion and escalating housing prices are by-products of Orange County's rapid growth. If Orange County were not perceived as a better place, the hundreds of thousands of people who immigrated here in the 1980s would not have come. Orange County would then have been less populous, less costly, and less congested.

The combination of postsuburban spatial organization, information capitalism, consumerism, and cosmopolitanism signals the birth of a new social formation that may turn out to be far less than utopian. In particular, the county is segmented spatially, economically, ethnically, and socially in ways that cannot sustain utopian aspirations. The chapters of this book examine the inescapable tensions inherent in Orange County's emerging economy and society, tensions that presage the result of metropolitan growth elsewhere in the United States.

NOTES

1. See Edward Soja, Rebecca Morales, and Goetz Wolf, "Urban Restructuring: An Analysis of Social and Spatial Change in Los Angeles," *Economic Geography* 59 (April 1979): 80–106. For more general studies of the American sunbelt, see Peter Wiley and Robert Gottlieb, *Empires in the Sun: The Rise of the New American West* (New York: Putnam's, 1982); Richard M. Bernard and Bradley R. Rice, eds., *Sunbelt Cities: Politics and Growth since World War II* (Austin: University of Texas Press, 1983); and Larry Sawers and William K. Tabb, eds., *Sunbelt/Snowbelt: Urban Development and Regional Restructuring* (New York: Oxford University Press, 1984).

2. An oversimplified account of this development, as well as sketches of the incorporation efforts of various cities, can be found in Pamela Hallan-Gibson, *The Golden Promise: An Illustrated History of Orange County* (Northridge, Calif.: Windsor, 1986). Our book differs substantially from Hallan-Gibson's account, which is an "official" business-oriented chronology of Orange County's development from the earliest days of Spanish settlement in the late eighteenth century to the 1980s.

3. There were major naval facilities near Los Angeles in San Pedro, as well as 150 miles south in San Diego.

4. See Ian Todd and Michael Wheeler, *Utopia* (New York: Harmony Books, 1978), 120–25.

5. See *Orange County Business First*, 13 June 1988. For an overview of the Orange County high-technology complex, see Allen J. Scott, *Metropolis: From the Division of Labor to Urban Form* (Berkeley: University of California Press, 1988), 160–202. However, the lack of a major international airport within Orange County inhibits the rate at which business can become international. Orange County's main airport serves as a regional node in the airline system. There are direct daily flights from Orange County to San Francisco, San Diego, Dallas–Fort Worth, Phoenix, Chicago, Denver, Salt Lake City, and Los Angeles. There are one-stop flights daily to all major American cities and many major foreign cities. There have been several attempts since the early 1970s to find a new location for an international airport within the county, but none has been successful.

6. See Evan Maxwell and Peter King, "In Orange County: A New Identity," *Los Angeles Times,* 4 July 1982.

7. See Chapter 2 for a discussion of employment and residential patterns in Orange County and twenty-one similar counties nationwide. Many Orange County workers also commute from nearby Riverside County, where they find housing more affordable.

8. As in other metropolitan areas most of Orange County's poor neighborhoods were originally middle-class neighborhoods that declined in comparative value over time.

9. According to Hallan-Gibson, *Golden Promise,* 244, Orange County's conservative image was formed in the late 1950s and early 1960s, when a small number of right-wing politicians and political activists gained national attention. The John Birch Society claimed five thousand members in Orange County. And Congressman James B. Utt vigorously attacked the income tax, welfare, civil rights, and the United Nations until his death in 1970. A national survey of newspaper editors found that conservative politics is a key element in their overall image of Orange County. See Larry Peterson, "Stereotype: OC's Image as Bastion of Conservatism Dies Hard," *Orange County Register,* 29 June 1987. But Orange County's vocal right-wing zealots have created an unbalanced picture of its citizens' political orientations, which are diverse. Although the county is by no means as liberal as San Francisco, or even Los Angeles, in the elections of 1988 Democrats constituted nearly 35 percent of registered voters (410,644, the second largest concentration of Democrats in California) as opposed to 55 percent for Republicans (650,348). The remaining voters were scattered among the American Independent Party, the Libertarian Party, and the Peace and Freedom Party. See Larry Peterson, "GOP Voter Registration Leads Democrats by Record 240,000," *Orange County Register,* 25 Oct. 1988.

10. Mark Baldassare, *Trouble in Paradise: The Suburban Transformation in America* (New York: Columbia University Press, 1986), 46–47.

11. Robert Fishman, *Bourgeois Utopias: The Rise and Fall of Suburbia* (New York: Basic Books, 1987), 184; emphasis in original.

12. Fishman (*Bourgeois Utopias*) labels this new formation a *techno-city* and *techno-burb.* We are uncomfortable with these terms because they focus on the technological infrastructure, especially automobiles. Transportation and communication technologies are central facilitators of postsuburban development, but other features, such as spatial decentralization, are also salient. Others have labeled these new formations *outer cities, urban villages,* or *exurbs.* Baldassare (*Trouble in Paradise*) simply calls them *transformed suburbs.* Each of these labels has connotations we believe to be inappropriate.

With some reluctance we have coined yet another term—the somewhat vaguer *postsuburban region,* which implies that the new formation follows the development of suburbs in time. Postsuburban regions are neither better nor worse than traditional cities; they are simply different. And we find them much more interesting than traditional suburbs.

13. Gottdiener and Kephart (Chapter 2) characterize social formations like Orange County as "deconcentrated" and "polynucleated." They prefer the term

fully urbanized county to *postsuburban county.* Despite these differences in terminology we see Orange County in essentially identical ways. See also M. Gottdiener, *The Social Production of Urban Space* (Austin: University of Texas Press, 1985).

14. Levittown on Long Island exemplifies this strategy of homogeneous residential-tract developments.

15. In the South County, where some of the newer (and more expensive) homes are located on terraced hillsides, the private patios often overlook other homes lower down the hillsides. But they are still private households.

16. Paul Goodman and Percival Goodman, *Communitas: Means of Livelihood and Ways of Life* (New York: Vintage Books, 1947), pt. 2.

17. See, for example, Fishman, *Bourgeois Utopias*; Peter Muller, *Contemporary Suburban America* (Englewood Cliffs, N.J.: Prentice-Hall, 1981); Carl Abbott, *The New Urban America: Growth and Politics in Sunbelt Cities* (Chapel Hill: University of North Carolina Press, 1981); Kenneth Jackson, *The Crabgrass Frontier: The Suburbanization of the United States* (New York: Oxford University Press, 1985); and Gottdiener, *Social Production of Urban Space.* Also see Christopher Leinberger and Charles Lockwood, "How Business Is Reshaping America," *Atlantic Monthly,* October 1986; and Christopher Leinberger and Charles Lockwood, "The Boom Towns," *Time,* 15 June 1987.

18. Paul Goldberger, "Orange County: Tomorrowland—Wall to Wall," *New York Times,* 11 Dec. 1988.

19. See Leinberger and Lockwood, "How Business Is Reshaping America," 44.

20. Goldberger, "Orange County."

21. See John R. Logan and Harvey Molotch, *Urban Fortunes: The Political Economy of Place* (Los Angeles: University of California Press, 1987).

22. See David Plotke, "The United States in Transition: Toward a New Order?" *Socialist Review* 54 (November-December 1980): 72–76. Also Patrick Brantlinger, *Bread and Circuses: Theories of Mass Culture and Social Decay* (Ithaca, N.Y.: Cornell University Press, 1984). An early entrant into this debate, with whose views we largely disagree, was Daniel Bell, *The Coming of Post-industrial Society* (New York: Basic Books, 1973). Bell's vision is appropriately criticized by Krishan Kumar in *Prophesy and Progress* (London: Allen Lane, 1978) and by David Lyon in *The Information Society: Issues and Illusions* (New York: Harper & Row, 1988).

23. See Marc Uri Porat, *The Information Economy: Definition and Measurement,* U.S. Office of Technology Special Publication 77-12(1) (Washington: Department of Commerce, 1977).

24. Gottdiener and Kephart develop a careful definition of high-tech workers in Chapter 2. They estimate the number of high-tech workers in Orange County and twenty-one other postsuburban counties in 1975 and 1980. More recent data come from less analytical sources. A business writer, Eric Herman, estimated that there were 94,900 high-tech workers in Orange County in 1986; "High Technology in Orange County: A Historical Perspective," *Special Resource Magazine, High Technology,* 1988, p. 25.

25. See Chapter 4 for a thorough discussion of information capitalism. Also see Timothy W. Luke and Stephen K. White, "Critical Theory, the Informational

Revolution, and an Ecological Path to Modernity," in *Critical Theory and Public Life*, ed. John Forester (Cambridge, Mass.: MIT Press, 1985), 22–53.

26. Some service businesses have actually developed information services as adjuncts to their main lines of business. The best example is American Airlines, a provider of transportation that sells access to its airline reservation system (Sabre) to other airlines. It has organized Sabre so that it gives American Airlines a competitive edge.

27. Scott (*Metropolis*) points out that after a long period of decline in federal defense and space spending in Orange County during the 1970s, defense expenditures rose again in the early 1980s. The defense sector clearly serves as an important source of employment in the county, yet Scott erroneously claims that defense jobs constitute the major source. We do not believe this claim. Defense spending amounted to $3.23 billion in 1987, less than 10 percent of Orange County's expected 1988 gross national product of $50 billion. Orange County's manufacturing sector employs a bit more than 20 percent of the work force, and about 40 percent of those jobs are high-tech jobs. About 40 percent of the county's eight hundred high-tech electronics firms have defense contracts. For the large aerospace-defense firms defense contracts constitute a major fraction of revenues; for small firms such contracts often constitute a much smaller percentage of business. Undeniably, defense firms have a high profile in Orange County because they are the county's largest high-tech manufacturing firms (for example, Hughes Aircraft, Rockwell International, Ford Aerospace and Communications, and McDonnell Douglas). See Scott, *Metropolis*, 163–66, and Richard V. Simon, "Security—Our National Defense," *Special Resource Magazine, High Technology*, 1988, pp. 48–49.

28. See, for example, Chris Barnett, "The Ripening of Orange County: How It's Stealing the L.A. Dream," *Los Angeles Magazine*, March 1978; Ruth Walker, "Tomorrowland in the World's 30th Largest Economy," *Christian Science Monitor*, 12 Sept. 1982; and Frederick Muir, "An Economy That Reflects the Shape of Things to Come," *Los Angeles Times*, 3 May 1987. The Orange County employment base by industry in 1986 was as follows: manufacturing, 24.1 percent; wholesale and retail trade, 24.7 percent; services, 23.7 percent; finance, insurance, and real estate, 7.3 percent; government/public, 10.9 percent; construction, 4.7 percent; agriculture, 0.9 percent; and other, 3.7 percent. See Orange County Chamber of Commerce, *Orange County Fact Sheet* (Orange, 1986).

29. See Chapter 9 for a thorough discussion of the participation of undocumented Mexican immigrants in grass-roots politics in Santa Ana during the 1980s. Also see Cathleen Decker, "1980 Census Shows Minorities Up to 14% of County Population," *Los Angeles Times*, 28 Mar. 1981; Lynn Smith, "Conference Focuses on Problems of Immigrants," *Los Angeles Times*, 13 Dec. 1985; and Carla Lazzareschi, "Immigrants Are Vital Part of Economy, Businesses Say," *Los Angeles Times*, 27 July 1986. Orange County's Latino residents were recorded by census officials in a separate category for the first time in 1980 but were included in the white totals.

30. See Stuart Ewen and Elizabeth Ewen, *Channels of Desire: Mass Images and the Shaping of American Consciousness* (New York: McGraw-Hill, 1982); Roland

Marchand, *Advertising the American Dream: Making Way for Modernity, 1920–1940* (Berkeley: University of California Press, 1985); and Adrian Forty, *Objects of Desire: Design and Society from Wedgewood to IBM* (New York: Pantheon, 1986).

31. Henri Lefebvre, *Everyday Life in the Modern World*, as quoted in William Severini Kowinski, *The Malling of America: An Inside Look at the Great Consumer Paradise* (New York: Morrow, 1985), 335.

32. See Steve Emmons and Mark Landsbaum, "Shop Til You Drop: When It Comes to Spending, Orange County Ranks No. 1," *Los Angeles Times*, 5 Dec. 1987; and "Almanac: Retail Sales in 1987 Third Quarter," *Los Angeles Times*, 26 Apr. 1988.

33. According to the National Association of Realtors, the ten most expensive housing markets in the United States in the second quarter of 1989 were: San Francisco ($265,700 median resale home price), Honolulu ($262,500), Orange County ($247,636), Los Angeles ($218,000), Boston ($188,600), New York ($185,000), San Diego ($176,000), Hartford ($165,100), New Haven ($156,100), and Washington, D.C. ($139,900). In 1988 Orange County had the most expensive housing market in the nation. In San Francisco, surprisingly, only 9 percent of families could afford to buy a home. These figures contrast with the national average of 44 percent of families who can afford to buy a home, and the California statewide average of 22 percent. During the 1980s the percentage of families who could afford to buy a home fell dramatically, even with the sharp rise in two-income households. See John O'Dell, "Orange County Leads Nation in Cost of Homes," *Los Angeles Times*, 15 Feb. 1989.

The relative expense of housing in Orange County also is important. Nearby Riverside County's median resale home price was $122,200 in the second quarter of 1989, which 29 percent of that county's families could afford. Consequently, many Orange County workers have been moving to Riverside and commuting one to two hours daily to work. See Michael Flagg, "Median Home Price Increases to $255,897," *Los Angeles Times*, 30 Aug. 1989, Orange County Business section.

34. Eugene Burdick, *The 480* (New York: McGraw-Hill, 1964). In this novel, Burdick satirized a marketing firm that advances a presidential candidate through a scheme in which the United States is segmented into 480 distinct political markets defined by demographic characteristics and voting behavior.

35. Scott (*Metropolis*, chap. 9) provides a nice historical analysis of the move of aerospace firms to Orange County and their role in spawning other industrial developments.

36. Examples include the Fluor Corporation, Allergan Pharmaceuticals, and Beatrice Foods.

37. Examples include Printronix (a computer-printer manufacturer), AST Research (a manufacturer of components for microcomputers), and Western Digital (also a manufacturer of microcomputer components).

38. According to the 1988 *Orange County Annual Survey*, adults who lived in Orange County less than five years differ substantially from those who have lived in Orange County for more than ten years on several characteristics, among others: college education (29 percent of recent immigrants versus 23 percent of long-term residents); graduate degrees (14 percent of recent immigrants versus

12 percent of long-term residents); political affiliation (45 percent of recent immigrants are registered as Republicans, 23 percent are registered as Democrats, and 5 percent are independent, compared with 54 percent of long-term residents registered as Republicans, 30 percent registered as Democrats, and 4 percent independent). Mark Baldassare and Cheryl Katz, *Orange County Annual Survey: 1988 Final Report* (Irvine: Public Policy Research Organization, University of California, 1988).

39. See Robert V. Hine, *California's Utopian Colonies* (Berkeley: University of California Press, 1983).

40. See Spencer C. Olin, "Bible Communism and the Origins of Orange County," *California History* 48 (Fall 1979): 220–33.

41. See Baldassare, *Trouble in Paradise*. See also Lynn Smith, "A Nice Place to Live, but Freeway Phobia Prevails," *Los Angeles Times*, 11 Dec. 1987.

42. These perceptions differ significantly from those that Baldassare found in his *Orange County Annual Survey* in 1985. In 1985 more than 40 percent of his respondents reported that Orange County would be a better place to live in the future and about 35 percent complained that the quality of life would diminish. By 1987 only 26 percent reported optimism about their future lives in Orange County, while 54 percent expected the quality of life to decline. These data are reported in Mark Baldassare and Cheryl Katz, *Orange County Annual Survey: 1987 Final Report* (Irvine: Public Policy Research Organization, University of California, 1987).

REFERENCES

Abbott, Carl. *The New Urban America: Growth and Politics in Sunbelt Cities.* Chapel Hill: University of North Carolina Press, 1981.

"Almanac: Retail Sales in 1987 Third Quarter." *Los Angeles Times*, 26 Apr. 1988.

Baldassare, Mark. *Trouble in Paradise: The Suburban Transformation in America.* New York: Columbia University Press, 1986.

Baldassare, Mark, and Cheryl Katz. *Orange County Annual Survey: 1987 Final Report.* Irvine: Public Policy Research Organization, University of California, 1987.

———. *Orange County Annual Survey: 1988 Final Report.* Irvine: Public Policy Research Organization, University of California, 1988.

Barnett, Chris. "The Ripening of Orange County: How It's Stealing the L.A. Dream." *Los Angeles Magazine*, March 1978.

Bell, Daniel. *The Coming of Post-industrial Society.* New York: Basic Books, 1973.

Bernard, Richard M., and Bradley R. Rice, eds. *Sunbelt Cities: Politics and Growth since World War II.* Austin: University of Texas Press, 1983.

Brantlinger, Patrick. *Bread and Circuses: Theories of Mass Culture and Social Decay.* Ithaca, N.Y.: Cornell University Press, 1984.

Burdick, Eugene. *The 480.* New York: McGraw-Hill, 1964.

Decker, Cathleen. "1980 Census Shows Minorities Up to 14% of County Population." *Los Angeles Times*, 28 Mar. 1981.

Emmons, Steve, and Mark Landsbaum. "Shop Til You Drop: When It Comes to Spending, Orange County Ranks No. 1." *Los Angeles Times*, 5 Dec. 1987.

Ewen, Stuart, and Elizabeth Ewen. *Channels of Desire: Mass Images and the Shaping of American Consciousness*. New York: McGraw-Hill, 1982.

Fishman, Robert. *Bourgeois Utopias: The Rise and Fall of Suburbia*. New York: Basic Books, 1987.

Flagg, Michael. "Median Home Price Increases to $255,897." *Los Angeles Times*, 30 Aug. 1989, Orange County Business section.

Forty, Adrian. *Objects of Desire: Design and Society from Wedgewood to IBM*. New York: Pantheon, 1986.

Goldberger, Paul. "Orange County: Tomorrowland—Wall to Wall." *New York Times*, 11 Dec. 1988.

Goodman, Paul, and Percival Goodman. *Communitas: Means of Livelihood and Ways of Life*. New York: Vintage Books, 1947.

Gottdiener, M. *The Social Production of Urban Space*. Austin: University of Texas Press, 1985.

Hallan-Gibson, Pamela. *The Golden Promise: An Illustrated History of Orange County*. Northridge, Calif.: Windsor, 1986.

Herman, Eric. "High Technology in Orange County: A Historical Perspective." *Special Resource Magazine, High Technology*, 1988.

Hine, Robert V. *California's Utopian Colonies*. Berkeley: University of California Press, 1983.

Jackson, Kenneth. *The Crabgrass Frontier: The Suburbanization of the United States*. New York: Oxford University Press, 1985.

Kowinski, William Severini. *The Malling of America: An Inside Look at the Great Consumer Paradise*. New York: Morrow, 1985.

Kumar, Krishan. *Prophesy and Progress*. London: Allen Lane, 1978.

Lazzareschi, Carla. "Immigrants Are Vital Part of Economy, Businesses Say." *Los Angeles Times*, 27 July 1986.

Leinberger, Christopher, and Charles Lockwood. "The Boom Towns." *Time*, 15 June 1987.

————. "How Business Is Reshaping America." *Atlantic Monthly*, October 1986.

Logan, John R., and Harvey Molotch. *Urban Fortunes: The Political Economy of Place*. Los Angeles: University of California Press, 1987.

Luke, Timothy W., and Stephen K. White. "Critical Theory, the Informational Revolution, and an Ecological Path to Modernity." In *Critical Theory and Public Life*, ed. John Forester, 22–53. Cambridge, Mass.: MIT Press, 1985.

Lyon, David. *The Information Society: Issues and Illusions*. New York: Harper & Row, 1988.

Marchand, Roland. *Advertising the American Dream: Making Way for Modernity, 1920–1940*. Berkeley: University of California Press, 1985.

Maxwell, Evan, and Peter King. "In Orange County: A New Identity." *Los Angeles Times*, 4 July 1982.

Muir, Frederick. "An Economy That Reflects the Shape of Things to Come." *Los Angeles Times*, 3 May 1987.

Muller, Peter. *Contemporary Suburban America.* Englewood Cliffs, N.J.: Prentice-Hall, 1981.

O'Dell, John. "Orange County Leads Nation in Cost of Homes." *Los Angeles Times,* 15 Feb. 1989.

Olin, Spencer C. "Bible Communism and the Origins of Orange County." *California History* 48 (Fall 1979): 220–33.

Orange County Business First (Irving, Calif.) 13 June 1988.

Orange County Chamber of Commerce. *Orange County Fact Sheet.* Orange, Calif., 1986.

Peterson, Larry. "GOP Voter Registration Leads Democrats by Record 240,000." *Orange County Register,* 25 Oct. 1988.

———. "Stereotype: OC's Image as Bastion of Conservatism Dies Hard." *Orange County Register,* 29 June 1987.

Plotke, David. "The United States in Transition: Toward a New Order?" *Socialist Review* 54 (November-December 1980): 72–76.

Porat, Marc Uri. 1977. *The Information Economy: Definition and Measurement.* U.S. Office of Technology Special Publication 77-12(1). Washington: Department of Commerce.

Sawers, Larry, and William K. Tabb, eds. *Sunbelt/Snowbelt: Urban Development and Regional Restructuring.* New York: Oxford University Press, 1984.

Scott, Allen J. *Metropolis: From the Division of Labor to Urban Form.* Berkeley: University of California Press, 1988.

Simon, Richard V. "Security—Our National Defense." *Special Resource Magazine, High Technology,* 1988.

Smith, Lynn. "Conference Focuses on Problems of Immigrants." *Los Angeles Times,* 13 Dec. 1985.

———. "A Nice Place to Live, but Freeway Phobia Prevails." *Los Angeles Times,* 11 Dec. 1987.

Soja, Edward, Rebecca Morales, and Goetz Wolf. "Urban Restructuring: An Analysis of Social and Spatial Change in Los Angeles." *Economic Geography* 59 (April 1979): 80–106.

Todd, Ian, and Michael Wheeler. *Utopia.* New York: Harmony Books, 1978.

Walker, Ruth. "Tomorrowland in the World's 30th Largest Economy." *Christian Science Monitor,* 12 Sept. 1982.

Wiley, Peter, and Robert Gottlieb. *Empires in the Sun: The Rise of the New American West.* New York: Putnam's, 1982.

TWO

The Multinucleated
Metropolitan Region:
A Comparative Analysis

M. Gottdiener and George Kephart

Prior to the 1950s and for many centuries the city, as a form of settlement space, and urbanization, as the social process of city formation, were both well understood. The internal differentiation of an industrialized society was often expressed in urban/rural terms. Cities were bounded spatial forms with distinct centers that dominated, in both an emotional and an economic sense, the urbanized areas surrounding them. The economic growth of cities took place through war, commerce, and industry, while population swelled accordingly by the absorption of migrants from the hinterland and immigrants from places elsewhere. In effect cities were huge magnets that concentrated both people and economic activity or wealth in well-defined, bounded spaces. These processes were so distinct, were taking place on such a massive scale, and were so typical of cities everywhere that an urban science could be articulated with well-defined laws that explained urban location decisions and urban social interaction as distinct from processes taking place outside the city.

Early analyses of urbanization were aided greatly by census taking. This practice followed closely the urban/rural dichotomy in characterizing the population according to rural/farm and city/nonfarm dwellers. By the turn of the century, however, growth beyond central-city borders was a common occurrence on the American scene (Warner 1962). These suburban districts sometimes acquired separate political jurisdiction and sometimes remained merely as unincorporated land; however, they were recognized as being neither country nor city. In fact, land speculators promoted development outside the city as fulfilling some vague Arcadian ideal that integrated the best of city and rural living (see Jackson 1985, Lundberg et al. 1934).

Initially, locating a private residence outside the city was an act of

31

the relatively well-off. By the late 1800s, however, ambitious developers opened up for the majority vast tracts of land adjacent to cities. Surprisingly, real estate schemes often fit with the plans of railroad tycoons to expand their own dominance of the turn-of-the-century transportation boom because the sale of suburban land created demand for commuter lines. Such a pattern of suburban expansion was especially true for Los Angeles (Crump 1962).

As growth beyond central cities progressed, functional differentiation of the suburbs quickly followed, giving rise to our earliest pictures of regional metropolitan development (see, for example, Burgess 1925, Harris and Ullman 1945). By the 1930s it was well recognized that suburban areas possessed commercial and industrial facilities that made them somewhat autonomous from central cities. Yet, the functional importance of the center and its political, economic, and cultural dominance of the hinterland did not wane during the years prior to World War II. In this period a consistent image of suburbia emerged as a bedroom commuter shed housing those who traveled to work in the city.

By the 1950s the pace of suburbanization quickened considerably. The causes for this change are now well known (see Gottdiener 1985); they include easy financing and subsidized loans for houses; tax write-offs for homeowners; ambitious highway-construction schemes; innovations in modular home construction; and, not the least, the growing popularity of the suburban life-style. Relocation to suburbia blossomed into a mass movement at this time as housing developers became able to build entire communities at once (see Gans 1967). As the predominantly white population took up residence outside the city, the center's minority population began to increase. White flight to the hinterland brought drastic and profound changes to city neighborhoods and their ways of life.

THE EMERGENCE OF THE MULTINUCLEATED METROPOLITAN REGION

Following the censuses of 1950 and 1960, the images of both city and suburb changed irrevocably in the United States. In particular, the generalized view of the suburb as a commuter shed was abandoned in favor of a conception of suburban areas as differentiated with regard to class, income, and life-style (Schnore 1957, 1963; Dobriner 1958, 1963). Most important, the approach to urbanization itself shifted fundamentally at this time, as the concepts of metropolitanization and regional development replaced the idea of city-based growth. The metropolitan region was conceived of as comprising a large, concentrated central city containing the most important industrial, administrative, and commercial functions; the city then dominated a surrounding and sprawling region of homes and dispersed social activities. Working in New York City, the Regional Plan Association (1962) coined the terms *slab city* and *spread city* to capture the new image of the fully urbanized metropolitan region.

As early as 1949 the Bureau of the Census moved to obtain a more accurate picture of urban/suburban sprawl than it had previously had by using a separate technique for classifying what it called a Standard Metropolitan Area (SMA). This concept was changed in 1959 to the Standard Metropolitan Statistical Area (SMSA) (see Federal Commission on Standard Metropolitan Statistical Areas 1980). The SMSA cuts up the space surrounding a large metropolitan center, or possibly two or more centers adjacent to each other, into a core and a periphery by aggregating all counties (townships in New England) that are linked together economically. The link is determined principally through assessing the extent of commutation between counties. By using journey-to-work data, one can consider all linked counties part of a metropolitan region or "daily urban system" (Berry and Kasarda 1977) that forms the base for the economic growth of the region. The 1960 census, by using the concepts of the SMSA and the daily urban system, replaced the image of the compact, bounded city that historically signified urban space with a new picture of an agglomerated and sprawling region anchored by the traditional city and extending for many miles across county lines that we call the multinucleated metropolitan region.

Metropolitan expansion and hinterland development have persisted since the 1960s. By the 1970s researchers began to marvel at the level of suburban development. The regional hinterland had surpassed the city as the site for the most rapid growth. Even though cities continued to attract population, suburban and exurban areas were the primary beneficiaries of population movements. The population residing outside central cities began to outstrip that of the city itself. In fact, between 1970 and 1980 traditional urban centers such as New York, Chicago, San Francisco, and Philadelphia experienced net population declines. At present, nearly half the total U.S. population resides in suburban areas.

In addition to population, significant components of industry as well as banking and corporate administration shifted to suburban areas (Berry and Kasarda 1977, 228–47). Indeed, even administrative functions were becoming dispersed (Armstrong 1979). Suburban areas emerged not just as the hubs of population but also as the hubs of metropolitan activity in general, thereby calling into question the mainstream urbanist's concept of central-city dominance.

We call this process of becoming a fully urbanized region *deconcentration,* and we call the new space it produces the *multinucleated metropolitan region* (Gottdiener 1985). Deconcentration includes the restructuring of both the central city and the outlying areas. Because of the massive regional dispersal of population, industry, and commerce, we now have vast urbanized areas for which the concept of urban dominance is becoming obsolete. These areas constitute a settlement-space form that is polynucleated, functionally dispersed, culturally fragmented, yet hierarchically organized, and that extends for tens and even hundreds of miles.

A multinucleated metropolitan region is a qualitatively new form of settlement space. Although analysts of deconcentration have made considerable strides in documenting the general process associated with this phenomenon, the mainstream understanding of a multinucleated metropolitan region as a new form of sociospatial organization lags behind. For us the traditional concept of the city has become obsolete. Instead, we believe that urban life is now organized in metropolitan regions composed of polynucleated and functionally differentiated spaces that are no longer extensions of the traditional city. They are neither suburbs nor satellite cities; rather, they are fully urbanized and independent spaces that are not dominated by any central city (Gottdiener 1985).

The multinucleated metropolitan region is perhaps best exemplified by the relatively recent fully urbanized, yet independent county located within an expanding metropolitan region, such as Orange County in California or Suffolk County in New York. These counties seem to grow and prosper independently of the traditional city centers adjacent to them. Orange County in particular is a phenomenon. It is polynucleated, with no clear urban center that dominates the others. In fact, 70 percent of its population lives outside its three largest cities. Orange County employs nearly one million people—more than several states—and has a complete functional complement of industry, commerce, banking, corporate headquarters, and even farming. It has acquired a first-rate cultural center that rivals the facilities of Los Angeles. In sum, Orange County can hardly be viewed as a satellite of Los Angeles. It provides the full array of functions and services associated with the concentrated cities of the past, except that it is a prime example of the force of deconcentration and the way that force has been reshaping our lives.

Conceptualizing deconcentration in this manner departs fundamentally from the way it has been viewed in the mainstream urban literature. Many mainstream observers continue to view metropolitan regions as simply larger versions of cities (see in particular Long and DeAre 1982). They use deconcentration most commonly to refer to a regional leveling of population, and their belief in the dominance of the central city persists. Our conceptualization of deconcentration also departs from the mainstream view in that we see it as a sociospatial form of late capitalism. Accordingly our understanding of its causes and historical origins differs completely from the ideas of mainstream urban ecologists, who do not specify in their work the relation between space and the mode of production (see Gottdiener 1985 for a detailed discussion of these conceptual differences).

THEORIES OF DECONCENTRATION

Several theories have emerged in the literature to account for the new pattern of metropolitan deconcentration. We will refer to these theories loosely as the human ecological, the high technology, and the postindustrial.

The human-ecological approach is an expanded version of the traditional theory of metropolitan expansion (Sly and Tayman 1980). It retains the focus on suburban growth but acknowledges that mature suburbs, while still performing a bedroom, commuter-shed function, have increasingly become the home for industry. The ecological approach has long appreciated the important power of mature suburban areas as sources of employment in manufacturing, service, commerce, and banking (see Schnore 1957, 1963). It suggests, however, that there is nothing unique about the economy of multinucleated metropolitan regions. Deconcentration is the result primarily of improved transportation and communications and the functional differentiation and decentralization of the activities that they lead to (Sly and Tayman 1980). However, as we have suggested, this approach continues to view deconcentration within the traditional framework, and the notion of the dominance of the city is retained.

Another general theory alleges that deconcentration is the result of the structural transformation to a postindustrial society (Bell 1980, Touraine 1971). The principal hallmark of the new era, it is argued, is the replacement of an economic base dominated by manufacturing with one dominated by service and information industries. This process results in deconcentration in several ways. First, it causes the decline of certain types of industries (manufacturing) and the growth of others (services). To the extent that there are differences, for whatever reason, in where declining and growing industries are located (centralized versus multinucleated metropolitan region, central city versus suburb), geographic restructuring will occur. Some evidence supports this contention. Analysts of growth outside major central cities have commonly observed the important role of service industries in the suburban economic base, even if such analysts do not subscribe to the postindustrial thesis (Calhoun 1984, Leven 1979, Richards 1978). Second, constraints on where work and production can be located are lifted. Production in service and information industries is less tied to particular locations for both the firm and the worker than it is in manufacturing industries (Calhoun 1984). Third, the location of firms relative to their markets may be altered in a way that contributes to deconcentration (Leven 1979).

Finally, there is the high-technology thesis, which has been inspired by the advent of "silicon landscapes." At least since 1970 military spending, coupled with the microelectronics industry, has sustained the economy of a number of locations outside traditional cities. Orange County and Silicon Valley in California are among the best examples. Adherents of this approach allege that such areas are the product of a new stage of capitalism in which technology has become a principal source of sociospatial change for both cities and suburbs. The high-technology thesis has focused explicitly on the role of high-technology firms in restructuring settlement space (Markusen, Hall, and Glassmeier 1986, Castells 1985, Scott 1986). According to this perspective, the importance of high technology does not have to do as much with the product as with high technology as a means of production. Automation, robotics, and computers have revolutionized the production process, increasing the capital intensiveness of firms, expanding information processing, and even transforming financial strategies (Bluestone and Harrison 1982). High technology, it is argued, is emerging as a new means of production that is altering firms' decisions regarding location and organization (Castells 1985, 11–40). The growth of high technology is closely linked to large federal outlays for defense and for research and development. In fact, as we shall see later in this chapter, it is often difficult to separate out the growth of high-tech firms from economic development that has been sustained by the massive spending associated with what Ernest Mandel (1975) calls the "permanent war economy."

Allen Scott (1986) has applied this perspective explicitly to the case of Orange County. Scott sees high technology and military spending as providing the economic base for Orange County—a base that differs from the classic industrial profile of the capitalist city. Scott explains the patterns of internal differentiation of space within Orange County according to a classic concentric-zone model of development, which assumes "perfect competition" among capitalists and adopts the view that regions are organized around their large central cities. He does not include in his explanation reasons connected with politics, state regulation, land development, or speculation. Scott sees the development of Orange County solely as a result of economic competition, which produces vertical disintegration of industry and agglomeration tendencies that are a function of differing capital intensities among firms and that, in turn, lead to deconcentrating location decisions.

We will assess these three explanations by comparing a sample of twenty-one counties that are like Orange County in that they are multinucleated, highly urbanized, and prosper adjacent to traditional urban centers. We compare these counties with respect to their economic base and the degree to which they are employment or residential centers, and on a number of basic demographic and social variables. From these results we will suggest that no simple, single-factor theory can account for the growth of counties like Orange County. In particular, we will argue that far too much has been made of the high technology thesis and that other equally important factors, such as real estate development and the deconcentration of "ordinary" labor-intensive manufacturing, must be considered.

SOURCES OF DATA

The counties we examined were selected because they were similar to Orange County in four respects. First, they were all located adjacent to major traditional urban centers including New York, Boston, Washington, Baltimore, Philadelphia, Atlanta, Detroit, Chicago, Miami, Los Angeles, and San Francisco. Second, they were all areas that were growing, both in total population and in number of civilian jobs. Third, all the counties were large and highly urbanized. With two exceptions, they had populations over 500,000 in 1980 and employed more than 100,000 civilians over age sixteen. All counties were also located within a Consolidated Metropolitan Statistical Area or Metropolitan Statistical Area of more than one million people. The exceptions were two counties located outside Atlanta (Gwinnett and De Kalb) that are adjacent to each other and when combined totaled more than 500,000 population in 1980. Finally, with one exception, none of the counties we selected was dominated by a large urban center. The one exception was Santa Clara County in California, which contains a large central city, San Jose. This county was included because it contains Silicon Valley and is heralded as the type of settlement space we examine here. Furthermore, despite the presence of a single large city, over half the county population is located outside San Jose; so Santa Clara County does in fact possess aspects of deconcentration that are comparable to those of Orange County.

The selection of counties with more than 500,000 people excludes many counties that are also highly urbanized and located outside major urban centers. This exclusion occurs because counties in the United States display a great deal of variation in land area. For example, metropolitan counties in Texas are typically quite small. Small land areas precluded any of these counties from meeting the size cutoff, and it was not feasible to combine counties. We have two reasons for our use of this size cutoff. First, the county is a somewhat arbitrary unit of analysis, and many of the variables on which we wished to compare counties are not independent of the size of the county. For example, as land area and population become smaller, the county will tend to become more specialized in employment and in the degree to which it is an employment or residential center. We wished to choose only counties that were large enough to display diversity. Second, our desire was simply to contrast Orange County with other similar counties, not to make generalizations for all areas in the United States. The twenty-one counties we have chosen provide the opportunity for interesting and informative comparisons with Orange County.

County-level data were obtained from three different sources. First, a number of basic variables such as decennial growth, racial composition, and median income were obtained from the Area Resource File (Bureau of Health Professions 1980). These data are a compilation of statistics at the county level. Second, journey-to-work data from the Bureau of the Census were utilized to compute employment-to-residence ratios for each county (Census of Population 1985). This is a ratio of the number of workers, age sixteen and over, who are employed in a county to the number of workers, age sixteen and over, who reside within a county. It is an index of the extent to which a county is an employment or residential center. Finally, county-business-patterns (Bureau of the Census 1975, 1980) data were used to gauge employment changes in various industries. In county-business-patterns data employment counts are tabulated according to the 1973 Standard Industrial Classification (SIC), which classifies all industries by detailed three- or four-digit codes rather than the standard two-digit scheme employed in tabulated census data. Using these data enabled us to identify high-technology manufacturing industries as well as military-related high-technology industries.

There has been considerable debate as to what constitutes a high-technology industry, and a number of measures have been used (Markusen, Hall, and Glassmeier 1986). Here, high-technology industries are defined according to the proportion of technical occupations in the total labor force of an industry. We used a list of SIC codes from Glassmeier (1985) that is based on the overall average proportion of employees in each industry who are engineers, engineering technicians, computer scientists, mathematicians, and life scientists, including geologists, physicists, and chemists. In contrast to measures based on the technical sophistication of the product or research-and-development intensity, this measure defines high technology as a means of production. Markusen and Bloch (1985) provide a list of such high-technology industries that are related to the military. Utilizing this list, we also tabulated employment counts for military-related high-technology industries. In addition to tabulations for high-technology industries, we include employment figures for other manufacturing sectors (those that are not classified as high technology), finance, construction and real estate, transportation and communication, wholesaling and retailing, and services.

County employment patterns for two years, 1975 and 1980, were used so that the contribution of different industrial categories to total employment change could be established. It would perhaps have been more desirable to examine employment change for the period between 1970 to 1980; however, changes in the SIC scheme precluded this. In 1972 the scheme was revised, which resulted in incompatibilities for three- and four-digit categories.

EVIDENCE FOR DECONCENTRATION

The counties we examine generally prospered over the two-decade period from 1960 to 1980, often in contrast to declines in the traditional urban cores to which they are adjacent. All the counties selected experienced population growth during this period (table 2.1). Percentage increase in population was generally much higher in the 1960–70 period, ranging from 2.1 percent annually for Fairfield County in Connecticut and for Montgomery County in Pennsylvania to a spectacular 10.2 percent annualized increase for Orange County. In contrast, between 1970 and 1980 a number of counties—including Norfolk, Massachusetts; Fairfield, Connecticut; Middlesex, New Jersey; and Prince Georges, Maryland— experienced very modest annual growth of less than 0.2 percent. Although all the counties we selected were growing, they experienced a variety of growth patterns. Some counties grew relatively rapidly in both decades (for example, Gwinnett/De Kalb, Georgia; Broward, Florida); some grew relatively modestly in both decades (Fairfield, Connecticut; Montgomery, Pennsylvania); some modestly in 1960–70 and rapidly in 1970–80 (Hillsborough, Florida); and some rapidly in 1960–70 and modestly in 1970–80 (Prince Georges, Maryland).

All the counties also sustained increasing civilian-employment growth between 1975 and 1980 (table 2.2). Annual percentage increases varied from a high of 11.1 percent for Orange County, which was once again a growth leader, to 2.5 percent for Montgomery County in Pennsylvania. Generally, this employment growth appears to be correlated with population growth. An exception, however, was Hillsborough, Florida, which experienced low employment growth but a relatively large population increase between 1970 and 1980. Additionally, the counties for the most part had only moderate levels of unemployment, with all but Macomb and Oakland counties in Michigan experiencing unemployment rates of less than 10 percent (table 2.3). Total civilian employment (table 2.4) for each county was also quite respectable during this same period. At the low end, Ventura County, California, was very much like a medium-sized city

TABLE 2.1 County Demographic Characteristics

County	Total Population 1960	1970	1980	Growth, % 1960–70	1970–80	Area, mi², 1980	Employment/ Residence, 1980	Size of Largest Place, 1980
Norfolk, Mass.	510,256	605,100	606,587	19	1	400	.77	84,743
Fairfield, Conn.	653,589	792,800	807,143	21	2	632	.93	142,546
Suffolk, N.Y.	666,784	1,125,000	1,284,231	69	14	911	.70	44,321
Middlesex, N.J.	433,856	583,900	595,893	35	2	316	.89	41,422
Monmouth, N.J.	334,401	459,400	503,173	37	10	472	.75	29,819
Montgomery, Pa.	516,682	623,900	643,621	21	3	486	.99	59,651
Du Page, Ill.	313,459	491,900	658,835	57	34	337	.73	43,043
Macomb, Mich.	405,804	625,300	694,600	54	11	482	.80	161,134
Oakland, Mich.	690,259	907,900	1,011,793	32	11	875	.93	76,715
Baltimore, Md.	492,428	621,100	655,615	26	6	598	.66	48,301
Montgomery, Md.	340,928	522,800	579,053	53	11	495	.84	72,893
Prince Georges, Md.	357,395	660,500	665,071	85	1	487	.63	35,793
Fairfax, Va.	285,194	487,700	625,806	71	28	402	.54	103,217
Gwinnett/De Kalb, Ga.	300,323	487,700	649,927	62	82	705	.76	37,283
Broward, Fla.	333,946	620,200	1,013,200	86	64	1211	.80	153,266
Hillsborough, Fla.	397,788	490,300	646,960	23	32	1053	.93	271,515
Contra Costa, Calif.	409,030	558,400	656,380	37	18	730	.65	103,225
Orange, Calif.	703,925	1,420,400	1,932,709	102	36	798	.84	219,311
San Mateo, Calif.	444,387	556,300	587,329	25	6	447	.74	77,561
Santa Clara, Calif.	624,315	1,064,700	1,295,071	66	22	1293	.94	629,442
Ventura, Calif.	199,138	376,600	529,174	89	41	1862	.71	108,095

TABLE 2.2 Annual County Employment Growth by Sector, 1975–80, as Percentage of Growth in Total Employment

County	Change in Total Employment	Manufacturing I			Manufacturing II			Transportation and Communication	Retail and Wholesale	Finance	Service	Land Development (Construction and Real Estate)	All Other
		Total	High-Tech	Other	Total	Defense	Other						
Norfolk, Mass.	3.96	14.79	-1.81	16.60	14.79	-0.48	15.27	4.93	33.32	8.30	33.91	4.0	0.59
Fairfield, Conn.	4.33	35.32	-1.35	36.67	35.32	4.03	31.29	5.66	20.32	-2.65	30.32	8.1	2.50
Suffolk, N.Y.	5.70	38.23	20.74	17.49	38.23	20.16	18.07	4.64	21.29	2.42	26.67	5.3	1.39
Middlesex, N.J.	3.72	14.10	6.21	7.89	14.10	1.69	12.41	14.15	32.53	6.77	29.17	2.6	0.66
Monmouth, N.J.	4.01	24.32	17.61	6.71	24.32	15.79	8.53	4.40	25.07	14.74	26.06	4.1	1.31
Montgomery, Pa.	2.46	0.53	0.18	0.35	0.53	-2.62	3.15	0.80	22.68	6.23	54.42	13.7	1.59
Du Page, Ill.	6.93	29.27	11.27	18.00	29.27	4.06	25.21	6.89	29.30	3.90	28.75	1.6	0.27
Macomb, Mich.	5.12	26.60	1.84	24.76	26.60	7.17	19.43	3.92	29.21	4.00	29.27	5.8	1.18
Oakland, Mich.	6.49	19.04	4.08	14.96	19.04	4.99	14.05	7.10	31.00	6.15	29.95	6.1	0.57
Baltimore, Md.	3.51	11.54	12.64	-1.10	11.54	6.92	4.62	-1.19	33.98	10.33	32.86	11.4	1.04
Montgomery, Md.	4.99	6.29	3.62	2.67	6.29	-2.14	8.43	6.63	20.40	5.42	48.83	11.0	1.44
Prince Georges, Md.	4.38	2.62	2.54	0.08	2.62	0.39	2.23	3.72	33.21	3.58	43.09	12.8	0.90
Fairfax, Va.	10.55	5.68	3.55	2.13	5.68	1.15	4.53	5.55	25.33	4.98	42.24	14.7	1.49
Gwinnett/De Kalb, Ga.	6.84	16.43	6.74	9.69	16.43	1.34	15.09	7.03	33.06	1.74	29.19	8.9	1.92
Broward, Fla.	7.65	16.06	6.84	9.22	16.06	4.04	12.02	3.53	32.93	7.99	23.34	14.6	1.50
Hillsborough, Fla.	3.01	7.83	3.35	4.48	7.83	-1.30	9.13	15.66	40.56	8.55	42.68	14.1	1.96
Contra Costa, Calif.	6.82	4.22	3.37	0.85	4.22	2.46	1.76	4.90	34.35	11.30	27.90	15.1	2.17
Orange, Calif.	11.14	24.74	11.39	13.35	24.74	6.53	18.21	5.41	23.86	6.43	23.27	14.3	1.93
San Mateo, Calif.	5.62	10.18	6.28	3.90	10.18	4.09	2.26	16.09	32.29	3.31	25.54	10.7	1.90
Santa Clara, Calif.	10.78	42.68	39.85	2.83	42.68	30.86	11.82	1.25	18.48	3.67	26.52	6.6	0.82
Ventura, Calif.	8.42	19.40	8.91	10.49	19.40	3.36	16.04	4.84	27.03	4.63	25.21	13.7	5.13

TABLE 2.3   County Socioeconomic Characteristics, 1980

County	White, %	Median Family Income, $	Poverty, %	Median Home Value, $	Unemployment, %
Norfolk, Mass.	97.7	25,435	4.2	56,600	4.2
Fairfield, Conn.	88.9	26,604	5.9	92,300	5.2
Suffolk, N.Y.	92.4	24,195	5.3	45,600	6.2
Middlesex, N.J.	89.9	25,603	4.7	62,600	6.3
Monmouth, N.J.	89.6	24,526	6.0	65,500	7.2
Montgomery, Pa.	93.9	25,803	3.3	60,600	6.3
Du Page, Ill.	95.0	30,431	2.3	78,100	5.6
Macomb, Mich.	97.5	26,666	3.9	51,000	13.6
Oakland, Mich.	93.2	28,807	4.1	58,100	10.9
Baltimore, Md.	90.2	24,414	4.1	56,700	7.7
Montgomery, Md.	85.9	33,711	3.0	97,400	3.2
Prince Georges, Md.	59.2	25,525	4.9	64,500	4.4
Fairfax, Va.	89.3	30,962	3.0	94,622	9.9
Gwinnett/De Kalb, Ga.	77.8	23,697	6.6	53,226	4.9
Broward, Fla.	87.8	19,610	6.3	62,900	4.7
Hillsborough, Fla.	84.8	17,697	10.7	37,400	5.1
Contra Costa, Calif.	82.1	26,513	6.1	94,600	9.0
Orange, Calif.	87.2	25,919	5.2	108,100	4.3
San Mateo, Calif.	79.3	27,279	4.5	124,400	3.6
Santa Clara, Calif.	79.6	26,662	5.3	109,400	5.3
Ventura, Calif.	82.7	23,612	6.1	93,300	7.2

with total civilian employment levels of 77,901 in 1975 and 117,238 in 1980. At the high end, Orange County generated a level of civilian employment comparable to that of many states with 471,659 employed in 1975 and 786,814 working in 1980.

All the counties in our sample were major population and employment centers to such an extent that they can hardly be viewed as satellites or suburbs of the traditional urban cores to which they are adjacent. In addition to containing large residential populations, they also employed a large number of people (see table 2.4). The extent to which these counties were not specialized residential areas can be seen by examining their employment-to-residence (E/R) ratios (see table 2.1). An E/R ratio greater than one implies that the area is a net employing region with commutation adding to the labor force. A ratio of less than one implies that the area still performs a significant function as a residential center and does not employ all its eligible occupants. Such an area might possess many of the functions

traditionally associated with suburbia in addition to an industrial infrastructure of some kind.

The industrial strength of the counties in our sample was so robust that
with one exception, Fairfax, Virginia, they can be characterized as having
significant employment as well as residential functions (see table 2.1).
Although these counties were not net employing areas, they have taken
on the employment diversity usually associated with cities. Among our
twenty-one counties (considering Gwinnett/De Kalb as one county), for
example, ten had E/R ratios of 0.80 or higher, and seventeen had E/R
ratios of 0.70 or higher, indicating the presence of a strong employment
base. Additionally, it can be seen in table 2.4 that the employment base of
these counties is diverse; they host manufacturing, service, retail, and
financial activities.

It can also be seen in table 2.1 that most of the counties we examined
did not contain any large central places. Only nine of the counties contained a place larger than 100,000, and only three counties contained a
place larger than 200,000. Unique among these counties is Santa Clara in
California, which contains Silicon Valley. San Jose, its largest city, at over
600,000 total population, is an older, more traditional urban center. As
indicated, we included this county in our sample both because of its
similarities to Orange County and because it remains an example of
deconcentration since over half of the population is outside San Jose.

However, other features of the twenty-one counties are characteristic
of traditional suburban areas. In particular and with one exception they
have a predominance of whites in the population (see table 2.3). Although Prince Georges, Maryland, had a white population of 59.2 percent in 1980, in the remainder of the counties approximately 80 percent
of the population was white. This type of distribution contrasts markedly
with that in traditional urban centers, which are more racially heterogeneous, even if they are in many cases fragmented into segregated areas.

In several other respects, however, these counties displayed diversity in
some of the standard suburban stereotypes. To consider table 2.3, for
example, there is substantial variation in home values and rates of poverty. In 1980 Orange County's median home value was a staggering
$108,100, and its poverty level was 5.2 percent. Other counties—such as
Macomb, Michigan; Montgomery, Maryland; Montgomery, Pennsylvania; and Fairfax, Virginia—had poverty rates under 4 percent. However,
not all these counties were affluent. Hillsborough, Florida, had a median
home value of only $37,400, while its poverty level was 10.7 percent. De
Kalb/Gwinnett, Georgia; Baltimore County, Maryland; Norfolk, Massachusetts; Macomb, Michigan; Oakland, Michigan; and Suffolk, New
York, all had median home values under $60,000 in 1980. In short, many

TABLE 2.4 Composition of County Employment, 1975 and 1980

County	Year	Total	Agriculture and Mining, %	Manufacturing, %			Transportation and Communication, %	Wholesale, %	Retail, %
				Total	High-Tech	Other			
Norfolk, Mass.	1975	175,687	0.4	29.5	12.3	17.2	4.1	9.3	24.0
	1980	217,403	0.4	26.7	9.6	17.1	4.3	9.2	24.1
Fairfield, Conn.	1975	275,942	0.4	41.9	21.5	20.4	3.6	6.0	17.7
	1980	347,665	0.6	40.5	17.0	23.5	4.0	6.5	16.5
Suffolk, N.Y.	1975	222,894	0.5	26.4	15.4	11.0	5.5	7.3	26.7
	1980	299,111	0.6	29.4	17.1	12.3	5.3	8.1	22.7
Middlesex, N.J.	1975	188,957	0.3	42.0	16.2	25.7	8.1	9.1	18.6
	1980	232,081	0.4	36.8	14.8	22.0	9.2	9.6	19.0
Monmouth, N.J.	1975	100,162	0.5	24.6	9.2	15.4	5.2	4.0	28.0
	1980	124,279	0.6	24.5	10.7	13.8	5.1	4.2	26.5
Montgomery, Pa.	1975	277,191	0.5	37.9	13.1	24.8	4.4	7.8	17.1
	1980	318,142	0.6	33.1	11.1	22.0	3.9	7.6	17.1
Du Page, Ill.	1975	185,930	0.3	25.0	7.2	17.9	4.7	10.1	24.3
	1980	263,191	0.3	26.3	8.7	17.6	5.3	11.7	21.2
Macomb, Mich.	1975	167,241	0.2	54.1	8.8	45.3	2.4	4.1	19.8
	1980	218,634	0.3	47.6	8.8	38.8	2.8	4.1	21.0
Oakland, Mich.	1975	301,237	0.3	28.4	6.7	21.7	2.9	7.7	21.9
	1980	418,450	0.4	25.8	6.9	18.8	4.1	8.4	21.5

Location	Year							
Baltimore, Md.	1975	183,879	0.6	31.8	5.2	26.6	3.8	5.5	25.4
	1980	222,573	0.6	28.3	6.6	21.7	2.9	5.7	25.7
Montgomery, Md.	1975	166,790	0.6	8.6	3.3	5.4	3.1	4.0	25.7
	1980	216,687	0.7	8.1	3.3	4.8	3.9	4.0	23.6
Prince Georges, Md.	1975	127,190	0.5	8.9	2.0	6.8	5.9	7.0	38.0
	1980	160,609	0.6	7.6	2.2	5.4	5.5	7.4	35.2
Fairfax, Va.	1975	92,164	0.7	7.3	4.1	3.2	3.4	4.9	33.1
	1980	150,485	0.8	6.7	3.7	3.0	4.2	4.7	28.4
Gwinnett/De Kalb, Ga.	1975	168,555	0.5	19.9	3.3	16.6	5.4	13.1	22.8
	1980	237,708	0.7	18.9	4.1	14.8	5.9	13.8	21.3
Broward, Fla.	1975	218,066	0.8	11.8	4.9	6.8	6.2	4.7	29.7
	1980	318,154	0.7	13.1	5.8	7.3	5.4	5.5	28.5
Hillsborough, Fla.	1975	188,759	0.8	17.4	1.3	16.1	11.6	10.7	21.7
	1980	222,874	0.9	15.9	1.5	14.4	7.4	11.1	22.6
Contra Costa, Calif.	1975	112,193	0.8	24.7	8.5	16.2	4.8	4.6	28.6
	1980	158,087	0.9	18.8	7.0	11.8	4.9	4.8	28.7
Orange, Calif.	1975	471,659	1.1	31.9	16.4	15.5	3.6	5.3	24.2
	1980	786,814	1.1	29.1	14.7	14.4	4.3	6.1	21.1
San Mateo, Calif.	1975	175,130	0.5	18.7	7.1	11.6	14.4	10.8	19.7
	1980	230,431	0.5	16.6	6.7	9.9	14.8	10.1	20.9
Santa Clara, Calif.	1975	370,764	0.6	41.6	25.3	16.2	4.2	5.4	18.2
	1980	610,494	0.5	42.0	30.5	11.5	3.1	5.5	16.1
Ventura, Calif.	1975	77,901	3.5	20.6	10.71	9.9	5.1	6.2	28.4
	1980	117,238	3.4	20.2	10.6	9.6	5.0	5.6	26.4

TABLE 2.4 (*continued*)

County	Year	Finance, %			Service, %	Land Development, % (Real Estate and Construction)	Unclassified, %	Employment/ Residence, 1980
		Total	Banking, Credit	Insurance				
Norfolk, Mass.	1975	5.2	1.7	3.3	20.8	6.0	0.6	0.77
	1980	5.8	2.0	2.8	23.3	5.7	0.6	
Fairfield, Conn.	1975	6.5	4.8	1.2	18.9	4.4	0.5	0.93
	1980	4.6	2.8	1.3	21.2	5.3	0.6	
Suffolk, N.Y.	1975	5.6	3.1	2.4	21.2	5.5	1.1	0.70
	1980	4.8	2.3	2.3	22.6	5.5	1.0	
Middlesex, N.J.	1975	3.0	1.8	1.1	13.2	5.1	0.6	0.89
	1980	3.7	1.6	1.8	16.1	4.6	0.5	
Monmouth, N.J.	1975	3.7	2.4	1.1	26.8	6.0	1.0	0.75
	1980	5.9	2.5	3.0	26.6	5.7	0.9	
Montgomery, Pa.	1975	4.6	1.9	2.3	20.0	7.2	0.6	0.99
	1980	4.8	1.9	2.3	24.4	8.0	0.5	
Du Page, Ill.	1975	4.3	1.8	1.5	22.0	8.4	1.0	0.73
	1980	4.2	2.1	1.8	24.0	6.4	0.6	
Macomb, Mich.	1975	2.3	1.2	0.8	12.6	3.8	0.7	0.80
	1980	3.2	1.6	0.9	16.5	4.3	0.6	
Oakland, Mich.	1975	5.9	2.2	2.8	23.1	8.8	0.9	0.93
	1980	6.0	2.2	3.2	25.1	8.0	0.7	

Location	Year						
Baltimore, Md.	1975	3.5	1.1	2.1	20.4	8.3	0.6	0.66
	1980	4.7	1.8	2.4	22.6	8.9	0.5	
Montgomery, Md.	1975	5.8	2.0	3.2	32.8	18.5	0.6	0.84
	1980	5.2	2.3	2.7	36.5	16.8	0.6	
Prince Georges, Md.	1975	3.76	2.0	1.0	20.9	13.6	0.7	0.63
	1980	3.7	2.3	0.7	25.5	14.0	0.6	
Fairfax, Va.	1975	5.3	3.3	1.2	30.8	13.6	0.8	0.54
	1980	5.2	2.8	1.7	35.2	14.0	0.7	
Gwinnett/De Kalb, Ga.	1975	6.3	2.5	3.4	20.3	11.0	0.7	0.76
	1980	5.5	2.0	3.0	22.9	10.3	0.7	
Broward, Fla.	1975	5.0	3.0	1.5	26.7	13.5	1.4	0.80
	1980	6.0	3.8	1.4	25.7	13.9	1.3	
Hillsborough, Fla.	1975	5.5	2.4	2.7	21.8	9.6	0.8	0.93
	1980	6.5	2.5	2.9	25.0	10.3	0.8	
Contra Costa, Calif.	1975	4.3	2.7	1.3	20.6	10.4	1.1	0.65
	1980	6.4	3.6	2.2	22.7	11.8	1.1	
Orange, Calif.	1975	5.4	2.3	2.5	21.0	6.3	1.0	0.84
	1980	5.8	2.8	2.4	21.9	9.5	1.0	
San Mateo, Calif.	1975	5.8	2.1	2.9	20.7	8.7	0.6	0.74
	1980	5.2	2.6	2.2	21.9	9.1	0.8	
Santa Clara, Calif.	1975	3.1	1.8	1.0	20.4	1.6	0.8	0.94
	1980	3.4	1.8	1.1	22.8	6.0	0.7	
Ventura, Calif.	1975	6.1	2.8	2.6	23.6	6.0	1.0	0.71
	1980	5.2	2.7	2.1	24.1	8.6	1.3	

of the counties in our sample were less like affluent suburbs and more like industrialized cities with devalorized housing and relatively significant poverty rates. Others fit well the stereotypical socioeconomic profile of suburbia.

With regard to a wide range of factors, the counties in our sample exhibit diversity as well as consistency when compared with Orange County. They are generally fast-growing, strong-employment areas that do not contain large, dominant cities. For the most part they depart from the characteristic profile of the suburban commuter shed. They are highly industrialized and suburban at the same time with employment bases comparable to those of cities, if not states. Yet, most are predominantly white and affluent and some at least have a sizable resident population that commutes elsewhere to work. Orange County, like the others in our group, therefore, cannot be characterized in the manner typically employed by urban ecologists. It is neither a suburb nor a city. It is both a powerhouse of employment and a vast market for housing. For this reason such areas can best be described as multinucleated yet fully urbanized regions that in many ways have assumed the functions traditionally associated with cities but that lack their concentrated form.

EVALUATION OF DECONCENTRATION HYPOTHESES

As indicated at the beginning of this chapter, the emergence of such highly urbanized and deconcentrated counties lying outside our large central city regions has begun to receive attention from developmental theorists. We noted several hypotheses that attempt to explain this phenomenon by stressing one or two causes, such as manufacturing decentralization or the rise of high technology. It is possible to evaluate these alternative hypotheses in a fashion by examining further the characteristics of our sample. The following discussion is a comparative one. To be sure, not every county in our sample might be accepted by other spatial-restructuring theorists as an appropriate area for testing these alternate theories. However, this is a matter of judgment that can always be debated. More significant is the fact that we have utilized a comparative approach while other restructuring theories currently circulating have typically been launched by reasoning from single cases, such as the high-technology, silicon landscapes or the growth of the military industry.

The Role of High-Technology Industries

The role of high-technology manufacturing industries must be seen against the background of the growth of manufacturing industries in general. Among our counties, the contribution of growth in total manufacturing employment to growth in total employment varied considerably (see table 2.2). In seven of the counties, growth in manufacturing accounted for more than 20 percent of total growth in employment. Manufacturing in Santa Clara County, in particular, accounted for 42 percent of a very large increase in total employment. However, in six other counties growth in manufacturing accounted for less than 10 percent of total employment growth. Counties in which manufacturing was a major component tended to be those in which employment grew most rapidly. This was markedly the case for Orange and Santa Clara counties. However, there were clear exceptions to this tendency. Fairfax, Virginia, experienced large increases in employment, but manufacturing played only a small role in this growth. Fairfield, Connecticut, and Suffolk, New York, experienced only moderate employment growth, despite the fact that manufacturing growth was the dominant component. Thus, although some of our counties clearly experienced large growth because of manufacturing, there is no consistent link between employment growth and manufacturing growth.

The same pattern also seems to hold for high-technology manufacturing. No clear relationship is apparent. In some instances, such as Orange and Santa Clara counties, high-technology manufacturing played the dominant role in manufacturing employment growth; however, in Fairfield, Connecticut, high-technology manufacturing actually declined while other forms of manufacturing grew markedly. Overall, in only nine of the counties did high-technology growth exceed the growth of other forms of manufacturing. Among the seven counties in which manufacturing played a paramount role, growth in high technology was the principal factor in three.

In summary, for several of the counties (but not for others) manufacturing growth dominated other types of employment growth. In some of these counties high-technology manufacturing dominated, while in others it did not. Thus, neither the decentralization of manufacturing in general nor the growth in high-technology manufacturing can alone explain the emergence of highly urbanized and multinucleated counties such as the ones we examine here.

The Role of Military-Related Manufacturing
Arguments that stress the role of high technology as the generator of growth, such as those advanced by urban ecologists, do not always acknowledge the close connection between high-tech industries and government-subsidized military spending. Yet, without such an appreciation the role of high-tech as an economic force cannot be understood. Urban ecologists have particularly asserted, in keeping with the nature of their approach, that the emergence of high-tech industries and their importance for new urban growth are quite natural consequences of techno-

logical innovation, especially microcomputing, robotics, and automation. This assertion of organicism is falsified once we acknowledge the role of the permanent war economy in U.S. capitalism. To be sure technology is a central force of production; however, approaches that focus principally on this force as the key, contemporary source of sociospatial restructuring while neglecting other causes as well as the social context of growth are quite limited.

As indicated in table 2.2, employment in military-related manufacturing industries grew between 1975 and 1980 in all but four of the counties in our sample. In six counties the share of employment in such industrial activity was greater than the share in all other forms of manufacturing. Perhaps most interesting, however, is the fact that many of the counties that are high-tech growth centers are dominated by military-related manufacturing. In short, publicly subsidized military-related manufacturing is closely connected to the growth of high-tech manufacturing in these multinucleated urban regions. Rather than an organic or ecological theory of sociospatial restructuring that emphasizes the special role of high technology as a force of production, the data here indicate that we need a theory that emphasizes the role of high-technology manufacturing in the permanent war economy subsidized by the state.

The Role of Service Industries

A separate thesis regarding contemporary regional restructuring stresses the role of service employment. The relative role of service versus manufacturing employment needs to be considered in this regard. Among our sample of twenty-one counties, nine had service sectors in 1980 that were larger than the manufacturing sector (see table 2.4). Even more revealing is the observation that for sixteen of the twenty-one counties service employment was a larger component of total employment growth than was manufacturing in the period between 1975 and 1980 (see table 2.2). Service thus plays a dominant role in the employment growth of these counties. In fact, the role of service employment is at least as significant as that of high-technology employment.

It can be argued that although service employment plays an important role, its growth is tied to both the original presence of and the increase in basic manufacturing activity. Clearly there is a strong connection between these sectors. However, as our data show, no direct ratio links the two. Furthermore, in several cases service sectors have expanded while manufacturing has declined. Because service employment is related more directly to a combination of residential and industrial needs (than to the growth of manufacturing) and because our counties are most often diverse employment and housing areas, we cannot attribute the growth in service employment simply to the expansion of manufacturing.

It could also be argued that the role of service employment is related to the extent to which counties are the sites of extensive residential development. A check against the E/R ratios, however, does not bear this supposition out. Among the five counties in which service employment made the largest contribution to total employment growth, three had E/R ratios greater than 0.80 (Montgomery, Pennsylvania; Hillsborough, Florida; and Montgomery, Maryland).

Consequently, service employment probably possesses a relatively independent role in the growth of multinucleated metropolitan regions, and the base of the service sector is a diverse one rather than one dependent on manufacturing or high technology on one hand or residential development on the other.

CONCLUSION

Considerable attention is now being focused on the ways industry and the economy have been restructured to meet the challenges of modernization, international competition, declining productivity, and falling profit rates. Urban analysts have also tried to connect changes arising from such restructuring with equally profound alterations in the social organization of space. The dimensions of a new spatial science are being determined by this ongoing effort.

Work so far, however, has been hampered by two key limitations. The first is that observers persist in talking about growth as a city-based phenomenon, even one that assumes the 1920s pattern of concentric circles emanating from a single city center. These observers see multinucleated metropolitan regions not as a qualitatively new form of settlement space but simply as a spatially sprawled version of a dominant central city and its hinterland. We have described here a departure from this pattern. We have focused on what we consider to be a new form of settlement space— the fully urbanized, multinucleated, and independent county. Such areas possess relatively large populations; they are polynucleated, with no single center that dominates development as it does in the traditional urban model; and they possess relatively robust employment bases and also serve as residential areas, especially for the white middle class. The counties we have chosen to consider are formally separated from but adjacent to large, well-known metropolitan regions such as Atlanta, Los Angeles, and New York. As a new form of settlement space, they are the first such occurrence in five thousand years of urban history; these places function very much like cities, yet they do so with a multinucleated form of sociospatial organization. Orange County is clearly one of these new forms of settlement.

A second key limitation is that we are subjected to single-cause explanations. In particular, there is a vein of technological determinism emerging in the literature, a current of thought that has epitomized for decades the limitations of mainstream work on social and ecological change. Clearly, high technology is the primary base of economic growth in a number of the counties we examined. We do not deny this fact. However, in some of the multinucleated counties technology plays a minimal role. High technology and the permanent war economy cannot alone account for the growth of the counties in our sample, including Orange County. In a similar fashion, growth in services cannot alone account for the emergence of the multinucleated county.

Through a comparative analysis of these fully urbanized counties, we have been able to comment on the diverse nature of their growth. Following a hypothesis derived from arguments laid out elsewhere (see Gottdiener 1985, 1989), we believe that growth in our sample of counties derives from a variety of separate but contingent sources. A focus on high technology, postindustrial services, or the power of manufacturing alone cannot account for the patterns that have been observed. Rather, many social forces—military-related spending in the permanent war economy, the growth in high technology, the robust real estate market, racism, the flight of the white industrial working class to the hinterland, the construction of traditional (non-high-technology) manufacturing plants, the hypertrophic expansion of service-related industries, and new arrangements in the corporate business structure—have all combined in several distinct ways to produce the new form of settlement space (see Gottdiener 1985, 1989). What remains constant in this process is not some single economic or technological cause at the level of production but changes in contemporary social organization involving production, circulation, and reproductive relations. These are the changes that are producing multinucleated metropolitan regions independent of the large and bounded central city.

REFERENCES

Armstrong, R. 1979. "National Trends in Office Construction, Employment and Headquarters Location in the U.S. Metropolitan Areas." In *Spatial Patterns of Office Growth and Location,* ed. P. Daniels. New York: Wiley.
Bell, D. 1980. "The Social Framework of the Information Society." In *The Microelectronics Revolution,* ed. T. Forester, 500–550. Cambridge, Mass.: MIT Press.
Berry, B., and J. Kasarda. 1977. *Contemporary Urban Ecology.* New York: Macmillan.
Bluestone, B., and B. Harrison. 1982. *The Deindustrialization of America.* New York: Basic Books.
Bureau of the Census. 1975. County Business Patterns. File 2 (County). Machine-readable data file. Washington.
———. 1980. County Business Patterns. File 2 (County). Machine-readable data file. Washington.

Bureau of Health Professions. 1980. *Area Resource File.* Washington.

Burgess, E. 1925. "The Growth of the City." In *The City*, ed. R. Park, E. Burgess, and R. McKenzie, 1–49. Chicago: University of Chicago Press.

Calhoun, C. 1984. "Communications, Community and the City of the Computer Age." Paper presented at the American Conference of Arts and Sciences meeting, Meaning of the City.

Castells, M. 1985. *High Technology, Space and Society.* Beverly Hills, Calif.: Sage.

Census of Population. 1985. *Journey-to-Work, 1980.* Washington: Bureau of the Census.

Crump. 1962. *Ride the Red Cars.* Los Angeles: Crest.

Dobriner, W., ed. 1958. *The Suburban Community.* New York: Putnam's.

———. 1963. *Class in Suburbia.* Englewood Cliffs, N.J.: Prentice-Hall.

Federal Commission on Standard Metropolitan Statistical Areas. 1980. *Documents Relating to the Metropolitan Statistical Area Classification.* Washington: Office of Management and Budget, Office of Statistical Standards.

Gans, H. 1967. *The Levittowners.* New York: Pantheon.

Glassmeier, A. 1985. "Innovative Manufacturing Industries: Spatial Incidence in the United States." In *High Technology, Space and Society*, ed. M. Castells, 55–79. Beverly Hills, Calif.: Sage.

Gottdiener, M. 1985. *The Social Production of Urban Space.* Austin: University of Texas Press.

———. 1989. "Crisis Theory and Socio-spatial Restructuring: The Case of the U.S." In *Capitalist Development and Crisis Theory: Accumulation, Regulation and the Restructuring of Space*, ed. M. Gottdiener and N. Komninos, 365–90. London and New York: Macmillan.

Harris, C., and E. Ullman. 1945. "The Nature of Cities." *Annals of the Academy of Political and Social Science* 242:7–17.

Jackson, K. 1985. *The Crabgrass Frontier.* New York: Oxford University Press.

Leven, C. 1979. "Economic Maturity and the Metropolis' Evolving Physical Form." In *The Changing Structure of the City: What Happened to the Urban Crisis*, ed. G. A. Tobin, 2–44. Beverly Hills, Calif.: Sage.

Long, L., and D. DeAre. 1982. "The Slowing of Urbanization in the U.S." *Scientific American* 249:33–41.

Lundberg, G., M. Kamorousky, and M. McInery. 1934. *Leisure.* New York: Columbia University Press.

Mandel, Ernest. 1975. *Late Capitalism.* London: Verso.

Markusen, A., and R. Bloch. 1985. "Defensive Cities: Military Spending, High Technology and Human Settlements." In *High Technology, Space and Technology*, ed. M. Castells, 106–20. Beverly Hills, Calif.: Sage.

Markusen, A., P. Hall, and A. Glassmeier. 1986. *High Tech America.* Boston: Allen & Unwin.

Regional Plan Association. 1962. *Spread City.* New York.

Richards, R. 1978. "Urbanization of Rural Areas." In *Handbook of Contemporary Urban Life*, ed. D. Street and associates, 551–91. San Francisco: Jossey-Bass.

Schnore, L. 1957. "Metropolitan Growth and Decentralization." *American Journal of Sociology* 63:171–80.

————. 1963. "The Socio-economic Status of Cities and Suburbs." *American Socio-logical Review* 28:76–85.

Scott, A. 1986. "High Technology Industry and Territorial Development: The Rise of the Orange County Complex, 1955–1984." *Urban Geography* 7(1):3–45.

Sly, D., and J. Tayman. 1980. "Metropolitan Morphology and Population Mobility." *American Journal of Sociology* 86:119–138.

Touraine, A. 1971. *The Post Industrial Society.* New York: Random House.

Warner, Sam B. 1962. *Street Car Suburbs.* Cambridge, Mass.: Harvard University Press.

THREE

Designing the Model Community: The Irvine Company and Suburban Development, 1950–88

Martin J. Schiesl

Few large organizations have played a greater role in the postwar economic and social evolution of Orange County than the Irvine Company. M. Gottdiener and George Kephart show in Chapter 2 that the county's spatial structure, unlike the structure of many older metropolitan regions that are based on a dominant central city surrounded by residential and industrial areas, is a new form of regional deconcentrated space consisting of several independent and highly specialized centers. Much of this important development can be attributed to the policies and activities of the Irvine Company. Holding the largest piece of undeveloped land in the county, company leaders decided to reorganize their business from a successful farming operation into a professional land-management corporation with community planning and building accorded highest priority. The result was the creation of a postsuburban system possessing remarkable commercial specialization, technological expertise, and much residential homogeneity and self-sufficiency.[1] In the process, serious questions emerged concerning population balance and diversity, environmental integrity, and regional obligations and responsibilities. Dealing with these various issues meant continual tension between the determination of the company to maximize profits on land development and the desire of citizen groups and public officials to maintain a higher quality of life than that found elsewhere in metropolitan California.

The history of the Irvine Company goes back to California's pastoral era. Two brothers, Benjamin and Thomas Flint, and their cousin, Llewellyn Bixby, operated a large sheep ranch in Monterey County under the name of Flint, Bixby and Company in the 1850s. The outbreak of the Civil War greatly increased the demand for California wool. Flint, Bixby and Company proceeded to extend its business farther south and sought to purchase some cattle ranches located in the Los Angeles area. A severe drought in the early 1860s had brought devastation to the cattle industry and left Mexican-American rancheros financially destitute. James Irvine, a wealthy merchant from San Francisco, accepted an invitation from the sheepmen to take a half interest in their investment in the empty cattle lands. They purchased the Rancho San Joaquin, Rancho Lomas de Santiago, and part of the Rancho Santiago de Santa Ana. Irvine bought out his partners for $150,000 in 1876 and got title to all three properties. He died in 1886. Three years later the California legislature, responding to pressure from merchants and prominent landowners from towns in the Santa Ana Valley, voted in favor of creating a new county out of the southern part of Los Angeles County and authorized a special election to decide whether it should be formed. The voters in the proposed County of Orange approved separation by a huge margin. Mindful of the new county's growing economic importance, James Irvine II, who had inherited all his father's estate, decided to consolidate the properties and incorporated them as the Irvine Company under the laws of West Virginia in 1894.[2]

Incorporation sparked a gradual transition of the ranch from a grazing enterprise to an agricultural business. Much land formerly devoted to sheep pasture was planted in the late 1890s to field crops such as beans, barley, and corn. Farm operations diversified further in the following decade with the planting and cultivation of celery, cabbage, peas, lettuce, and other vegetables. In the 1910s and 1920s the Irvine Company entered the citrus industry and devoted hundreds of acres to lemon and orange trees. All this activity put heavy demands on the ranch's water resources; obtaining an adequate and continual supply of water was a major problem. In response, the company in the 1920s and 1930s drilled hundreds of wells and laid nearly a thousand miles of pipeline. It also built several dams and reservoirs for purposes of conservation and flood control.[3]

BEGINNING OF SUBURBAN DEVELOPMENT

Residential demands in the postwar decade placed new pressures on the Irvine Company to devote portions of the ranch to urban uses. One of the greatest assets of the organization was its ocean frontage, which stretched for eight miles along the coast from Newport Bay to Laguna Beach. The rapid increase of population in southern California and the growing demand for recreational opportunities gave the land a value that an older generation never contemplated. Rather than sell this precious property outright, Myford Irvine, who had become company president upon the death of his father in 1947, moved the company into the development business. It subdivided a large number of tracts, contracted with building firms to construct single-family housing, and offered long-term leases for the houses and lots. Tennis courts, club houses, and other amenities were also provided. Several enclaves, dubbed with idyllic names like Irvine Cove, Cameo Shores, and Harbor View Hills, sprouted up around Newport Bay and along the coast in the 1950s. The affluent residents lived in well-designed homes, frequented superior recreational facilities, and enjoyed panoramic views of the Pacific Ocean. They also belonged to homeowners associations organized by Irvine executives. Residents were given the right to use an association's property and to vote for its officers and, in return, were obliged to pay an association's assessments and follow its rules and regulations. The result was an effective system of land-use control through which the company kept community amenities in good condition and maintained certain architectural standards.[4]

Urban growth in the northern and western parts of the county proceeded along far different lines. Federal Housing Authority insurance and liberal loans from the Veterans Administration enabled large numbers of low- and moderate-income families to buy homes and generated hundreds of new real estate developments in suburban areas. By the early 1950s these bedroom communities were heavily dependent on Los Angeles County for jobs, goods, and services. As a result, much of the housing, commercial, and industrial development occurred in those places closest to or with good access to Los Angeles. The 1955 opening of Disneyland at Anaheim and the completion of the Santa Ana freeway changed these arrangements considerably. Many companies, expecting a strong market for consumer goods and personal services, entered the Anaheim area and provided hundreds of new jobs that beckoned to people in every corner of southern California. The county's population rose from 220,000 in 1950 to 704,000 in 1960, an increase of 220 percent. Large-scale merchant builders made the most effective response to the demand for housing. They bought up vast areas of farmland, subdivided their property into different-sized lots, and sold scores of identical homes to middle- and working-class families. This residential expansion gradually spread south and pushed toward the northern edge of the property of the Irvine Company, which received attractive offers from experienced developers who were interested in buying all or portions of the ranch.[5]

The University of California was also interested in the Irvine property. Shopping around for a new campus in the south, the regents commissioned architects Charles Luckman and William Pereira in 1957 to study various prospective sites. Their staff visited a few outstanding universities in the United States and Europe and did research on the kind of relationship that existed between the schools and their surrounding areas. They concluded that a great university, in addition to having a superior faculty and gifted students, had to provide housing on or near the campus, enjoy the support of a sympathetic community, and be close to a cosmopolitan urban center. It also should possess enough land to avoid congestion in the future. Numerous locations in southern California could meet these requirements reasonably well. The regents accompanied Pereira on a tour of some of them, ending with the one he considered most suitable. It was a stretch of gentle rolling hills on the Irvine Ranch, just east of the northern tip of Newport Bay. Pereira pointed out that this location offered a unique opportunity to build around the campus a city that would fulfill all the needs of the university. The regents agreed and unanimously approved the campus site.[6]

Joan Irvine Smith was delighted with their decision. The strong-minded daughter of James Irvine III and holder of the largest amount of stock in the company, Smith replaced her mother on the board of directors in 1957. She strongly urged Irvine officials to donate the land to the university. Her plea was a familiar mixture of altruism and self-interest. She talked about great intellectual and cultural benefits for nearby cities. She had also observed the building boom that accompanied the completion of the campus of the University of California at Los Angeles. The Janss family, among other groups, got rich developing the village of Westwood near the school. Neither factor, however, weighed heavily with Irvine officials. They felt that it would be quite unbusinesslike to give ranch property away and decided to reject Smith's generous proposal. Enraged over their decision, she took her case to the general public. She held formal press conferences, gave several radio and television interviews, and helped organize mass rallies at which she spoke out fervently in support of the Irvine campus.[7]

Such publicity became embarrassing for Irvine officials; Smith made them look like penny-pinching opponents of higher education and the public interest. They also had serious financial problems to worry about. With residential and business development moving close to the northern edge of the ranch, taxes on the company's agricultural property were raised considerably to reflect its growing value for urban use. This situation led the company in the direction of comprehensive land planning, and as a result it donated one thousand acres to the University of California for the new campus. The company then proposed that a land-use plan be prepared for the area adjoining the school to ensure proper integration of community and university life. Not having sufficient space and adequate housing on some other campuses, the regents also saw planning as vital to the interests of the university population and surrounding areas. They and company officials requested Pereira and his staff to make a detailed study of the Irvine site.[8]

Few architects in southern California were better qualified than Pereira for the job. After graduating from the University of Illinois in 1930, he joined an architectural company in Chicago and helped plan a number of public-works projects for recently unemployed people. His wife, a top photographer's model, accepted an offer in a Hollywood film and moved to Los Angeles with her husband in 1938. Pereira signed on as a set designer and producer for Paramount Studios and also established his own architectural practice, designing department stores, medical centers, and military installations. Charles Luckman, a former college classmate and ex-president of Lever Brothers, joined his firm in 1950. Together they designed the space-exploration complex at Cape Canaveral, Los Angeles International Airport, Marineland on the Palos Verdes Peninsula, and dozens of other multimillion-dollar facilities. By the late 1950s Pereira felt that his artistic integrity had been compromised by too much commercial business and decided to break up the lucrative partnership. "It is not that we were doing bad work," he recalled later, "it's just that I knew I wasn't doing my best work. With our volume, I couldn't give each job the individual attention it deserved."[9]

PLANNING A COMMUNITY

The Irvine contract demanded nearly all of Pereira's attention and expertise. His initial report, finished in the fall of 1959, established the economic feasibility of building a major campus on the ranch. It also recorded promises of support from various governmental agencies and surrounding cities.[10] A second report, finished in the spring of 1960, mapped ten thousand acres of undeveloped land and presented a master plan for a university-oriented community to be organized along the lines of the venerable garden-city model. The garden city was the brainchild of Ebeneezer Howard, a London court stenographer and reformer. Howard, writing in the last decade of the nineteenth century, worried about the waste and social disorganization that rapid industrialization brought to large European cities and proposed a new kind of community that would be self-sufficient and would combine the best features of city and countryside. His scheme had the support of a number of prominent American planners during the early twentieth century and reached its fullest expression in the New Deal's famous greenbelt towns. Garden-city principles reappeared in the late 1950s as part of various proposals for new communities by leading architects and academic consultants who specialized in urban and regional land-use planning. Close observation of the patterns of suburbanization convinced them that most metropolitan areas suffered from too-rapid change and considerable instability and obsolescence. The remedy to this situation appeared to lie in the direction of structured and interdependent urban development. Kevin Lynch, a professor of city planning at the Massachusetts Institute of Technology, contended that such arrangements would encourage "the use of intensive centers, variety . . . and a differentiated but well-patterned flow system."[11]

Pereira's plan for the university community met some of these criteria almost perfectly. It designated certain land surrounding the campus as inclusion areas to be interlocked with the central core. Roughly two hundred acres each, these parcels would provide apartments and single-family dwellings for faculty and staff, residences for single and married students, churches, schools, and shops. Land was also reserved for a new town center, which would serve as the focus of commercial, cultural, and social activity in the community. Shops, offices, restaurants, and entertainment facilities were to be closely grouped, resembling the structure of older university towns in America and Europe with their "intimate pedestrian scale." Pereira devoted equal attention to environmental and recreational needs. He proposed that various low lands on the site be converted into a lake, open greenbelts, a golf course, and public parks.[12]

Irvine Company officials saw great merit and value in Pereira's plan. They watched nervously as merchant builders continued to transform adjacent areas from citrus groves to sprawling subdivisions. Their property also sat at a central point in the state's network of roads. The state legislature in 1959 approved new highway plans and appropriated ten billion dollars for their completion; three major freeways linking the Irvine Ranch with the rest of the Los Angeles metropolitan area were slated for future construction. Pereira's scheme for the new campus gave permanent assurance against encroachment. It also pointed the way to avoidance of uncontrolled suburbanization of ranch property. Pereira had introduced into southern Orange County a new version of the garden city, complete with shopping centers, greenbelts, and parks. The Irvine Company retained him to prepare a master land-use plan for the rest of the ranch.[13]

Joining Pereira and his staff in the project were a group of new Irvine Company employees unfamiliar with farming operations. Irvine officials created a new land-development division in 1961 and recruited several landscape architects and planning consultants to staff it. Raymond Watson, a highly respected architectural planner, left a lucrative partnership in San Francisco and joined the company because the job possessed "a lot of romantic appeal." The ranch, with its thousands of acres of virtually untouched wilderness, appeared to him to be a "planner's dream."[14] Watson and his colleagues gave the lowest priority to the remote mountainous areas to the east. The central tier, some thirty-two thousand acres of lush fields and citrus groves, received more attention in order to maintain income from farming activity as long as possible. Highest priority went to the southern sector, which covered about forty thousand acres from the ocean to the northern boundary of the proposed university community. As an extension of existing residential enclaves located around Newport Bay, it was the logical location for initial development. The planners talked about new communities in the southern sector that would feature attractive and comfortable residences for people at all income levels and that would provide a variety of jobs and services. There would also be less dependence on the automobile, with people easily able to walk to shops, restaurants, and recreational facilities. Pereira believed that there was nothing "more ugly" than vast areas of open land paved for parking lots and spoke fervently of neighborhood and regional parks that would "restore the land to the pedestrian."[15]

Merchant builders in the 1950s seldom bothered with these considerations. Concentrating on the broad middle- and lower-income segment of the housing market, they bought land in the urban outskirts and applied techniques of mass production to the housing industry, offering homes at lower prices than similar structures would cost if built individually. Land was set aside for various community functions, but its actual development was often left to the whims of local government and the marketplace. The Irvine Company pursued different and broader goals. It represented what two authorities on postwar California suburbanization have described as the "new community builders" of the early 1960s. The others in southern California included the Newhall Land and Farming Company, which would develop the community of Valencia on some four thousand acres of ranch land in northeastern Los Angeles County, the Janss Corporation, builder of Janss/Canejo in Ventura County, and the Mission Viejo Company, which would develop a planned community on ten thousand acres of rolling hills in southern Orange County. They and the Irvine Company were strongly influenced by the writings of prominent urban critics who viewed the rapid expansion of suburban America as a crisis. Lumping all suburbs together without regard to differences in class composition and living conditions, they argued that profit-oriented building companies had scarred the countryside, produced waste and economic inefficiency, and completely disregarded human and social needs. It followed that development in the future could be spared these deplorable consequences only if it were based on thorough and comprehensive planning.[16]

This critique of suburbia convinced Irvine executives that it would be possible to create a better living and working environment than that typically found throughout metropolitan California. They could also expect to make a great deal of money doing it. The supposed unrest with the quality of suburban life suggested to them the existence of a strong market for amenity-packed, planned communities. They intended to be a leader in offering consumers a product that had not been available in most conventional suburbs.

Orange County planning officials had no objections to their goals. They worried that the aimless urban sprawl in other areas of the county would be repeated throughout its southern tier. "The growth of western Orange County was a piece-meal process of one subdivision after another, and the consequent related piece-meal zoning problems of residential, commercial, and industrial areas," Planning Director Harry Bergh told the county Board of Supervisors in 1963. "It was not characterized by a preconceived master plan of development, nor even a series of master plans, such as must be prepared to guide the growth of large holdings." The alternative to this disturbing situation, he felt, lay in flexibility in development and attention to the interrelationship of land uses.[17] Accordingly, he and his staff drafted a planned-community ordinance and persuaded the board to adopt these regulations for future urban and suburban expansion. The ordinance permitted much more flexibility in community planning and site design than did traditional zoning regulations. Land uses could be mixed on the same site. Cluster development on small lots was also allowed in exchange for large amounts of open space in the community. The developer, in return for this increased flexibility, was required to get approval of a master plan for the entire area and subsequently submit detailed site plans for each part of the holding to be developed.[18] Pereira and his colleagues proceeded to incorporate the original university-community scheme into a master plan for the southern part of the ranch and confidently presented the entire package to the county for its consideration and approval.

The Board of Supervisors did not quarrel with the plan; they saw it largely as enhancing the county's financial interests. The plan was designed to create an attractive environment, which would encourage a rise in land values. Taxes would rise accordingly on any developed lands to reflect their growing value for urban uses. The supervisors also believed the plan could be completed. Irvine Company executives, unlike many merchant builders who generally bypassed architects and planning consultants, had the expert staff to carry out their ambitious plan. Moreover, they seemed financially capable of providing and managing facilities that would otherwise be the responsibility of the county, such as golf courses, swimming clubs, and parks.[19] Impressed with these points, the supervisors adopted the south Irvine Ranch general plan in the winter of 1964 as the county's guide for future urban and suburban development. Shortly afterward, a full-time professional planning staff was established in the Irvine Company to assure consistency of concepts, continuity of projects, and design control. They took over responsibility for master planning from Pereira and hired several engineers, economists, and market analysts.[20]

Garden-city principles were at the heart of Irvine's southern-sector plan. It proposed a system of "balanced communities" that would foster social heterogeneity and achieve "a measure of economic and functional independence." Each community would contain distinctive residential districts to which inhabitants could relate in an intimate way. The housing for these areas would not be monotonous and repetitive as it was elsewhere in the county. Instead, the plan provided for a diversity of building types— garden apartments, single-family housing, and cluster home developments. In addition, each village would have its own schools, churches, and shopping centers. Environmental considerations, too, were part of the plan. It identified certain sites as open-space preserves and reserved them for greenbelts and community parks.[21]

Company planners also gave attention to employment opportunities. They called for the immediate development of two major industrial areas on the ranch. One was a site southwest of the university campus ringing the Aeronutronics Division of Ford Motor Company; the other extended north of the campus, near the Orange County airport. Both sites were served by four freeways and two railroad lines. Land was also reserved for supportive commercial areas. The most ambitious project was the Newport Center. Envisioning a "downtown" for the Irvine development and the south coast of Orange County, the plan proposed a seven-hundred-acre complex to consist of high-rise office buildings, medical centers, service businesses, and other commercial facilities arranged around a regional shopping center. Irvine Company president Charles Thomas, talking about Newport Center and other proposed projects in the master plan at a special press conference held on the ranch, proclaimed that his organization was undertaking the "finest land development in the world" and expected to see "enormous progress and prosperity" for nearby communities as well as the company.[22]

Developments in the late 1960s confirmed Thomas's optimism. The county gradually evolved from an agricultural to an industrial base, with contract construction and manufacturing accounting for the largest share of growth. Many aerospace companies, electronic firms, and research-and-development industries found their way south and located in the four-thousand-acre Irvine Industrial Complex. They provided thousands of new jobs and attracted large numbers of people from different parts of southern California. The county's population rose from 704,000 in 1960 to 1.4 million in 1970, an increase of 100 percent. Most conspicuous among the newcomers were affluent white-collar employees and their families, who shared with their counterparts in other suburban regions certain high living standards. They wanted comfortable housing, ready access to the outdoors, proximity to work, and better-than-average educational and recreational opportunities.[23]

Providing such amenities on the Irvine property demanded a style and strategy different from those of older real estate developments in southern California. Unlike merchant builders, who usually marketed homes first and the community second, the Irvine Company sought reputable homebuilders and concentrated on marketing an amenity-packed community. Some large builders in the county specialized in the middle- and lower-income segment of the housing market, while others preferred to build relatively expensive homes. Irvine officials accepted offers only from those building expensive homes and informed them that ranch land would be leased for real estate development only. They also stipulated in contracts the minimum price for which homes to be constructed could be sold.[24]

The leaseholds also permitted orderly and coordinated urbanization. Developers were required to preservice ranch lands with roads, water supplies, and sewer systems. Company planners, moreover, closely supervised residential and commercial projects and made sure that they conformed to specific architectural and landscape styles outlined in the master plan. Many houses, for example, were clustered and located near open space and paths. Because of the company's special emphasis on leisure activity, it provided golf courses, tennis courts, lakes, and other recreational facilities.[25] Two consultants who wrote an extensive report on urbanization on the Irvine Ranch in 1968 observed that the residential villages provided a "more desirable living environment" than that available in most subdivisions elsewhere in California. The following year the Orange County chapter of the American Institute of Planners singled out the Irvine development as being "one of the most comprehensive and completely balanced new communities to be found in the United States."[26] Company officials deserved much of this recognition. Ten years of skillful planning and careful design made the residential enclaves on the ranch far more attractive and healthier than the drab rows of tract housing that permeated the northern and western sectors of the county.

PROBLEMS IN PARADISE

The Irvine design was not, however, a radical alternative to postwar California suburban sprawl. One close observer of the Irvine operation pointed out that the company was not concerned with providing any "utopian solution to urban problems" and saw its projects mostly as an "extension of professionalism in the development process and [as avoiding] the excesses of uncontrolled suburbanization." It was also less risky and more businesslike to promote generally accepted forms of development with assured returns rather than radical changes. Irvine vice-president Watson, in a paper read to a conference on community projects sponsored by the

American Association of Architects in 1971, talked about the reluctance of new community builders to commit all their available resources because of certain "financial constraints" within which they usually operated. The best policy, he continued, was to narrow down development to "one or two strategies" that held the "most promise of success."[27]

Least promising to him and other Irvine executives was low-income housing. They claimed to be committed to population diversity and repeatedly spoke about a reasonable range of building types and prices in their residential projects. Most of the homes, however, were luxury dwellings with costly frills and were affordable only by upper-middle- and upper-class people. The average selling price of a single-family house on the Irvine property was thirty-five thousand dollars, more than twice the average for the county.[28] Urban studies scholars Raymond Burby and Shirley Weiss, writing in their monumental work on new communities in the United States since 1960, attribute this situation largely to the economics of the development process: "Development strategies are designed to escalate values as rapidly as possible. Not only may housing for lower income persons be seen as threatening necessary appreciation in land values, but rising prices themselves make it exceedingly difficult to build moderately priced housing units."[29] Acting on these considerations, the Irvine Company chose not to hold down the costs of new houses and continued to advertise its urban landscape as a high-income, homogeneous place to live.

The housing programs of noted community builders in the East proceeded along more equitable lines in the late 1960s than those of the Irvine Company. Builders in the East matched the Irvine Company's commitment to architectural design and amenities but added a concern for population balance and diversity. Most impressive in this regard was developer James Rouse of Columbia, Maryland. Rouse saw adequate dwellings for low-income families as necessary for a balanced and healthy community. One of his main goals in Columbia was income diversity through the provision of housing for blue-collar workers unable to find affordable homes in the area. He recruited planners who were committed to socioeconomic mixing, facilitated the construction of lower-priced housing by writing down the cost of developed land, and made use of certain federal assistance programs designed to help low-income families buy or rent decent homes. He also worked closely with civic groups and individual residents to maintain the credibility of such policies. Columbia's social diversity was emulated in Reston, Virginia, a planned community conceived and initiated by developer Robert Simon in 1962. Simon believed that changes in family structure, age, or financial situation should not force people to move out of the community. When Gulf-Reston, Inc., took over the development, it maintained Simon's commitment to population diversity. The company and other developers built lower-priced dwelling units, financed partly through federal housing-subsidy programs, for elderly people, working-class families, and moderate-income groups.[30]

This program of income diversity in Reston and Columbia aroused little interest among Irvine executives and planners. They directed most of their attention and energy to broad questions concerning the distribution of population, resources, and institutions. The 1964 plan had proposed a new city of ten thousand acres with a projected population of 100,000 to be created around the University of California campus. Further planning and development activity in the late 1960s convinced them that interest in the central portion of the ranch was greater than originally thought and the goal of orderly development in this area would be better served by greatly expanding the size of the proposed city. They unveiled a new master plan in 1970 for a fifty-three-thousand-acre development with a population of 430,000 by the year 2000. The plan, covering an area twice the size of the city of San Francisco, provided for twenty-four separate residential villages, reserved twenty-four hundred acres for parks and recreation, and suggested numerous sites for elementary and secondary schools. It also proposed a thirty-three-mile network of landscaped environmental corridors for nonresidental use and set aside seventy-five hundred acres for industrial and commercial activity. Political considerations, too, were given close attention. The plan evaluated different jurisdictional alternatives and concluded that the goals and unity of purpose desired for Irvine could be best met with a single municipal-level government. It was expected that the city would be incorporated within five years.[31]

County planning officials greeted the Irvine scheme with great interest. They had adopted a new countywide program that expanded the usual process of general planning to include economic, physical, and human considerations. The program also emphasized intergovernmental cooperation and coordination of public and private development activity. Irvine's master plan provided county planners with their first opportunity to apply some of these criteria to proposed suburban development.[32] They were particularly concerned with the overdependence on automobile transportation. Company planners, while reserving land for a few bus routes, gave little attention to mass transit and put most of their effort into providing for an efficient flow of auto traffic on local streets and roads. "The inability of the automobile centered circulation structure to meet the transportation needs of a significant minority, especially the too young, the too old, and the low income citizens, impairs the movement of a substantial proportion of the county's citizens," the officials stated. "Thus, programs must be developed to meet the overall transportation needs of the county." They urged the Irvine Company to consider building mass-transit facilities in its proposed villages.[33]

Little attention was also given in the plan to protection of the natural landscape. The planning department invited UCI-Project 21, a group of local businesspeople, university professors, and various public officials concerned with improving the suburban environment, to do an extensive study of open-space needs in the county. Their report contained a number of proposals for creating open-space preserves in shoreline and undisturbed natural areas, many of them on the Irvine Ranch. Drawing heavily on this document, the planners recommended that certain protections for the environment be added to the plan. These included a system of riding and hiking trails, wetlands preservation, additional greenbelts, and the conservation of prime agricultural soils.[34]

Far more disturbing to the planners than the lack of protection for the environment was the company's elitist housing program. The county was quite concerned that dwellings be available for low- and moderate-income families whose services would be needed in the new community. Irvine's scheme, however, said nothing about income diversity and subsidized housing. Planning officials pointed out that only about half the families in the county could afford a new apartment, while single-family houses were beyond the reach of two-thirds of the population. "Unless Irvine deliberately sets out to utilize federal or state programs which enable it to develop housing for lower and middle income families," they observed, "only upper middle and upper income families will be able to live at Irvine." The result could be increased "polarization" in certain residential areas and more "social envy and social strife."[35] Similar concerns were expressed by the planning department's equal-opportunity subpanel, which consisted of civil rights activists and representatives of minority organizations. Most of their clients resided in the barrios and ghettos of the county's older cities and had low-paying jobs, poor housing, and inferior schools and health care. One remedy to this depressing situation was to open portions of newly developed suburbs like Irvine to low- and moderate-income nonwhite families. "The handwriting is on the wall," subpanel members observed. "Los Angeles has a large Black population, Orange County has a ten to fourteen per cent Chicano population, and the Oriental has long been a resident of Orange County. Thus, the City of Irvine must also share this mixed population."[36]

Class and racial diversity had been of little concern to company officials however. Like other new community builders in California, they considered nonwhite families to be a relatively unimportant segment of the housing market and chose not to incorporate open-occupancy provisions into their master plan. "It [Irvine] will be a white, upper-middle class, sterile, suburban ghetto," Alan Kreditor, a professor of urban and regional planning at the University of Southern California and former consultant to the Irvine Company, bluntly stated. "They will just build a subdivision a little bit better and a whole lot bigger than the last one."[37] Other critics singled out Columbia and Reston for special praise because of their commitment to some degree of racial balance. Developers in both communities, backed by local business and civic groups, used nonwhite models in their promotional literature and attracted a substantial proportion of black residents. The black population accounted for 18 percent of Columbia households in 1970, the highest rate for any new American town.[38] Irvine's Watson saw little chance of racial integration in his community however. "When Columbia started, they ran full-page newspaper ads showing pictures of interracial couples," he noted. "Back there, that went over great. But if I tried it here, I would scare off every white person I had even the slightest hope of getting."[39]

A survey of Irvine's population by a group of urban specialists at Claremont College gave him no reason to worry. It revealed that 95 percent of the 10,500 persons living in the residential villages were white, with blacks and Asians comprising less than 1 percent of the total population.[40] One minority member of the equal-opportunity subpanel attributed this severe imbalance to certain policies prevalent in suburban southern California in general and the Irvine operation in particular. "The creation of the suburbs and their growth is directly related to the process of relegating nonwhite minorities to the rundown core of the cities," he pointed out. "In the Irvine Plan, as in all those I have heard of, there is implied the idea that 'quality [natural] environment costs a lot.' This implication carried to its logical extension means those unable to pay for a quality environment aren't going to get one." He and other subpanel members strongly recommended against approval of the master plan on the grounds that it would permit company officials to keep the prices of their homes above what most nonwhite families could afford and would thus foster increased racial segregation in the county.[41]

Coastal development was another serious problem confronting the Irvine Company. The late 1960s saw environmental concerns and issues gain widespread support in California, as elsewhere in the country. Watson, speaking before the American Institute of Real Estate Appraisers in 1975, recalled that those proposing planning and controls had in the past taken "a back seat to the growth advocates." The results of this situation were traffic congestion, polluted air and water, and needless destruction of the natural landscape.[42] The debate in southern Orange County centered on Upper Newport Bay, one of the few remaining large estuaries along the California coast. Irvine executives talked about an extensive development of the shoreline of the interior portion of the bay to include a recreational harbor and adjoining water-oriented residental communities. Their project, however, depended on a land swap with the county. They agreed to transfer company-owned islands on the bay for county-owned tidelands. A large group of local residents greeted the exchange with considerable resentment and charged that the Irvine project would seriously infringe on public access to the bay. The Sierra Club, a highly influential organization of environmentalists and conservationists, added its voice to the chorus of protest. Seeing the bay as an irreplaceable natural resource, the club denounced the project as a threat to marine life and certain migratory birds.[43]

Irvine Company president William Mason reacted angrily to this opposition. Convinced that the project would be beneficial for the county, he portrayed Sierra Club leaders and their supporters as misguided and irresponsible zealots. His intemperate remarks helped fuel a growing environmental movement dedicated to the preservation of the natural features of the coastal landscape. Some participants entered the 1970 race for the Board of Supervisors on an anti–Irvine Company platform and won election by a fairly wide margin. They immediately voted to rescind the land-exchange agreement in Upper Newport Bay and appointed conservation-minded people to the planning commission. The new commissioners endorsed the criticisms of Irvine's master plan regarding open space and affordable housing and sent the document back to company planners for extensive revisions.[44]

THE FIGHT OVER INCORPORATION

Making things more difficult for the company were the territorial ambitions of surrounding cities. The 1950s and early 1960s saw several communities in the county incorporate to protect themselves from encroaching urbanization and annexation threats. Irvine executives faced the same situation in 1969 and 1970. Newport Beach proposed to annex a large portion of the Irvine Industrial Complex; Costa Mesa wanted some of the company's commercial property located near the county airport; and Tustin eyed several hundred acres of prime industrial land on the ranch. Company executives, in response, accelerated their cityhood timetable and called for the incorporation of Irvine as soon as possible. The alternatives, either partition of the planning area by adjacent suburban municipalities or a multiplicity of new jurisdictions, held forth the unpleasant prospect of the abandonment of large-scale development in favor of local, provincial development. Incorporation would also transfer control of development in the affected areas from the county planning agency to a city planning agency that could be expected to work cooperatively with the company in the pursuit of its plans, independent of regional social and environmental considerations.[45]

These views and expectations found considerable support among the
homeowners associations. They believed that incorporation was necessary to preserve the economic viability and territorial integrity of the
proposed city. Some thirty associations joined together in the Council of
the Communities of Irvine (CCI) to investigate and determine the feasibility of cityhood.[46] Headed by John Burton, a local businessman, CCI
worked closely with Irvine Company personnel and prepared an extensive report that included information on public services, tax estimates,
and development goals. The report convinced CCI that cityhood was the
best choice for Irvine residents. Piecemeal annexations, CCI contended,
would allow adjoining towns to usurp the community's tax base and cause
a considerable rise in homeowners' taxes. They also claimed that incorporation would reduce the costs of urban services being offered by the
county. The alternative of several existing cities could lead to a "patchwork of conflicting jurisdictions" with inconsistent levels of service and
taxation. In addition, CCI argued the importance of protecting the "balance and promise" of the Irvine master plan and stressed the supposed
advantages of having major land-use decisions made by local authorities
rather than by county bureaucrats and officials operating many miles
away. All these points, along with some statistical data and boundary
maps, were integrated into an incorporation petition drafted jointly by
CCI leaders and the Irvine Company. They submitted the petition to the
Orange County Local Agency Formation Commission (LAFCO) in late
1970 and expected that it would be approved without any serious revision
or long delay.[47]

Some neighboring cities felt uncomfortable with the proposed incorporation. The Irvine Company had assured them for some time that they
could annex certain portions of its undeveloped property. Santa Ana, for
instance, claimed nine hundred acres of prime industrial land near the
Marine Air Corps Station at El Toro. The boundaries of the new city
would cancel this and other annexation agreements. Irvine executives,
uneasy over the prospect of continuing opposition to incorporation, met
with the leaders of CCI and persuaded them to reduce the proposed
boundaries in their petition from fifty-six thousand to nineteen thousand
acres. The new borders did not exclude the area claimed by Santa Ana
however; and Santa Ana officials decided to oppose the proposed incorporation until the company honored its long-standing annexation agreement with their community.[48]

More troublesome than annexation agreements were the fiscal hardships that could arise for Santa Ana because of the creation of a new
suburban municipality. Irvine's residential developments had attracted
some middle- and upper-income families from Santa Ana and other older
cities in the county. Santa Ana officials worried that incorporation might

lure even more of these people from their community and deprive it of important tax revenues needed to finance services for a growing population of low-income, minority families. The city in 1970 contained 68 percent of the county's black population and 30 percent of its Mexican American residents. "If we could be assured that Irvine would take care of its fair share of low-income families, we would have no position on incorporation," City Manager Carl Thornton stated in January 1971. "But there is no such guarantee on record and we would wind up at the mercy of people with no direct interest in the problem."[49]

Thornton persuaded the city council to hire a prominent Chicago consulting firm to study and assess the impact of incorporation on the county in general and on Santa Ana in particular. Its report confirmed his anxieties about the cityhood proposal. "A city of Irvine could capture virtually all of the major new tax resources to be created in the county," said the report, "and at the same time reject groups and activities that represent a drain on values or resources." The Irvine area, however, also possessed "great potentials" which could be used for the benefit of neighboring cities and the entire county. "The size, newness, economic base, and good design of a new city could provide an environment in which a rich variety of life styles, income groups, and activity are accommodated in truly balanced and compatible ways," the report pointed out. It called for Irvine Company officials to take increased responsibility for areawide social and environmental problems and urged that their master plan be amended to match county policies regarding affordable housing, mass transportation, and open-space reserves.[50]

None of these considerations weighed heavily with the LAFCO commissioners however. After some debate over the economic impact of the new city on surrounding communities, they voted three to two in favor of the incorporation proposal and sent written notice of their action to the Board of Supervisors. The next step required that petitions for cityhood be signed by 25 percent of the property owners in the area proposed for incorporation. CCI members, with the help of City of Irvine Now (COIN), a group of several dozen residents, circulated incorporation forms among subdivision communities on the ranch and signed up 67 percent of the area's property owners, including the top executives of the Irvine Company. After receiving the petitions, the Board of Supervisors held a public hearing on Irvine's incorporation at which Santa Ana officials charged that the new city would hoard valuable industrial land and contribute to the "economic degradation" of their community. The board, however, voted four to one to approve the municipal boundaries and authorized an election in the proposed city at the end of 1971.[51]

Some local opposition to incorporation soon surfaced. Forum Against Cityhood Today (FACT), a group of homeowners attracted to the area by various amenities, held that the community's existing tax base was not sufficient to support an independent city. They predicted a large increase in property taxes for financing municipal services. FACT also found fault with the Irvine master plan and pointed out that it gave no attention to serious environmental problems such as air pollution and flood control.[52]

Meanwhile, CCI and COIN conducted a vigorous campaign in which they talked glowingly about the alleged virtues of local autonomy and self-determination. Irvine Company executives made available to them space in their weekly newspaper, the *Irvine World News*, and time on a local television station owned by the company. Both organizations proclaimed in numerous articles and television speeches that cityhood would deliver Irvine homeowners from the supposed bad influence of Santa Ana and the county government. They also held that the new city could offer one of the lowest tax rates among California municipalities and provide a higher level of public services and facilities. Irvine residents were sufficiently impressed. They approved incorporation by a margin of two to one in December 1971.[53]

THE FIGHT OVER GROWTH

Coincident with the cityhood vote was an election for Irvine's first five-member council. The central issue in the campaign was the Irvine Company master plan for the future growth and development of the area. Irvine executives financed and strongly promoted several candidates. Among them was Burton, the local businessman who had been a leading figure in the incorporation drive. Burton strongly supported the Irvine plan mainly on the grounds that it would assure an orderly and productive environment, and he pledged to secure the adoption of the scheme without any major changes.[54] Running against him and other company-backed candidates were several persons affiliated with the Irvine Tomorrow organization. It consisted mostly of upper-middle-class activists who shared a new environmental philosophy described by historian Carl Abbott in his major work on postwar sunbelt cities as "quality-of-life liberalism." The Irvine Company, like other new community builders, did not always come through on its promises regarding parks, greenbelts, and other amenities.[55] Irvine Tomorrow leaders worried that the public would not have permanent access to recreational land and cared deeply about the preservation of the natural environment. The group was also concerned with the lack of population balance and diversity. They were most bothered by the inability of local residents to affect private planning and to control or slow down the pace of community development. Irvine Tomorrow candidates stuck mostly to this issue and conducted highly effective, door-to-door campaigns. Especially candid and persuasive was

Gabrielle Pryor, a member of the board of directors of a local home-owners' association. Pryor expressed strong reservations about the environmental elements of the Irvine Company master plan, pledged support for fair housing, and vowed to oppose certain large-scale projects that could put the community "on the road to bad growth." She and two other Irvine Tomorrow candidates, along with Burton, won seats on the council. "All Southern California will be watching to see if the promise of Irvine is fulfilled," reported the *Los Angeles Times* shortly after the election. "If projections are correct, it could become the county's biggest city. More important, it has the chance to be a better city than any other created here."[56]

The new council quickly took advantage of this opportunity. It voted a temporary moratorium on all construction in the city and told the Irvine Company to expect major revisions in its master plan. The council also established a planning commission and brought in a group of conservationists and environmentalists to staff it.[57] Most outspoken in the group was Wesley Marx, a visiting lecturer in social ecology at the University of California at Irvine. Marx questioned the basic premises of the Irvine Company master plan and wondered whether the county could afford another upper-class suburbia with a projected population of 430,000. The council hired the consulting firm of Wilsey and Ham to help him and the other commissioners prepare land-use plans for the city. Wilsey and Ham in the 1960s did the master planning for several new communities in different parts of the country, including Foster City, located twenty-five miles south of San Francisco. Joining them in the Irvine project were a number of people from local homeowners' associations. The council placed them on several committees and encouraged them to share their ideas and views with the professional planners.[58]

Out of the activity came the Irvine general plan in 1973. It covered the city, its sphere of influence, and a ten-thousand-acre coastal section south of Newport Beach. Three development options were presented in the plan. Option 1 closely followed the proposals of the Irvine Company for a series of villages and activity corridors, with an additional industrial complex and a regional commercial center located at the junction of the San Diego and Santa Ana freeways. It projected a midrange population of 337,000 people. Maximum urbanization was assured in the second option with a projected population of 453,000. Option 3, based on minimum urbanization estimates, reserved all the coastal-hills zone as open space and projected a population of 194,000.[59]

The plan also established goals and policies to guide future development. Particular attention was given to having a range of convenient and attractively grouped community facilities. The plan outlined a circulation system of bicycle, hiking, and equestrian trails to link recreation areas together. Such a system was expected to reduce dependence on the automobile and provide residents with increased access to recreation land. The plan also reserved various sites for schools, churches, and shopping facilities. More impressive was a concern and support for social diversity. The plan proposed the establishment of an information network that could closely monitor housing developments to be sure they filled the residential needs of all people who worked in the community. The plan also outlined specific procedures for builders to follow so that they provided housing in different price ranges and for different income groups in specific areas of the city.[60]

Irvine Company executives did not quarrel with these particular arrangements. The stinging criticism of their residential projects in 1970 and 1971 had led them to pay increased attention to the middle-income segment of the housing market. Furthermore, the nearby communities of Laguna Niguel and Mission Viejo offered many of the same features and conveniences found in Irvine. The place was no longer the only destination in the county for upper-class buyers seeking a planned environment with a wide range of leisure and natural amenities.[61] Accordingly, company executives decided on a policy of allocating a certain number of units in their housing construction program for moderate-income families. They submitted to the planning commission in early 1973 a proposal to provide housing for about eleven thousand people on a 484-acre site to be named the Village of Valley View, 200 acres of which would be developed within the first year. The housing would be for families earning incomes from eight to twelve thousand dollars a year. Included were proposals for 375 apartment units, 504 detached homes, and a townhouse section of 912 units. The planning commission voted in favor of the project with the recommendation that the total number of units be reduced from 1,791 to 1,358 to achieve a lower density.[62]

Homeowners living near the proposed Village of Valley View were not happy with the commission's decision. "In order for integration policies to be implemented successfully, resident support is vital," Burby and Weiss point out. "It is important that residents are aware of the integration goals and if possible, involved in the decisions regarding integration."[63] Neither of these procedures was followed by Irvine Company leaders and city planning officials. As a result, planned development in this case was not the same thing to them as it was to the homeowners in the affected area. These residents and many other Irvine homeowners believed that one of the basic purposes of planning was to minimize the threat that unknown changes would present to their social status and monetary investment. The change most feared by them was the construction of markedly less expensive housing nearby. Their concerns were voiced in several heated hearings held by the council on the proposed project. Some residents argued that the densities were too high. Others charged that the project would adversely affect traffic and surrounding property values and also incur huge costs for flood control. Still others expressed opposition to class and racial integration. One resident worried that most of his new neighbors would be on food stamps. Another strongly objected to making room in the new city for minority groups, families on welfare rolls, and transient young adults. In the face of all this prejudice and protest, the council voted unanimously against the Valley View project.[64]

Subsidized housing was an equally troublesome issue for Irvine officials. The Federal Housing Administration Section 235 interest-supplement and Section 236 rental-supplement programs were being extensively used by builders and developers in cities across the nation to increase the supply of decent dwellings for low- and moderate-income families.[65] Irvine Company leaders announced in late 1972 that they were considering participation in both programs and hoped to provide a certain amount of low-cost housing in new villages. Their intentions aroused some vigorous debate among members of the council. Burton strongly opposed joining federal housing programs and argued that they were generally unworkable and sometimes disastrous. Recent resident polls in the city, he noted, showed much resistance to housing subsidies, particularly those for low-income groups. Pryor was not impressed. Decrying opposition to subsidized housing as a "socialist bugaboo," she pointed out that the quality and management of 235 and 236 projects in many cities were improving and urged that housing subsidies be actively considered, short of using city tax monies. The council, however, voted three to two against participation in federally assisted housing in March 1973. Shortly afterward, Pryor consulted with the liberal-minded planning commission and helped them organize a study committee to develop alternative ways of providing housing for moderate-income families. Out of the committee's work came a recommendation that pointed the city in the direction of income diversity. They proposed that a certain number of lower-priced rental and sale units be built in large developments. The council, after some debate over density requirements, approved the measure in early 1974. It was first applied to the Irvine Company's new 8,900-unit Woodbridge Village. The council required that 10 percent of the units be moderate-income housing. One year later, they imposed the same income allocation on the company's 5,000-unit University Town Center proposal. Irvine, in the process, became the first city in the county to require that some inexpensive housing be permanently available in residential developments.[66]

Such a policy, while admirable and long overdue, fell far short of meeting the city's responsibility to the regional housing market. The Irvine Company's industrial parks had lured a large number of manufacturing firms and service businesses from older cities in the county and

other parts of southern California. Many employees could not find affordable housing and commuted an hour or more to their jobs.[67] This
disturbing situation was not of great concern to Irvine city officials however. They generally subscribed to the progrowth philosophy of the
Irvine Company and considered large-scale commercial and industrial
expansion to be essential to the continued economic health and social
cohesiveness of the community. Irvine Company executives made sure
the politicians did not change their minds. They lobbied hard for approval of the Irvine Industrial Complex–East (IIC-East), a two-thousand-
acre site located just east of the El Toro Marine Air Corps Station. The
council voted four to one to approve zoning for the project in early 1975.
IIC-East, in combination with the existing western complex, made the
company the owner of the largest industrial development in the nation. It
was expected that the new project would employ over fifty thousand
people and provide tax revenues of ten million dollars a year to the city.
Company and city officials regretfully reported that only a small number
of workers would find moderate-income housing in the area and saw little
chance of any low-income units being built over the next several years.[68]

     This bleak announcement aroused much concern among some liberal-
minded activists in the community. The continual movement of industry
to suburban areas, they pointed out, was creating severe hardships for
workers who were not able to afford the costs of extended journeys to
work. Backed by the Orange County Fair Housing Council, environmen-
talist Marx and six other Irvine residents filed a lawsuit against the zoning
of the IIC-East site. The suit accused the city of abandoning the principles
of its general plan and violating new state regulations regarding affordable housing. Irvine officials, in response, reaffirmed their moderate-
income allocations, which applied to five villages. They also adopted
incentives for developers to build low-cost housing; these incentives included waivers on density levels and park fees.[69] Marx and the other
plaintiffs were not satisfied with these actions. They asked that the Irvine
Company provide 644 low-income projects over a ten-year period, regardless of whether state or federal assistance were available. Their request was firmly rejected by city and company officials in 1976.

     The following year brought a breakthrough in the housing debate. Fol-
lowing several months of negotiation, a financial consortium outbid the
Mobil Corporation and bought out the Irvine Company for $337 million.
Among the new owners were shopping-center developer A. Alfred Taubman, Joan Irvine Smith, and Donald L. Bren, a wealthy southern California developer who had conceived and initiated the community of Mission
Viejo.[70] They were eager to get IIC-East under way and negotiated an out-
of-court accord that was signed by all the parties involved in the housing
suit. The Irvine Company agreed to provide 725 low-income units for

workers and their families over a five-year period in five separate villages. The accord also committed company officials to providing $2.8 million for off-site improvements such as streets, sidewalks, and various utilities.[71]

These concessions indicated some shift in the development policies of the Irvine Company. The intense controversy over affordable housing for industrial workers made the new owners more receptive than the previous ones to class integration and income diversity. Taubman talked about having a "balanced community" on the ranch and promised construction of "all kinds of housing." He and his colleagues also believed that the company had become too diversified and announced that certain land would be sold rather than leased to reputable building firms. The builders were responsible for developing portions of residential villages under strict guidelines and supervision by company planners and engineers. Little was said about slowing down the pace of development however. Watson had resigned as company president and moved on to a top position at Walt Disney Productions. His replacement was corporate executive Peter Kremer, a long-time business acquaintance of Bren. Kremer had headed a residential-development subsidiary of the Newhall Land and Farming Company, which was responsible for the creation of the new town of Valencia, a high-amenity suburb not unlike Irvine.[72] He listened to complaints from local critics that the Irvine development was a perpetuation of aimless California suburban sprawl. His rebuttal emphasized the marketing and financial aspects of new community building. "Sociologists may want them to live that way, but the vast majority of Southern Californians don't like high density urban development," he maintained. "And when you are in business, you have to respond to the market." Kremer told company stockholders that all existing residential projects would be completed and promised a considerable expansion of commercial and industrial construction.[73]

His assurances might not have been completely in line with the development programs and goals of the city of Irvine. The 1978 council election, in which several candidates vied for two open seats, revolved largely around this crucial matter. Arthur Anthony, former mayor of Irvine, argued strongly in favor of the city's general plan as "one of the best in California" and stressed the need to maintain a healthy balance of commercial, industrial, and residential development. He promised to work cooperatively with Irvine Company directors and continue the implementation of the plan in a "rational and just manner." His support did not extend to the city's fair-housing program however. He pledged firm opposition to any attempt of county and state agencies to force the city to provide additional subsidized housing.[74] Larry Agran, a local attorney and active member of various community organizations, presented different views regarding the future growth of Irvine. "The City Council's present General Plan would cause Irvine to explode in size, doubling to over 100,000 people by 1982," he pointed out. "This excessive rate of growth threatens our beautiful, uncrowded environment." He called for some fundamental changes in the general plan and urged extensive use of zoning powers to slow the intense pace of suburban growth, with particular attention to open-space protection. He also argued in favor of increased class integration and talked about getting additional state and federal funding for moderate-income housing. His candidacy attracted considerable support from Irvine Tomorrow, the influential citizens group strongly committed to the preservation of open space. They conducted an effective door-to-door campaign and helped elect Agran to the council. Anthony, backed by local developers and construction companies, won the other seat.[75]

The elections prompted no major reduction in Irvine's economic and physical expansion. Anthony expressed concern that the city's retail business was lagging behind that of surrounding cities and sent a letter to the Irvine Company in which he urged it to build additional commercial facilities. He talked about a serious shortage of furniture, plumbing fixtures, electrical supplies, and other retail goods. Increased commercial development would also provide badly needed sales-tax revenue for various public services. The council in 1980 approved the urban design for the commercial portion of Irvine Center, a 480-acre site located within a triangle created by the intersection of the Santa Ana, San Diego, and Laguna freeways. Irvine Center was to contain several large office buildings, a regional shopping mall, and three hotels. The council also approved company plans for the construction of offices and retail facilities in University Town Center, the Irvine Home and Garden Center, and Woodbridge Village Center.[76]

Development in Newport Beach proceeded along different and controversial lines. The Irvine Company had leased a large amount of residential land in the city in the 1960s. By the end of the 1970s the rapid rise in Orange County land prices greatly increased the value of the leases. Some four thousand residents in 1981 received rent adjustments called for in their long-standing agreement with the company. They protested vehemently against the increases and pleaded with Irvine directors to sell the land to them at prices well below current market value. Seeing their request as unfair to other tenants on the ranch, the directors offered them a variety of land-purchase plans and rent-reduction packages. Several leaseholders, however, decided to file a lawsuit against the company. Further controversy erupted over the proposed expansion of Newport Center, a financial area. The city council voted in favor of company plans for a three-hundred-room luxury hotel and 200,000 square feet of commercial facilities. Its decision met with much resentment from many

Newport Beach residents. Fearful of increased traffic congestion in their picturesque community, they organized themselves into a number of citizens' groups and conducted an effective referendum campaign to give residents a chance to vote on the Newport Center proposal. Irvine Company directors, uncomfortable over the prospect of continuing opposition to their other projects in the city, scrapped the development plans and promised a scaled-down version if they expanded the center in the future.[77]

A CHANGE OF DIRECTION

This agitation over the growth of Newport Center, coupled with the leasehold controversy, seriously damaged the public image of the Irvine Company. County Supervisor Thomas Riley, whose district included Newport Beach, reported that many of his constituents considered the company to be an "insensitive big corporation." Irvine city officials were also upset with the organization for dragging its feet on certain promised development. Particularly irritating to them was the failure to start a shopping complex in Irvine Center. Making things worse was renewed agitation over the development of ocean property between Corona del Mar and Laguna Beach. The company presented a plan to build two ten-story office towers and twenty-one thousand homes on the site and won approval from the Board of Supervisors and the state Coastal Commission. Friends of the Irvine Coast, a conservation organization boasting a membership of two thousand, complained about a serious lack of open-space provisions and filed a lawsuit against the plan in 1981.[78]

The result of all of this criticism was a major executive shake-up in the fall of 1982. Bren, the company's largest stockholder, joined Taubman as cochairman of the board of directors. Kremer resigned as president to "pursue personal business interests" and was succeeded by Thomas Nielsen, who had a good reputation among local public officials and civic organizations. Nielsen had served as assistant secretary of the Air Force for business management in the late 1960s and had worked in various real estate enterprises for the Newhall Land and Farming Company in the 1970s. He joined the executive ranks of the Irvine Company in 1978 and held the position of vice-president for community development at the time of his appointment to the top post.[79]

Company tactics and attitudes changed considerably under Nielsen's direction. Kremer had been content to muscle company plans past local residents and treated certain projects on the ranch as feudal fiefdoms. Nielsen operated in a friendly manner and gave priority to flexibility and conciliation. He told a gathering of county and municipal officials in early 1983 that the company was "sincerely concerned with the future of communities" and assured them that it would be more "constructive and cooperative" than it had been in the past. These points were repeated in numerous speeches given to citizen groups and various community organizations. He also made extensive use of public relations managers and instructed them to help explain various proposals to the governments of six cities responsible for different portions of the company's development activity.[80]

Less visible but more significant was Bren's strong dissatisfaction with the company's general development program. His colleagues on the board of directors, unlike their predecessors, who followed a long-term growth plan and invested heavily in community infrastructure such as improved roads and water facilities, were content to continue the practice of selling land to builders and putting most of the proceeds in the bank. The problem with this policy, Bren complained, was that the company was not sufficiently expanding its investment in income-producing office buildings, shopping centers, and apartments. Worried about the effect of these conditions on his investment, he bought out five members of the 1977 consortium for $500 million and acquired majority ownership of the company in 1983. His takeover led to the drafting of a new, comprehensive plan designed to dramatically increase the pace of development on the ranch. The largest projects included 740,000 square feet of additional office space in the John Wayne Airport area, a two-hundred-acre medical complex on the western edge of Irvine Center, and three new shopping malls in Irvine. Company leaders also proposed to provide in Irvine over a five-year period 3,888 apartments renting for between $500 and $950 a month and 10,000 homes of which 1,700 were to be priced from $80,000 to $150,000. The apartments and moderately priced homes, Nielsen noted, were vital to keeping businesses in the city's industrial parks. He and other company executives were concerned that many manufacturing firms might leave the area because of a shortage of affordable housing for their workers.[81]

Such ambitious proposals served as the dominant topic in the 1984 council elections in Irvine. Six candidates vied for three open seats. Incumbent David Sills campaigned in support of continual, large-scale building as long as the projects followed the "guidelines and controls" contained in the city's general plan. David Baker, a local attorney, called for shorter, five-year plans that would allow the city to initiate development programs rather than simply respond to the "Irvine Company's concerns." Both candidates endorsed the controversial Proposition A. Drafted by the Orange County Transportation Commission, Proposition A provided for a 1 percent countywide sales tax to finance street and road maintenance, new freeway construction, and the development of a mass-transit system. The centerpiece of the measure was a proposal calling for freeways along the San Joaquin Hills and Foothill transportation corridors bordering Irvine. Irvine Company leaders worried about losing the ability to sustain growth without new transportation facilities and endorsed the measure. Mary Ann Gaido, running for a third term, argued strongly against Proposition A on the grounds that it would allow developers to bulldoze the remaining hills and canyons with "little respect for the environment" and would result in a substantial deterioration of air quality in the area. Enough voters shared her concerns. The measure went down to defeat by a margin of two to one. Gaido lost her bid for another term however. Sills, Baker, and another progrowth candidate won the elections.[82]

Irvine Company planners and public relations experts wasted little time in getting down to business with the council. They lobbied for various building permits with a skillful blend of deference and determination and won approval of certain commercial and industrial schemes. Especially impressive was Irvine Spectrum, a twenty-two-hundred-acre business and technology community near the junction of the Santa Ana and San Diego freeways in Irvine. Helped along by a boom in federal aerospace and military expenditures, Orange County, with its high-quality labor force and superior amenities, continued to attract a large number of growth industries such as electronic firms, research-and-development enterprises, and biotechnical companies. Richard Sim, president of the newly formed Irvine Industrial Research and Development Division, saw Spectrum as the final home of many of these businesses. He expected the project to become the key to both the company's financial future and the county's continued economic prosperity.[83] Developments in 1985 and 1986 confirmed Sim's optimism. Many industrial concerns requiring additional space as the result of opening new subsidiaries moved most of their equipment and personnel to Irvine Spectrum. The complex housed over 160 companies with twelve thousand employees. Plans were also being made to provide hotels, restaurants, and other supportive commercial facilities.[84]

This expansion, along with the company's numerous other projects, served as the major issue in the Irvine council elections in 1986. One candidate, Tom Jones, president of the Irvine Chamber of Commerce, argued in favor of continual residential and industrial construction and firmly endorsed the proposed San Joaquin Hills and Foothill freeways. His campaign enjoyed considerable support from the Irvine Company; many of its employees tirelessly walked precincts on Jones's behalf and solicited substantial financial contributions.[85] Incumbent Agran and his supporters conducted an equally vigorous campaign in which they stressed the need to effectively restrain "excessive growth" and proposed basic changes in the city's general plan that would reduce increasing residential densities and guarantee permanent preservation of certain hillsides and farmlands. Agran also argued against new freeways in the Irvine area as potential sources of additional congestion and "unbearable air pollution" and advocated the withdrawal of the city from the Joint Powers Agreement as soon as possible. The agreement was entered into by Irvine and surrounding cities to oversee the design and financing of the Foothill, San Joaquin Hills, and Eastern freeways. Similar views and proposals were voiced by Ed Dornan, a member of the city planning commission. Dornan criticized the council for some "hasty and unwise development" in certain parts of the city. He promised to work aggressively for open-space preservation, spoke in favor of widening existing freeways to relieve traffic snarls, and called for the enactment of new ordinances designed to reduce the rate of physical growth to manageable proportions. Irvine voters, concerned that their pleasant community might become one more smoggy, congested suburb on the road between Los Angeles and San Diego, elected Dornan and Agran to the council by wide margins. They and incumbent Ray Catalano, a professor of urban planning at the University of California at Irvine, composed, for the first time in the council's history, a slow-growth majority.[86]

Irvine Company leaders greeted the new council with resignation and a spirit of cooperation. "We read the election outcome in Irvine as an expression of public support for controlled growth," Nielsen told a local newspaper journalist. He reported that the company was willing to work with the slow-growth coalition and hoped to assist them in furthering "public understanding" on open space, transportation, and other development issues. The actions of the new council left little room for any consultation or cooperation however. It voted in favor of changes in the city's general plan to rezone hundreds of acres of land as permanent open space. It also withdrew Irvine from the consortium of cities collecting fees for the construction of three freeways until a citywide vote could be held on the matter.[87]

Further disappointment for Irvine Company executives came over their commercial property in Newport Beach. They won council approval of a proposed $300 million expansion of Newport Center to include three office towers, homes, shops, and cultural facilities. A large number of residents greeted the plan with considerable resentment and organized a citizens group called Gridlock to protest the company's actions. Charging that the office towers would add forty thousand car trips a day to already congested roads and further transform the community into an overcrowded urban center, Gridlock successfully circulated a petition calling for a referendum on the expansion as an amendment to the city's general plan. The Irvine Company vigorously promoted the plan and spent $100,000 on public-opinion surveys, campaign brochures, and television advertisements. Newport Beach voters, fearful of increased traffic congestion and seeing no major benefits to their community from the expansion, soundly defeated the proposal.[88]

Coastal planning proceeded along more hospitable lines than did plans for Newport Center. Irvine Company executives had not forgotten the 1981 lawsuit against their original plan. They also believed that it would not make enough money for the company.[89] Consequently, they decided to shelve the plan and met with representatives of the Friends of the Irvine Coast and other conservation groups to discuss and evaluate alternative building proposals. Out of the talks came a comprehensive scheme for the development of a ten-thousand-acre stretch of oceanfront property just north of Laguna Beach. The plan called for four hotels, two golf courses, and twenty-six hundred homes. It also set aside 76 percent of the site as open-space preserves to include parks and trails. The Board of Supervisors unanimously adopted the plan in 1987 as the county's guide for future coastal development. The following year a coalition of environmentalists appeared before the supervisors and persuaded them to approve a development agreement to protect the project from land-use changes for twenty years. It required that the Irvine Company pay $22.7 million for road improvements and contribute about $2 million toward the construction of a fire station, police facilities, and a public library in the area. Carol Hoffman, a member of the company's board of directors, hailed the coastal arrangements as a "very thoughtful balance" and declared that developers were finally "seeing how to include the community upfront."[90]

Slow-growth advocates in Orange County and other parts of southern California did not share her sentiments. Ten years of debate over questions of traffic flow, open-space preservation, and density levels had convinced them that big developers, with their eyes primarily on lucrative profits rather than environmental integrity, could not be relied on to make any fundamental changes in their land-use policies and programs. They were also greatly disappointed with the performance of city and county elected officials and faulted them for not using enough regulatory power to alleviate growing traffic congestion and unnecessary destruction of natural terrains. Their criticisms and frustration found expression in various slow-growth proposals that reached the ballot in 1987 and 1988.

Orange County's controversial Measure A was the most far-reaching proposal. Drafted by Orange County Tomorrow, a coalition of affluent property owners, environmental activists, and liberal and conservative politicians, Measure A prohibited any new construction where traffic moved at speeds slower than thirty to thirty-five miles per hour at peak hours on roads between the proposed development and the nearest freeway, state highway, or major artery. It also required developers to set aside an increased amount of land for parks. As expected, the initiative met with strong opposition from building firms, the Irvine Company, and other development companies in the region. They spent two million dollars on direct-mail brochures, personal phone calls to homeowners, and strategically placed highway billboards. Measure A, they charged, would halt most construction, greatly increase the cost of housing, and eliminate many jobs in various areas. Orange County voters were sufficiently convinced. They rejected the proposition by a comfortable margin.[91]

The 1988 elections in Irvine, however, clearly indicated that rapid suburban growth would remain the dominant issue in South County public affairs. Agran, promising increased regulation of certain development projects, won the city's first election for mayor, while three council seats went to slow-growth candidates.[92] Irvine Company executives could also expect close scrutiny and criticism of their development activities on other parts of the ranch. The postwar decades saw the company, equipped with a remarkable amount of planning expertise and technical skills, transform a vast agricultural landscape into a postsuburban complex organized around a number of distinct centers, portions of which lie within the boundaries of several incorporated cities. These jurisdictions continue to be protective of their turf and work to advance their own economic and social welfare.

The toughest challenge for the Irvine Company is to modify its preoccupation with private profit and to help create a consensus that can transcend such partisan interests and deal with serious regional problems such as aimless commercial sprawl, maddening traffic congestion, and random destruction of natural landscapes. An equally disturbing problem is that much of the housing provided by the company and other South County developers, while available to a limited number of middle-income people, remains beyond the reach of most low-income workers and their families. This lack of population balance deserves the same degree of concern as environmental health and preservation.

One important step in the right direction is the Ad Hoc Advisory Committee formed by the Board of Supervisors to develop a countywide growth-management plan. The committee welcomes the advice and proposals of municipal officials, civic leaders, and representatives of the Irvine Company and other business organizations in the region. In a position paper presented to the committee, the company stated:

> Sound growth management requires an ongoing partnership between the developer, governments, and communities to resolve competing and sometimes conflicting public policy goals. We hope the result of your Committee's efforts will be a growth management process that accommodates new growth in a manner that . . . insures rates and types of growth that are

adequate to meet the housing, employment, economic development, and cultural needs of the county.[93]

Such expectations can be seen as additional confirmation of the important fact that the Irvine Company, along with other leading members of the development industry, has brought into existence a highly deconcentrated form of metropolitan settlement that places enormous strains on the region's economic and social resources. The ability of the company and other corporate organizations, citizens' groups, and public officials to work cooperatively to relieve these strains will greatly determine the future quality of life for all people who work and live in southern Orange County.

NOTES

1. Good discussions of the economic and spatial development of postsuburban centers in certain areas of the sunbelt can be found in Peter O. Muller, *Contemporary Suburban America* (Englewood Cliffs, N.J.: Prentice-Hall, 1981), 1–17, 120–81; Kenneth T. Jackson, *Crabgrass Frontier: The Suburbanization of the United States* (New York: Oxford University Press, 1985), 246–71; Carl Abbott, *The New Urban America: Growth and Politics in Sunbelt Cities*, 2d ed. (Chapel Hill: University of North Carolina Press, 1987), 60–100.

2. Robert Glass Cleland, *The Irvine Ranch*, 3d ed. (San Marino, Calif.: Huntington Library, 1962), 43–45, 57–59, 67–71, 87–88, 101.

3. Ibid., 104–10, 120–22.

4. Ibid., 132–33, 150; Nathaniel M. Griffin, *Irvine: The Genesis of a New Community* (Washington, D.C.: Urban Land Institute, 1974), 10, 62.

5. Leo J. Friis, *Orange County through Four Centuries* (Santa Ana, Calif.: Pioneer, 1965), 171–72; Pamela Hallan-Gibson, *The Golden Promise: An Illustrated History of Orange County* (Northridge, Calif.: Windsor, 1986), 237.

6. Cleland, *Irvine Ranch*, 151–52.

7. Stephen Birmingham, *California Rich* (New York: Simon & Schuster, 1980), 218–19.

8. Griffin, *Irvine*, 9–10; William L. Pereira and Associates, *A Preliminary Report for a University-Community Development in Orange County*, 1959, Government Publications Files, University of California, Irvine (hereafter referred to as UCI), 1.

9. "The Man with the Plan," *Time*, 6 Sept. 1963, 70–71; quoted in David Shaw, "Architect Pereira: Working for Third Millennium," *Los Angeles Times*, 14 Sept. 1969.

10. Pereira and Associates, *Preliminary Report*, 3–5.

11. Edward P. Eichler and Marshall Kaplan, *The Community Builders* (Berkeley: University of California Press, 1967), 2–4, 8; Kevin Lynch, "The Pattern of the Metropolis," *Daedalus* 90 (Winter 1961): 94.

12. William L. Pereira and Associates, *Second Phase Report for a University-Community Development in Orange County*, 1960, Government Publications Files, UCI, 9–10, 12–13, 17–22.

13. Eichler and Kaplan, *Community Builders*, 28; Griffin, *Irvine*, 16.

14. Quoted in Wyndham Robertson, "The Greening of the Irvine Company," *Fortune* 94 (December 1976): 89.

15. Quoted in Griffin, *Irvine*, 16–17; "Man with the Plan," 69.

16. Eichler and Kaplan, *Community Builders*, 5–9, 36–43; Raymond J. Burby and Shirley F. Weiss, *New Communities U.S.A.* (Lexington, Mass.: Heath, Lexington Books, 1976), 49–50.

17. Harry E. Bergh, *The Diminishing County Myth*, statement to the Orange County Board of Supervisors and the Orange County Planning Commission, April 1963, Government Publications Files, UCI, 6.

18. Eichler and Kaplan, *Community Builders*, 95; Burby and Weiss, *New Communities U.S.A.*, 52.

19. Eichler and Kaplan, *Community Builders*, 100.

20. Griffin, *Irvine*, 17; Martin A. Brower, "A Time for People: How an Old Company Moved into the New Era," *New Worlds* 7 (June/July 1976): 63–64.

21. Alan Kreditor and Kenneth L. Kraemer, *Final Report: Southern Sector General Plan*, May 1968, Government Publications Files, UCI, pt. 2, 3; pt. 4, 3–4; Don Smith, "Irvine Master Plan Unveiled," *Los Angeles Times*, 19 Jan. 1964.

22. Quoted in Ray Hebert, "Master Plan Set for Irvine Ranch," *Los Angeles Times*, 5 May 1964.

23. Kreditor and Kraemer, *Final Report*, pt. 3, 14–15; Hallan-Gibson, *Golden Promise*, 237–38, 258–59.

24. Eichler and Kaplan, *Community Builders*, 104.

25. "New Town Rises Back at the Ranch," *Business Week*, 23 Sept. 1967, 278, 282; "Huge Giant Awakens," *Los Angeles Herald Examiner*, 16 June 1968.

26. Kreditor and Kraemer, *Final Report*, pt. 4, 3; "Ranch Cited for Planning Achievement," *Irvine Ranch Newsletter* 4 (March 1969): 1.

27. Griffin, *Irvine*, 16; Raymond L. Watson, "Phasing Growth: How Fast? Where Next?" Reprinted in *New Towns in America: The Design and Development Process*, ed. James Bailey (New York: Wiley, 1973), 88.

28. Irvine Company, *Housing Element Data for Central Area Irvine General Plan*, November 1970, Government Publications Files, UCI, 4, 6–7, 8–11.

29. Burby and Weiss, *New Communities U.S.A.*, 108.

30. Ibid., 109–10; Carlos C. Campbell, *New Towns: Another Way to Live* (Reston, Va.: Reston Publishing, 1976), 32, 73–74.

31. Irvine Company, *Irvine General Plan*, 1970, Government Publications Files, UCI, 9–18.

32. Orange County Planning Department, General Planning Program, *Summary Report: Part I*, 3 June 1969, Government Publications Files, UCI, 7–8.

33. Orange County Planning Department, *Staff Report on the Proposed City of Irvine Plan*, 12 Nov. 1970, Government Publications Files, UCI, 16–17.

34. David Curry, "Irvine: The Case for a New Kind of Planning," *Cry California* 6 (Winter 1970/71): 25–27; Orange County Planning Department, *Preliminary Recommendation Package: Proposed Irvine General Plan: A Staff Report to the Orange County Planning Commission*, 14 Oct. 1970, Government Publications Files, UCI, 21–22.

35. Orange County Planning Department, *First Phase Impact Analysis: Proposed City of Irvine General Plan*, 1 July 1970, Government Publications Files, UCI, 183–84.

36. Orange County Planning Department, Equal Opportunity Subpanel, *Irvine General Plan: Analysis Sheet*, 1970, Government Publications Files, UCI, 3–4.

37. Quoted in David Shaw, "Irvine—City or Super Subdivision?" *Los Angeles Times*, 14 June 1970.

38. Campbell, *New Towns*, 42–43, 97.

39. Quoted in Shaw, "Irvine."

40. John Blackburn, "Irvine Atypical, Survey Claims," *Santa Ana Register*, 7 Oct. 1971.

41. Orange County Planning Department, *Irvine General Plan*, 17–18.

42. Raymond L. Watson, *How One Developer Lives with Government Controls*, address delivered to the Southwest Regional Conference, American Institute of Real Estate Appraisers, Anaheim, California, 17 Apr. 1975, Government Publications Files, UCI, 3.

43. Robertson, "Greening of the Irvine Company," 90; Brower, "Time for People," 69.

44. Robertson, "Greening of the Irvine Company," 91; Don Smith, "Two Days of Setbacks Leave Irvine Co. Officials Reeling," *Los Angeles Times*, 8 Jan. 1971.

45. Hallan-Gibson, *Golden Promise*, 240–41, 243; "Annexation Wars Hit," *Orange Coast Daily Pilot*, 14 Sept. 1970; Irvine Company, *Environmental Reasons for Proposing a Unified City*, November 1970, Government Publications Files, UCI, 2–5.

46. Don Smith, "Homeowner Unit Makes Bid for Cityhood," *Los Angeles Times*, 12 Sept. 1970; Curry, "Irvine," 30–31.

47. Irvine Citizen Study Committees, *Irvine Incorporation Feasibility Analysis: A Summary Report Prepared for the Council of the Communities of Irvine*, October 1970, Government Publications Files, UCI, pt. 3, 2–3, 5; Curry, "Irvine," 31–33.

48. "Irvine Officials Agree to Amend Boundary," *Orange Coast Daily Pilot*, 19 Oct. 1970; "Santa Ana Vows Scuffle on Incorporation," *Santa Ana Register*, 27 Sept. 1970.

49. Quoted in Don Smith, "LAFCO Ends Hearing on Irvine City Plan," *Los Angeles Times*, 14 Jan. 1971.

50. Barton-Aschman Associates, *Orange County, Santa Ana, and Irvine: Making the Development of Irvine a Countywide Success* (Chicago, 1971), 12–13, 66–68.

51. Don Smith, "LAFCO Approves Incorporation for City of Irvine," *Los Angeles Times*, 11 Feb. 1971; "Irvine Incorporation Petitions Filed," *Los Angeles Times*, 13 May 1971; Mike Colwell, "City of Irvine's Boundaries Okayed," *Santa Ana Register*, 9 Sept. 1971.

52. "Anti-Cityhood Flyers Distributed by Newly Formed 'Fact' Group," *Irvine World News*, 11 Nov. 1971; Forum Against Cityhood Today, *Ballot Pamphlet against Proposed City of Irvine Incorporation Election, December 21, 1971*, Government Publications Files, UCI, 2.

53. Mark Northcross, "Incorporation: Irvinian Birth Pangs," *New University*, 22 Oct. 1971, 1; idem, "Tippecanoe and Irvine Too," *New University*, 19 Nov. 1971,

12; W. B. Rood, "Residents of Irvine Vote to Incorporate by Margin of 2 to 1," *Los Angeles Times,* 22 Dec. 1971.

54. *Statements by Candidates for Proposed City of Irvine Council Elections,* 30 Nov. 1971, Government Publications Files, UCI, 1, 3; Mark Northcross, "Irvine Election: You Can't See the Game without a Program," *New University,* 3 Dec. 1971, 6.

55. Abbott, *New Urban America,* 216.

56. Northcross, "Irvine Election," 6; Herman Wong, "New Irvine Council Moves to Set Up a City," *Los Angeles Times,* 23 Dec. 1971; Editorial, "The Future of the City of Irvine," *Los Angeles Times,* 24 Dec. 1971.

57. Robertson, "Greening of the Irvine Company," 92; Chris Welles, "The Graying of Orange County," *New West,* 29 Aug. 1977, 30.

58. Wilsey and Ham, *Irvine General Plan,* December 1973, Government Publications Files, UCI, pt. 1, 5–6.

59. Ibid., pt. 1, 9–10.

60. Ibid., pt. 2, 1, 3, 7; pt. 4, 10–13.

61. Burby and Weiss, *New Communities U.S.A.,* 85; William A. Boyer, "A Tale of Two Cities: Mission Viejo, Too, Was a Planned Site," *Orange County Register,* 9 Nov. 1986.

62. Campbell, *New Towns,* 184–85.

63. Burby and Weiss, *New Communities U.S.A.,* 116.

64. George Leidel, "Seeds of Intolerance Find Fertility in Irvine," *Orange Coast Daily Pilot,* 4 Feb. 1973.

65. R. Allan Hays, *The Federal Government and Urban Housing: Ideology and Change in Public Policy* (Albany: State University of New York Press, 1985), 112–29.

66. Campbell, *New Towns,* 185; Herman Wong, "Irvine's Housing Battle: A Cease-Fire but No Peace Treaty," *Los Angeles Times,* 2 Oct. 1977.

67. Welles, "Graying of Orange County," 28. Two years after the council required the building of inexpensive housing, a survey of housing opportunities by an Anaheim firm found that 90 percent of individuals working in Irvine lived elsewhere. Envista, Inc., *Housing Demand/Preference Study for the City of Irvine,* August 1976, Government Publications Files, UCI, 54.

68. Wong, "Irvine's Housing Battle."

69. Douglas Fritzsche, "Irvine Seeking End to Housing Suits," *Orange Coast Daily Pilot,* 3 Mar. 1976; Wong, "Irvine's Housing Battle."

70. Tom Barley, "Directors Okay Sale of Irvine Company," *Orange Coast Daily Pilot,* 25 May 1977; Larry Peterson, "Irvine Co. New Principal Owner Coming Home," *Santa Ana Register,* 9 Aug. 1977.

71. Herman Wong, "Irvine Housing Accord to Be Filed in Court," *Los Angeles Times,* 21 Nov. 1977. Some of the housing units would be partly financed with subsidies from the mortgage-financing and rental-assistance programs of the state and federal governments. The City of Irvine, Community Development Department, *Implementation of the Fair Housing Council Lawsuit Settlement,* 25 Nov. 1979, Government Publications Files, UCI, 2–4.

72. Quoted phrases in Forest Kimler and Art Barrett, "Heiress Vows No Fragmentation of Irvine Ranch," *Santa Ana Register,* 27 July 1977; Leslie Berk-

man, "The Winning of Irvine Company—and What Lies Ahead," *Los Angeles Times*, 14 Aug. 1977.

73. Quoted in Welles, "Graying of Orange County," 32; "No Irvine Changes," *Orange Coast Daily Pilot*, 11 Sept. 1977.

74. Quoted in "Campaign '78," *Irvine World News*, 2 Mar. 1978; Philip Rosmarin, "Seven Vie for 2 Irvine Seats," *Orange Coast Daily Pilot*, 6 Mar. 1978.

75. Quoted in "Campaign '78," *Irvine World News*, 2 Mar. 1978; "Ex-Mayor Tops in Spending," *Orange Coast Daily Pilot*, 6 Mar. 1978; "Agran and Anthony Win Council Seats," *Irvine World News*, 9 Mar. 1978.

76. "Irvine Commercial Needs Stressed," *Orange Coast Daily Pilot*, 23 May 1980; Ronald J. Foreman, "Irvine Company Enters 1981 with Unprecedented Wave of Development," *Los Angeles Business Journal*, 26 Jan. 1981, 1–2.

77. Jeanne Wright, "Troubles Surround Irvine Company," *Orange County Register*, 2 Feb. 1982.

78. Ibid.; Dave Lesher, "Longtime Irvine Coast Antagonists Hail Agreement," *Los Angeles Times*, 27 Apr. 1988.

79. Carla Lazzareschi, "Shake-Up at Irvine Company Adds a Co-chairman," *Orange County Register*, 17 Sept. 1982; Tom Furlong, "Nielsen Will Succeed Kremer at Irvine Company," *Los Angeles Times*, 22 Oct. 1982.

80. Steve Emmons, "Irvine Co. Polishes Public Image," *Los Angeles Times*, 27 Jan. 1983; Lynn O'Dell, "Size Is a Boon and Burden to Irvine Company," *Orange County Register*, 26 Feb. 1984.

81. John O'Dell, "Bren Buys Control of Irvine Company," *Los Angeles Times*, 16 Apr. 1983; Jane Glenn Haas, "Irvine Co. Thinks Big on Building," *Orange County Register*, 12 Apr. 1983. Much of this information on Bren's discontent with company policies appears in court testimony he has given in a lawsuit filed against the company by Joan Irvine Smith and her mother. The suit will settle a dispute over how much money they will get for the stock they held in the company before Bren's buyout in 1983. See Leslie Berkman, "Bren's Battles on the Stand," *Los Angeles Times*, 8 Nov. 1987.

82. "Council Candidates Speak Out on Community Issues," *Irvine World News*, 31 May 1984; "Nielsen Discusses Irvine Company's View of Proposition A," *Irvine World News*, 24 May 1984; Amy Starke, "Baker, Miller Join Incumbent Sills in Victory," *Irvine World News*, 6 June 1984. Various citizen-sponsored measures dealing with the management of urban and suburban growth found their way onto the ballot and won voter approval in several cities and counties in northern California in the early 1980s. See Larry Ordman, "Ballot-Box Planning: The Boom in Electoral Land-Use Control," *Public Affairs Report* (Bulletin of the Institute of Governmental Studies, University of California, Berkeley) 25 (December 1984): 1–10.

83. Jane Glenn Haas, "Sim Powers Job Development Program," *Orange County Register*, 4 Nov. 1984.

84. Martin A. Brower, "Irvine—It's Special," *The Executive*, July 1985, 39; Irvine Company, *Fact Sheet*, August 1986, 6.

85. Heidi Evans, "A Discreet Distance Is Political Key for Irvine Company," *Los*

Angeles Times, 19 May 1986; "Council Candidates Sound Off on Critical City Issues," *Irvine World News,* 22 May 1986.

86. "Council Candidates Sound Off"; "Candidate Profiles," *Irvine World News,* 29 May 1986; Tracy Childs, "Winners Call Their Victory a Mandate," *Irvine World News,* 6 June 1986.

87. Quoted in Heidi Evans, "Council Winner Expects to Put Brakes on Irvine Growth," *Los Angeles Times,* 5 June 1986; Bob Schwartz, "Grass-Roots Efforts to Slow Development Are Gaining Ground," *Los Angeles Times,* 22 Sept. 1986.

88. Heidi Evans, "Newport Beach Voters Reject Center Expansion," *Los Angeles Times,* 26 Nov. 1986.

89. Leslie Berkman, "Smith-Irvine Co. Trial Bares Firm's Internal Secrets," *Los Angeles Times,* 23 Aug. 1987.

90. Dave Lesher, "Irvine Coast Development Plan Okayed," *Los Angeles Times,* 2 Nov. 1987; idem, "Longtime Irvine Coast Antagonists Hail Agreement."

91. Jeffrey A. Perlman, "Initiative Seeks Slow Growth in Orange County," *Los Angeles Times,* 14 June 1987; Richard Breene, "Downturn in Growth Initiative," *Los Angeles Times,* 5 May 1988; Jeffrey A. Perlman and Michael Flagg, "Money Beat Measure A, Foes, Supporters Agree," *Los Angeles Times,* 6 June 1988. The largest contribution came from the Irvine Company, which gave $150,000 to the campaign against Measure A. See Dave Lesher, "Slow-Growth Foes Had 20–1 Spending Edge over Backers," *Los Angeles Times,* 2 Aug. 1988. On slow-growth propositions in cities in Orange County and other urban centers in southern California, see Steve Glennon, "Growth Problems: We Are Not Alone," *Saddleback Valley News,* 20 May 1988.

92. Jim Carlton, "Agran Calls Irvine Vote 'Validation' of His View," *Los Angeles Times,* 6 June 1988.

93. Irvine Company, *TIC's Input to the County Ad Hoc Advisory Committee on the Growth Management Plan,* 21 Apr. 1988, 2.

REFERENCES

Abbott, Carl. *The New Urban America: Growth and Politics in Sunbelt Cities.* 2d ed. Chapel Hill: University of North Carolina Press, 1987.

Barton-Aschman Associates. *Orange County, Santa Ana, and Irvine: Making the Development of Irvine a Countywide Success.* Chicago, 1971.

Birmingham, Stephen. *California Rich.* New York: Simon & Schuster, 1980.

Brower, Martin A. "A Time for People: How an Old Company Moved into the New Era." *New Worlds* 7 (June/July 1976): 59–74.

Burby, Raymond J., and Shirley F. Weiss. *New Communities U.S.A.* Lexington, Mass.: Heath, Lexington Books, 1976.

Campbell, Carlos C. *New Towns: Another Way to Live.* Reston, Va.: Reston Publishing, 1976.

Cleland, Robert Glass. *The Irvine Ranch.* 3d ed. San Marino, Calif.: Huntington Library, 1962.

Curry, David. "Irvine: The Case for a New Kind of Planning." *Cry California* 6 (Winter 1970/71): 18–40.

Eichler, Edward P., and Marshall Kaplan. *The Community Builders.* Berkeley: University of California Press, 1967.

Friis, Leo J. *Orange County through Four Centuries.* Santa Ana, Calif.: Pioneer, 1965.

Griffin, Nathaniel M. *Irvine: The Genesis of a New Community.* Washington, D.C.: Urban Land Institute, 1974.

Hallan-Gibson, Pamela. *The Golden Promise: An Illustrated History of Orange County.* Northridge, Calif.: Windsor, 1986.

Hays, R. Allen. *The Federal Government and Urban Housing: Ideology and Change in Public Policy.* Albany: State University of New York Press, 1985.

Jackson, Kenneth T. *Crabgrass Frontier: The Suburbanization of the United States.* New York: Oxford University Press, 1985.

Lynch, Kevin. "The Pattern of the Metropolis." *Daedalus* 90 (Winter 1961): 79–98.

Muller, Peter O. *Contemporary Suburban America.* Englewood Cliffs, N.J.: Prentice-Hall, 1981.

Northcross, Mark. "Incorporation: Irvinian Birth Pangs." *New University,* 22 Oct. 1971, 1, 6.

———. "Irvine Election: You Can't See the Game without a Program." *New University,* 3 Dec. 1971, 6.

———. "Tippecanoe and Irvine Too." *New University,* 19 Nov. 1971, 1, 12.

Ordman, Larry. "Ballot-Box Planning: The Boom in Electoral Land-Use Control." *Public Affairs Report* (Bulletin of the Institute of Governmental Studies, University of California, Berkeley) 25 (December 1984): 1–15.

Robertson, Wyndham. "The Greening of the Irvine Company." *Fortune* 94 (December 1976): 84–94, 96.

Watson, Raymond L. "Phasing Growth: How Fast? Where Next?" In *New Towns in America: The Design and Development Process,* edited by James Bailey, 87–89. New York: Wiley, 1973.

Welles, Chris. "The Graying of Orange County." *New West,* 29 Aug. 1977, 25–32.

FOUR

The Information
Labor Force

Rob Kling and Clark Turner

WORK IN ORANGE COUNTY

Is Orange County's economy producing a large number of relatively good jobs, relatively poor jobs, or some mix? Are there increasing opportunities for mobility across occupations and labor submarkets, or are occupations and labor markets sharply segmented? This chapter answers these questions by examining the changing patterns of employment in Orange County and in the United States.

In this chapter we examine the restructuring of labor markets in Orange County since the end of World War II, when the county was primarily an agricultural area. It would be easiest to measure employment trends in the traditional economic sectors—agriculture, manufacturing, and services—and examine how jobs have shifted between sectors and altered within them.[1] However, because we are interested in Orange County's trajectory of social development, we decided to examine work in ways that best characterize this development. Employment patterns in the Orange County information sector were the avenues we selected for study.

The information sector is a relatively new construct. It is composed of those jobs in which people record, process, or communicate information as a substantial part of their work. These occupations include manager, lawyer, accountant, realtor, stockbroker, and clerk. Although all workers—including truck drivers, trapeze artists, and machinists—process information in important ways, "information" jobs are those in which information is a key product or in which the person is likely to spend a substantial part of each workweek communicating, reading, searching for information, or handling paperwork in its various forms, including electronic transactions.

The information work force differs significantly from the hi-tech work force, which M. Gottdiener and George Kephart examine in Chapter 2 and which other analysts have examined in studies of hi-tech areas like Silicon Valley (Markusen and Bloch 1985). The hi-tech work force is composed of people who work in a variety of jobs within hi-tech manufacturing firms. These firms have over half their work force in hi-tech occupations, such as engineer and biologist. But 30 to 40 percent of their work forces can be composed of people in other occupations, such as secretary, accountant, assembler, and truck driver. The approximately 100,000 hi-tech workers in Orange County in 1988 constituted about 40 percent of its manufacturing work force and less than 10 percent of the county's total work force. Orange County developed a manufacturing dynamo in the 1960s that is still growing in absolute size and in national importance. But in the 1980s manufacturing was no longer the largest sector of Orange County's economy.

In contrast with the hi-tech work force, the information work force is composed of a specific set of occupations, such as clerk, engineer, accountant, and manager. As we shall see, most of Orange County's workers belong to its information work force. (See also the discussion in Chapter 1.) The information work force gives us a complementary but larger window than the hi-tech work force through which to examine social change in Orange County.

Information-processing jobs play a major role in today's economy. Several analysts have argued that information handling is not simply a feature of existing jobs, or even a central element in a few jobs, but a key dimension for characterizing labor markets and urban economies. Manuel Castells (n.d.), for example, simply declares that information handling is a defining activity in new metropolitan formations and dubs leading-edge urban development as an "informational city."[2] Robert Fishman (1987) labels postsuburban regions *technoburbs* and thereby indicates that their dependence on transportation and communication technologies undergirds their social and spatial forms. Richard Knight (1986) follows Daniel Bell's (1973) characterization of postindustrial societies and argues that knowledge work is a core activity in a transformed urban economy.

These provocative theses are worthy of investigation. They provide an important entry point to the study of the work force in advanced economic areas in contrast to the traditional trichotomy of agriculture, manufacturing, and services. Unfortunately, analysts who write about the primacy of information work usually treat it as a social fact rather than carefully examining the meanings of information work in new social formations. In contrast, David Lyon (1988) argues persuasively that information work should be examined anew rather than being taken for granted. Shoshana Zuboff (1988), for example, argues that an organization with highly "informated" jobs requires especially skilled workers who can challenge traditional managerial styles and whose skill is a novel resource for managers to cherish.

The information sector is a relatively new analytical category that we believe is worth exploring. Orange County's work force, like the U.S. work force, is composed of people in hundreds of occupations. Every simple categorization mixes diverse occupations and working conditions. The traditional scheme mixes field hands and agribusiness accountants (agriculture); welders, stock clerks, and industrial engineers (manufacturing); cabdrivers, waitresses, and lawyers (services). Distinctions between union and nonunion cut across occupations and depend on local circumstances. Similarly, the crude distinction between information work and other kinds of work mixes diverse workers such as postal clerks and lawyers. But this chapter goes beyond the usual accounts of information work by grouping information workers into five occupational strata that differ according to the quality of the jobs within them. We examine here the composition of the information work force with special attention to simple differences between better and worse jobs. And we look at the changing composition of different strata in the information work force primarily by using demographic data.

WORK IN AN INFORMATION ECONOMY

Social analysts characterize the major economic transformations of this era according to two different rubrics: as a postindustrial society (Bell 1973; Ginzberg, Noyelle, and Stanback 1986) and as an information society (Porat 1973; Bell 1980; Huppes 1987). Some analysts loosely mix these terms (Naisbitt 1984; Huppes 1987), even though they have different connotations. The service sector dominates in Bell's (1973) characterization of postindustrial economies. He argues that postindustrial societies also depend critically on credentialed experts, especially "knowledge producers" such as scientists and engineers. But scientific and engineering occupations form only a small fraction of the jobs in even the most technologically advanced societies. The service sector is dominated by a variety of industries, from transportation to restaurants, from insurance and banking to utilities (Ginzberg, Noyelle, and Stanback 1986). These service industries are composed of two key kinds of jobs: jobs where people provide direct service (such as bank teller, waitress, stockbroker, lawyer, security guard, bus driver, and insurance agent) and jobs in the administrative core of these organizations (such as clerk, accountant, and office managers of various kinds as well as specialists in marketing, computers, and so on). These jobs are found in all industries, not just service industries.

In contrast, the concept of an information economy focuses on occupations in which the processing of information is a central and time-consuming activity. All jobs require that people process some information, even if only sensory information to know where they stand and where they are going. But some workers also provide information as a central element of the services they provide. These jobs include certain service jobs such as teacher, lawyer, and researcher.[3] They also include core administrative jobs such as clerk, accountant, and computer programmer wherever they may be found—in agriculture, manufacturing, or services. For example, Allen Scott (1988, 178) notes that over 60 percent of Orange County's manufacturing work force is composed of white-collar workers. And most of these are information workers such as engineers, inspectors, clerks, and accountants.[4]

Timothy Luke and Stephen White (1985, 31) argue that capitalism has entered a new phase, "informational capitalism," in which "data-intensive techniques, cybernetic knowledge, and electronic technologies" are the new strategic resources for corporate production.[5] They point out that core information services have expanded (banking, insurance, telecommunications, mass media, advertising, education). In addition, managers of service, industrial, and agricultural firms have invested heavily in systems that base production on information: banks invest in data processing and electronic funds transfer; manufacturing plants invest in automated inventory control and robotics; agricultural firms invest in computer-based farm-management programs; and managers in all sectors invest in information systems to support basic accounting and cash-flow management. Behind these systems lie the workers—from the specialists who design them to the wide variety of people who use them.

Marc Porat (1977) estimated that the information sector accounted for more employment than manufacturing or services by 1950 and that approximately 46 percent of the work force was employed in the information sector in 1970 (table 4.1).[6] Although most of the occupations in the information sector are white-collar jobs and although the terms *white-collar work force* and *information work force* overlap substantially, they are not identical.[7] However, much of the growth of the information sector in this century was driven by the same forces that drove the growth of white-collar employment: the substantial gains in productivity in agriculture and manufacturing; the rise of services; and (especially) the rise of large bureaucracies, both public and private (Mills 1951, 68–69). The white-collar work force mushroomed nationwide by the late 1940s, when Orange County was just emerging as a manufacturing center. There were few big businesses or big government agencies in Orange County until the late 1950s. So it is possible that the Orange County work force did not change in ways that paralleled previous national trends. In addition,

TABLE 4.1 Four-Sector Aggregation of the U.S. Experienced Civilian Labor Force

Year	Information Sector N	%	Agriculture Sector N	%	Industry Sector N	%	Service Sector N	%	Total
1860	480,604	5.8	3,364,230	40.6	3,065,024	37.0	1,375,525	16.6	8,285,383
1870	601,018	4.8	5,884,971	47.0	4,006,789	32.0	2,028,438	16.2	12,521,216
1880	1,131,415	6.5	7,606,590	43.7	4,386,409	25.2	4,281,970	24.6	17,406,384
1890	2,821,500	12.4	8,464,500	37.2	6,393,883	28.1	5,074,149	22.3	22,754,032
1900	3,732,371	12.8	10,293,179	35.3	7,814,652	26.8	7,318,947	25.1	29,159,149
1910	5,930,193	14.9	12,377,785	31.1	14,447,382	36.3	7,044,592	17.7	39,799,952
1920	8,016,054	17.7	14,718,742	32.5	14,492,300	32.0	8,061,342	17.8	45,288,438
1930	12,508,959	24.5	10,415,623	20.4	18,023,113	35.3	10,109,284	19.8	51,056,979
1940	13,337,958	24.9	8,233,624	15.4	19,928,422	37.2	12,082,376	22.5	53,582,380
1950	17,815,978	30.8	6,883,446	11.9	22,154,285	38.3	10,990,378	19.0	57,844,087
1960	28,478,317	42.0	4,068,511	6.0	23,597,364	34.8	11,661,326	17.2	67,805,518
1970	37,167,513	46.4	2,466,883	3.1	22,925,095	28.6	17,511,639	21.9	80,071,130
1980	44,650,721	46.6	2,012,157	2.1	21,558,824	22.5	27,595,297	28.8	95,816,999

SOURCE: Data from Table 9.2 in Bell (1981, 522). Based on Bell's median definition of the information economy, which differs somewhat from our own definition as reflected in other tables.

approaches to managing business and government changed in the 1960s and 1970s, the formative years of Orange County's development as a complex economic region with a broad mix of manufacturing and services.

Even though the terms *information economy* and *information work* are becoming commonplace, they often are used loosely. We see three problems with these casual usages. First, many authors talk about the information age and the information economy as social facts that have no conceptual problems (for example, Naisbitt 1984; Huppes 1987; Strassman 1985; Luke and White 1985). These accounts usually draw on Porat's (1977) pioneering analysis, which segmented the U.S. economy into four sectors. The national data used by Porat, and often repeated in other publications, aggregate workers across regions with widely disparate industrial mixes and misses any distinguishing regional characteristics. Employment in rural regions such as California's San Joaquin Valley, centers of smokestack industry such as Gary, Indiana, and service centers such as Hartford, Connecticut, are all mixed together. Some metropolitan economies are much more information intensive than others. For example, we are interested in the character and mix of information jobs in a particular regional economy, Orange County, which should be more information intensive than are rural or manufacturing economies.

Second, many analysts who examine the information economy focus on the best jobs, particularly professional, technical, and managerial jobs.[8] Some of them ignore the poorer jobs, such as clerical work in its various forms (Strassman 1985). Or they treat poorer jobs as transitional occupations that may soon disappear (Giuliano 1982).[9] Or they argue that office automation will eliminate a substantial portion of the least-skilled entry-level jobs (Rosenberg 1986, 234).

Third, some authors assume that the sequence from agricultural to manufacturing to service economies is a natural one and that information economies are simply the fourth step in the sequence (Huppes 1987). Bell (1980) argues that agricultural economies naturally evolve into post-industrial (service) economies and sees the information sector as part of the infrastructure for a postindustrial society.[10] We do not assume that there is a four-stage evolutionary sequence from agricultural societies to information societies.[11] Rather, we treat the information sector as an important economic sector that *crosscuts* the traditional three sectors and whose occupational structure may shed interesting light on work in modern society.

Many commentators confuse the meaning of information work by confounding it with the use of some form of information technology, especially advanced computer systems. For example, Vincent Giuliano (1982) advances a typical interpretation of information work and information-age offices when he examines the shift of office technologies from pen and paper through typewriters and mechanical devices to interactive computer-based systems available on every desk. He argues that the social organization of office work is evolving through three stages: an informal "preindustrial" office, a highly regimented "industrial" office, and a flexible "information-age" office in which computerized information systems are much more integrated than in his industrial office. There are major technological differences in his illustrations of these archetypical offices. His preindustrial office relies on telephones, paper, and organized files. His industrial office relies on batch-run computerized information systems, as well as paper and telephones. His information-age office relies on universal desktop computing linked to interactive data bases.[12] He characterizes the information-age office as one that

> exploits new technology to preserve the best aspects of the preindustrial office and avoid [its] failings. At its best, it combines terminal-based work stations, a continuously updated data base, and communications to attain high efficiency along with a return to people-centered work rather than machine-centered work. In the information age office the machine is paced to the needs and abilities of the person who works with it. . . . The mechanization of office work is an essential element in the transformation of American society to one in which information work is the chief economic activity. (p. 86).

Giuliano's article illustrates the typical confusion of information work and specific technologies. All his illustrations depict offices that are exclusively devoted to information handling in some form, but there is no reason for labeling any of these office forms as information-age offices. The label glamorizes the kind of office technology that Giuliano would like to see become widespread—interactive computer systems linked to integrated data bases. As Porat's study of the information work force shows, there was a substantial information work force in the United States by 1900, and it grew to 30 percent of the work force by 1950—long before electronic computer systems of any kind were routine fixtures of white-collar work.

We believe that these computer technologies can be interesting and may become indispensable. But the way in which they transform work is still open to question and investigation. Suzanne Iacono and Rob Kling (1987) observe:

> Despite the dramatic improvements in office technologies over the past 100 years, career opportunities and working conditions for clerks have not similarly improved. Although clerical tasks today require more skills in using a complex array of technologies, these skills are not reflected in status or pay. A new generation of integrated computer-based office systems will

not automatically alter the pay, status, and careers of clerks without explicit attention. (p. 75)

These issues of pay, status, and career lines are peripheral to understanding how information work differs from other kinds of work, such as craftwork; we return to them in the next section when we examine the occupational structure of the information work force.

Zuboff's *In the Age of the Smart Machine* (1988) is the most daunting and serious study to examine the processes and phenomenology of work with computer-based systems. She provides vivid and often brilliant descriptions of such work in specific work settings.[13] Superficially, her account differs substantially from Giuliano's. For example, her illustrations portray workplaces like his "industrial" office as much less pleasant workplaces than information-age offices.[14] But she makes similar errors by not carefully distinguishing between computer-based work and information work in general.[15] Like Giuliano, Zuboff coins a special term (*informate*) with broad informational connotations to describe some special aspects of work with computers (pp. 9–10).

Zuboff identifies abstraction as a special feature of computerization rather than as a generic feature of symbol systems, whether represented by cuneiform on papyrus, quill pen marks on parchment, pencil marks on paper, or data displays on an electronic screen (pp. 69, 79, 83–84). Moreover, important kinds of information work do not always entail the use of abstract symbol systems. A good deal of information work involves interpersonal negotiation, often face to face, but sometimes mediated by telephone—between students and teachers, judges and defendants, clerks and clients.

Although it is difficult to find occupations in which participants do not rely on any symbol systems, workers vary in the extent to which their world is mediated by symbol systems rather than by communication of personal experience. Hotel concierges and realtors, for example, often work with a good deal of key information based on their personal knowledge of localities and provide it to clients verbally. In contrast, other information workers, such as stockbrokers, are much more wrapped in a complex world of abstract symbols and systems of relationships between them (stock prices, trading volumes, market averages, interest rates, transaction costs). Through the 1970s and even early 1980s, most stockbrokers relied on paper systems, telephones, and narrow-range information services such as Quotron. By the 1980s, most stockbrokers gained access to complex information systems that provide a wide array of data fast and in comparative formats. They can also routinely monitor and trade in a wide variety of financial instruments and international markets, ranging from Eurodollars to the Japanese stock market. Information technologies have helped reshape the job of stockbrokers. However, although their work may have been much simpler in the 1960s than in the 1990s, their knowledge was anchored in complex symbolic systems, albeit based on paper. The routine dynamics of stock markets and their relationships to other markets, such as money and bond markets, have not substantially changed because of computer systems, except for the special phenomenon of program trading.

Zuboff views computerized work as a major transformation in labor processes that substantially reduces, even almost eliminates, the importance of the physical body as an acting and knowing agent. This transformation applies to information work in general. But Zuboff glosses over key similarities between information work and computer-based work because she focuses on a small set of cases in which relatively low-level paper-plant operators and clerks were beginning to use computer-based systems that were thrust upon them. Her sensitive observations about the phenomenology of computerized work in these special settings can often apply just as well to many forms of information work.

We have discussed Giuliano's and Zuboff's accounts because they illustrate common arguments about the kinds of labor processes that undergird information work. We find both these accounts misleading because they confuse information work with special kinds of work that use advanced computer systems.

We will not further examine the phenomenology of information work here. Although a careful investigation would be useful, it would apply to information work wherever it is done and in whatever historical period: London, England, in the 1600s and Irvine, California, in the 1990s. It would not teach us about changes in the work and labor markets within Orange County since World War II without important additional information about the distribution of jobs, occupations, and technologies in the region.

CHANGES IN THE DISTRIBUTION OF
INFORMATION OCCUPATIONS

Studies based on several different units of analysis could shed special light on changes in a regional labor market—studies of changes in specific occupations within the region, studies of changes in information work at the firm level, and studies of the occupational mix in a specific labor market. In this chapter we focus on changes in the distribution of jobs within the information sector of Orange County's labor market as a way to understand the changing mix of good and bad jobs. Our first reason for this choice is that it helps shed light on the structure of information labor markets by using the same kinds of data that protagonists of the information economy use. Second, we found that adequate, quality employment data for Orange County were available through public sources. These data made our study financially feasible.

Our basic strategy in this chapter is simple. We have adopted Porat's (1977) characterization of information workers and his list of information workers, which he used for estimating the size of the information work force in the United States.[16] Porat's list is as follows:

Professionals

    Accountants
    Architects
    Lawyers and judges
    Life scientists
    Operations researchers
    Physical scientists
    Physicians, dentists, and related occupations
    Social scientists
    Teachers, college and university

Semiprofessionals

    Bank officers
    Computer specialists
    Engineers
    Financial managers
    Foresters and conservationists
    Health administrators
    Librarians, archivists, and curators
    Managers and administrators (nec)[17]
    Nurses, dietitians, and therapists
    Office managers
    Officials and administrators (public)
    Personnel and labor-relations workers
    Research workers
    School administrators
    Social and recreation workers
    Teachers, except college
    Technical workers (nec)
    Vocational and educational counselors
    Writers, artists, and entertainers

Clerical Workers

    Bank tellers
    Billing clerks

Bookkeepers
Cashiers
Clerical workers (nec)
Collectors, bill and account
Counter clerks, except food
Demonstrators
Dispatchers and starters, vehicle
Enumerators and interviewers
Estimators and investigators (nec)
Expediters and production controllers
File clerks
Hucksters and peddlers
Library attendants and assistants
Mail carriers, post office
Mail handlers, except post office
Messengers and office helpers
Newspaper carriers and vendors
Office-machine operators
Payroll and timekeeping clerks
Postal clerks
Receptionists
Salesclerks, retail trade
Sales workers, except clerks
Secretaries
Shipping and receiving clerks
Statistical clerks
Stenographers
Teacher aides, except school monitors
Telephone operators
Ticket, station, and express agents
Typists
Welfare-service aides

Sales and Supervisory Personnel

Advertising agents and sales workers
Blue-collar-worker supervisors (nec)
Buyers and purchasing agents
Clerical supervisors (nec)
Credit and collection managers
Engineering and science technicians
Health technologists and technicians
Inspectors
Insurance adjusters and examiners

Insurance agents and brokers
Insurance investigators
Insurance underwriters
Officials of lodges and societies
Real estate agents and brokers
Sales managers, including retail trade
Sales representatives, manufacturing
Sales representatives, wholesale
Stock and bond sales agents
Union officials

Blue-Collar Workers

Checkers and examiners, manufacturing
Data-processing-machine repairers
Inspectors, manufacturing
Office-machine repairers
Photographic-process workers
Printing craftworkers
Radio and televison repairers
Telephone line installers
Telephone repairers

We use a similar list of occupations to estimate the overall size of the information work force in the United States and Orange County in 1980.[18] These are aggregate estimates of employment.

Many analysts treat the information work force as relatively homogeneous. But because we are particularly concerned with the mix of good jobs and bad jobs, we have divided information jobs into five status strata—professional, semiprofessional, supervisory and upper-level sales, clerical, and blue collar. We examine the number of jobs in each of these strata in order to answer such questions as, Are professional jobs, such as accountant and lawyer, the largest stratum of jobs in the information sector?

We are also concerned with changes in the information sector over time. Is the information sector still increasing relative to other occupational sectors?[19] Is the mix of good jobs and bad jobs within the information sector changing over time? To answer these questions, we examine the information sector in the U.S. economy from 1900 to 1980. We also examine Orange County's trends through official California state projections of its work force through 1990 (State of California 1985).

No one has asked these questions about the character of jobs in the information economy so directly. But possible answers appear implicit in key writing about the information labor force: (1) It is relatively large and is the dominant sector of the U.S. labor force (Porat 1977; Bell 1980;

Huppes 1987; Strassman 1985). (2) It is continuing to grow. (3) It is composed of generally good jobs (Strassman 1985; Giuliano 1982). We will critically examine these ideas in this chapter.

STRATIFICATION OF JOBS IN AN INFORMATION ECONOMY

Optimistic themes of universal progress undergird most accounts of the information economy.[20] However, few authors carefully explain how good jobs come to replace bad ones. Giuliano (1982) implies that jobs will be upskilled. In three diagrams that illustrate his article, he indicates that highly specialized accounting clerks will become "account managers" when work is electronically integrated through the use of advanced information systems.[21] Giuliano's claim goes beyond the arguments about upskilling and deskilling because he implies that jobholders take on new jobs, moving from narrow clerical jobs like posting clerk to much broader jobs like account manager.[22] In bureaucratic terms, these information-oriented jobs have simply been reclassified.[23]

Accounts of information work like Giuliano's casually assumed that clerical jobs would be replaced by semiprofessional jobs. In fact, however, during the twentieth century, there has been a white-collar revolution in the United States. White-collar workers increased from about 18 percent of the work force in 1900 to about 48 percent in 1974.[24] In contrast, manual workers remained at 35 to 40 percent of the work force during these seventy-five years. And farmworkers declined from 38 percent of the work force in 1900 to 3 percent in 1974.

We are also critical of accounts that focus on professionals and ignore clerks; clerks are a major occupational group in the United States. Clerks grew from 3 percent of the national work force in 1900 to 18 percent in 1974, a sixfold increase. In contrast, professional workers grew from 4 percent of the work force in 1900 to 14 percent in 1974, a growth factor of 3.5. Managers grew from 6 percent of the work force in 1900 to 10 percent in 1974, a factor of about 1.6. In 1900 managers outnumbered clerks by two to one; in 1974 clerks outnumbered managers by 1.6 to 1. Clerical jobs constituted about 25 percent of white-collar jobs by 1974. Information jobs are not the same as white-collar jobs, but they are similar enough to suggest that clerks could form 20 to 30 percent of the information work force.

There are at least five kinds of valid criteria for ranking jobs from better to worse: economic criteria such as pay, benefits, security, and career opportunities; psychological criteria such as challenge, autonomy, and variety; social criteria such as prestige and control; health and safety criteria such as routine exposure to toxic materials or dangerous situations; situational criteria such as fit with one's personal life, flexibility of work schedules, and length of time spent commuting to work. These characteristics are not fixed for all people in a specific occupation. Ranking of jobs by these criteria can depend on the specific practices of particular employers and the specific preferences of particular employees. Also, particular jobs may be ranked high on one set of criteria, yet be mediocre or poor on other criteria. In addition, some industries, such as transportation and aerospace, pay their workers more for comparable jobs than do other industries, such as banking and insurance. Although we recognize these complexities, we sought some simple strategies for characterizing the quality of jobs and comparing them over time. Any classification scheme that places some occupations into a "better" category and other occupations into a "worse" category necessarily simplifies complex criteria by which people assess specific jobs.

We considered two major ways to characterize the quality of jobs: by economic criteria such as income and by social criteria such as status and autonomy. We could not locate adequately detailed income data for each of the occupations in the information work force for 1900 to 1980 at the federal level and for more recent periods in Orange County. As a consequence we turned to social criteria for comparing the quality of jobs in the information sector.

Following Porat (1977), we divided information-sector occupations into five broad strata: four white-collar strata and one blue-collar group. The white-collar strata range from full-fledged professions at one extreme to clerical jobs at the other. They do not include all white-collar jobs (for example, dentists) because we are examining the information sector rather than white-collar work generally. We used standard sociological categories for professions and semiprofessions.[25] In addition, we identified one occupational stratum between clerks and semiprofessionals.

Professional occupations include the eight most highly professionalized jobs in the United States in the information work force. It includes accountants,[26] architects, lawyers, and physicians. The most highly developed professions have legal monopolies over legitimate practice and credentialing requirements. These are usually the most prestigious occupations, and many pay relatively well. Jobs within these occupations vary considerably on other criteria, such as amount of stress.

Semiprofessional occupations include sixteen groups that have some professional standing but that are not full-fledged professions. These groups include computer specialists, engineers, managers, school administrators, social workers, and teachers. Semiprofessional occupations are usually less prestigious and less well paid, on average, than the full-fledged professions. But they are usually much more autonomous and and are more prestigious than the occupations in the next stratum.

Supervisory and upper-level sales occupations constitute a category whose

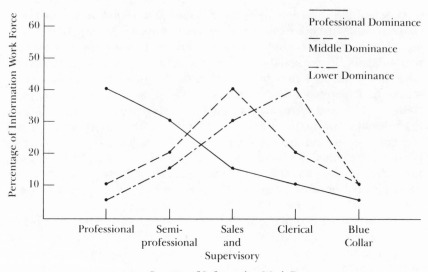

Stratum of Information Work Force

Fig. 4.1. Theoretical distributions of occupations within strata of the information sector

status lies between that of semiprofessionals and that of clerical workers. It includes advertising agents, health technologists, insurance agents, office managers, purchasing agents, real estate agents, and stockbrokers.[27] This complex stratum lies between the moderately prestigious semiprofessional occupations and the clerical occupations, which are less prestigious, provide less autonomy, and are lower-paid.

Clerical occupations include clerical jobs of all kinds (including cashier and salesclerk).[28] They usually pay poorly compared with other information jobs. Clerical jobs—from telephone operator to executive secretary—vary considerably in the autonomy they provide, but they are often fairly regimented. And they usually allow few opportunities for moving to jobs that provide substantially more autonomy or better pay.

Blue-collar occupations include technicians who install or repair communications, printing, and other information-processing equipment.

We classified each occupation in the information sector into one of these five strata in the preceding section and report their employment levels in table 4.2. Optimistic and pessimistic theories about the quality of jobs in the information economy can be evaluated by looking at how good jobs and bad jobs are distributed across the five strata of the information work force. In figure 4.1 we graph the three alternative theoretical distributions that are most commonly discussed in the literature about information work: (1) Professional jobs dominate the information work force.

Most information workers hold highly professionalized jobs like accountant, scientist, and lawyer; a smaller group holds semiprofessional jobs such as engineer and schoolteacher. (2) Middle-level jobs dominate the information work force. Most information workers hold middle-level jobs. We portray the alternative in which the most dominant middle-level jobs are the sales and supervisory jobs. The other information occupations are less numerous than these occupations.[29] (3) Lower-level jobs dominate the information work force. Most workers hold clerical jobs. The higher-level occupational strata employ relatively fewer people, inversely proportional to their status.

Thus, these theoretical distributions range from optimistic portraits of an information sector characterized by generally good (professional) jobs to a pessimistic portrait of the same sector characterized by predominantly poorer (clerical) jobs. These distributions are static, but some of the theories describe the current distribution of information occupations as moving toward one of these three end points. In the next section we examine how well the data about employment fit these three theories.

SCALE, GROWTH, AND STRUCTURE
OF THE INFORMATION WORK FORCE

The information occupations mushroomed from 1900, when they constituted 17 percent of the United States work force, to 1980, when they made up over 50 percent (table 4.3).[30] In this period, the United States moved from a dominantly agricultural economy to a service economy.[31] Orange County was rapidly transformed from an agricultural economy to a service-based economy between 1940 and 1970. In 1940 about 22 percent of the work force was employed in agriculture and 24 percent was employed in services—the two dominant sectors. Manufacturing accounted for 10 percent of the work force. By 1960 agricultural employment plummeted to less than 1 percent of the work force and manufacturing zoomed ahead of services (table 4.4). Orange County's manufacturing sector reached a peak share of 40 percent of the work force in 1964. After 1964 it declined in relative size, reaching about 22 percent in 1988, even though it has generally grown in absolute size and in national importance because of its hi-tech component. Service employment grew steadily in relative size after the 1950s and surpassed manufacturing employment in 1988. By 1980, 59 percent of Orange County's work force held jobs in its information sector (table 4.5).[32] This percentage was approximately 10 percent larger (in relative size) than the percentage at the national level.

Table 4.3 reports the percentage of workers in each stratum of the information work force at the federal level between 1900 and 1980. Professional and semiprofessional workers composed a remarkably stable

TABLE 4.2   Federal and Orange County Employment
in the Information Sector, by Occupation, 1980 and 1990

Occupation	Federal, 1980 (000)	Orange County, 1980	Orange County, 1990 (Projected)
Fully Professional			
Accountants	1,076	7,371	9,997
Physicians and related practitioners	803	4,519	6,092
Teachers, college and university	564	5,101	4,437
Lawyers and judges	558	1,548	2,774
Life and physical scientists	309	1,085	1,355
Social scientists	285	1,082	1,354
Operations and systems researchers and analysts	173	1,990	3,353
Architects	92	567	773
Semiprofessional			
All other managers and administrators	6,621	68,713	84,658
Teachers, except college and university	3,209	26,519	27,478
Nurses, dietitians, and therapists	1,607	8,553	11,709
Engineers	1,472	21,530	27,992
Writers, artists, and entertainers	1,313	6,071	7,694
Bank officers and financial managers	659	5,509	6,861
Computer specialists	598	3,059	4,713
Social and recreation workers	509	3,264	3,918
School administrators	435	—	—
Officials and administrators (public)	433	1,565	1,999
Health administrators	213	1,781	2,218
Librarians, archivists, and curators	201	1,037	1,076
Vocational and educational counselors	183	1,441	1,352
Research workers	180	unlisted	unlisted
Foresters and conservationists	67	28	35
All other professional and technical workers	62	20,176	26,318
Upper-Level Sales and Supervisory			
Blue-collar worker supervisors (nec)	1,754	10,445	12,686
Engineering and science technicians	1,127	14,859	19,518
Sales representatives, wholesale trade	935	5,741	7,356
Sales managers, including retail trade	721	2,015	2,570
Real estate agents and brokers	598	3,423	4,062
Health technologists and technicians	588	1,748	2,340
Insurance agents, brokers, and underwriters	543	3,676	5,006
Personnel and labor-relations workers	461	2,024	2,614
Buyers and purchasing agents	460	2,260	2,658
Sales representatives, manufacturing	434	12,071	15,276
Clerical supervisors (nec)	245	4,391	5,717
Insurance adjusters, examiners, and investigators	179	1,937	3,121
Stock and bond sales agents	137	504	591
Advertising agents and sales workers	112	936	1,166
Inspectors, except construction and public	111	928	1,156
Officials of lodges, societies, and unions	108	903	1,124
Credit and collection managers	69	577	718

TABLE 4.2   (*continued*)

Occupation	Federal, 1980 (000)	Orange County, 1980	Orange County, 1990 (Projected)
Clerical			
Secretaries	3,944	23,337	31,848
Sales workers (nom)	3,149	40,149	51,088
Bookkeepers	1,942	14,533	17,736
All other clerical workers	1,899	53,829	68,276
Cashiers	1,592	16,302	23,177
Typists	1,043	10,755	13,483
Office-machine operators	959	8,121	9,655
Receptionists	644	4,216	5,378
Estimators and investigators (nec)	545	1,845	2,794
Bank tellers	542	4,973	6,409
Shipping and receiving clerks	515	4,003	4,970
Statistical clerks	396	2,306	2,890
Teacher aides, except school monitors	391	3,263	3,681
Counter clerks, except food	358	4,613	6,011
File clerks	332	2,856	3,676
Telephone operators	323	4,288	4,974
Postal clerks	291	2,206	2,480
Mail carriers, post office	247	2,955	3,323
Expediters and production controllers	238	1,990	2,478
Payroll and timekeeping clerks	237	1,646	2,034
Hucksters and peddlers	181	unlisted	unlisted
Mail handlers, except post office	168	323	417
Billing clerks	165	31	44
Library attendants and assistants	155	1,381	1,458
Ticket, station, and express agents	144	587	834
Newspaper carriers and vendors	112	unlisted	unlisted
Dispatchers and starters, vehicle	105	847	1,083
Messengers and office helpers	98	310	401
Demonstrators	92	14	18
Welfare service aides	89	669	860
Enumerators and interviewers	87	727	906
Collectors, bill and account	81	680	978
Stenographers	66	1,404	1,418
Blue Collar			
Checkers, examiners, and inspectors, manufacturing	750	155	152
Printing craftworkers	415	4,696	5,684
Telephone line installers and repairers	390	2,124	2,710
Inspectors	150	5,534	6,327
Radio and television repairers	122	706	851
Photographic-process workers	90	732	986
Data-processing-machine repairers	86	93	190
Office-machine repairers	82	866	1,541

SOURCE: Data from Table 3 in State of California (1985) and from Table B20 in Bureau of Labor Statistics (1982: 664–67).
NOTE: "nec" means not elsewhere classified; "nom" means not otherwise matchable.

TABLE 4.3 Distribution of Occupational Strata within the U.S. Information Sector, 1900–1980

Year	Professional	Semiprofessional	Sales and Supervisory	Clerical	Blue Collar	Total Information Work Force	Total Work Force
Employment Levels by Stratum, in Thousands							
1980	3,328	16,997	8,047	21,583	1,249	50,108	99,303
1970	2,152	9,995	6,796	16,600	1,192	36,735	80,603
1960	1,338	7,553	5,803	12,286	913	27,893	67,990
1950	1,065	5,473	4,900	9,508	786	21,732	59,230
1940	687	4,195	3,773	6,992	506	16,153	51,742
1930	595	3,972	3,469	5,952	469	14,457	48,686
1920	437	2,803	2,586	4,438	344	10,607	42,206
1910	338	2,296	2,126	2,933	288	7,981	37,291
1900	280	1,395	1,557	1,604	209	5,045	29,030
Occupational Strata as Percentage of Information Work Force							
1980	6.5	33.2	15.7	42.4	2.4		
1970	5.9	27.2	18.5	45.2	3.2		
1960	4.8	27.1	20.8	44.0	3.3		

1950	4.9	25.2	22.5	43.8	3.6
1940	4.3	26.0	23.4	43.3	3.1
1930	4.1	27.5	24.0	41.2	3.2
1920	4.1	26.4	24.4	41.8	3.2
1910	4.2	28.8	26.6	36.8	3.6
1900	5.6	27.7	30.9	31.8	4.1

Occupational Strata as Percentage of Total U.S. Work Force

1980	3.4	17.1	8.1	21.7	1.3	50.5
1970	2.7	12.4	8.4	20.6	1.5	45.6
1960	2.0	11.1	8.5	18.1	1.3	41.0
1950	1.8	9.2	8.3	16.1	1.3	36.7
1940	1.3	8.1	7.3	13.5	1.0	31.2
1930	1.2	8.2	7.1	12.2	1.0	29.7
1920	1.0	6.6	6.1	10.5	0.8	25.1
1910	0.9	6.2	5.7	7.9	0.8	21.4
1900	1.0	4.8	5.4	5.5	0.7	17.4

SOURCE: 1900–1970 data come from Series D-182 through D-682, Bureau of the Census (1976, 139–145); 1980 data come from Table B20 in Bureau of Labor Statistics (1982, 664–67) and Table 276 in Bureau of the Census (1984) and are selected to match the smaller number of occupational categories from this time series. The resulting 1980 data do not match other tables but are comparable with the data in this table.

TABLE 4.4 Estimated Wage and Salary Workers by Industry, Anaheim–Santa Ana Metropolitan Statistical Area (Orange County), Selected Years, 1960–88

Industry	1960	1962	1972	1974	1976	1978	1980	1982	1984	1988
Number of Jobs, in Thousands										
Total, All Industries	136	169	480	565	617	756	844	856	962	1103
Total Agriculture	1	1	6	6	7	9	7	8	9	9
Production	—	—	6	6	6	7	6	7	7	—
Services	—	—	1	1	1	1	2	1	2	—
Total, Nonagriculture	135	169	474	559	610	747	836	849	953	1094
Mining	2	2	2	2	2	2	2	4	4	2
Construction	17	17	28	30	29	42	45	32	45	56
Manufacturing	47	69	133	159	162	198	221	212	232	239
Nondurable goods	—	—	31	36	40	50	55	54	60	64
Durable goods	—	—	102	123	122	149	166	158	172	175
Transportation and Public Utilities	—	7	16	17	19	23	27	30	31	36
Transportation	—	—	7	8	9	12	14	15	17	—
Utilities	—	—	9	10	10	11	14	15	15	—
Wholesale and Retail Trade	38	42	112	130	148	181	201	210	238	282
Wholesale	—	—	17	23	27	34	40	45	55	69
Retail	—	—	94	107	121	147	161	166	183	213
Finance, Insurance, and Real Estate	—	8	25	29	34	47	57	61	70	87
Finance	—	—	9	11	13	17	22	24	29	—
Insurance, real estate	—	—	16	19	21	30	36	37	41	—
Services	19	24	85	106	121	152	177	195	228	279
Government	—	—	74	86	97	102	106	104	105	114
Federal	—	—	8	9	9	10	12	12	13	15
State and local	—	—	66	77	87	92	93	92	91	99
County	—	—	10	11	12	11	11	12	12	—
City	—	—	10	13	15	16	15	14	14	—
Other	—	—	46	53	60	66	67	66	65	—
Other	13	0	—	—	—	—	—	—	—	—

Percentage of Jobs

Total, All Industries	100	100	100	100	100	100	100	100	100	100
Total Agriculture	0.6	0.5	1.3	1.1	1.2	1.1	0.9	0.9	0.9	0.8
Production	—	—	1.1	1.0	1.0	0.9	0.7	0.8	0.7	—
Services	—	—	0.2	0.1	0.2	0.2	0.2	0.1	0.2	—
Total, Nonagriculture	99.4	99.6	98.7	98.9	98.8	98.9	99.1	99.1	99.1	99.2
Mining	1.3	0.9	0.4	0.4	0.3	0.3	0.3	0.5	0.4	0.2
Construction	12.3	10.0	5.8	5.2	4.6	5.6	5.4	3.7	4.7	5.0
Manufacturing	34.6	40.8	27.6	28.1	26.2	26.2	26.1	24.8	24.1	21.7
Nondurable goods	—	—	6.4	6.4	6.4	6.5	6.5	6.3	6.3	5.8
Durable goods	—	—	21.2	21.7	19.7	19.6	19.7	18.5	17.8	15.9
Transportation and Public Utilities	—	4.1	3.3	3.1	3.1	3.0	3.2	3.5	3.3	3.3
Transportation	—	—	1.4	1.4	1.5	1.6	1.6	1.8	1.7	—
Utilities	—	—	2.0	1.7	1.6	1.5	1.6	1.7	1.5	—
Wholesale and Retail Trade	27.9	24.6	23.2	22.9	23.9	23.9	23.9	24.5	24.7	25.5
Wholesale	—	—	3.6	4.1	4.3	4.5	4.8	5.2	5.7	6.2
Retail	—	—	19.6	18.9	19.6	19.5	19.1	19.3	19.0	19.3
Finance, Insurance, and Real Estate	0.0	4.7	5.2	5.2	5.4	6.2	6.8	7.1	7.3	7.9
Finance	—	—	1.9	1.9	2.1	2.3	2.5	2.8	3.0	—
Insurance, real estate	—	—	3.3	3.3	3.4	3.9	4.2	4.4	4.3	—
Services	14.0	14.2	17.6	18.8	19.6	20.1	21.0	22.8	23.7	25.3
Government	—	—	15.5	15.2	15.7	13.5	12.5	12.2	10.9	10.4
Federal	—	—	1.7	1.7	1.5	1.3	1.5	1.4	1.4	1.4
State and local	—	—	13.8	13.6	14.2	12.2	11.0	10.8	9.5	9.0
County	—	—	2.0	2.0	1.9	1.4	1.3	1.4	1.3	—
City	—	—	2.2	2.2	2.5	2.1	1.8	1.7	1.5	—
Other	—	—	9.6	9.4	9.8	8.7	8.0	7.7	6.7	—
Other	9.3	0.2	—	—	—	—	—	—	—	—

SOURCE: Table 44 in State of California (1986, s10–s11); 1988 data are projected in that report.
NOTE: Some subtotals are imprecise because of rounding.

TABLE 4.5   Distribution of Occupational Strata
within the Information Sector, 1980

	Orange County		Federal	
Occupational Stratum	N	% of Information Work Force	N (000)	% of Information Work Force
Professional	23,263	4.7	3,501	6.5
Semiprofessional	169,246	34.5	17,762	33.2
Sales and supervisory	68,438	13.9	9,044	16.9
Clerical	215,158	43.8	21,130	39.5
Blue collar	14,906	3.0	2,085	3.9
Total information work force	491,011		53,522	
Total work force	830,193		99,303	
Information work force as % of total work force		59.1		53.9

SOURCE: Data come from Table 3 in State of California (1985) and Table B20 in Bureau of Labor Statistics (1982, 664–67). This table contains a slightly different estimate for the total Orange County work force than does Table 4.4, which is based on State of California (1986).

proportion of the information work force between 1900 and 1970: 4 to 6 percent and 25 to 29 percent, respectively. Together, these professional strata formed a minority of the information work force—between 30 and 33 percent. Blue-collar information workers slowly declined from about 4 percent in 1900 to 3 percent in 1970.

Since 1900 clerks have been the largest stratum of information workers. They rose from 32 percent of the information work force in 1900 to about 42 percent in 1920. Clerical employment grew at a slightly faster rate than overall employment in the information sector between 1920 and 1970, when it peaked at about 45 percent. At the same time, the higher-level sales and supervisory stratum fell from 31 to 19 percent of the information work force. These two lower-level white-collar strata comprised the majority of information workers, although the relative number of mid-level jobs has declined significantly since 1900, while clerical jobs have risen.

There are signs of a different pattern of occupational growth and decline between 1970 and 1980.[33] As in the previous seventy years, the number of information workers continued to increase in all five strata. However, the relative size of some strata shifted in small but noticeable ways. The proportion of professional and semiprofessional workers rose to about 40 percent of the information work force. Clerical workers declined somewhat in relative size to 42 percent,[34] although they continued to grow as a proportion of the total work force. In addition, the strata of supervisors and higher-level sales personnel continued to decline. And the blue-collar strata continued to decline in relative size.

Overall, the information work force mushroomed since the turn of the century so that by 1980 it composed about 54 percent of the national work force and about 59 percent of Orange County's work force. Its lower-level white-collar workers outnumber professional workers. But this distribution has been masked by the steady growth of information-sector jobs in the highly professional and semiprofessional strata, as well as at the clerical level. The occupational stratum between clerks and semiprofessionals— supervisory and upper-level sales workers—has steadily declined in relative size. In 1900 it was twice as large in relative size as it was in 1980.

Thus we can see that two lower strata—clerks and sales and supervisory workers—account for more than 55 percent of the jobs in the information sector, and semiprofessionals also account for a substantial fraction of the jobs, about 33 percent. But there is a large kink in the distribution of jobs across the three strata because the number of sales and supervisory jobs is about half the number in the semiprofessional stratum and less than half the number in the clerical stratum. This pattern is replicated in Orange County (see table 4.5), although there are some subtle differences that we discuss later in this chapter.

The relative size of the five occupational strata therefore does not fit any of the three theoretical models that we discussed—professional, middle, or lower-level jobs dominating in a monotonic pattern. This distribution comes as a surprise because we expected that either middle or clerical strata dominated the information work force. Although we did not have strong expectations about trends in the relative size of strata, we were astounded by the stability in relative size between 1900 and 1970 (except for the steady decline in the sales and supervisory stratum). These kinked occupational distributions provide interesting evidence for segmentation in information labor markets in both the United States and Orange County (Berger and Piore 1980). We examine the segmented character of information labor markets generally in the next section and then turn back to Orange County in the following section.

THE SEGMENTATION OF NATIONAL
INFORMATION LABOR MARKETS

In this section we argue that information labor markets are divided into four relatively impermeable segments: clerical work, supervisory and higher-level sales jobs, the two strata of professional jobs, and blue-collar jobs. Our thinking has been influenced strongly by dual labor-market theorists, even though their emphasis has often been different. Dual labor-market theorists have focused mostly on the segmentation between jobs in the primary and secondary labor markets.[35] (Most information-sector jobs are primary-sector jobs.) Dual labor-market theorists often mention that jobs in the primary labor markets are also segmented, but they rarely examine segmentation in the primary sector.[36] The key element of segmentation patterns in labor markets is that significant structural barriers inhibit people's mobility from one labor market to another— or, in our case, from one occupational stratum to another (Berger and Piore 1980).

Our arguments that the information labor markets are segmented are simple. Most occupations in the professional and semiprofessional strata are segmented by special education and licensing requirements. All the occupations that we have listed as professions (see table 4.2) require specialized college or postgraduate degrees. Some professions, such as law and medicine, impose stringent licensing requirements.

Many of the semiprofessions have similar barriers that inhibit people from moving up into them, although some of them do not require formal training or licensing—for example, managers and administrators, who account for the largest number of semiprofessional jobs in the United States (and in Orange County). "Writers, artists, and entertainers" is perhaps the most intriguing category because theoretically anyone can write, paint, or play.

Our data reveal a less apparent structural barrier that seals many women into clerical careers.[37] First, women who wish to rise from clerical jobs to something better often lack the special education and credentials required for fully professional and semiprofessional jobs.[38] Second, managerial jobs are the main source of semiprofessional employment where credentialing does not play a major role, but historically managerial jobs have been male dominated (many clerical specialties became female dominated by 1900). Although managerial jobs have become increasingly open to women since 1980, they have remained male dominated (Taeuber and Valdisera 1986) because some structural barriers still exist (Kanter 1977).

For all clerical workers (male and female) the supervisory and higher-level sales jobs are more within reach than are semiprofessional jobs because they do not have significant educational and credentialing barriers. Some pay more than semiprofessional jobs.[39] But they have steadily declined in number, from being approximately equal to clerical jobs in 1900 to being approximately one-third the number of clerical jobs in 1980. Our argument is based on the relative number of slots for clerical workers in the next stratum: clerical workers who want to move up in the information sector will see a significantly smaller number of jobs they can qualify for.

Several questions might weaken this numerical argument. We do not believe that these counterarguments have substantial force, but they are worth noting. We have no specific data about the occupational mobility of workers between these strata in 1900 or 1980 or at times in between, although indirect evidence indicates that clerks often do not move into other kinds of careers (Kanter 1977). An argument that two occupational strata are segmented depends on mobility data. However, such data would not reveal the number of clerical workers who sought jobs in higher-level information-sector strata but did not find them or were not recruited into them. Nor do we know the extent to which clerks would find the various jobs in the stratum attractive and would have sought them if they thought they were readily available. For example, although sex discrimination in hiring has continued to impede women's access to certain professional and semiprofessional jobs, their conceptions of attractive jobs also influence where they work. The higher-strata jobs were probably not equally desirable to clerical workers at all times between 1900 and 1980. Perceptions have almost certainly changed. In the early twentieth century, most clerks were men, and they may have viewed sales jobs and supervisory jobs that require more initiative than many clerical jobs as acceptable if not attractive. Traditional women, who dominated the clerical work force by the 1950s, may have found these higher-level sales and supervisory jobs less attractive. However, since the mid-1970s the women's movement has influenced women's conceptions of acceptable careers.[40] As a consequence, we suspect that more women clerical workers would find these jobs attractive today than in 1960 if they could move into them. However, these better jobs have been declining precisely during the time that they could become a move up for many clerks.

Although the information labor force became more segmented, access to many information jobs has become more difficult. The educational and credentialing requirements for jobs in all strata in the information sector have generally tightened during this century. College degrees were once the prerequisites for only the most specialized and technical or most professional occupations. Since World War II there has been a form of credential inflation; bachelor's (and sometimes graduate) degrees have become commonplace requirements for many semiprofessional jobs. Some employers are beginning to selectively hire people with college degrees for clerical jobs. Clerical work is probably the primary occupational opportunity for college-educated women with degrees in the liberal arts who do not acquire professional or graduate degrees.

THE SEGMENTATION OF INFORMATION
LABOR MARKETS IN ORANGE COUNTY

Orange County's information work force is similar in structure to that of the United States as a whole (see table 4.5). But it differs in two details. First, it is larger in relative size than the nation's information sector. In 1980 it employed about 59 percent of the county's work force in contrast with the national sector, which employed about 54 percent of the nation's work force.[41] Second, Orange County's information work force is substantially more segmented than the national information work force. In 1980 its clerical stratum was 10 percent larger in relative size (44 percent versus 40 percent). But its stratum of upper-level sales and supervisory workers was almost 20 percent smaller in relative size. (The ratio of clerical workers to sales and supervisory workers was about 3:1 for Orange County but about 2.3:1 for the United States overall.) In Orange County, the percentage of the information work force that was semi-professional was about four points above the comparable percentage of the national information work force, and the percentage that was fully professional was about thirty points above. Orange County also employed (in relative size) about 25 percent fewer blue-collar information workers than the national sector did.

We wanted to examine temporal changes in Orange County's information work force but were hampered by a lack of time-series data for specific occupations prior to 1980.[42] We did, however, find two data sources for trends in Orange County's information work force in the 1980s and 1990: a projection of the occupational structure of Orange County in 1990 (State of California 1985)[43] and a series of annual counts and estimates of employment by industrial sector (State of California 1986).[44]

These data indicate that the structure of Orange County's information labor market will remain relatively unchanged through at least 1990 (table 4.6). In the State of California (1985) projection, Orange County's full work force is expected to grow by about 25 percent between 1980 and 1990. Using these data, we estimate that the information sector will grow slightly faster than the overall economy and will encompass almost 60 percent of Orange County's jobs by 1990. Table 4.7 lists projected job openings for the Orange County information sector between 1980 and 1990. These projections indicate that the relative size of the five enlarged strata of information-sector jobs will be similar to their distribution in 1980.[45] In absolute terms the fifty-five thousand clerical job openings exceed the forty-four thousand highly professional and semiprofessional openings; and the projected clerical openings are almost three times as numerous as the nineteen thousand openings projected for higher-level

TABLE 4.6   Projected Growth of Orange County
Information Work Force, 1980–90

Occupational Stratum	N, *1980*	% of Information Work Force	N, *1990*	% of Information Work Force	Openings, *1980–90*
Professional	23,263	4.7	30,135	4.9	6,872
Semiprofessional	169,246	34.5	208,011	33.6	38,765
Sales and super-					
visory	68,438	13.9	87,679	14.2	19,241
Clerical	215,158	43.8	274,778	44.4	59,620
Blue collar	14,906	3.0	18,441	3.0	3,535
Total information					
work force	480,281		602,283		122,003
Total work force	830,193		1,033,931		203,738
Information work					
force as % of					
total work force		59.1		59.9	

SOURCE: Data come from Table 3 in State of California (1985). This table contains a slightly different estimate for the total Orange County work force than does table 4.4, which is based on State of California (1986).

sales and supervisory positions. The largest single category, about sixteen thousand openings, is a residual category of semiprofessionals—"all other managers and administrators." However, the next four largest categories are all clerical—other sales workers, other clerical workers, secretaries, and cashiers—and they account for about thirty-six thousand jobs.

Accounting is projected to provide the largest number of fully professional jobs—about twenty-six hundred—and about 40 percent of all professional openings. The next sets of fully professional occupations—operations and systems researchers and lawyers and judges—together account for about twenty-six hundred jobs, or another 40 percent of the fully professional jobs.

The clerical stratum may grow even more than these projections indicate (especially relative to upper-level sales and supervisory jobs) for another reason. We view information-sector jobs as being distributed through the other sectors. Over 80 percent of the job growth projected for Orange County between 1980 and 1988 was expected to occur in three industrial clusters: wholesale and retail trade (31 percent); finance, insurance, and real estate (11.6 percent); services (including health, education, business services, hotels, repairs, and recreation) (39 percent) (see table 4.4). In the service industries, health care and business services were projected to account for about two-thirds of the growth of new jobs.[46] In

TABLE 4.7 Projected Growth of Orange County Information Work Force, by Occupation, 1980–90

Occupation	N, 1980	N, 1990	Total Job Growth		Rate of Growth Relative to Information Growth, %[b]
			Openings, 1980–90	% of Information Jobs Open[a]	
Fully Professional					
Accountants	7,371	9,997	2,626	2.1	137
Operations and systems researchers and analysts	1,990	3,353	1,363	1.1	263
Lawyers and judges	1,548	2,774	1,226	1.0	304
Physicians and related practitioners	4,519	6,092	1,573	1.2	133
Social scientists	1,082	1,354	272	0.2	96
Life and physical scientists	1,085	1,355	270	0.2	95
Architects	567	773	206	0.2	139
Teachers, college and university	5,101	4,437	(664)	-0.5	-50
Semiprofessional					
All other managers and administrators	68,713	84,658	15,945	12.5	89
Engineers	21,530	27,992	6,462	5.0	115
All other professional and technical workers	20,176	26,318	6,142	4.8	117
Nurses, dietitians, and therapists	8,553	11,709	3,156	2.5	142
Computer specialists	3,059	4,713	1,654	1.3	207
Writers, artists, and entertainers	6,071	7,694	1,623	1.3	103
Bank officers and financial managers	5,509	6,861	1,352	1.1	94
Teachers, except college and university	26,519	27,478	959	0.7	14
Social and recreation workers	3,264	3,918	654	0.5	77

Officials and administrators (public)	1,565	1,999	434	0.3	106
Librarians, archivists, and curators	1,037	1,076	39	0.0	14
Foresters and conservationists	28	35	7	0.0	96
Research workers	unlisted	unlisted			
Health administrators	1,781	2,208	427	0.3	92
School administrators	unlisted	unlisted			
Vocational and educational counselors	1,441	1,352	(89)	−0.1	−24
Upper-Level Sales and Supervisory					
Engineering and science technicians	14,859	19,518	4,659	3.6	120
Sales representatives, manufacturing	12,071	15,276	3,205	2.5	102
Blue-collar-worker supervisors (nec)	10,445	12,686	2,241	1.8	82
Sales representatives, wholesale trade	5,741	7,356	1,615	1.3	108
Insurance agents, brokers, and underwriters	3,676	5,006	1,330	1.0	139
Clerical supervisors (nec)	4,391	5,717	1,326	1.0	116
Insurance adjusters, examiners, and investigators	1,937	3,121	1,184	0.9	234
Real estate agents and brokers	3,423	4,062	639	0.5	72
Health technologists and technicians	1,748	2,340	592	0.5	130
Personnel and labor-relations workers	2,024	2,614	590	0.5	112
Sales managers, including retail trade	2,015	2,570	555	0.4	106
Buyers and purchasing agents	2,260	2,658	398	0.3	68
Advertising agents and sales workers	936	1,166	230	0.2	94
Inspectors, except construction and public	928	1,156	228	0.2	94
Officials of lodges, societies, and unions	903	1,124	221	0.2	94
Credit and collection managers	577	718	141	0.1	94
Stock and bond sales agents	504	591	87	0.1	66
Office managers	unlisted	unlisted			

TABLE 4.7 (continued)

Occupation	N, 1980	N, 1990	Openings, 1980–90	% of Information Jobs Open[a]	Rate of Growth Relative to Information Growth, %[b]
Clerical					
Sales workers (nom)	40,149	51,088	10,939	8.5	104
All other clerical workers	53,829	68,276	14,447	11.3	103
Secretaries	23,337	31,848	8,511	6.6	140
Cashiers	16,302	23,177	6,875	5.4	162
Bookkeepers	14,533	17,736	3,203	2.5	85
Typists	10,755	13,483	2,728	2.1	97
Office-machine operators	8,121	9,655	1,534	1.2	72
Bank tellers	4,973	6,409	1,436	1.1	111
Counter clerks, except food	4,613	6,011	1,398	1.1	116
Receptionists	4,216	5,378	1,162	0.9	106
Shipping and receiving clerks	4,003	4,970	967	0.8	93
Estimators and investigators (nec)	1,845	2,794	949	0.7	197
File clerks	2,856	3,676	820	0.6	110
Telephone operators	4,288	4,974	686	0.5	61
Statistical clerks	2,306	2,890	584	0.5	97
Expediters and production controllers	1,989	2,478	489	0.4	94
Teacher aides, except school monitors	3,263	3,681	418	0.3	49
Payroll and timekeeping clerks	1,646	2,034	388	0.3	90
Mail carriers, post office	2,955	3,323	368	0.3	48
Collectors, bill and account	680	978	298	0.2	168

				[a]	[b]
Postal clerks	2,206	2,480	274	0.2	48
Ticket, station, and express agents	587	834	247	0.2	161
Dispatchers and starters, vehicle	847	1,083	236	0.2	107
Welfare-service aides	669	860	191	0.1	109
Enumerators and interviewers	727	906	179	0.1	94
Mail handlers, except post office	323	417	94	0.1	112
Messengers and office helpers	310	401	91	0.1	113
Library attendants and assistants	1,381	1,458	77	0.1	21
Stenographers	1,404	1,418	14	0.0	4
Billing clerks	31	44	13	0.0	161
Demonstrators	14	18	4	0.0	110
Hucksters and peddlers	unlisted	unlisted			
Newspaper carriers and vendors	unlisted	unlisted			
Blue Collar					
Printing craftworkers	4,696	5,684	988	0.8	81
Inspectors	5,534	6,327	793	0.6	55
Office-machine repairers	866	1,541	675	0.5	299
Telephone line installers and repairers	2,124	2,710	586	0.5	106
Photographic-process workers	732	986	254	0.2	133
Radio and television repairers	706	851	145	0.1	79
Data-processing-machine repairers	93	190	97	0.1	400
Checkers, examiners, and inspectors, manufacturing	155	152	(3)	−0.0	− 7

SOURCE: Data come from Table 3 in State of California (1985).
[a] Percentage of the 122,003 information-sector jobs to be added between 1980 and 1990.
[b] Rate of growth of the occupation relative to the 26.1 percent growth rate of the information work force between 1980 and 1990. A 100 percent relative growth indicates growth at the same rate, while 150 percent is 50 percent faster (39 percent).
NOTE: "nec" means not elsewhere classified; "nom" means not otherwise matchable.

contrast, about 7 percent of the new jobs opening between 1980 and 1988 were expected to be in manufacturing.[47] These high-growth service and trade industries employ disproportionately more clerical workers than other industrial sectors. The three largest upper-level sales and supervisory jobs, for example, are driven by manufacturing rather than by services, while the largest clerical jobs are linked to sales and a variety of industries.[48] Consequently, we may have underestimated the absolute and relative size of Orange County's clerical stratum in tables 4.2, 4.5, 4.6, and 4.7.

CONCLUSIONS

We found that the information sector provides most of the jobs in the U.S. work force and a somewhat larger fraction of jobs in Orange County. Over a forty-year period Orange County was transformed from an agricultural to a service economy with an important information sector. This shift parallels the shift from a local to an international economy that Spencer Olin describes in Chapter 8.

Information-sector jobs vary widely in quality. We have characterized the quality of jobs by one dimension: location in the status hierarchy of occupations. This simplified conception captures important aspects of pay, status, autonomy, and other working conditions. Relatively few information-sector jobs are fully professional, and clerical jobs form the largest occupational stratum. When we examined the growth of the various strata between 1900 and 1980, we found that clerical jobs became more dominant not less dominant.

We do not have direct data about occupational mobility. But our data suggest that the mobility of clerical workers is significantly limited by structural features of the information sector, which is internally segmented, not just differentiated. We expect that these patterns will continue in Orange County. The information sector will grow somewhat in overall importance, and clerical jobs will continue to grow in absolute and relative size. In Orange County clerical jobs provided more new openings between 1980 and 1990 than any other occupational stratum in the information sector (see table 4.7).

It is common to use a male professional such as an accountant, urban planner, or engineer to represent the information worker. This representation misleads. A female clerical worker is a more accurate representative, although no stratum is so dominant that the other strata can be ignored. Contrary to the argument that the information work force is becoming professionalized through the use of information technologies (Giuliano 1982), we have observed a steady growth in the relative size of the clerical stratum between 1900 and 1970 (see table 4.3). Moreover, the relative size of the clerical stratum in Orange County is unlikely to decline soon (see table 4.6). The growth of the semiprofessional stratum has been less marked. It was relatively stable between 1900 and 1970, compared with the other strata in the information sector, and it swelled disproportionately between 1970 and 1980 (see table 4.3). However, it was expected to decline slightly in relative size in Orange County by 1990 (see table 4.6).

It is ironic that clerical jobs are still expanding when the education level of women, as measured by the number of college degrees awarded, is at an all-time high.[49] Our own observations suggest that certain clerical jobs, like secretary and bookkeeper, have become increasingly varied as a by-product of computer technologies and higher education.[50] In fact, some managers report quite happily that they are now recruiting college-educated women into clerical jobs that formerly drew only high school or junior college graduates. However, other clerical jobs, such as cashier and counter clerk, may remain relatively routinized, even when they have automated support through specialized point-of-sales terminals.

This labor-market organization has important repercussions for the lives of women in Orange County. Many women in Orange County take clerical jobs, and mobility to more lucrative careers is limited for them. In the late 1980s clerical salaries were usually $15,000 to $20,000 per year. In contrast, a condominium usually cost well over $100,000, and a single-family house cost over $175,000 in most areas of Orange County. In 1989 a household required well over $80,000 per year in income to qualify for a loan on the median-priced new house, and less than 20 percent of households could afford to buy a first home. The average costs of homes were usually much higher than these minimum figures. Housing is a household purchase, and many households in Orange County have two adult incomes. However, when female clerks are single or self-supporting single heads of households, they may find homeownership a distant dream.

We had not expected to find the information sector structured like a dual labor market for such a long period of time. Because we focus on the information sector, our data do not tell us about key aspects of dual labor markets, such as the employment of skilled craftspeople or even of mobility between other sectors and the information sector. Moreover, we do not have the kind of income data to definitely answer key questions about "the declining middle class" (Lerman and Salzman 1987). These questions were outside the scope of this study. Even so, our data lend support to the declining-middle thesis. Moreover, our data cast doubt on arguments that office workers are becoming more paraprofessional and professional (Noyelle 1987). Based on our own field studies of computerization in white-collar work, we believe that office work is becoming increasingly skilled (Iacono and Kling 1987). But we do not see evidence in our data (see table 4.3) that there are substantially more opportunities than before for office workers to enter semiprofessional and professional occupations, which normally require college degrees. Even the high-skill information jobs above the clerical stratum that do not require college degrees are in relatively short supply.

Robert Reich (1989) identifies three major segments of the U.S. labor force that parallel our own categories. His three segments account for about 75 percent of U.S. employment: symbolic analysts (lawyers, investment bankers, management consultants, research scientists, academics), providers of routine production services (clerks), and providers of routine personal services (barbers, retail-sales personnel, cabdrivers). He argues that the United States is situated in international markets in such a way that symbolic analysts are relatively valuable and well paid while providers of routine production services are often competing with low-wage labor elsewhere in the world. In contrast, providers of personal services have captive local markets and can fare better than clerks. After all, one does not fly to Taiwan just for a haircut or a cab ride, even if it is cheap! But a publisher may well have a book typeset in Southeast Asia and thus displace clerical jobs in the United States. Reich's symbolic analysts parallel our professional and semiprofessional information workers. Although his thesis is loosely argued, it suggests an important dynamism that may reinforce the dual structure of information labor markets. It certainly merits further investigation.

In this chapter we have not addressed the question of whether substantial technological change, particularly in the form of computerization and the use of advanced telecommunications systems, will alter the structure of the information occupations. Although some economists predict substantial declines in the size of the clerical work force (see, for example, Leontieff and Duchin 1984), these projections rest on narrow studies of technological efficiency and simple assumptions about the substitution of capital for labor.[51]

As the information sector continues to expand, it has taken on many characteristics of the overall economy. It offers a substantial mix of jobs in terms of pay, status, and power. Moreover, its internal divisions reflect patterns of segmentation that have developed elsewhere. Overall, the information sector has become sufficiently large so that it is not an alternative to the dominant order; it simply reproduces many of its structural features.

APPENDIX A: MEASURING THE SCOPE
OF THE INFORMATION WORK FORCE

In his landmark study, which provides the most widely used basis for defining and measuring the size of the information economy, Porat realized that "stating precisely who is an information worker and who is not is a risky proposition" (1977, 105). He identified information workers by asking, "Which occupations are *primarily* engaged in the production, processing, or distribution of information as the output, and which occupations perform information processing tasks as activities ancillary to the primary function?" (p. 105). We agree that an answer to this question yields a meaningful list of information jobs.

We based our typology of information workers on Porat's. We began with his list of information occupations to produce a list that is substantially similar to his. Porat identifies 188 information occupations, while we identify 82. This difference is an indication only of the finer occupational distinctions in Porat's list,[52] as many of our single occupational titles are composed of some combination of separate titles from his list.[53] We match Porat's list closely.[54]

Porat's "knowledge producers" consist of "scientific and technical workers" and "private information services." We find the categories "mathematical scientists" and the subcategory "actuaries" in the official Orange County data. We find the categories "mathematical scientists" and "actuaries" in Porat's occupational-category list. We do not match the categories because the official Orange County data indicate there were only about three hundred jobs under these headings, which account for a mere 0.1 percent of the total in 1980. We find the occupational categories "farm management advisors" and "home management advisors" in Porat's list, but we do not match them because the similar categories in the official Orange County data indicate zero jobs for them. We find categories "farm management advisors" and "home management advisors" in Porat's list under "counselors and advisors." All similar categories from the official Orange County data show zeroes.

Porat's "knowledge distributors" are all matched to occupations on our list. Under "market search and coordination specialists" we do not match "office managers" and "foremen" because they do not appear anywhere in our Orange County data. "School administrators" are listed in those data, but no numbers are provided. We do not include "postmasters, mail superintendents" as they account for only a tiny fraction of the information work force in Orange County (there were ninety in 1980). "Enumerators and interviewers," "advertising agents and sales workers," "health administrators," and "expediters and production controllers" were not listed in our Orange County data, but we considered these occupations important enough to place estimates based on federal proportions in their places.

We match all Porat's "information processors" with the exceptions of "health-record technicians" and "railroad conductors," which were not listed in our data. "Motion-picture projectionists" are included in our data, but we did not match the occupation as it accounted for so few workers (eighty-eight in 1980) in Orange County.

We match "information workers" except for "sign painters," which were not listed in our data, and "data-processing-machine repairers," which were listed but not matched because the number was insignificant (ninety-three in 1980 in Orange County). Note that "radio operators" are included in our count but in the noninformation sector under "technicians, except health, science and engineering."

Porat (1977, 118) uses "restrictive" and "inclusive" definitions of information workers. Basically, he believes that 28 of his 188 listed occupations are "mixed" in nature, and he is uncomfortable including them as wholly information occupations. He thus allocates the "ambiguous" occupations proportionately to separate sectors. For example, he allocates "physicians" 50 percent to information and 50 percent to service under his "inclusive" definition, and 100 percent to service under his "restrictive" definition.[55]

Porat (1977, 121) reports his data on the growth of the information work force exclusively in his (often-reproduced) graph of the four-sector aggregation of the U.S. work force, 1860–1980, using "median estimates." For these estimates the data points on the graph are the median of the restrictive and inclusive figures for the given year.[56]

Our own approach to counting information workers is more straightforward than Porat's. We include Porat's twenty-eight ambiguous occupations as information occupations without ambiguity. We believe it is reasonable to include them; for example, physicians and registered nurses appear to be primarily information workers.[57] We also believe that salesclerks increasingly perform roles as information workers—for instance, as operators of point-of-sale terminals. Similarly, "miscellaneous clerical" workers (such as general office clerks and medical-insurance clerks) are generally employed to enter, file, or move information for their employers. We perceive the managerial occupations to be highly information oriented and define them as information occupations. In the blue-collar stratum, we identify inspectors and examiners as primarily information workers, as the titles imply.

APPENDIX B: NOTES ON SOURCES OF DATA AND METHODS

We drew data for our tables from these sources: Table 4.1 data from Bell (1981, Table 9.2). Table 4.2 data from State of California (1985, table 3) and Bureau of Labor Statistics (1982, table B20). For Table 4.3, 1900–1970 data come from Series D-182 through D-682, Bureau of the Census (1976, 139–45). Data for 1980 come from Bureau of Labor Statistics (1982, Table B20; 1984, table 276) selected to match the smaller number of occupational categories from this time-series. The resulting 1980 data do not match those in other tables but are comparable with the data in this table. Table 4.4 data are from State of California (1986, Table 44); 1988 data are projected in that report. Tables 4.5 and 4.6 data are from State of California (1985, Table 3) and Bureau of Labor Statistics (1982, Table B20). These tables contain a slightly different estimate for the total Orange County work force than does Table 4.4, which is based on the State of California (1986). Table 4.7 data are from State of California (1985, Table 3).

Occupational data are complex because each source provides a somewhat different grouping of occupations and somewhat conflicting data for the same year. There are three sets of data about employment in the United States economy in our tables. These three sets of numbers come from different sources and are not directly comparable. They are, however, comparable with other labor data within the tables in which they appear. Two of these data sets are designed to match time-series developed by others, and these pose special problems, which we outline here.

In Table 4.1 the 1980 data are from Bell (1981). Bell's 1980 data are comparable to his labor data from 1860 to 1970. We cannot readily reconstruct his four-sector breakdown of the United States economy with better 1980 data. Bell's breakdowns within this table are internally consistent.

Table 4.2 uses data from the 1980 census (Bureau of Labor Statistics, 1982) to calculate our best estimate of the size of the different occupations and strata within the information labor force.

Table 4.3 is based on a 1900–1970 times-series of occupations that we obtained from the Bureau of the Census (1976). We added 1980 data from the Bureau of Labor Statistics (1982) to best match the specific occupational titles in the 1900–1970 time-series. Because the time-series data do not contain all the occupational titles that appeared in the 1980 census, the total employment in the information sector is somewhat smaller than our best estimate, which appears in Table 4.2. Our breakdowns of occupations into five strata within this table are internally consistent and extend the time-series to 1980.

Occupational Comparisons, 1900–1980, Federal Data
In assembling our historical series of federal data of 1900–1980 for the five strata of the information work force (see table 4.3), we relied primarily on the Bureau of the Census (1976) but were forced to use data from other sources to fill in some unexplainable gaps in the series and to add data for 1980. (For example, teachers and nurses are counted for all years except 1970!) We also dealt with some apparent reclassifications of occupations across categories for given years.

Because our main task was to track the proportions of workers within a given stratum, our job was simplified. Even if the job was reclassified with others, as long as they all remained within the same occupational stratum the crucial total is correct. We explain key examples of our calculations below. We used Bureau of the Census (1976) data for 1900–1970 unless otherwise noted. We used Bureau of Labor Statistics (1982) as our source for 1980 data unless otherwise noted.

In the professional stratum, there are no figures for "teachers, college and university" in 1970. We estimate the figures for this year from Bureau of the Census (1985). The figures for "physicians" from the Bureau of the Census (1976) include "osteopaths" before 1960. They include "chiropractors" and "therapists and healers" for 1900. "Life and physical scientists" are a combination of the Bureau of the Census (1976) categories of "chemists" and "natural scientists (nec)" for 1900–1970. The category "operations and systems researchers" is not listed in Bureau of the Census (1976), but we obtained data from the Bureau of the Census (1984) for 1970 and 1980.

In the semiprofessional stratum, the number of "all other managers and administrators" had to be calculated from the Bureau of the Census (1976) by subtracting the number of all ten managerial occupations already included in our list from the total. "Teachers, except college and university" were estimated from Bureau of the Census (1985). The category "all other professional and technical" has no entry for 1970, and the data gave us no basis for estimating the size of this occupational category in 1970. We left it as 0. But we estimate the size of this category for 1980 from the Bureau of Labor Statistics (1982), which includes not only "all other . . ." but also the semiprofessional categories "research workers" and "vocational and educational counselors," which were not counted separately in the Bureau of the Census (1976) data.

The category "writers, artists, and entertainers" is a composite in both the Bureau of the Census (1976) and the Bureau of Labor Statistics (1982) estimates. In the Bureau of the Census (1976) tables, it is composed of "actors and actresses," "dancers and dancing teachers," "entertainers (nec)," "artists and art teachers," "authors," "editors and reporters," "designers," "musicians and music teachers," and "photographers." From the Bureau of Labor Statistics (1982) table we derive an estimate from the difference between the "writers, artists, and entertainers" category and the excluded subcategory "athletes and kindred." The category "computer specialists" is not included in the Bureau of the Census (1976) data. We record the 1970 and 1980 estimates from the Bureau of the Census (1985), which consist of the sum of the estimates for "computer systems analysts and scientists" and "computer programmers."

For 1900–1940 the "sales representatives" and "sales workers (nom)" (clerks and low-level salespeople) are matched in the Bureau of the Census (1976) data by "salesmen and salesclerks (nec), manufacturing and wholesale" and "salesmen and salesclerks (nec), retail," respectively (even though sales representatives are upper-level sales workers and sales workers are clerical workers. We estimate their proportions for these years by the ratio from 1950 and enter the data separately.

The category "all other clerical workers" comes from "clerical and kindred workers (nec)" in the Bureau of the Census (1976) data. We carefully calculated a Bureau of Labor Statistics (1982) figure by subtracting the sum of all the seventeen other clerical categories that were included in the total clerical estimate.

Federal vs. Orange County Data

In setting up our federal/Orange County comparison tables (tables 4.2 and 4.5), we began with federal categories as derived from Porat's list of information workers.[58] The State of California has its own list of occupations, which does not exactly match the federal list. Fortunately, matches were frequent and mismatches were reasonably resolved. We discuss here only the matches that were not simple and mechanical.

"Teachers, except college and university" is calculated by subtracting the Orange County figure for "college and university teachers" from the overall category "teachers." "All other managers and administrators" was hard to track and match because little information is provided on the breakdown in the Orange County data. Because most of our study concerns what happens within a given stratum, this lack of an exact match poses no serious problem. The "all other professional and technical" federal category is matched by subtracting all the Orange County "professional and technical" occupations counted elsewhere (eleven in all) from the total. The federal category "officials and administrators, public" becomes the Orange County category "administrators and public inspectors."

The federal category "clerical supervisors (nec)" becomes the Orange County category "clerical supervisors." We used the federal category "personnel and labor-relations workers" to match the Orange County category "personnel and employment workers."

The "all other clerical" category is a large one. We had to construct a figure by taking the total "other clerical" Orange County category and subtracting the subcategories (twenty-four in all) that were counted elsewhere. The Orange County category "sales workers (nom)" is composed of the categories "salesclerks" and "all other sales workers." The federal category "teacher aides, except school monitors" becomes the Orange County category "teachers' aides/educational assistants." The federal category "library attendants and assistants" is matched with the Orange County category "library assistants." The federal category "collectors, bill and account" is matched by the Orange County category "collectors."

The federal category "welfare-service aides" is matched with the Orange County category "eligibility workers, welfare."

"Printing craftworkers" in the federal list are matched by "printing-trade craftworkers" in the Orange County list. The federal category "telephone line installers and repairers" is matched by the Orange County category "telephone installers, repairers" (including "cable installers"). "Office-machine repairers" in the federal list is matched with the Orange County category "office machine servicers/cash register servicers." We match federal "photographic-process workers" with "other photo-process workers" in the Orange County list.

Estimates of the Number of Clerical Workers
Our clerical stratum of information occupations differs from the usual list of clerical occupations. In trying to capture the lower end of the white-collar information jobs, we include the low-level sales workers, such as salesclerks (who are usually counted in other grosser categories, such as "sales workers"). This category is large in size relative to the others. For example, the Bureau of Labor Statistics (1982) reports about 2.4 million salesclerks in 1980. This different way of categorizing salesclerks produces a significant difference in the reported size of the clerical work force.[59]

Another explanation for possible differences between our count and other counts is the differing data sources. We were surprised (and unfortunately enlightened) to find large disparities in different data sources for single occupational titles.[60]

NOTES

Acknowledgments: Our thinking about information work and postsuburban development has been helped by continuing discussions with Mark Poster and Spencer Olin. In addition, Paul Attewell, Craig Calhoun, Suzanne Iacono, Ken Laudon, Hal Salzman, and Karen Wieckert have helped us think through some key aspects of our analysis. Alta Yetter Gale and Donald Johnson of the California State Department of Employment have provided invaluable data about Orange County's work force and economy.

1. According to our data, Orange County's economy was primarily agricultural in the early 1940s and primarily manufacturing in the 1960s; it shifted to a service base in the 1980s (see table 4.4). Bob Kuttner (1983) argues that Department of Labor projections for the U.S. economy indicate that the service sector now dominates expected job openings and that as a result the United States is producing a large number of low-end dead-end jobs.

2. Castells takes a more timid position in his 1985 essay. There, he discusses the increasing role of computers and telecommunications in work life; business

services, and home entertainment. He also argues that information technologies have played a major role in the spatial and economic restructuring of modern cities. But he does not explicitly define an "informational city."

3. Information jobs do not include all service jobs. The dividing line is not sharp. But at the extremes, driving a bus, washing dishes, and working as a cook are service jobs in which processing or providing information plays a small part.

4. Scott also notes that about 35 percent of the national manufacturing work force is composed of white-collar workers. Thus, Orange County's manufacturing work force is almost twice as information intensive as the national average. This difference may be a by-product of the importance of engineering in Orange County's substantial hi-tech manufacturing sector and the importance of administration in some of the large aerospace firms that have huge plants and laboratories in Orange County.

5. In their central image, "the computer console has replaced the factory smokestack as the determinant sign of economic power." They go on to assert that "informationalization has reconstituted labor and management" (Luke and White 1985, 32).

6. Although Porat's study provides the data that are most widely used, he reports them in graphics. Bell (1980) reports his estimates of employment in the four economic sectors in a more precise numerical format, and that is why we have reproduced his data in table 4.1.

7. The information work force includes some blue-collar workers who operate and repair computer, communications, and office equipment. The white-collar work force includes some jobs like salesclerk that have a strong information component but that are not wholly information-handling jobs.

8. John Naisbett (1984) is an interesting exception. He characterizes the transformations of the U.S. work force from agriculture to information with the terms "farmer, laborer, clerk." We do not share his belief in a linear progression of dominant sectors, which ends with an information sector. He is forthright in arguing that clerks play a central role in the information sector. But he does not examine the size of their role and its possible changes over time.

9. In contrast, some writers, like Kuttner (1983), argue that the service sector is generating a much larger number of low-end dead-end service jobs than professional, managerial, and technical jobs. For example, the Department of Labor estimated that the occupations with the ten largest number of job openings in 1980 would be retail salesclerks, miscellaneous managers and administrators, cashiers, secretaries, waiters, cooks, stock handlers, bookkeepers, and "miscellaneous" clerical workers. Six of these occupations are in the information sector. Kuttner's analysis is controversial because he examines only the absolute number of openings in jobs with relatively high turnover. Even so, we find his analysis suggestive.

10. Paul Strassman (1985) follows Bell (1980) in arguing that information work is part of the infrastructure for a service economy. Strassman makes his links much more explicit than does Bell.

11. Bell's evolutionary approach to postindustrial societies is best critiqued by Krishan Kumar (1978). Kumar observes that the service sector employed more

people in England than the manufacturing sector from before the industrial revolution through the 1970s.

12. The information-age office is the only office type that Giuliano illustrates with computer terminals; and computer terminals are located on every desk. It is also the only office with plants. The one photograph of a computerized office in his article combines an "industrial" organization of work space (a matrix of desks in an open area) with his information-age elements of a terminal on every desk and plants!

13. Zuboff examines three cases in substantial detail. In each case some sort of information system was imposed on the work groups she studied. This type of implementation process is commonplace for large-scale systems and those used by many clerks and blue-collar workers. However, many work groups have actually fought to get computer technologies. These grass-roots implementations have different dynamics, which Zuboff ignores.

14. Unlike Giuliano, Zuboff is sensitive to the problems that people and organizations can face in computerization projects. However, like Giuliano, she usually portrays computerization as a relatively homogeneous process that has similar consequences for most workers. Giuliano views computerization as economically efficient and psychologically satisfying. Zuboff portrays computerization as a process that usually disorients, isolates, and demoralizes workers. Both of them ignore key contingencies that can lead to different outcomes.

15. On p. 171 Zuboff does try to distinguish between the work in mechanized and in computerized offices. She argues that computer systems can be much more expansive than mechanical systems. This is a small point relative to her major theses, and she does not carefully distinguish between computer-based work and other forms of information work or office work when she makes her major arguments.

16. Porat estimated the number of workers in each occupation from U.S. census data and industry-occupation matrices of the 1967 National Income Accounts.

17. The abbreviation "nec" means not elsewhere classified.

18. See table 4.2 for a list of our information occupations and a description of the ways in which our list differs from Porat's. Although some of Porat's occupational assignments can be seriously questioned, they do not substantially alter his estimates of the size of the information work force. By using his categories, we can readily compare our results with his and with those of other studies.

19. Michael Cooper (1983) argues that the information economy is no longer expanding rapidly at the national level. In this chapter we examine its growth in Orange County.

20. Lyon's (1988) critique and Judith Perrolle's (1987) textbook are rare exceptions.

21. There are major debates about the extent to which computerization upskills or deskills jobs. Judith Gregory and Karen Nussbaum (1982), Robert Howard (1985), and Abbe Mowshowitz (1986) argue that organizations are most likely to computerize in order to deskill jobs, while Strassman (1985) and Tom Forester (1987) argue that computerization almost universally upskills jobs. We believe that

organizations computerize in ways that upskill some jobs and deskill other jobs. We find that the bulk of available evidence supports the position that most jobs are upskilled, even if that is an unconscious by-product of practices chosen for other reasons (Iacono and Kling 1987). A small fraction of clerical jobs may be deskilled. But because there are over twenty million clerical jobs in the United States, a small fraction can be a large number (for example, 3 percent of the clerical jobs is six hundred thousand jobs, not a tiny number).

22. Giuliano's account is sketchy. He does not indicate whether clerks move up into the new jobs or whether new applicants fill the improved jobs.

23. Kuttner (1983) argues that many jobs actually become worse while their titles are upgraded.

24. The labor data in this paragraph and the next come from George Ritzer (1977, 14). We have rounded percentages to the nearest point. Ritzer uses conventional Department of Labor occupational classifications, which we do not accept. See note 26.

25. The Department of Labor lists a set of diverse occupations under the label "professional workers": athlete, engineer, librarian, lawyer, physician, schoolteacher, vocational counselor, writer, and so forth. These groups have not all made an equally convincing claim to the label *professional,* even though they can make a convincing case that some occupational practices are more professional than others. We have divided these occupations into two groups: higher-status professionals, who often have a legal monopoly on educating practitioners and licensing; and semiprofessionals, who have some of the characteristics of professionals but not all.

26. The Department of Labor classifies accounting as a management-related specialty. We classify most managers in the semiprofessional stratum and treat accounting as a fully professionalized occupation.

27. Some of these workers, especially sellers who work as independent agents, can be much better paid than many salaried semiprofessionals and professionals.

28. We see clerical jobs as poorer jobs than the upper-level sales and supervisory jobs because they are relatively low paid and consist primarily of routinized or delegated work (or both). Clerical work is not all of one kind. Secretaries, the aristocrats of the clerical work force, may have substantial discretion in how to carry out their work, while billing clerks may have little. Moreover, some clerical work is becoming more technically complex and, at times, more interesting. Despite these variations within clerical occupations and improvements in some elements of the job, clerical workers are less well paid and can exercise less initiative than workers in other occupational strata. We do not believe that most clerical jobs are becoming degraded or deskilled. We believe that they are simply poor jobs relative to others in the economy for many workers.

29. A variation of this theory would place the bulk of information workers in the other middle category—semiprofessional jobs such as engineer, schoolteacher, and social worker.

30. See Appendix B for a discussion of our methods.

31. In 1900, 38 percent of the U.S. labor force was employed in agriculture, fishing, and forestry; 30 percent was employed in industry; and 31 percent was

employed in services. By 1970, 3 percent of the labor force was employed in agriculture, fishing, and forestry; 31 percent was employed in industry; and 60 percent was employed in services (Ritzer 1977, 15).

32. Unfortunately, there are no reliable and detailed occupational statistics for Orange County before 1980 that can be used to calculate the relative size of its labor force in different economic sectors (see table 4.4).

33. We are cautious in identifying this shift as a significant trend because there are problems in comparing these data.

34. The relative decline of clerical workers is influenced by a substantial rise in the group of "all other professional and technical workers" in our data. However, a comprehensive study of computerization and clerical work also projects decreased growth of clerical jobs between 1982 and 1995 (Hartman, Kraut, and Tilly 1986).

35. There are several forms of dual labor-market theory (Berger and Piore 1980, 17). All of them divide the (national) labor market into two distinct sectors and hold that workers rarely move between the two sectors. One, the primary sector, provides the most attractive and better-paying jobs. The other, the secondary sector, provides poorer jobs—jobs that are worse in pay, status, security. Labor economists originally used dual labor-market theories in the United States to help understand why the unemployment rate of urban blacks was relatively high and difficult to change.

36. For example, Suzanne Berger and Michael Piore (1980, 18) note that primary-sector occupations are divided into upper and lower tiers. They identify the upper tier as jobs that are "managerial and professional" and the lower tier as jobs that are "blue collar" and "certain ones that are white collar." They place craft jobs in a third, intermediate tier. David Montagna (1977) treats clerical jobs simply as secondary-sector jobs.

37. About 80 percent of the clerks in the U.S. labor force are women. Specific clerical occupations vary considerably in the extent to which they are primarily female occupations, from 11 percent of mail carriers to 99 percent of secretaries. Most clerical occupations are over 70 percent female. Bureau of Labor Statistics (1982, Table B20); also see Taeuber and Valdisera (1986, 23) and Hartmann, Kraut, and Tilly (1986, 20).

38. In his studies of computerization and office work, the senior author has met women who wish to find a "better job" but who have substantial problems in figuring out exactly what they might do. Many of these women only vaguely articulate what kind of better job they would like, and they are unsure how to locate and prepare for nonclerical jobs. Sometimes they take computer classes in the hope that technical skills will increase their career opportunities. If they must support themselves while qualifying for alternative careers, few women in this predicament can afford to attend college for substantial periods of time. Some can, and do, take night courses, but these women are a minority.

39. For example, some realtors and stockbrokers earn much more than school-teachers and social workers.

40. For example, many more women take degrees in traditionally male fields such as engineering, architecture, law, and business today than they did in 1967 (Taeuber and Valdisera 1986). See also Burris (1983).

41. The data in table 4.3 are not directly comparable with the data in table 4.5 because they come from different federal sources. The data in table 4.3 come from the 1980 census (Bureau of Census, 1984). The data in table 4.5 come from special time-series designed to make occupational categories comparable from 1900 to 1970, despite substantial changes in census codings in that period (Bureau of the Census, 1976). We matched the occupational titles of this series as closely as possible with 1980 data to extend the series.

42. Although we have been troubled by gaps, relabelings of occupations, and inconsistencies in federal data, those data are far better than no systematic data.

43. This projection is one of a series published by the State of California. Similar projections were created for the state economy as a whole and for San Diego County.

44. These two sources provide somewhat conflicting estimates of actual employment. The data on annual employment by industrial sector is more accurate because it relies on actual counts between 1980 and 1985. It estimates employment for 1986, 1987, and 1988 based on local trends. But it does not break down employment by individual occupations. The 1990 projections are based on a forecasting model developed for the State of California, and it is less accurate for individual counties. For example, the 1985 report estimated that Orange County's total work force would be about 1,033,000 in 1990—a size that was exceeded in 1986! Moreover, the report significantly overestimates the size of Orange County's manufacturing work force and underestimates employment in sales and services. Unfortunately, we had to use the 1990 projections of employment in specific occupations as our primary data source. We temper these projections with the information about employment within industries.

45. These projections differ somewhat from the national occupational trends between 1900 and 1980 (see table 4.3). And these projections of a slightly enlarged clerical sector differ substantially from several forecasts that see relative reductions in clerical work in the future (compare Hartmann, Kraut, and Tilly 1986).

46. We base this estimate on the proportion of job growth within industries that is reported with the 1990 occupational projections (State of California 1985). This study estimates 62,000 new service jobs in Orange County between 1980 and 1990. Among these, it estimates 20,000 new jobs in business services and 17,100 in health care. These are significant underestimates. By 1984 Orange County had already added 51,400 new service jobs, and the Employment Development Department was projecting 102,000 new service jobs overall between 1980 and 1988 in its studies of employment by industry (State of California 1986).

47. These data are more accurate than the 1990 occupational projections. They estimate significantly higher growth rates for services and trade and significantly lower growth rates for manufacturing than do the 1990 projections.

48. This pattern suggests that cross-stratum mobility may require sectoral mobility—for example, salesclerk to a job in manufacturing—not just occupational mobility.

49. Since 1981 women have received more bachelor's degrees and master's degrees annually than men. In 1960, they received about one-third of the bachelor's degrees and less than one-third of the master's degrees.

50. Some of the variety comes in the skills and practices needed to work around gaps in imperfect computer systems. See Iacono and Kling (1987). Our position differs considerably from Zuboff's (1988) argument that computerization has almost always led to socially isolated jobs in which the abstractness of computerized data disorients workers.

51. For a review of the debates and detailed comparisons of several studies, see Heidi Hartmann, Robert Kraut, and Louise Tilly (1986).

52. But note that Porat's granularity is not quite as fine as others. For example, Bureau of Labor Statistics data break the clerical stratum into ninety-five specific occupations (Hartmann, Kraut, and Tilly 1986, Table 3-18, p. 112). These distinctions are fine enough to distinguish between "desk clerks, bowling floor" and "desk clerks, except bowling floor." We found it unnecessary to distinguish between who was on the bowling floor and who was not.

53. For example, our occupational title "life and physical scientists" corresponds to the (sub)titles "agricultural scientists," "meteorologists," "life scientists" (further consisting of "biologists" and "medical scientists"), "chemists," "geologists and geophysicists" (including "oceanographers"), "physicists," and "life and physical scientists (nec)." The corresponding occupational titles under Porat's "natural and physical sciences" are "agricultural scientists," "atmospheric, space scientists," "biological scientists," "chemists," "geologists," "marine scientists," "physicists and astronomers," and "life and physical scientists."

54. We did not match seventeen occupational titles on his list, but we estimate six of them that appear to account for some significant proportion of workers from federal data. Our estimates are obtained by calculating the percentage of the total work force that can be attributed to the particular occupation and multiplying this percentage by the total Orange County work force; the result is our estimate (in lieu of no number at all).

55. He does this even though he notes that "time budget studies of physicians' offices revealed that over 70% of a physician's time is spent . . . in information tasks" (Porat 1977, 118).

56. The median is usually the middle number between the two numbers considered, but in Porat's estimation procedure the twenty-eight ambiguous occupations are counted as 25 percent information and 75 percent some other sector.

57. One wonders, in fact, whether the information component of such occupations is not growing with time. Computers are a nontrivial part of record-keeping, expert systems, therapy machines; and it requires special knowledge to use them properly.

58. See Appendix A.

59. For example, compare Table 3-18 in Hartmann, Kraut, and Tilly (1986, p. 112). We count about 3 million more clerical workers in 1980 than the 18.7 million that they count for 1982. Our larger count is due almost entirely to our inclusion of sales workers.

60. For example, the figure for "receptionists" for 1982 reported in Hartmann, Kraut, and Tilly (1986, Table 3-18) is 381,100, based on Bureau of Labor Statistics data. But the Bureau of Labor Statistics (1982) reports a figure of 644,000 for 1980! There is clearly a difference in definition or method of mea-

surement. And we cannot readily explain other anomalies in official federal data sources that cite the Bureau of Labor Statistics.

REFERENCES

Bell, Daniel. 1973. *The Coming of Post Industrial Society.* New York: Basic Books.
————. 1981. "The Social Framework of the Information Society." In *The Micro-electronics Revolution,* ed. Tom Forester, 500–550. Cambridge, Mass.: MIT Press.
Berger, Suzanne, and Michael Piore. 1980. *Dualism and Discontinuity in Industrial Societies.* Cambridge: Cambridge University Press.
Bureau of Labor Statistics. 1982. *Labor Force Statistics Derived from the Current Population Survey: A Databook, Volume 1.* Bulletin 2096. Washington.
Bureau of the Census. 1976. *Bicentennial Edition, Historical Statistics of the United States, Colonial Times to 1970, Part 1.* Washington.
————. 1984. *1980 Census of the Population, Detailed Population Characteristics, United States Summary, Section A: U.S.* Washington.
————. 1985. *Statistical Abstract of the United States 1986, 106th Edition.* Washington.
Burris, Beverly. 1983. *No Room at the Top.* New York: Praeger.
Castells, Manuel. 1985. "High Technology, Economic Restructuring, and the Urban-Regional Process in the United States." In *High Technology, Space, and Society,* ed. Manuel Castells. Beverly Hills, Calif.: Sage.
————. n.d. "The Information City." Berkeley, Calif.
Cooper, Michael D. 1983. "The Structure of the Information Economy." *Information Processing and Management* 19:9–26.
Dunlop, Charles, and Rob Kling, eds. 1991. *Computerization and Controversy: Value Conflicts and Social Choices.* New York: Academic Press.
Fishman, Robert. 1987. *Bourgeois Utopias: The Rise and Fall of Suburbia.* New York: Basic Books.
Forester, Tom, ed. 1980. *The Microelectronics Revolution.* Cambridge, Mass.: MIT Press.
————. 1987. *High Tech Society.* Cambridge, Mass.: MIT Press.
"Gender Wage Gap Narrows, but Women Still Shortchanged." 1987. *Orange County Register,* Sept. 4, 1.
Ginzberg, Eli, Thierry Noyelle, and Thomas Stanback. 1986. *Technology and Employment.* Boulder, Colo.: Westview.
Giuliano, Vincent. 1982. "The Mechanization of Office Work." *Scientific American,* 247(3):148–64.
Goldthorpe, John H., and Keith Hope. 1974. *The Social Grading of Occupations: A New Approach and Scale.* Oxford: Clarendon Press.
Gordon, David M., Richard Edwards, and Michael Reich. 1982. *Segmented Work, Divided Workers: The Historical Transformation of Labor in the United States.* Cambridge: Cambridge University Press.
Gregory, Judith, and Karen Nussbaum. 1982. "Race against Time: An Analysis of the Trends in Office Automation and the Impact on the Office Workforce." *Office: Technology and People* 1:197–236.

Hartmann, Heidi, Robert E. Kraut, and Louise A. Tilly, eds. 1986. *Computer Chips and Paper Clips: Technology and Women's Employment*, vol. 1. Washington, D.C.: National Academy Press.

Howard, Robert. 1985. *Brave New Workplace*. New York: Viking Press.

Huppes, Tjerk. 1987. *The Western Edge: Work and Management in the Information Age*. Boston: Kluwer.

Iacono, Suzanne, and Rob Kling. 1987. "Changing Office Technologies and Transformations of Clerical Jobs." In *Technology and the Transformation of White Collar Work*, ed. Robert Kraut. Hillsdale, N.J.: Erlbaum.

Kanter, Rosabeth Moss. 1977. *Men and Women of the Corporation*. New York: Basic Books.

Katz, Raul L. 1986. "Measurement and Cross-National Comparisons of the Information Work Force." *The Information Society*, 4(4):231–77.

Knight, Richard V. 1986. "The Advanced Industrial Metropolis: A New Type of World City." In *The Future of the Metropolis: Economic Aspects*, ed. Hans-Jurgen Ewers, John B. Goddard, and Horst Matzerath. New York: de Gruyter.

Kumar, Krishan. 1978. *Prophecy and Progress: The Sociology of Industrial and Post-industrial Society*. New York: Penguin Books.

Kuttner, Bob. 1983. "The Declining Middle." *Atlantic Monthly*, 252(1):60–72.

Leontief, Wassily, and Faye Duchin. 1984. *The Impacts of Automation on Employment, 1963–2000*. New York: Institute for Economic Analysis, New York University.

Lerman, Robert, and Harold Salzman. 1987. *Deskilling and Declassing: Whither the Middle Stratum?* Boston: Center for Applied Social Science, Boston University.

Luke, Timothy, and Stephen K. White. 1985. "Critical Theory, the Informational Revolution, and an Ecological Path to Modernity." In *Critical Theory and Public Life*, ed. John Forster. Cambridge, Mass.: MIT Press.

Lyon, David. 1986. "From 'Post-industrialism' to 'Information Society': A New Social Transformation?" *Sociology* 20(4):577–88.

———. 1988. *The Information Society: Issues and Illusions*. New York: Blackwell.

Markusen, Anne Roell, and Robin Bloch. 1985. "Defensive Cities: Military Spending, High Technology, and Human Settlements." In *High Technology, Space, and Society*, ed. Manuel Castells. Beverly Hills, Calif.: Sage.

Mills, C. Wright. 1951. *White Collar*. New York: Oxford University Press.

Montagna, David. 1977. *Occupations and Society: Towards a Sociology of the Labor Market*. New York: Wiley.

Mowshowitz, Abbe. 1986. "The Social Dimensions of Office Automation." In *Advances in Computers*, vol. 25, ed. Marshall Yovits. New York: Academic Press.

Naisbitt, John. 1984. *Megatrends: Ten Directions Transforming Our Lives*. New York: Warner Books.

Noyelle, Thierry J. 1987. *Beyond Industrial Dualism: Market and Job Segmentation in the New Economy*. Boulder, Colo.: Westview.

Perrolle, Judith A. 1987. *Computers and Social Change: Information, Property, and Power*. Belmont, Calif.: Wadsworth.

Porat, Marc Uri. 1977. *The Information Economy: Definition and Measurement*. U.S. Office of Technology Special Publication 77-12(1). Washington: Department of Commerce.

Reich, Robert. 1989. "As the World Turns: U.S. Inequality Keeps on Rising." *New Republic* 3876(1 May):23, 26–28.

Ritzer, George. 1977. *Working: Conflict and Change.* 2d ed. Englewood Cliffs, N.J.: Prentice-Hall.

Rosenberg, Richard. 1986. *Computers and the Information Society.* New York: Wiley.

Scott, Allen. 1988. *Metropolis: From the Division of Labor to Urban Form.* Berkeley: University of California Press.

State of California, Employment Development Department. 1985. *Projections of Employment by Industry and Occupation, 1980–1990, Anaheim–Santa Ana–Garden Grove Metropolitan Statistical Area (Orange County).* Sacramento.

———. 1986. *Annual Planning Information, Anaheim–Santa Ana Metropolitan Statistical Area (Orange County), 1986–1987.* Sacramento.

Stonier, Tom. 1983. *The Wealth of Information: A Profile of the Post-industrial Economy.* London: Thames Methuen.

Strassman, Paul. 1985. *Information Payoff.* New York: Free Press.

Taeuber, Cynthia, and Victor Valdisera. 1986. *Women in the American Economy.* Current Population Reports, Special Studies Series P-23, no. 146. Washington: Department of Commerce.

Zuboff, Shoshana. 1988. *In the Age of the Smart Machine: The Future of Work and Power.* New York: Basic Books.

FIVE

Changing Consumption Patterns

Alladi Venkatesh

In Chapter 4 Rob Kling and Clark Turner show how the production sector is evolving as a result of both changing patterns of employment and growth in the information and service sectors. Here I examine a complementary aspect of the regional economy: Orange County's consumption sector. A pertinent question is whether changes in the consumption sector are as significant and far-reaching as those that Kling, Turner, and other contributors to this book claim for the production sector.

In attempting to answer that question, we must recognize at the outset that developments in these two sectors may not be symmetrical during the early stages of major shifts. There may be lags, or the inherent characteristics of these two sectors may differentiate the pace of change. The production sector, for example, is generally considered organized, which means that, by a process of careful planning and technological and capital infusion, significant changes can be brought about in a relatively short period of time. These changes can especially result if the existing production processes are not well entrenched and a new infrastructure can be built without having to replace an existing one. The consumption sector, however, operates according to well-established social and cultural norms and is based in stratification systems that evolve over time. E. Hirschman (1985) has analyzed the continuities and discontinuities in consumption in a changing environment and the essential tension between the two.[1] She argues that even in the so-called postindustrial age, people cling to primitive aspects of consumption as an effective defense against the forces of change. Changes occurring in the consumption sector, therefore, may or may not be as dramatic or visible as those in the production sector, but they are nonetheless extremely important as anticipatory or confirming processes. Our analysis attempts to uncover those processes. However, there are two aspects of our study that need some explanation: one pertains to the paucity of data, the other to the scope of the analysis.

Our experience shows that government agencies and private research institutions collect much better and more complex data about production- and employment-related developments than about consumption trends. This bias is no accident. First, it is a direct consequence of the institutional capitalism that supports all activities that promote industry's interests. Second, by their very nature, consumer data are generally more diffuse and less easily obtainable than production data. Because of the sparse nature of reliable data, we have to rely on limited information and resort to informed speculation, accepting weak signals as plausible evidence of change.

Although Orange County has been incorporated for more than one hundred years, it has only recently come out of relative obscurity into national prominence. Today, Orange County is a mixture of older communities that still retain some of their historical character and newer communities that have a distinctly modern feel, with homogenized tract housing, broad boulevards, well-groomed industrial parks, and shopping malls. In this chapter, the focus is on the rapid transformation of Orange County and on the forces that have caused that transformation. A large part of the county's development has been the product of deliberate social experimentation and careful planning. The scale and scope of this experimentation are unprecedented, whether one refers to the shopping environments, the industrial establishments, the educational and cultural institutions, the medical facilities, or the residential communities. The underlying theme of this chapter is the tension between the forces behind this social experimentation and the people who live under that experimentation as consumers of its output.

I make no attempt to present a comprehensive account of all the consumption processes in the county but attempt instead to show how the consumption process at the region's core contributes to its diversity and dynamism. The "core consumption culture" is the upper-middle-class and middle-class ownership patterns that are celebrated in many mass media—owning a home, a fancy car, stylish furniture and clothes.

THE ROOTS OF AN AFFLUENT SETTLEMENT CULTURE

Since World War II Orange County's population has become increasingly diverse, multicultural, and multilingual. Its economic strata vary widely from upper- to lower-income groups. Because of the high proportion of relative newcomers in the population, Orange County can be appropriately called a settlement culture.

It is also an affluent culture. The county's consumer economy can be

TABLE 5.1 Population and Various Statistics for Consumer Product Sales, Selected Metropolitan Areas, 1986

	1986 Population (000s)	Consumer Product Sales ($ million)						
		Groceries	Major Household Appliances	Women's Clothes	Drug, Health, and Beauty Products	Eating and Drinking Places	Furniture and Sleeping Equipment	Total Retail
New York	8,527 (1)	8,379 (2)	642 (1)	3,791 (1)	2,093 (2)	5,707 (1)	1,186 (2)	44,722 (2)
Los Angeles	8,312 (2)	8,651 (1)	429 (2)	3,111 (2)	2,146 (1)	5,653 (2)	1,305 (1)	53,977 (1)
Chicago	6,166 (3)	5,658 (3)	381 (3)	2,868 (3)	1,552 (3)	3,873 (4)	923 (3)	37,545 (3)
Philadelphia	4,827 (4)	5,146 (4)	335 (4)	2,025 (4)	1,447 (4)	2,809 (5)	689 (4)	31,122 (4)
Detroit	4,359 (5)	4,956 (5)	287 (6)	1,612 (6)	1,340 (5)	2,700 (7)	578 (7)	28,365 (6)
Boston (metro)	3,724 (6)	4,816 (6)	296 (5)	1,941 (5)	1,005 (6)	3,880 (3)	593 (6)	30,511 (5)
Washington, D.C.	3,544 (7)	4,001 (7)	262 (7)	1,569 (7)	980 (7)	2,738 (6)	670 (5)	26,757 (7)
Houston	3,232 (8)	3,349 (9)	257 (8)	1,220 (9)	813 (8)	2,450 (8)	497 (8)	21,801 (8)
Nassau/Suffolk	2,664 (9)	3,915 (8)	211 (9)	1,295 (8)	808 (9)	1,603 (13)	487 (9)	20,979 (9)
Atlanta	2,543 (10)	2,549 (12)	182 (13)	1,089 (10)	729 (10)	2,003 (10)	418 (10)	19,050 (10)
St. Louis	2,451 (11)	2,714 (11)	183 (12)	889 (15)	595 (13)	1,505 (16)	308 (17)	16,174 (13)
Dallas	2,378 (12)	2,438 (13)	208 (10)	1,032 (11)	609 (12)	1,977 (11)	329 (13)	17,259 (11)

Minneapolis	2,323 (13)	2,811 (10)	179 (14)	954 (14)	580 (14)	1,542 (15)	326 (14)	16,837 (12)
Baltimore	2,306 (14)	2,316 (16)	153 (18)	—	576 (15)	1,371 (19)	—	14,264 (17)
San Diego	2,217 (15)	2,159 (19)	174 (15)	813 (17)	550 (20)	1,565 (14)	336 (12)	14,346 (16)
Orange County	**2,177 (16)**	**2,386 (14)**	**160 (16)**	**1,007 (12)**	**621 (11)**	**1,818 (12)**	**337 (11)**	**16,117 (14)**
Pittsburg	2,139 (17)	2,196 (17)	—	767 (19)	528 (21)	—	—	—
Riverside	2,005 (18)	2,053 (23)	—	—	—	—	—	—
Oakland	1,949 (19)	2,192 (18)	153 (17)	759 (20)	558 (19)	—	300 (18)	13,458 (19)
Phoenix	1,916 (20)	—	—	—	567 (17)	1,275 (20)	—	—
Tampa	1,916 (20)	—	189 (11)	—	—	—	—	—
Newark	1,899 (22)	2,321 (15)	—	—	—	—	—	—
Cleveland	1,853 (23)	—	—	—	565 (18)	—	313 (16)	12,444 (20)
Miami	1,780 (24)	—	—	860 (16)	576 (16)	—	300 (18)	13,594 (18)
Seattle	1,758 (25)	—	—	—	—	1,374 (18)	—	—
Denver	1,649 (26)	—	150 (19)	—	—	1,411 (17)	—	—
San Francisco	1,584 (27)	2,113 (21)	—	960 (13)	508 (22)	2,178 (9)	323 (15)	14,541 (15)
Bergen/Passaic	1,303 (35)	—	147 (20)	807 (18)	—	—	—	—

SOURCE: "Survey of Buying Power," 1987.
NOTE: Ranks are shown in parentheses. A dash indicates that a city is not among the top twenty-five in sales.

TABLE 5.2   Buying Power of Selected Regions in the United States, 1986

	Households with EBI of $50,000 and over (000s)	Effective Buying Income (EBI) ($ billion)	Effective Buying Median Household Income ($)
Los Angeles	651 (1)	121.15 (1)	27,017 (84)
New York	632 (2)	114.13 (2)	23,666 (178)
Chicago	495 (3)	86.72 (3)	29,481 (34)
Washington, D.C.	449 (4)	61.48 (5)	37,209 (5)
Boston	352 (5)	57.66 (6)	31,333 (24)
Nassau/Suffolk	339 (6)	46.26 (8)	41,990 (1)
Philadelphia	327 (7)	63.47 (4)	27,233 (80)
Detroit	292 (8)	56.74 (7)	28,160 (54)
Houston	236 (9)	43.57 (9)	28,821 (43)
Orange County	**234 (10)**	**34.57 (10)**	**35,181 (8)**
Oakland	209 (11)	31.33 (16)	32,670 (15)
Atlanta	201 (12)	34.28 (11)	29,025 (40)
Newark	191 (13)	29.69 (17)	32,145 (18)
Dallas	190 (14)	33.67 (13)	28,471 (49)
San Francisco	189 (15)	29.04 (18)	32,092 (19)
Minneapolis/St. Paul	186 (16)	33.98 (12)	30,927 (26)
San Diego	174 (17)	31.68 (14)	27,773 (66)
San Jose	164 (18)	22.16 (21)	37,517 (3)
Seattle	162 (19)	26.67 (20)	30,814 (31)
St. Louis	158 (20)	31.45 (15)	27,518 (75)

SOURCE: "Survey of Buying Power," 1987.
NOTE: EBI is a classification developed by *Sales and Marketing Management* and equals personal household income less personal tax (federal, state, and local), nontax payments (of fines, fees, and penalties), and personal contributions to social insurance. Ranks are shown in parentheses.

described in terms of its population, income, and spending characteristics. Tables 5.1 and 5.2 compare Orange County with other major metropolitan regions in the United States. Table 5.3 gives a direct comparison with the Los Angeles region regarding certain key factors. Table 5.4 shows consumption trends within the county for certain product categories. The population of Orange County is more than two million, making it the sixteenth largest metropolitan region in the country (see table 5.1). Although 14.8 percent of the population is Hispanic, the county is less ethnically diverse than Los Angeles County (see table 5.3). The national image of Orange County as an affluent community is borne out by some key figures. At forty-three thousand dollars in 1988, the county's median

TABLE 5.3   A Comparison of Orange County
with the Los Angeles Metropolitan Area, 1986

	Orange County	Los Angeles
Population	2,177,300 (16)	8,312,300 (2)
White	93.5%	67.9%
Black	1.3%	12.6%
Other	5.2%	19.5%
(Hispanic)	(14.8%)	(27.6%)
Buying power (000)	$34,579,535 (10)	$121,150,626 (1)
Median household spendable		
income	$35,181 (8)	$27,017 (84)
Households with incomes over		
$50,000	30.3% (10)	21.4% (35)
Total retail sales (000)	$16,116,998 (14)	$53,977,936 (1)
Per household retail sales	$20,828	$17,602
Per capita spending on dining out	$835	$680
Per household supermarket sales	$1,235	$1,162
Per capita spending on apparel,		
women	$463	$374
Per capita spending on apparel,		
men	$238	$200

SOURCE: *Shopping Profile 1989* (the *Orange County Register*'s annual survey of consumer shopping).
NOTE: Figures in parentheses denote national rank among the major metropolitan areas. Hispanic population also includes those who label themselves as whites.

annual family income was the eighth highest in the nation and ranked first among the twenty most populated metropolitan regions. The county also ranked tenth in the United States in the total number of households with an effective buying income of fifty thousand dollars or more (see table 5.2). Effective buying income is gross income minus taxes (federal, state, and local) and nontax payments (fines, fees, penalties, and social security).

Orange County is also one of the most important centers of retail trade in the country. Although it is only sixteenth in population, it ranks fourteenth in retail sales, ahead of San Francisco, ranked fifteenth, and San Diego, ranked sixteenth (see table 5.1). For expenditures on specific product groups, the region ranks fourteenth in grocery products, eleventh in drug/health/beauty products, eleventh in food consumed outside the home, and eleventh in furniture and sleeping equipment. Expenditures on beauty aids, furniture, and dining out indicate relative affluence. Longitudinal retail trends are equally revealing. Table 5.4 provides a six-year summary of the growth patterns in five selected retail businesses:

TABLE 5.4   Retail Trade in Orange County, 1981–86,
in Billions of Dollars

	General Merchandise	Specialty Products	Apparel and Shoes	Drugstore Products	Food
1981	1.263	0.971	0.554	0.193	1.029
1982	1.271	1.091	0.570	0.222	1.088
1983	1.456	1.335	0.529	0.234	1.142
1984	1.648	1.602	0.689	0.253	1.182
1985	1.868	1.725	0.632	0.267	1.217
1986	1.979	1.737	0.673	0.280	1.248
Average annual change	+9.4%	+12.6%	+5.5%	+7.8%	+4%

SOURCE: Compiled from statistical tables provided by the Orange County Administrative Offices.

general merchandise, specialty (luxury) goods, apparel and shoes, drug-store products, and food products (groceries). Although the rate of growth across all the categories is impressive, it is reasonably uniform from year to year, except for specialty products. In this category, the average rate of increase has been dramatic—12.6 percent compared with 9.3 percent for the next highest category, general merchandise.

Two other indicators, automobiles and housing, also point to the rela-tive economic position of Orange County. The county is a major market for automobiles, especially expensive imported ones. The county has the two top Mercedes-Benz dealers in the nation, and many brands of luxury cars are common in the county's affluent neighborhoods.[2] The median price of a single-family home in Orange County in mid-1989 surpassed $247,000, which ranks among the highest home prices in the nation.[3]

These factors suggest Orange County's affluence, but they do not indicate how much its population values consumption as a way of life or to what extent consumption is a defining activity. All groups consume food, clothing, transportation, entertainment, and shelter. But some groups create their social identities from highly conspicuous consumption— wearing stylish clothes, driving trendy cars, living in high-status neigh-borhoods. Some social theorists have argued that the United States has become a predominantly consuming culture during this century (Ewen 1976, Douglas and Isherwood 1978, Leiss 1976, Fox and Lears 1983, Ewen and Ewen 1987). But the intensity of consumption varies from one locale to another. I will refer to a region in which consumption is an important cultural value as a "consumer region." In its extreme form, such a region comprises financial profligates who borrow freely, spend in-dulgently, save little, and live far beyond their means. In more formal terms, several factors typify consumer regions: (1) The culture values consumption as a social accomplishment. (2) There are high levels and much distribution (as opposed to concentration) of wealth, which translates into buying power. (3) There is a nonhomogeneous marketplace, which results in highly differentiated consumer-choice patterns. (4) There are high levels of education, which allow for market sophistication, market experimentation, and market innovation.

Orange County is characterized by all these factors. Its consumption pattern also has an additional element: As we have seen, most of the county's population consists of relative newcomers, both from within the United States and from abroad. Newcomers are less bound by established consumer traditions and are therefore more likely to experiment. In fact, this feature distinguishes Orange County from most other postsuburban areas in the United States.

Orange County's overall affluence masks significant variations. There are noticeable disparities in income distribution because of large numbers of single-parent families and poor immigrants. Thirty-five percent of the households earn less than twenty-five thousand dollars a year, and 11 percent earn less than ten thousand dollars, which is the poverty line (Southern California Association of Governments 1984). Although average household income has risen significantly, this rise has been due mainly to an increasing proportion of dual-income middle-class families. The income disparities also have a geographical character. The county can be divided into northern and southern regions, with a greater proportion of poor families, often Latino, living in the north. In 1986 the median family income of South County residents was estimated to be forty-four thousand dollars, compared with forty thousand dollars for North County residents. The gap widened dramatically in 1987, with reported incomes for these groups of, respectively, forty-eight thousand dollars and forty thousand dollars. Such disparities affect the nature of consumption and people's perception of well-being. In Orange County, the percentage of residents in single-family homes slipped from 57 percent in 1982 to 49 percent in 1987.[4]

With such variations in income distribution, how can one justify an analysis that treats Orange County as if it were monolithic? Orange County is no more monolithic than the rest of the United States or, for that matter, other so-called developed societies of the world. However, from Thorstein Veblen (1925) to J. Baudrillard (1981) to D. Miller (1987), it has been customary and even necessary to treat the elitism of consumer culture as an analytical construct and subject it to a critical examination. In this chapter, such a construct is embodied in the notion of a *core*, which is as much a state of mind as it is a physical reality. We are not so much concerned here with the actual size of the core as with its dominant position in the cultural ethos of Orange County. Unlike other urban

communities that have a core that represents a relatively stable component (usually called the establishment), Orange County does not have a
core with an established past on which to base its dominant position. The
core consists instead of recently formed groups—entrepreneurs of one
sort or another, political leaders, media personalities, professionals, and
educators—or, to use the terminology of L. Althusser (1971), the ideological apparatuses. The core may even consist of people who are not
privileged by current economic standards but who are striving to attain
higher standards. The possibility of doing so is the essence of the settlement culture. By understanding the core one eventually makes sense of
the periphery.

THE EFFECTS OF POSTSUBURBAN TRANSFORMATION
ON CONSUMER PATTERNS

Consumer patterns change for both micro and macro reasons. At the
micro level, changes are attributable to individual consumer's changing
tastes. At the macro level, such changes occur because of structural shifts
in the environment. The second type of change has characterized Orange
County's growth since 1975. In the remainder of this chapter, I focus on
macro-level shifts and draw implications for micro-level behavior.

Since World War II the region has been transformed from a rural
community of farm towns into a postsuburban metropolis (see Chapter
1). It has become cosmopolitan in its links to an international economy
and also in consumer tastes. (For example, the new performing arts
center now hosts world-class performers.) The region's commerce has
shifted from locally owned downtown stores to shopping malls that house
national chain stores selling international brands. The diversity of the
population is itself a major source of complexity in the consumption
system. Underlying these changes are two distinct movements: urbanized
consumerism and information capitalism. At present, these two seem to
be developing in a parallel fashion and do not seem to be closely related.
Yet, they are fundamental to our understanding of the changes taking
place in Orange County.

Urbanized Consumerism

The nature of Orange County's urbanization is fully explored by other
contributors to this book. Of particular interest is M. Gottdiener and
George Kephart's (Chapter 2) description of urbanization in Orange
County as an example of deconcentration. To these authors, deconcentration is the formation of a settlement space that is "polynucleated, functionally dispersed, culturally fragmented, yet hierarchically organized."

What are the consumption implications of deconcentration? At the theoretical level, this question reflects the current debate on postmodernism (Venkatesh 1989). A development of postmodern culture that has engaged the attention of many social theorists is the juxtaposition of opposites and the creation of seemingly incompatible objects and images for consumption. To quote Elizabeth Wilson (1988), "Postmodernism refuses to privilege any one perspective and recognizes only difference, never inequality, only fragments, never conflict." In such an environment, the consumer has infinite options, but the options remain unconnected (Firat 1989). The objects of consumption are no longer embedded in a centrally identifiable part of human life but exist in free-floating symbolic environments filled with contradictions and juxtapositions. The individual is therefore a consumer of symbols rather than objects. The symbols are made available through a complex interaction of high-technology production and sociospatial configuration. The forces behind deconcentration in modern urbanized societies, such as Orange County, are the same forces that create the symbolic environments of consumption.

At the practical level, deconcentration means that multiple-consumption environments can be designed to create multiple-consumption experiences. The consumption experiences are, in turn, located in a wide assortment of activities: shopping, dining, entertainment, leisure, and recreation. Deconcentration also means that people lead fragmented lives while struggling to create new networks and establish new roots. Family structures assume new forms to permit the delicate balancing of work life and home life within a social space that remains in a state of continuous flux.

Let us look at two examples of deconcentration that affect consumerism in Orange County: (1) the emerging shopping environments and the ubiquity of consumerism and (2) the changing consumption patterns caused by structural shifts in family patterns. The first example dramatizes the semiotics of consumption in a fast-paced economy. The second example provides insights into the realities of daily life in a complex, financially demanding economy.

Orange County is dotted with neighborhood shopping centers, shopping malls, swap meets, and consumer warehouses (for example, the Price Club), each of which plays a different role in the postsuburban consumer marketplace. Neighborhood shopping centers are traditional outlets for marketing products and services, and they are functional shopping areas in that they do not carry any special symbolic meaning, and the shopping activity in them tends to be quite straightforward.

The shopping malls, however, are not only centers of shopping in the conventional sense but highly organized social spaces for entertainment, interaction, and other types of consumer excitement. Some of them (for example, South Coast Plaza and Fashion Island) have acquired a post-modern theatrical character by engaging in relentless marketing activism. A perfect example of a store that embodies such theatricality is Nord-strom's (at the South Coast Plaza), which is both a shopping complex and a fantasy land. It is not uncommon for a shopper at this store to try on a pair of Italian shoes while a live pianist gives a rendition of Chopin. Piped-in music has been replaced by something more authentic, and such a juxtaposition of opposites—high art and mundane consumption—has become a matter-of-fact event. Nordstrom's is not the only instance of a public commercial space in which, for the modernist, the "sacred" and the "profane" meet, but it typifies a trend in this postsuburban culture. Par-ticipation in the shopping mall is not cost free. Although many customers may visit the malls for fun and entertainment, the shops could not survive without substantial sales. The stores need customers to spend money, which they encourage through an elaborate credit system. A high per-centage of shopping-mall revenues are not cash-based; in fact, Orange County residents possess an average of 3.31 department-store credit cards.[5]

In contrast to the shopping malls, Orange County also has swap meets and consumer warehouses. These are alternatives to both the manufac-tured fantasy of the shopping malls and the unstimulating neighborhood shopping centers. Swap meets allow buyers and sellers to interact at a personal level so that shopping is not an alienated activity. Buyers are able to deal with sellers on their own terms, without necessarily feeling power-less in the economic exchange. Consumer warehouses are mega-shopping spaces and highly efficient assembly-line operations. Their main attrac-tion is low prices, possibly the lowest prices one can obtain in the local market. Their clientele includes middle-income to low-income families.

On the face of it, both swap meets and consumer warehouses are uncomplicated economies attempting to survive in the face of shopping-mall capitalism. This picture is only partially true because both enter-prises are, in reality, highly organized ventures designed to create myths of their own. Swap meets supposedly symbolize counterculture move-ments. The bazaar look and the disorganization give them the appear-ance of a medieval marketplace. Behind this seeming spontaneity, how-ever, one finds that they are highly dependent on the local political machinery for their survival. Similarly, consumer warehouses provide their own symbols through giant storage spaces and membership privi-leges. Giant storage spaces give the impression that the consumer has abundance at his or her fingertips, while the idea of exclusive member-ship privileges is as much a part of the Price Club as it is of American Express.

Some important themes emerge from the consumer environment in Orange County. The alternatives offered to the consumer are not simple shopping choices but experiences that elevate the ordinary consumer to a new state as metaconsumer (Firat 1989). A metaconsumer is not only a consumer of products and symbols but also an active participant in the shopping spectacle. The participating individual is thus both the consumer and the consumed. By the same token, the shopping mall is not merely an economic space where exchanges take place but a symbolic social space for everyone to come alive in. Stretching a bit, we might even say that the shopping environment becomes a metaphor for other aspects of life in Orange County. The shopping-mall spectacle is pervasive; it can be seen in offices, health spas, restaurants, fast-food places, universities, and religious establishments. A few examples should suffice to illustrate the point.

Orange County has witnessed a phenomenal growth in ethnic restaurants in the past ten years. There are basically two kinds of ethnic restaurants: those that serve ethnic immigrants and those that cater to upscale consumers. The first variety is a natural result of the arrival of new immigrant groups. The second type of restaurant, however, is transforming Orange County in a major way. The ethnic restaurants that cater to the nonethnics are part of a national gourmet movement that was virtually nonexistent in Orange County in the 1970s. This phenomenon is the result of the postsuburbanization and internationalization of Orange County's consumer culture. It is not merely that people are after delicious food, which they certainly are, but that they are after delicious life-styles, of which food is just a manifestation. Eating exotic foods is a simulated adventure in a theatrical society. Eating different types of food in different settings—by the ocean, on a rooftop, or in an elegant shopping-mall garden—adds flavor to choice. There are also places in Orange County where one can eat foods from different nations under one roof. Gone are the days when Orange Countians would go to Los Angeles for a special meal. It is almost unfashionable, besides being a matter of pride, for a resident of Orange County to boast of a trip to Los Angeles for a dinner engagement. In these days of much-heralded choice within the county (not to mention the freeway traffic), it may even sound a bit foolish.

A second example of the shopping spectacle as metaphor lies in the religious arena. The Crystal Cathedral in Anaheim is an important case in point. Its proximity to Disneyland may not be altogether coincidental. As one enters the grounds, one can see the bold architecture of a religious palace that boasts a thousand windows and an aviary inside. The combination of religious magnificence and material grandeur resembles Nordstrom's mix of high culture with consumerism. In their own way, both the

Crystal Cathedral and Nordstrom's are examples of the postmodern sub-
version of reality.

In addition to shopping environments, the effects of deconcentration
on consumerism can be seen by examining shifting family patterns. A
major social and economic development has been the revolution caused by
the entry of women into the labor force. This process has not only altered
the production side of the economy but, more significantly, has shifted
consumption into new directions. Historically, most marketing efforts of
consumer-product companies were directed toward single-income households in which women acted in the traditional wife/mother roles while men
were the breadwinners. The ethos of consumption was clearly defined by
traditional values. The new work patterns of women, however, have
resulted in a number of significant changes.

An overall change in life-styles is borne out by studies showing that
although the earnings of women working part-time constitute only 25
percent of their families' total income, the earnings of women working
full-time account for about 40 percent (Department of Commerce 1987,
70). Because many married women are working full-time today, the impact
of dual-income families has been quite substantial. As a result, 26 percent
of dual-income families are now classified as upper class, compared with
only 8 percent of single-income families (Bloom 1987). A second development is that the average working woman now spends nine hours per day
on her job if one includes the commute back and forth (Townsend 1985).
These two developments—rising discretionary incomes and increased
hours spent on work-related activities—have had significant impacts on
standards of living, shopping habits, types of products and services consumed, the use and quality of family time, and child rearing.

The increasing number of women in the labor force has altered the
way that families shop for food and dine out. "About 37 percent of
supermarket spending is accounted for by those [families] in which both
husband and wife work," observes F. Linden (1985), "compared with 31
percent ten years ago [in 1975]." There has been a decline in the amount
of unprocessed foods consumed at home and an increase in frozen and
prepared foods and snacks (McLaughlin and German 1985). Families
with working wives spend more than one-third of the family food budget
in restaurants; whereas in households with a nonworking wife, only one-
quarter of a family's food budget goes toward dining out (McLaughlin
and German 1985).

Women's employment has made a difference in Americans' ability to
purchase homes. Beginning in the mid-1970s, sharply rising housing
prices and mortgage interest rates, coupled with stagnant family incomes,
threatened to strike at the heart of the American dream of home ownership. But while the housing-affordability crisis was beginning to emerge,

home ownership was increasing among young married couples. To investigate this paradox, D. Myers (1985) conducted a study using Housing and Urban Development Annual Housing Survey Data from 1974 through 1980. He found that, among couples in which the wife was twenty-five to thirty years old, wives' earnings became an increasingly important factor in financing home ownership.[6]

Although most of these trends are national in character, the current developments in Orange County substantiate these trends. From a series of articles published in the *Orange County Register* from 1987 through 1989, the following picture emerges.[7] Fifty-eight percent of the women with children in Orange County are in the labor force, compared with 60 percent nationally. This figure declines to 42 percent for married women with children under three years old. The participation rate of single women with children in the labor force is slightly higher than for married women with children, regardless of the age of the dependent children. Within the county, childbearing patterns underwent considerable changes during the ten-year period following 1976. The average age of Orange County mothers, which was 25.3 years in 1976, rose to 26.9 years in 1986. The percentage of mothers who are thirty years old or older increased dramatically, from 20 percent in 1976 to 30.8 percent in 1986. The significance of these changes is as much sociological as economic. The increasing importance of careers for women explains some of these shifts. From an economic standpoint, the cost of raising a child in Orange County must be one of the highest in the country, given the high cost of both housing and services. Women seem to be caught between the opportunities in and financial rewards of the workplace and the pleasures and obligations of home life. A number of women successfully manage both worlds. Others prefer not to juggle the two and make choices to fit their needs. These choices range from not having children at all to giving up their jobs (see Chapter 7).

The consumption consequences of women's choices regarding their work and home lives are quite profound. The economic independence of women, in some cases gradually approaching equality with men, gives them the ability to make decisions regarding household products and services without having to base these decisions solely on the income of their husbands. Women are no longer tied to their home lives as in the past and stay in marriage more by choice than by social dictate. Freedom in the social arena has transferred to the marketplace, which has recognized the wisdom of treating women not as suburban housewives but as postsuburban consumers.

This newly gained status of women has another side to it, however, that deserves some discussion. Women simply do not have the unstructured time that they once had. The increasing commitment to paid employment and the inability to maintain control over home life compel them to surrender their consumption decisions to outside market forces, much the same way that families have looked to schools for providing many services. Within the family itself, a great deal of responsibility for making decisions about products and services is shifting to children. Children are no longer considered consumers at an early or primitive stage of an evolutionary process but as independent agents playing a major role in the consumption process. A large part of advertising these days is directed toward the young consumer as the decision maker.

The structural shifts in family organization are themselves a postmodern development with all its contradictions and juxtapositions. Family life is fragmented but not necessarily fractured. Women are financially independent but at the same time subject to a system that places considerable demands on their time. In most respects, this is still a man's world, but men are unable to respond to the changes and remain confused in the process. The parent is now both the consumer and the consumed. The child is simultaneously an adolescent and an adult.

Information Capitalism

Orange County watchers generally agree that the county is as good an example of an information society as any other region in the United States. Kling and Turner (Chapter 4) have tested this claim by analyzing the employment patterns in the information sector. Following T. Luke and S. K. White (1985), they use the term *information capitalism* to describe the entry of capitalism into a new phase in which information and cybernetic knowledge become factors of production for capitalistic control.[8] In describing information-oriented economies, it is common to use such labels as *information worker* or *knowledge producer* to designate people engaged directly or indirectly in information-processing activities in the production sector. Such clearly identifiable analytical categories, however, are not available for configuring the information orientation of the consumption sector. The term *information consumer* sounds awkward at best. The lack of terminology does not mean that the concept of the information society has no implications for the consumption sector, however. Nor does it mean that there is no discussion of the role of new technologies in the lives of ordinary citizens—as is evident from writings on new consumer-oriented technologies such as electronic media, home computers, and videotext (Compaine 1981, Buzzell 1985, Rogers 1986, Venkatesh and Vitalari 1986). These and other writings characterize contemporary societies as shifting to both an information orientation and a service orientation. In this section, our discussion is centered primarily around the information orientation of the consumer economy of Orange County as it pertains to specific technologies and modes of information.

Several technologies compete in the marketplace for public attention. Predictions have been made that in the early 1990s American households will use a wealth of these new technologies: home computers, two-way cable and viewdata systems, electronic mail services, facsimile machines, microprocessors, direct-to-home satellite broadcasting equipment, on-line data banks, voice synthesis and recognition devices, and more. Some of these technologies are already in wide use, and others are being test-marketed. Although predictions of an information revolution were made during the early 1980s, there is now more caution and realism in assessing the impact of these technologies on the consumption sector.

Some rough estimates are available regarding the consumer ownership levels of new technologies in Orange County.[9] Eleven percent of the households use computers in the home, a rate of ownership lower than for VCRs (55 percent), telephone answering machines (18.5 percent), and programmed home-control systems (16.7 percent), but higher than for cordless telephones (4 percent) and automobile telephones (2 percent). (The ownership figures for traditional household technologies such as refrigerators, telephones, and automobiles range from 85 to 95 percent.) These figures suggest that, within the consumption sector, one cannot say that the current developments are a computer revolution as much as that they are a rite of passage into the information economy.

The capabilities of computer technology and the opportunities it presents for industrial expansion have been widely discussed since the 1960s in the social science literature. In particular, the social impact of computers on large organizations is the subject of ongoing research at the University of California at Irvine (King and Kraemer 1985, Danziger and Kraemer 1986, Kling 1987). The adoption of information technology has been seen as increasing the production efficiency of organizations, while its impact on the quality of work life is more complex and not univalent.

Studies of the impact of computer technology on individuals and households extend these lines of research. These inquiries can be broken down into two separate categories. First, there is a question of how consumers utilize computer and communication technologies in their personal lives, such as using home computers and telecommunications systems for work, social interaction, or entertainment. The second area to be explored is the effects of individuals' and households' dealings with businesses and public agencies that are becoming increasingly computerized. Both kinds of interactions with computer systems have strong implications for the emerging social order based on new technologies.

It seems clear that the impacts of information technologies on individuals and households are being felt at two levels, indirect and direct. At the indirect level computerization minimizes consumers' face-to-face contact with technological complexities but nevertheless has an impact on their lives. Examples are computerized systems in automobiles, microwave ovens, audio/video machines, and other similar household products. At the direct level we have technologies such as microcomputers, which require direct manipulation by the user. At the indirect level, users do not have to acquire special skills to operate the technology. At the direct level, effective use of the technology requires a level of training that only a segment of the population can claim to have.

In my previous research, I found that a growing number of people were using computers at home to do job-related work (Venkatesh and Vitalari 1989). This finding is significant because industrial societies segregate work life and domestic life. If computers enable or encourage people to bring work home, we will be faced with a technology that fundamentally blurs the two spheres of activity. With an increasing number of women in the labor force, there is a strong incentive for some people to work at home if possible. The primary impact of computers and related telecommunication technologies at home may lie in helping people integrate work life with family life, rather than separating the two. This integration is unlikely to be either smooth or seamless, in part because a significant portion of the family's disposable income has to be allocated to the purchase of computers. Computer systems are capital intensive, and when they cost several thousand dollars with peripherals, they are the most expensive items in the family budget after homes and automobiles. The costs increase even further when families acquire several computers to satisfy the needs of different family members. However, if computers become integrated into the social life of the family as automobiles have been, people will be more likely than they now are to accept them and their cost.

This new wave of technologies has the potential to transform home and work environments. Little over half a century ago a similar change was heralded, resulting in the transformation of the American home into what it is today. The modern home may be described as the product of this electromechanical revolution. The changes became so much a part of our lives that they are now taken for granted. The overwhelming presence of a wide range of household appliances in the average American home is a testimony to the successful implementation of the precomputer technology. Like the electromechanical revolution of the past, information technologies have the potential to cause a major social transformation by the end of this century. At present, the impact of these technologies is not visible because of the seemingly unconnected ways in which they are diffusing across society. A natural question in this regard is, how prepared are average citizens to survive and live meaningfully in this emerging technological milieu?

By virtue of their membership in a computerized society, individuals must become increasingly familiar with the use of technologically advanced devices in their daily lives. We know that consumers living in modern societies should be able to read such materials as product manuals, insurance policies, service contracts, and rental agreements. However, consumers' ability to understand the complexities of modern technology is impeded by low levels of human contact and assistance in using it. As services become computerized and knowledge sources become computer-based, consumers will face an increased challenge in dealing with the technologically intensive self-services, such as automated teller machines and ticket dispensers. To do well in this environment, consumers will need to be literate technologically. Technological illiteracy is not an unfounded concern. The average high school student in Orange County reads at the eighth-grade level; his or her skills are sufficient to read comic books and prepare TV dinners—hardly adequate to survive in a computerized society (Lynn 1986).

We now turn to a final way in which information capitalism affects consumerism in Orange County.[10] We have noted that Orange County represents an advanced state of consumer culture. What sustains that consumer culture is an elaborate credit system maintained by a rigorous application of information technologies. The role of information capitalism is quite critical in this context.

To use an engineering metaphor, credit is the fuel that drives the engine of the consumer economy. Many articles have commented on the role of credit in the consumer economy at both national and local levels (Slater 1987, Bloom and Steen 1987, Bloyd 1989, Teebom 1987). The tone of the articles ranges from guarded optimism to genuine concern. There is optimism because credit translates into buying power and energizes the economy through consumer spending. Concern about credit arises because of the growing number of consumers carrying unmanageable debts.

Statistics show that consumer credit is growing at an astounding rate. Generally speaking, consumer credit takes three forms: home mortgages, automobile loans, and plastic money (credit cards). In 1945 the consumer installment debt of the average American family was 2 percent of its annual income. By 1985 it had risen to 18 percent (Bloom and Steen 1987). According to C. Slater (1987), home mortgages are the largest form of household borrowing, with mortgage payments accounting for about 50 percent of the total household debt, followed by auto payments (20 percent) and credit cards (5 percent). The current trend seems to indicate rapid growth in credit-card purchases. When consumers reach a point where they depend on credit cards for their daily survival, the situation becomes pathological. Orange County has developed the reputation of being one of the highest credit-dependent regions in the country

(Teebom 1987). As S. Bloyd (1989) notes, "Orange County households with incomes of more than $15,000 a year receive an average of four credit card solicitations a month—three times the national average." A similar view is expressed by Teebom (1987):

> The credit system in Orange County is growing. Orange County on average has much higher credit balances than the national average. At a time of economic downturn, this high credit situation can have serious consequences. Not only are there more credit purchases and credit use based on credit cards, because the home in Orange County is appraised at a very high price, consumers are able to borrow more. Home equity loans are at an all-time high. (p. 17)

The link between this credit culture and information capitalism comes about in the following way. Consumers require financial power to participate effectively in the economy, although everyone can fantasize about acquiring products, services, and life-styles that are well beyond their means. Financial power is usually exercised through the acquisition of goods and the ability to access services. A common method of exercising this power is through participation in the credit system. Credit converts individuals into consumers by expanding their purchasing power. Additional purchasing power is created simply by binding the consumers into the credit system. When consumers enter the credit system, they are indexed and continually recertified. If they fail to discharge their obligations in a timely manner, they can be easily removed from the system. Although this sort of binding is not new, the process can occur with stunning swiftness in a highly organized information-monitoring environment. It is therefore not surprising that the credit culture is intimately linked to information capitalism.

In Orange County, as in the rest of the country, we are witnessing the instant creation of credit histories for individuals and the simultaneous exercise of control over consumers. Ironically, in this process, a person's credit rating, which should be an extremely private piece of information, becomes a matter of official record through a highly organized and efficient system of information processing. The technology of the credit culture is so total that there seems to be no escape from it—that is, not to have credit can be as problematical as having credit.[11] Without credit, the individual cannot participate in the consumer economy; with credit, he or she cannot escape it.

In sum, in rapidly changing, technologically oriented regions like Orange County, the credit system plays a critical role in organizing the consumption activities of individuals through a sophisticated information apparatus. To understand the full ramifications of the system, it is important to go beyond its economic aspects and examine the sociological implications. The system is designed, ostensibly, to create a social order in which everyone can participate as consumers. But this noble ideal dissipates quickly once the technological apparatus that serves information capitalism takes over, raising an important question regarding the relationship between the system and the individual—who serves whom?

CONCLUSIONS

Orange County has emerged as an important economic region in the nation as it has become a highly information-oriented, postsuburban society, with all the strains of such transformation. An important aspect of this transformation is its rapid expansion as a consumer economy. My attitude toward this phenomenon has been a negative one, for I see a danger in romanticizing the transformation of Orange County. The county's growth and development are not merely consumer-oriented; they have imposed consumerism on virtually every aspect of life. Thus I have likened life in Orange County to an endless spectacle made more intense by new technologies of control—the technologies of information and communication. I see the shopping environment both as a privileged reality and as a metaphor for life in general. It is not entirely clear, but there is some indication that the county is in fact becoming two counties, and the dichotomy splits in many ways—North County and South County, postmodern and nonpostmodern, or the core and the periphery.

I have focused on the dominant modes of consumption, that is, the consumption patterns of the core, because they represent more fully than those of the periphery the postsuburban transformation of Orange County. A sequel to this analysis should include the periphery as well, as a means of fully understanding the relationship between the two spheres. Some preliminary thoughts on this relationship seem to be in order here. The existence of a core and a periphery suggests a bias in the products and services that are marketed. The core, being more affluent and sophisticated in its tastes, is likely to respond to highly differentiated products and services. To quote N. Dholakia and A. Fuat Firat (1987):

> Products that are not differentiated toward elite consumption do not receive marketing support. For all its glamour and sophistication, marketing has little to offer for basic products like staple, nutritious foods or simple, protective clothing. . . . Marketing strategies are extremely difficult to devise for basic social needs like nutrition, substance abuse prevention, exercise, automobile safety or literacy. These are basic, undifferentiated, mass, social needs [which marketing does not find it profitable to exploit].

As Orange County moves into the next century, these issues will become extremely important and need to be addressed.

NOTES

Acknowledgments: Without the encouragement and assistance of Rob Kling and Spencer Olin, this chapter would not have materialized. I thank them sincerely for their support and advice.

1. Hirschman (1985) analyzes the structural factors that contribute to the continuities in consumption patterns. Besides the economic costs associated with change, they include subcultural or ethnic norms and resistance to the dominant patterns.

2. N. Welgarz, "Orange County Car Dealership Rolls Ahead," *Orange County Register,* 8 Dec. 1987.

3. "Home Sales Decline: Interest Rates Cited," *Los Angeles Times,* 16 Aug. 1989.

4. Gary A. Warner, "People Back Slow Growth, Dream of Detached Home," *Orange County Register,* Metro section, 11 Dec. 1987.

5. *Shopping Profile 1989* (the *Orange County Register*'s annual survey of consumer shopping).

6. Myers also draws policy conclusions from his studies. National policies aimed at encouraging homeownership, he observes, should be linked with policies for improving the welfare of working women.

7. "Career and Children," 31 Dec. 1987; "Moms Bring Home the Bacon," 19 Dec. 1987; "Lack of Time Is the Tie That Binds Busy Moms," 20 June 1989; "Parenting: Choosing to Stay Home," 21 Jan. 1989. (These references are selective, not exhaustive.)

8. For a more recent discussion of information capitalism, see T. Morris-Suzuki (1988).

9. These estimates are compiled from different sources; specifically, they are based on the *Los Angeles Times*'s *Marketing Research Reports* and the *Orange County Register*'s *Shopping Profile* for 1985 to 1989.

10. Parts of the discussion in this section were inspired by the writings of Michel Foucault, to which I was exposed in a graduate seminar at the University of California at Berkeley taught by Paul Rabinow during 1988–89. The notion that the credit system can be used to expand the financial power of individuals and to validate them as consumers is a logical application of the Foucauldian analysis of culture and power.

11. To quote Bloyd (1989, 123), "Credit cards are so much a part of today's financial world that you literally can't get around without one. You will find it difficult to rent a car, get a hotel room, buy theatre tickets, join a video tape rental club or cash a check without a valid piece of plastic in your hand. Even libraries ask you to leave your driver's license or credit card as security for the temporary checkout of some items."

REFERENCES

Althusser, L. 1971. "Ideology and Ideological State Apparatuses." In *Lenin and Philosophy,* trans. Ben Brewster, 127–86. New York: Monthly Review Press.

Baudrillard, J. 1981. *For a Critique of Political Economy of the Sign.* St. Louis: Telos Press.

Bloom, D. E. 1987. "Women at Work." *American Demographics* 9(9):25–30.

Bloom, D. E., and T. P. Steen. 1987. "Living on Credit." *American Demographics* 9(10):22–29.

Bloyd, S. 1989. "Credit Overload." *Orange Coast* 15(8):122–33.

Buzzell, R. 1985. *Marketing in an Electronic Age*. Boston: Harvard Business School Press.

Compaine, B. 1981. "Shifting Boundaries in the Information Market Place." *Journal of Communication* 13(1):132–42.

Danziger, J., and K. L. Kraemer. 1986. *People and Computers: The Impacts of Computers on End-Users in Organizations*. New York: Columbia University Press.

Department of Commerce. 1987. "Male-Female Differences in Work Experience, Occupation and Earnings." *Household Economic Studies Series*, no. 10. Washington.

Dholakia, N., and A. Fuat Firat. 1987. "Marketing and Class Interest: Can the Twain Separate?" Paper presented at the American Marketing Association Theory Conference, San Antonio, Tex., February.

Douglas, M., and B. Isherwood. 1978. *The World of Goods: Toward an Anthropology of Consumption*. New York: Norton.

Ewen, S. 1976. *Captains of Consciousness*. New York: McGraw-Hill.

Ewen, S., and E. Ewen. 1987. *Channels of Desire*. New York: McGraw-Hill.

Firat, A. Fuat. 1989. "Post-modern Culture, Marketing and the Consumer." Paper presented at the Marketing Meaning Conference, Indianapolis, July.

Fox, R. W., and T. J. Lears, eds. 1983. *The Culture of Consumption: Critical Essays in American History, 1880–1980*. New York: Pantheon.

Hirschman, E. 1985. "Primitive Aspects of Consumption in the Post-industrial Age." Paper presented at the Association for Consumer Research meeting, Las Vegas, October.

King, J. L., and K. L. Kraemer. 1985. *The Dynamics of Computing*. New York: Columbia University Press.

Kling, R. 1987. "Defining the Boundaries of Computing across Complex Organizations." In *Critical Issues in Information Systems Research*, ed. R. Boland and R. Hirschheim. New York: Wiley.

Leiss, W. 1976. *The Limits to Satisfaction*. Toronto: University of Toronto Press.

Linden, F. 1985. "Supermarket Shoppers." *American Demographics* 7(8):4.

Luke, T., and S. K. White. 1985. "Critical Theory, the Informational Revolution, and an Ecological Path to Modernity." In *Critical Theory and Public Life*, ed. John Forster, 22–53. Cambridge, Mass.: MIT Press.

Lynn, D. 1986. "400,000 People in Orange County Cannot Read This: How Literacy Affects You." *Orange Coast* 10(11):26–35.

McLaughlin, E. W., and G. A. German. 1985. "Supermarketing Success." *American Demographics* 7(8):34.

Miller, D. 1987. *Material Culture and Mass Consumption*. New York: Blackwell.

Morris-Suzuki, T. 1988. *Beyond Computopia*. London: Kegan Paul.

Myers, D. 1985. "The American Dream." *Social Science Quarterly* 66(2):312–29.

Rogers, E. M. 1986. *Communication Technology: The New Media in Society*. New York: Free Press.

Slater, C. 1987. "The Pause That Refreshes." *American Demographics* 9(5):4–6.

Southern California Association of Governments. 1984. *Profile of an Economic Transition: A Status Report on the Southern California Economy.* Los Angeles.

"Survey of Buying Power." 1987. *Sales and Marketing Management* 139(10):B23–27.

Teebom, L. 1987. "Credit Happy Consumers Are Maxed-Out." *Orange County Business Journal* 10(20):17.

Townsend, B. 1985. "Working Women." *American Demographics* 7(1):6–7.

Veblen, T. 1925. *The Theory of the Leisure Class.* London: Allen & Unwin.

Venkatesh, A. 1989. "Modernity and Postmodernity: A Synthesis or Antithesis?" Paper presented at the American Marketing Association Theory Conference, St. Petersburg, Fla., February.

Venkatesh, A., and N. P. Vitalari. 1986. "Computing Technology for the Home: Product Strategies for the Next Generation." *Journal of Product Innovation and Management* 3:171–86.

———. 1989. *A Longitudinal Analysis of Computing in the Home.* Irvine: Public Policy Research Organization, University of California.

Wilson, E. 1989. *Hallucinations: Life in the Post-modern City.* London: Hutchinson.

1. Modestly dressed young girls represent the original American colonies on this 1908 Fourth of July float. (Courtesy of the Huntington Beach Historical Society)

2. As suggested by this 1909 parade entry, ethnic minorities have often been limited to stereotyped roles in Orange County's public ceremonies. (Courtesy of the City of Huntington Beach Public Information Office)

3. By the 1950s, women's public participation in Independence Day activities centered on the annual beauty contest. In this 1949 photograph, William Gallienne, organizer of the Fourth of July festivities, poses with two female participants. (Courtesy of the Huntington Beach Historical Society)

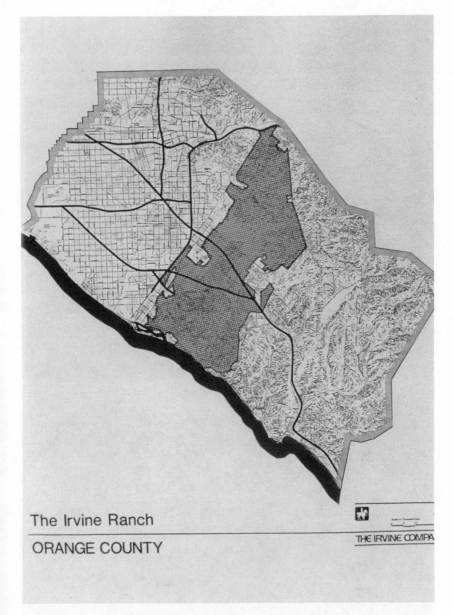

The Irvine Ranch

ORANGE COUNTY

THE IRVINE COMPA

4. Operated primarily as a sheep ranch in the late nineteenth century and a diversified agricultural business in the early twentieth century, the property of the Irvine Company developed after World War II into a postsuburban order consisting of residential communities, commercial facilities, and industrial parks. This map shows the vast extent of the company's property in 1970, covering nearly a fifth of Orange County. (Courtesy of the Irvine Company)

5. The urban development of the Irvine Ranch in the 1960s owed much to the ideas and energy of the architect William L. Pereira, shown here in 1964. Pereira introduced the concept of the self-contained community in his plan for the campus of the University of California at Irvine and played a major role in drafting a master plan for the southern part of the ranch. (Courtesy of Johnson Fain and Pereira Associates)

6. Former orange groves and agricultural land east of the Santa Ana freeway (1965) in what is now the city of Irvine, incorporated in 1971. (Courtesy of Special Collections, Main Library, University of California at Irvine)

7. The farmland, rolling hills, and attractive coastal landscape of southern Orange County underwent rapid and extensive suburbanization in the 1960s and 1970s. This aerial photograph shows exclusive housing and new business facilities (about 1970) on a section of the Irvine Ranch near two major freeways. (Courtesy of the Sherman Library, Corona del Mar)

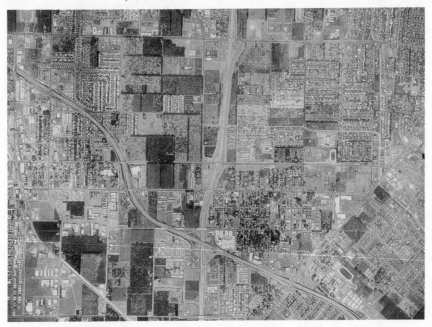

8. Interchange of the Santa Ana freeway and the Costa Mesa freeway (1965), with relatively sparse commercial, industrial, and residential development in Santa Ana and Tustin. (Courtesy of Special Collections, Main Library, University of California at Irvine)

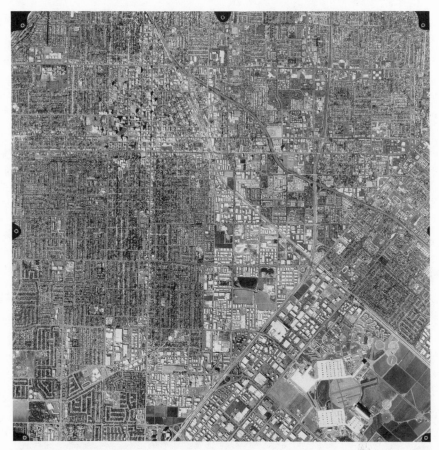

9. Interchange of the Santa Ana freeway and the Costa Mesa freeway (1988), with extensive commercial, industrial, and residential development in Santa Ana and Tustin. The County Civic Center is in the upper left and the Marine Helicopter Facility in the lower right. (Courtesy of Air Photo Services, Santa Ana, California)

10. The planned community of Mission Viejo (1988) in the southern portion of Orange County. (Courtesy of Air Photo Services, Santa Ana, California)

11. Between Corona del Mar and Laguna Beach stretches one of the last undeveloped portions of oceanfront land in southern California, the site of a political struggle between its owner, the Irvine Company, and environmental activists. The Irvine Company plans to build 2,600 dwellings, three hotels, and two golf courses on this 9,482-acre site. Seventy-six percent of the land will remain open space. (Courtesy of Air Photo Services, Santa Ana, California)

12. In the spring of 1985, more than five hundred Hispanic tenants involved in the citywide rent strike marched through the streets and patios of this large apartment complex on Minnie Street in Santa Ana to protest pressures exerted against strikers by the apartment owners. (Courtesy of the *Orange County Register*; photographer Chris Carlson)

13. Leaders of Orange County's Slow Growth campaign carry a casket bearing initiative petitions into the Santa Ana office of the County Registrar of Voters, February 1988. (Copyright, 1990, *Los Angeles Times*. Reprinted by permission. Photographer Gail Fisher)

14. Freeway scene of a field with an Irvine Spectrum sign at right. Near two major freeways, Irvine Spectrum is the site of a huge emerging industrial park that emphasizes the white-collar activities of high-tech manufacturing firms, such as engineering design, software development, accounting, and marketing. Agricultural land is being rapidly converted to support Orange County's information economy. Freeway proximity is critical for the success of regional centers—whether industrial centers or shopping centers. The specialized regional centers lend excitement to Orange County even though they also fragment ways of life and make the population extremely dependent on cars and high-capacity freeways. (Rob Kling)

15. Parking lots and stores of Tustin Marketplace, with light towers on far right. This large shopping center specializing in household goods illustrates the post-suburban trend of specialized retail malls. A general regional shopping center usually includes restaurants, movie theaters, and a wider variety of stores. The specialized shopping centers do not supplant, but rather complement, the general regional malls. (Rob Kling)

16. Irvine Auto Center—an immense shopping center specializing in the sale of cars and related services, such as car parts and repairs—illustrates specialized spatial organization. A commercial neighborhood about a mile away specializes in the sale of furniture and household fixtures (such as carpets, doors, and windows). More general shopping centers are one to two miles away. (Rob Kling)

17. House behind walls, park in foreground. A walled residential neighborhood with enclosed houses and a little-used park illustrates how private activities often take precedence over public life. The stone walls without a gate make the privacy "chosen" by the residents very inflexible. (Rob Kling)

18. Wide array of office buildings behind hilly pastureland. Orange County's emerging skyline in the Irvine–South Coast metro area contrasts with the Irvine Company's rural pastureland, which it is steadily converting to residential and commercial uses. (The lone white cow in the front center of the picture is part of a herd that is behind a hill off to the right of the photograph.) Orange County's information economy, embodied in office workers who inhabit the new multistory buildings, emerges as the rural economy passes into history. (Rob Kling)

SIX

Public Ceremony in a Private Culture: Orange County Celebrates the Fourth of July

Debra Gold Hansen and Mary P. Ryan

The chapters in this book are riddled with the twin themes of deconcentration and privatization, intersecting and reinforcing each other to
make social life in Orange County seem bereft of moorings in shared
central spaces. The flow of private automobiles through the net of freeways seems both a basic infrastructure and a fitting metaphor for social
life in postsuburbia. To M. Gottdiener and George Kephart (Chapter 2)
Orange County is the harbinger of a new stage in urban history, one in
which the bonded and centered city is replaced by a "polynucleated,
functionally dispersed, culturally fragmented" form of settlement. This
spatial pattern is echoed in politics, where civic authority is dispersed
throughout twenty-eight municipalities, and, according to Spencer Olin
(Chapter 8), power concentrates in secluded corporate boardrooms in
and outside the county. Even moments of social resistance, as described by
Lisbeth Haas (Chapter 9), are decentered—staged in detached neighborhoods by separate ethnic groups. Similarly, the issue that inspired mass
support in the postsuburban county, the taxpayer revolt described by
William Gayk (Chapter 10), congealed collective action around the private interests of homeowners. Even families, the narrowest and most
privatized of social groups, are becoming decentered, as the county's
children, according to Mark Poster (Chapter 7), are dispersed to multiple
locations for their primary socialization.

The decentralization and privatization endemic to postsuburban society fractures the local basis for generating a common culture. The
absence of a central political jurisdiction in which to deliberate about the
common good, combined with the paucity of sustained social connections
between residents, handicaps Orange Countians in their attempts to
create a local identity, common belief system, and home-grown values.

Consequently, students of Orange County are hard-pressed to breathe a spirit of self-generated local culture in these postsuburban communities.

This chapter employs anthropological theory and historical method to decipher the cultural meanings that Orange Countians attach to their place of shared residence with its decentralized social and political life. The strategy is to focus on those occasions set aside for common festivity and public ceremony, which, anthropologists tell us, can provide a capsule summary of a culture. As one theorist puts it, ceremony fulfills a society's need to say, "'Look, this is how things should be, this is the proper, ideal pattern of social life.' It gives to the people concerned an image of a harmonious, well-ordered, undisturbed social universe."[1]

This kind of centering cultural performance, which would seem especially necessary in postsuburban settlements, can provide us with a window through which to examine the belief system of the scattered residents of Orange County. Therefore, we have searched out historical records of local public holidays and analyzed reports on public ceremonies for evidence of the peculiar values that residents held in common. As it turns out, public ceremonies in Orange County were characteristically infrequent in number, narrow in function, confined in space, and subdued in mood. They were tightly organized and highly staged affairs, largely the creations of bureaucrats and businesspeople. Yet at least once every year, Orange County suspended its privatized business-as-usual and dedicated a day to the public commemoration of its civic identity. The one event that has consistently drawn Orange Countians together in common festivity is the Fourth of July. Orange County Independence Day ceremonies date from early in this century. By extending our investigation back to that time, we can trace the historical origins of some of the cultural characteristics of postsuburbia.

From early in this century, well before postsuburban formation was discernible, Orange County's celebration of July Fourth was imbued with the decentered and uprooted qualities that identify the county today. Rather than gathering at some civic institution like city hall, early residents scurried off to the beach or mountains in their private modes of transportation. Reported the *Anaheim Gazette* as early as 1905: "Not in years had so many vehicles been seen headed for Newport and Huntington Beaches, where thousands gathered to celebrate the nation's glorious holiday." Fifteen years later, that same newspaper noted how beach and mountain resorts were "crowded to suffocation." Highways were congested with automobiles, complained the editor, "all crowded with tired, dirty, wilted and peeved humanity, each trying to make himself believe that he had been having a good time."[2]

Although over the years different cities have vied to attract these roving Orange Countians to their separate Independence Day celebrations, the annual parade and fireworks extravaganza in Huntington Beach has gradually eclipsed all competitors. The Huntington Beach Fourth was inaugurated in 1904 when local businessmen, calling themselves the Board of Trade, organized to celebrate the opening of the Pacific Electric Railway line into the city. The occasion was used officially to change the town name from Pacific City to Huntington Beach, thereby linking the city's birthday with that of the nation.[3] Since then, the increasingly elaborate Huntington Beach Fourth of July has gained national attention as one of the largest and longest-running Independence Day celebrations in the country.

Owing both to its tradition and its self-promotion, the Huntington Beach Fourth affords an unusual opportunity to perceive how Orange County has presented itself over eighty years. By examining the changing organizations, activities, and symbols of Huntington's Fourth, one can begin to make sense of the development and meaning of public culture in Orange County. Before turning to the yearly festivities in Huntington Beach, however, we first provide a brief overview of American ceremonial tradition and describe how Orange Countians have adapted these festive rituals to suit the cultural milieu of their community.

EARLY CELEBRATIONS

Early American celebration was largely a carnivalesque takeover of the marketplace, organized by individuals outside of and often in opposition to existing forms of socioeconomic and political organization. Public festivity provided a period when local authority was suspended and the social hierarchy temporarily abandoned. The first half of the nineteenth century experienced an explosion of public sociability as cities invested in public ceremonies and public space. Public squares interrupted the grid of intersecting streets, and extensive parks like New York City's Central Park and Boston's Public Garden were laid out. At this time the rituals of the Fourth of July and St. Patrick's Day were created, and urban Americans regularly mounted public ceremonies to honor a national hero, inaugurate a civic improvement, commemorate a local anniversary, or celebrate a holiday.

Toward the middle of the nineteenth century, this golden age of American public life began to tarnish. The middle class was in retreat from social life in public, preferring to spend holidays and other special occasions in the company of family and friends. Their withdrawal from public space was also a consequence of the fierce, sometimes life-threatening, struggles that, beginning in the 1830s, periodically bloodied public space. These urban riots, which continued to occur into the 1870s, were often the consequence of ethnic conflicts and helped produce a critical reorganization of public life that splintered it into homogeneous ethnic and class components. As a result of this social conflict played out in American streets, leaders of the emerging urban social hierarchy began organizing orderly official ceremonies and professionalized and expanded police forces to control the excessive public conduct of the lower classes. Celebrations thus became a vehicle for local merchants and civic leaders to create a legitimate public presence by producing edifying spectacles that effectively communicated middle-class values and deportment as well as demonstrated the organizers' social prominence and political power.[4]

Early Orange County Independence Days and other local celebrations resembled these nineteenth-century public events but invested them with a distinctly Southern California flavor. As a rule, these occasions were more local than countywide in that different towns and settlements celebrated happenings significant to their particular communities. The City of Anaheim, for example, staged a picnic and barbecue in 1878 to celebrate the opening of the Cajon Irrigation Ditch and hosted a lavish party in 1895 to inaugurate the coming of electricity to the town.[5] Other communities held similar celebrations to honor the paving of streets, the laying of cornerstones of important buildings, or the organizing of local fire companies. Turn-of-the-century Orange, recollected long-time resident Garland Coltrane, held a Parade of Progress as well as an annual harvest festival to rejoice that "the good Lord was giving us a marketable crop so we could continue to live nicely in Southern California."[6] Early Orange County festivity, then, originated in local experiences and events and often commemorated the community's technological and economic progress.

If one were to believe newspaper accounts, these celebrations enjoyed universal popularity. Headlines boasted that every event attracted a "general turn-out of the people" or was patronized by all "public spirited citizens." In interviews given fifty years later, old-timers reflected on the general participation on these occasions. For example, Lucana Isch of San Juan Capistrano described how early in this century her grandfather put on barbecues "for the whole town." Fullerton's Otto Evans reminisced in the same fashion. Communitywide parades were quite "a big thing" then, he recalled. "They don't have anything like that anymore. The whole world has changed, and is changing fast."[7]

Early Orange County celebrations drew entertainment from the local population, and reviews of performances were intimate, affectionate, and noncritical, reinforcing the parochial nature of these public events. The *Anaheim Gazette* reported the performances commemorating the laying of the cornerstone for the Odd Fellows Hall in 1905 in a typical way. H. A. Dickel "never sang better," while Judge J. S. Howard, in his welcoming address, "was at his best." As for the evening's main speaker, Reverend

Knighten, he was in customary fine form. "No public speaker," enthused the *Gazette*, "has a stronger hold upon the people's hearts than this grand old Methodist preacher, Grand Army man, and Odd Fellow."[8]

As communal occasions, Orange County public events were determinedly apolitical. In fact, in 1897 a Fourth of July speaker was criticized for "allowing himself to be drawn into political matters."[9] In turn-of-the-century Talbert, Labor Day was treated as a grand fiesta. So while other late Victorian cities, especially in the East, witnessed politically pointed Labor Day parades and speeches,[10] Orange Countians were known to celebrate the occasion with a picnic highlighted by an egg-sucking contest.[11]

Reminiscences of long-time resident Frances Wright Bowen about early-twentieth-century Orange County festivities also suggest their apolitical nature. According to Bowen, social activists Fanny and Paulina Wright ventured into the county to attend Wright family picnics, at which they endeavored to enlighten their California relatives:

> The Wright sisters expounded their views on state and world affairs, alcohol, tobacco and religion; and many entered in or used it as a cover to release their lower level peeves. The finale always was Uncle Tom grabbing a megaphone away from Lizzie or Fanny or another as he leaped on [a] bench or table with: "Now see here . . . you girls! You do a lot of preachin' about the evils of tobacco and alcohol. But Dave and I are the only ones who do anything about it. We're drinking the country dry!" Everybody laughed no matter how tense their problem.[12]

As Bowen's recollections make clear, political discourse, especially by women, was not particularly welcomed at Orange County affairs.

Instead, public gatherings were recreational, social, and communal, designed to encourage and demonstrate harmony and solidarity among area residents. The most popular form of Orange County community activity was a picnic and barbecue held either at the beach or at some nearby rural retreat like Irvine Park (then called Orange County Park). A common form of the Orange County get-together was a fiesta, an occasion where people gathered to share food and drink, participate in competitive games, and socialize with neighbors. Paul Arbiso of San Juan Capistrano reminisced about these events: "They had a barbecue open for the town or anyone else who would come around. The Forsters or somebody would kill a steer or two, you know, and people around used to make potato salad, tortillas, salsa, and someone used to take the beans and cook them over there, a great big bucket of beans. Then they had kegs of beer, barrel kegs."[13] The day's activities centered on competitive events, such as horse and foot races of every sort, with participants divided by age and sex. Winners received small cash awards and had their victory printed in the local paper. Celebrants customarily spent the evening dancing to a hometown band on a makeshift pavilion.

Like the organizers of public events staged in towns across the United States, the planners of early Orange County celebrations stressed the respectability of the occasion. For example, a picnic held in Anaheim in 1871 was attended by 150 persons "embracing the best citizens." Likewise, the 1880 Fourth of July picnic held on the rural outskirts of Santa Ana was organized by men "all well and favorably known here."[14] Typically, ethnic and class lines were obscured during these mainstream occasions, while the existence of ethnic or lower-class celebrations was suppressed or ignored. Newspaper accounts and interviews provide only offhand suggestions that activities other than the upstanding, respectable kind took place, such as in 1876, when unidentified "drunken vandals" reportedly attacked an American flag, determined to tear down "the flaunting lie." The *Santa Ana Register* periodically mentioned a celebration by "Mexicans of northern Orange County" or "colorful ceremonies" held in the Mexican barrio, Delhi. More often, local newspapers were quick to report public disturbances and arrests made. The *Register*, for example, printed a small article in May 1925 about a "wild party" at the Bastanchury Ranch that was allegedly linked to Cinco de Mayo. Local police were summoned, and four Mexicans were arrested. In 1930 the Santa Ana paper listed a number of Mexicans arrested for drunkenness, reporting that their inebriated state was "closely connected with celebration of September 16, [a] Mexican national holiday."[15]

When ethnic diversity was acknowledged, it was often in stereotypical terms. One long-time Fullerton resident recalled that in 1912 the winner of the Fourth of July races was "a colored boy, they called him 'Gooba'; I don't know what his first name was. His last name was Smith; they were a well-known family. They were all great athletes."[16] In a similar vein, another old-timer remembered Anaheim's Chinatown as the place where illegal Chinese firecrackers could be purchased.[17] As suggested previously, Mexican Americans appeared in local news reports as prominent among those arrested for drunkenness and disorderly behavior. Accordingly, the Huntington Beach newspaper recorded that the celebrants at the 1915 Fourth of July gathering in the beach town entertained themselves, "except three Mexicans and one white man, who were entertained by City Marshal John Tinsley." A 1976 account of this episode notes that since the jail could hold only three inmates, the white man was released.[18] Orange County's ethnic world was thus typically portrayed as exotic and unlawful and was generally treated as beyond the community's cultural boundaries.

In sum, early Orange County celebrations were located within the dispersed municipalities of the county, convened a small population in face-

to-face conviviality, and paid homage to small-town American values—
civic pride, local achievement, cooperation, and homogeneity. The fiesta,
with its communitywide picnics and barbecues, was an indigenous form of
celebration that combined—if somewhat uncomfortably—Mexican food
and forms of sociability with Midwest customs of party giving while taking
advantage of the area's once stunning natural environment.[19] Thus when
Flume Number 8 of the Cajon Irrigation Ditch opened in 1878, the local
press proudly announced: "Had a stranger happened along he would
have had no difficulty in determining that the people he saw had come
together for a day of merry-making, and to celebrate some great triumph."[20] That is just what Orange Countians had in mind.

EARLY JULY FOURTH CELEBRATIONS

Early July Fourth celebrations were characteristic of these turn-of-the-
century public events in Orange County; they combined community
spirit and sociability with recreation and individual competition. The
Huntington Beach program was typical. The day began with a bomb
blast, followed by a rough-water swim around the Huntington Beach pier.
Afterward, public festivities would officially open with a convocation by a
local Protestant minister and a patriotic address by some local dignitary.
About 10 A.M. people from all over the county would crowd along Main
Street curbs to cheer the traditional parade.

Original Orange County Independence Day parades were small,
homemade affairs—a decorated wagon or buggy, little marching girls,
and parading lodge members. For example, the line-up of an 1885 Fourth
of July parade in Anaheim was listed in the local paper as follows:

GRAND PROCESSION
1. Grand Marshal
2. Anaheim Brass Band
3. Young Ladies Representing the Different States
4. Confidence Fire Company No. 1
5. Lodges and Civic Organizations
6. Cavalry Brigade
7. Display of Industries and Trades of the Town and County
8. Citizens and Strangers

After this official parade came the "Calithumpians" or "Horribles," a
procession of local men and boys who delighted the crowd with their
"hideous grotesqueness" by parading in silly masks and costumes and
ringing cow bells and horns.[21]

The July Fourth afternoon was spent picnicking, socializing, and competing in games and races: free-for-all swims, foot and horse races, and

(after 1910) automobile and motorcycle races. Customarily, these competitions were organized according to gender and age but did not exclude a little rivalry between the sexes. In fact, in 1920 a married woman won the seventy-five-yard dash. In addition to competitive races, afternoon activities frequently included a baseball game between local teams, an event that brought out fierce rivalries among Orange County towns. In the evening, revelers danced to the music of a local band and enjoyed fireworks displays.

Thus early Independence Day celebrations throughout Orange County were convivial, home-grown events. The official parade reinforced community involvement and solidarity, as both "citizens and strangers" were encouraged to participate in the procession. Moreover, the antics of groups such as Anaheim's Calithumpians, a time-honored feature of the festivity, symbolically broke down hierarchies implicit in the organization of the parade and, by extension, those in everyday social relations as well. Finally, postparade activities rewarded individual achievement and competition. When in 1885 the *Anaheim Gazette* announced that "everyone is invited to participate in the celebration," the emphasis was on participation.[22]

THE HUNTINGTON BEACH FOURTH

The Huntington Beach Fourth of July celebration arose out of these turn-of-the-century holiday traditions. Initially, Independence Day was only one of a series of events organized by the Huntington Beach Board of Trade (subsequently the Chamber of Commerce) in the early twentieth century to promote the beach town as Orange County's "great resort and playground." Early Huntington Beach business-sponsored events included Christmas parades, Black Gold Days, and an annual twins convention. In short, the Huntington Beach Independence Day celebration, like these other public occasions for profit, was designed in large measure to attract customers for businesses and real estate firms. Indeed, it was said that during the Fourth "an army of real estate agents" roamed among the picnickers and sunbathers.[23]

Because the Huntington Beach Fourth of July celebration was essentially a commercial venture, it was customary for promoters to calculate the holiday's success in dollars made. The 1915 Fourth was a huge success, newspapers declared: Downtown businesses "did a thriving business," and receipts taken at the local bathhouse (owned by the Huntington Beach Company[24]) were "higher than they had ever been." Similarly, in 1920 sales at stores "broke all records," and to demonstrate the success of the Fourth celebration the *Huntington Beach News* surveyed merchants as to their profits for the day. Forty years later, the paper continued to reflect the organizers' priorities. In bold type it proclaimed: "Dollarwise, the merchants of Huntington Beach never enjoyed better odds. For a municipal investment of only $6450 over the Friday, Saturday, Sunday and Monday holiday weekend, a gross take of over $100,000 was a conservative estimate." Commercial metaphors spilled over into general descriptions of the holiday, so that organizers were satisfied when "all the people got their money's worth" out of the celebration.[25]

Since the turn of the century, consumerism has assumed an increasingly prominent position not only in Huntington Beach's Independence Day festivities but in Orange County's ceremonial life in general. However, before 1940 the public holidays were not yet co-opted by profit concerns. "Business at a standstill for holiday tomorrow" ran the headline in the *Orange Daily News* in 1930, and initially even beach restaurants and grocery stores were reluctant to relinquish their day of vacation. Huntington Beach merchant W. R. Wharton, for example, stated that he had "always been opposed to keeping open on holidays," though he soon saw the "need of doing so in order to do his part in accommodating the visitors." Grocery owner H. F. Gibbs also had reservations about opening his Huntington Beach store, but the day's sales convinced him, too, of the "public service" he performed in keeping his business open over the Fourth. Although the local Safeway encouraged customers to "Vacation the Safeway," the grocery store remained closed for the 1925 holiday.[26]

In the early years of the twentieth century, Orange County merchants not only resisted opening their businesses during the holiday but also restricted special promotions to preholiday sales of only those goods closely associated with Independence Day. In 1905, for example, Anaheim's Asher & Falkenstein offered "especially low prices for the Fourth of July" on beach hats and bathing suits. Weber's Store, also in Anaheim, sold only holiday-oriented decorations in 1920, urging that "everyone should display a flag on the Fourth of July."[27]

Yet, even before World War II, the Orange County celebration was already beginning to be reshaped according to the county's unique social and economic structure, and these changes presaged postsuburban culture. For example, civic celebrations were increasingly organized by the promoters of county growth, who tied local festivities to commercial and real estate development and slowly wedded public occasions to an emergent culture of consumption. In the same vein, after 1940 county businesses began to appropriate Fourth of July rhetoric to promote larger sales and more varied products. Local car dealers were among the first to blatantly use the holiday for economic gain, as they admonished fellow Orange Countians to "show your independence on the Fourth with a new used car." In 1955 "Ole Pappy Hubbard" offered cars "hotter than a firecracker," while other car dealers advertised exciting "Holiday Sell-

A-Ramas." By the late 1950s and early 1960s general merchandise stores followed suit, "shooting the works" for the holiday by offering "July 4th Sizzlers." These business "Sellabrations," with extended hours, unbeatable sales, and in some cases clowns, balloons, and live circus-type shows, have come to rival, perhaps even replace, traditional Fourth of July celebrations.[28]

By the 1940s the Independence Day festivities of Huntington Beach had also inscribed special value to commerce and consumerism in the public culture of the county. From the outset, public activities on the Fourth were directed by area business associations—initially the Board of Trade, then for many years the Huntington Beach Chamber of Commerce, and more recently the Jaycees—which over the years have worked closely with local government officials. The City of Huntington Beach routinely budgeted funds for Fourth expenditures, increasing its outlay from $175 in 1919 to a whopping $17,000 in 1973. Sensitive to the taxpayers' revolt of the 1970s, however, organizers have since attempted to make the parade and its auxiliary activities self-supporting.[29]

For much of its eighty-year history, the city's Fourth of July was under the willing and capable direction of the Huntington Beach Chamber of Commerce secretary, William Gallienne. An immigrant from Guernsey, Gallienne owned and operated a local gas station until the Chamber of Commerce employed him full-time to run its public events. Bud Higgins, himself a long-time organizer of the annual activities, recalled that Gallienne "did not have very much formal education [but] was probably the best man to put on a parade that there was. He knew what it took to make a good parade. . . . He was a showman, a very good showman for public relations—to get people to the beach, to sell the city on celebrations, the beachfront, the pier, and this sort of thing."[30]

Gallienne was affectionately called El Generalissimo, a fitting nickname in light of the armies of people that invaded the beach area for the day. Whereas in 1905, 5,000 to 8,000 people showed up for the afternoon of free food and fireworks, by 1927 an estimated 67,000 people arrived for the day's entertainment, while in 1984, 250,000 celebrated the Fourth in Huntington Beach. In planning the increasingly complex and bureaucratic celebration, El Generalissimo commandeered dozens of committees, civic organizations, public safety agencies, and the local media, who, collectively, planned the holiday like military leaders devising strategies for an approaching battle. Using words and phrases like *invasion* and *period of emergency*, these dedicated individuals worked closely together to combat traffic, illegal fireworks, drunkenness, and the general mayhem accompanying the Fourth. The local police department, in particular, mobilized for the holiday, and by 1934 ninety-five officers were necessary to keep order. After three people drowned prior to 10 A.M. during the

1931 celebration, lifeguarding and other emergency services in Huntington Beach were professionalized. In addition, the city fire marshall (like those all over the county) yearly issued warnings and safety tips regarding the use of fireworks, and people were carefully advised about trash pickup schedules. Finally, newspapers delineated parade routes, street closures, parking areas, restroom facilities, and emergency stations. As the *Anaheim Bulletin* conceded after the 1900 celebration: "It is an awful good thing for any community that the Fourth of July only comes once a year."[31]

Participants in Fourth events have required as much organization as the general public. Whereas in 1930 it took only six committees to create the Huntington Beach Fourth of July, current planning for the celebration requires ten months, a paid coordinator, a full-time secretary, and thirty-five to forty separate committees.[32] Illustrative of the intensive and strategic planning that goes into staging a public festival like the annual Huntington Beach Fourth is a 1982 circular issued by the Anaheim Parks, Recreation, and Community Services Department concerning that city's "Olde Fashioned Fourth of July." This directive, sent out in April, explained registration fees, selection criteria for participants, the construction of booths (size, materials, and decoration), Orange County Health Department requirements regarding the preparation and packaging of food, and requisite State Board of Equalization tax permits for vendors.[33]

The movement to control the private purchase and use of fireworks in Huntington Beach—indeed throughout the county—is symptomatic of this bureaucratization and regulation of public celebration in postsuburban society. In the early years of this century, Orange Countians purchased fireworks at many local stores, markets, and small businesses. Residents of Orange, for example, bought their explosives at Harms Drug Store. By mid-century, individual cities had begun to control the availability of fireworks through restrictive legislation, editorials urging citizens to ring "the Liberty Bell instead of peppering the air with scraps of tin cans,"[34] and sponsorship of safe and affordable alternatives. By the mid-1980s most Orange County cities had banned the private purchase of fireworks within their boundaries.

The history of the fireworks display in Huntington Beach exemplifies this trend. In 1905 fireworks for the Fourth of July were donated and handled by the Japanese Association of Wintersburg (an area that is now part of Huntington Beach), which put on the show in a local baseball field. In 1930 the traditional fireworks were still free to the public but were moved away from the viewers and set off over the Pacific. Even this method, advertised as a "safe and sane" event, had its problems, as Harry "Cap" Sheue later recalled:

> On my first Fourth of July in Huntington Beach I helped the American
> Legion shoot firecrackers off the pier. This was the greatest (and shortest)
> fireworks demonstration ever given. We had all of the sky rockets, aerial
> bombs, etc. stacked in a huge pile in the center of the pier. As we attempted
> to set off the third air bomb, it exploded and backfired into the stack of
> fireworks. The next sixty seconds was magnificent bedlam. Rockets and
> bombs went off in every direction. Spectators on the shore cheered the
> wonderful display, but then suddenly it was all over.[35]

In the mid-1930s Huntington Beach turned over the direction of its
annual fireworks spectacular to Fire Chief Bud Higgins and hired a team
of experts, the Golden State Fireworks Company, to handle the display.
By the 1970s fireworks shows in Huntington Beach were safely ensconced
inside the local stadium and were designed so that only paying patrons
could see the show. Finally, in August 1987 the City of Huntington Beach
banned the sale of fireworks altogether, becoming one of the last municipalities in Orange County to prohibit the use of dangerous explosives.[36]
Today, pyrotechnic events are customarily confined to stadiums and
amusement parks, where families can gather and, for a price, safely enjoy
professional—indeed computer-controlled—fireworks entertainment.

In planning the annual fireworks show and other Fourth of July events,
Huntington Beach organizers, equating size with success, have sought
each year to surpass previous efforts by putting on increasingly elaborate
public spectacles. The 1930 program, for example, claimed that year's
event to be the "biggest ever," while the parades and fireworks of subsequent years were touted as the "biggest and best" in the history of the
event. The 1965 Fourth, according to news reports, was "easily the most
pretentious and grandiose celebration unleashed anywhere in Orange
County," and by the 1980s hundreds of thousands of revelers were crowd-
ing into the beach city to witness the anticipated spectacular.[37] Huntington Beach business leaders thus set up the machinery for extravagant
public ceremony well before Orange County had taken on the coloration
of a postsuburban society, using economies of scale and bureaucratic
efficiency as they marketed popular entertainment to an undifferentiated
mass of citizens.

Examination of specific cultural performances on these occasions reveals a set of emerging values characteristic of the new urban order. As
celebration organizers gradually converted the anniversary of American
independence into a kind of patriotic Disneyland for a day, local identity,
intimate sociability, and active participation slowly gave way to the icons
of national consumer culture, mass organization, and passive observation. These trends are especially evident in the evolution of the Huntington Beach parade, which over eighty years has been transformed from
an informal, homemade event into a Hollywood-style extravaganza re-

plete with movie stars, beauty queens, four-star generals, thousands of marching armed forces personnel, and hundreds of silver-adorned horses.

The grand marshals of the parade, for example, were initially Huntington Beach leaders—such men as Thomas Talbert, C. W. Warner, and W. T. Newland. After 1940, however, actors and other nonlocal media figures assumed the leading role in the celebration: western movie stars like Tom Mix (1930) and Leo Carrillo (1950); television figures such as Mouseketeers Jimmy Dodd and Roy Williams (1956); and radio personalities like Loman and Barkley (1957). During the 1950s and 1960s military authorities also played prominent parts in the parade. Today, the post of grand marshal is divided into four positions: the celebrity grand marshal; the resident grand marshal, a famous but local individual like former Los Angeles Ram football coach Ray Malavasi; the equestrian grand marshal, since 1950 the conservative television newscaster George Putnam; and the reviewing grand marshal, a role reserved for a visiting military dignitary. Honored heads of the Huntington Beach parade are thus no longer local authorities whose prestige derives from their economic and political power within the Huntington Beach and Orange County communities. Instead, symbolic leadership now resides with entertainment personalities and other media figures.

The incorporation of equestrians into the parade is another example of the glamorization of the celebration and its transformation into a form of passive, apolitical entertainment. As grand marshal in 1920, Mayor Thomas Talbert, leading the Orange County Board of Supervisors, was the first to ride a horse at the head of the procession. Throughout the 1920s and 1930s, Talbert continued to lead equestrian units, impressing Depression-era parade-goers with his "very expensive saddle and bridle" and his "couple of thousand dollars' worth of silver trappings."[38] Since then, equestrians have played an essential role in the development of the parade as public spectacle, as every year hundreds of men and women dressed in elaborate cowboy and Spanish outfits, their horses adorned with fine saddles and silver, vie for awards and prizes.[39] Meanwhile, parade-goers sit on the sidelines and marvel at the beautiful animals in their fancy trappings. Ostensibly the horses and their costumed riders link countians with their Old West heritage and values. But with land scarce and costly, horses in Orange County have become a luxury, an amusing pastime for the affluent. Equestrians perched on their saddled status symbols should remind viewers less of the Old West than of the exclusivity of the Orange County life-style and its annual parade.

The fashioning of the holiday into a mass spectacle has also effectively reduced the participation of ethnic minorities and women in the celebration. An unusual feature of early Huntington Beach Fourths was the recognition of local ethnic communities, particularly Huntington Beach's sizable Japanese American population, in the parade and other activities. During the early years of the twentieth century, resident Japanese entertained viewers with wrestling matches and dance exhibitions and, later in the day, handled the fireworks display.[40] In 1935 the Huntington Beach parade included full-fledged Japanese and Spanish divisions.[41]

Wartime evacuation temporarily destroyed the Huntington Beach Japanese American community, while the Cold War political climate discouraged displays of ethnic diversity in the annual procession thereafter. As a result, separate divisions of marching minorities all but disappeared from the Huntington Beach parade. In the 1950s and 1960s parade recognition of an ethnic presence in Orange County was limited largely to noncontroversial symbols like the best-dressed señor and Indian lady and nonideological themes such as the fiesta and the California heritage.

Initially, women also played a large part in local festivities, from the preparation of food to participating in competitive games, dancing, and general socializing. They were particularly prominent in early Fourth of July parades: younger girls grouped together to form a living flag or marched singly representing the different states, while older girls portrayed the Goddess of Liberty and Columbia or drove self-decorated buggies and carts.[42] However, starting in the 1920s, female participation in the Fourth was increasingly limited to bathing-suit-clad local beauties riding atop floats or uniformed girls marching in paramilitary musical and drill teams.

The centerpiece of women's participation in the Fourth eventually became the bathing-girl revue. The first Fourth of July beauty contest took place in 1920. Since two boys dressed as girls won prizes on that occasion, the contest was probably somewhat less than a serious event. However, over the next decade the beauty pageant steadily gained in popularity, so much so that by 1935 Boxie Huston, the "Ziegfeld of Huntington Beach," crowned Red, White, and Blue Queens, a Miss Independence, Miss Liberty, and Miss Freedom, as well as miscellaneous Ladies in Waiting.[43]

By the 1950s the Huntington Beach Fourth organizers had consolidated the presence of women into two major competitions, each representative of a different version of American femininity: woman as consumer and woman as sexpot. The first role was implicit in the competition for Fourth of July Queen, an honor awarded to the local high school girl who sold the most tickets to the beach city's celebration. As the holiday approached, newspapers printed stories and photographs concerning the competition, thus keeping the public informed as to who was in the lead and how many tickets had been sold. For her efforts, the most successful salesgirl not only got to ride atop a float in the parade and preside over a coronation ball but also received a cash award and a new wardrobe donated by local merchants.

While the competition for Fourth of July Queen honored the most enterprising female, the bathing-girl revue marketed women as sex kittens. On the afternoon of the Fourth, "shapely lovelies" and "bathing suit clad femmes" competed for the title of "Miss Out of This World" and "Miss Firecracker." This beauty contest, which was staged initially on the Huntington Beach pier and, after 1950, in a local stadium, allowed thousands of beach-goers to witness the spectacle of young women parading in their swim suits. Visiting "Hollywood personalities" and other "Hollywood notables" would then select the winner.[44]

In the weeks preceding the contest, "alluring" contestants were featured in a procession of Playboy-like newspaper photographs, such as one from the early 1950s depicting, against the backdrop of a huge unfurled American flag, four bathing beauties—their high-heeled shoes sinking in the sand—holding their ears while a fifth lights a gigantic firecracker.[45] As this picture illustrates, women continued to represent Americanism in Fourth of July celebrations. But where they had once stood for the best of American purity, freedom, and fertility, women in the 1950s and 1960s signified youth, sexiness, and self-display.

The trivialization and objectification of women's participation in the Huntington Beach Fourth can be correlated with their exclusion from the event's executive, decision-making responsibilities. Barred from Huntington Beach's Chamber of Commerce, effectively shut out from upper-level municipal employment, and even their traditional cooking tasks preempted by restaurants and barbecues managed by male-only fraternal groups, until recently women have played only a marginal role in the conceptualization and organization of Fourth of July activities. Officially, they have served on only those few organizing committees whose functions correspond to popular stereotypes about women's concerns. The first woman committee member was appointed in 1935 to organize the baby parade, and as late as 1960 women still could be found on only three committees—the Fourth of July Queen committee, the decorated automobiles committee, and the hostess committee. Not until the 1970s did women serve on the executive board overseeing the holiday extravaganza. Unofficially, however, Gallienne and his successors have credited Chamber of Commerce secretaries, who know "everything there is to know about the parade," with managing the day-to-day tasks necessary for putting on the event.[46] Moreover, behind the scenes, women volunteers generally have performed most of the work.

Because women's work traditionally has been behind the scenes, it is not surprising that women have held few prestigious or honorary posi-

tions in the parade over the years. The first female grand marshal was
Ruth Elder, the "famous aviatrix heroine" (1952). The next woman accorded the symbolic leadership of the procession was the buxom movie
queen Jayne Mansfield (1959). Other female notables have almost always
been media personalities as well: the sarong-attired actress Dorothy La-
mour (1971), the "brunette songstress" Gloria Grey (1955), and Hollywood starlets Rita Moreno and Yvette Dugay (1953).[47]

The rigidity of women's roles in public ceremonies was evident in a
newspaper article written in 1964 that reminisced about the time in the
1930s when the Huntington Beach Fourth organizers included a spelling
bee in the day's activities. The contest's moderator recalled:

> From the very beginning, it was evident that the winner was going to be an
> old maid school teacher from Arcadia. After the lady had won and had been
> awarded the prize, I said, . . . "Madame, you are just great on spelling. I
> wonder if you are as good on pronunciation?"
>
> "Yes," she replied, "I think I am."
>
> "Well then," I said, "I wonder if you would tell us how to pronounce the
> word which is spelled P O L O P O N Y?"
>
> "I never heard of the word," she said, "but I'm sure it is pronounced PO-
> LOP-O-Ne."
>
> The next two minutes were about the most uncomfortable moments I
> ever spent in public. I was informed that I not only was a "smart aleck" but
> was also "no gentleman."[48]

By drawing on negative stereotypes of the humorless old maid professional, the tale denigrates the woman's intelligence and competence,
punishing her for the crime of taking herself seriously. Whether apoc-
ryphal or not, the story illustrates the limits of women's participation in
the Huntington Beach Fourth and, by implication, in Orange County
public life.

The gradual militarization of Huntington Beach festivities further
restricted women's and, for that matter, men's participation in Fourth of
July activities. Early Orange County parades, especially on the Fourth of
July, customarily included a military component, often a company of local
war veterans. On the eve of the Second World War, however, the local
military establishment began to assume a much higher profile in Independence Day events. Between 1936 and 1938, for instance, part of the
day's excitement was the positioning of an American battleship off the
Huntington Beach shore, while in 1940 the parade was led by artillery
and antiaircraft units. Cold War military buildup intensified the presence
of the military in Orange County's celebration of the Fourth, so that by
1953 well over half the parade's participants were military personnel. As a
Huntington Beach News headline four years later announced: "Military
Units Dominate Annual July 4th Parade."[49] That year all but fifteen

hundred of forty-five hundred paraders were from the many military installations in Southern California. The prevalence of troops in the parade not only reflects the importance of the military in the local economy but also suggests a transformed meaning of American civic life and politics. Once a day to celebrate the republican ideals of the Declaration of Independence, the Fourth now celebrates the powerful military force of the state, as a mass, passive audience looks on.

Just as the general population withdrew from participating in the procession down Main Street to sit on the sidelines and cheer soldiers, equestrians, and beauty queens, the games and competitive events formerly held after the parade have gradually been supplanted by passive forms of entertainment. In 1930, for instance, holiday celebrants were treated to a rodeo starring western movie heroes Hoot Gibson, Ken Maynard, and Tom Mix. Five years later, Fourth revelers thrilled to the "Fearless Aldeline" and his "Sensational Slide for Life," the "Skating Demon," and the "Wonder Girl Frances Dexter, a de Luxe Novelty."[50] In subsequent years Huntington Beach offerings have become increasingly sophisticated and elaborate; they include vaudeville shows, carnivals, airplane exhibitions, the "classy" De Wayne Circus Troupe, and a variety of outdoor concerts.

If active participation in Fourth of July celebrations in postsuburban Orange County has gradually disappeared, so has much of the political meaning of the local holiday. Early Independence Days in Orange County routinely included a reading of the Declaration of Independence and a patriotic address, both by prominent local men. At the first Huntington Beach Fourth J. V. Vickers, president of the Huntington Beach Company, delivered an "inspired speech" in which he described his company's "growing plans to beautify and develop the community."[51] Subsequent orations were more typical patriotic fare, although, as noted, Orange Countians did not customarily intrude much political commentary into their public gatherings. As a result, patriotic oratory in Orange County was never particularly reflective or self-critical, and political comment frequently dwelt on events in Europe rather than on domestic problems or issues. In 1910, for example, Judge W. H. Anderson spoke on the "disease" of "money-seeking" currently disrupting Europe, while 1917 speeches discussed "the war, what for?" Post–World War I rhetoric focused on concerns such as the League of Nations, warning against the "propaganda" that sought to "restore this nation to the 'mother country.'"[52]

After the mid-twenties, patriotic oratory generally disappeared, replaced by other, contemporary forms of popular entertainment. In fact, when the John Birch Society tried to enter a float in the 1965 parade, Huntington Beach Fourth organizers successfully barred the ultraconservative association from participating. A day of recreation and entertainment, the Fourth of July in Huntington Beach avoids political controversy, preferring to elicit unexamined patriotic sentiment through the strategic use of popular symbols and images—a flag, a Marine, a cowboy—and leaving political discussion, however platitudinous, to the editorial pages.

PUBLIC CEREMONY IN ORANGE COUNTY

On July 4, 1915, the Anaheim Opera House opened its doors and invited Orange Countians to spend the holiday in the theater with all their "film favorites."[53] However unremarkable at the time, the newspaper notice of this event—buried on an inside page—prefigured some powerful changes in the nature of Orange County public life. The image of an individual celebrating Independence Day by sitting in a darkened theater and vicariously enjoying the pleasures and activities of media personalities symbolizes contemporary public life, especially in a place like post-suburban Orange County. Celebration, which once expressed the values and aspirations of the local community, now seems merely to project symbols mass-produced by a national culture industry.

The evolution of the Huntington Beach Independence Day celebration demonstrates that quite early in the history of the county local commercial elites utilized public space, popular images, and mass entertainment to develop and maintain a self-legitimating and profit-taking public culture. In doing so, Orange County businesspeople and government officials have transformed public ceremony into an apolitical, regimented, bureaucratic spectacle, a triumph of image over individual action and group interaction. In short, public festivity now seems to promote passivity and privatization, turning citizen into audience—an impassive consumer of images and products.

To talk of the simple demise of public life in Orange County is premature and myopic. Postsuburban society has also created new sites of sociability and has witnessed some attempts to reclaim public space and time. Celebration in the postsuburban era, like politics and social life, might best be described as a process of deconcentration rather than degeneration. Faced with the hollowness of mass-marketed celebrations like that of Huntington Beach, Orange Countians have developed new styles of sociability and have created different, more manageable, communities within which to celebrate the national holiday. For instance, in the 1930s local Arkansas natives started gathering for a private Fourth of July picnic, as did Huntington Beach "old-timers" who organized their own "old-fashioned" barbecue. Meanwhile, the Elks, Odd Fellows, Lions, and other Orange County civic and fraternal organizations have also begun holding their own holiday get-togethers, while the mayor of Huntington Beach hosts an exclusive postparade luncheon. In short, the increasing size and anonymity of the Huntington Beach Fourth of July (like other celebrations throughout the county) have all but destroyed the meaning and context of traditional communal festivity. As a result, Orange Countians have developed new definitions of community and different styles of sociability, ones based on family, ethnic, professional, and residential relationships.

Individual towns are also beginning to arrange small, local celebrations, usually designed as old-fashioned heritage days. The Irvine Harvest Festival is one such event. Established in 1973, the Harvest Festival is billed as a "home-grown fair" and attempts to re-create older festive occasions by bringing together the local population for informal socializing. Noticeably absent are elaborate and centralized ceremonial forms. But with its grand ball, symphony orchestra concerts, and ballet performances, as well as the financial support of local corporations like the Irvine Company, Fluor, and Armour, the Irvine Harvest Festival is, to a considerable extent, a more exclusive, upper-class version of the modern Orange County celebration. Moreover, the major public fixture of the celebration—a craft fair through which celebrants browse and make purchases—re-creates the sociability of a shopping mall.

In recent years, ethnic and other minority groups have also turned to local festivals to promote ethnic consciousness and to publicize current grievances. In 1984, for example, the Hispanic community of Santa Ana hastily and successfully organized their own Golden Brown City Days in competition with Santa Ana's official Golden City Days celebration. This separate ethnic event was designed to protest what local Hispanic leaders felt to be the city's discriminatory redevelopment programs and other civic efforts to "Anglocize" the downtown area.[54] On a rainy weekend in February 1989 Orange County's Vietnamese community held a Tet festival that attracted fifty thousand visitors. Yet, typical of modern celebration, festival coordinator Tony Lam at one point declared: "Next year we're going to start organizing right after Tet. None of this 3-month stuff. It's killing me."[55]

Finally, some Orange Countians keep alive the ancient Bacchanalian spirit of celebration. Particularly worrisome for local authorities, and the general public, has been the takeover of public spaces by riotous youths. Huntington Beach has been especially vulnerable to these sorts of crowd disturbances. On Labor Day 1986, forty people were injured, thirty-five arrested, and six police cars burned in what authorities and the media called a holiday melee.[56] The following May, five to six hundred youths gathered in an industrial parking lot, and when police attempted to disperse the "party," another riot ensued. "They were celebrating something out there tonight," one Huntington Beach officer commented to the press. "We're sure getting a lot of practice as far as riots go."[57]

Official reaction to these public disturbances has been immediate and concerted. In the local courts rioters have received severe sentences, and beefed-up police departments have begun to learn sophisticated riot-control techniques. Meanwhile, city governments are looking into the feasibility of eliminating events that attract "the wrong kinds of people to the beach."[58] Local television stations and newspapers have cooperated by widely publicizing these antiriot efforts. Unofficial, oppositional, and spontaneous festivity thus can still be found in Orange County, but it is confined to youth and takes chaotic and incoherent forms. To local authorities, moreover, this type of celebration is dangerous, embarrassing, and incomprehensible, something to be controlled or legislated out of existence.

We are left, then, with a blurred and fragmented picture of public celebration and public culture in postsuburban society. The organized centerpiece of the county's public celebration, Huntington Beach's Fourth of July spectacle, entertains thousands with a reaffirmation of mass culture. The homogeneous caricature of the county that the ceremony projects is patently false. For most county residents, the public stage has fractured; they now participate in deconcentrated festivities in the polynucleated spaces of separate ethnic groups, homogenized neighborhoods, and isolated families. The ultimate meaning of the day's events must be read in the scattered activities of Orange County inhabitants who make their private rounds to shopping centers and beaches or gather with their intimates around television sets.

The relative paucity of public life and vacuity of public symbols in Orange County may be the earmark of information capitalism, which leaves local citizens indifferent or powerless to challenge the control of the corporate economy and mass-culture industry over the creation and circulation of public values. Although the postsuburban county may spawn polynucleated centers for cultural expression and occasional resistance, it has not yet created a ceremonial platform from which to express a powerful, nuanced, diverse, and authentic local culture. Still, it is only in specific localities that people can gather together in common space to acknowledge one another and deliberate about their common goals. If American public life is to become resilient in the late twentieth century, it must find space to take root in places like Orange County.

NOTES

1. Quote from John Skorupski, *Symbol and Theory: A Philosophical Study of Theories of Religion in Social Anthropology* (Cambridge: Cambridge University Press, 1976), 164. See also Richard C. Trexler, *Public Life in Renaissance Florence* (New

York: Academic Press, 1980); Victor Turner, "Liminality and the Performative Genres," in *Rite, Drama, Festival, Spectacle: Rehearsals toward a Theory of Cultural Performance,* ed. John J. MacAloon (Philadelphia: Institute for the Study of Human Issues, 1984); and Mikhail Bakhtin, *Rabelais and His World,* trans. Helene Iswolsky (Bloomington: Indiana University Press, 1984), 255.

2. *Anaheim Gazette,* 6 July 1905; 8 July 1920.

3. See brief history of the Huntington Beach Fourth of July in an article in the *Huntington Beach News,* 28 June 1973.

4. For more information, see Susan Davis, *Parades and Power: Street Theatre in Nineteenth-Century Philadelphia* (Philadelphia: Temple University Press, 1986); Mary P. Ryan, "The American Parade: The Representation of the Nineteenth-Century Social Order," in *The New Cultural History,* ed. Lynn Hunt (Berkeley: University of California Press, 1989), 131–75; and Frank E. Manning, *The Celebration of Society: Perspectives on Contemporary Cultural Performance* (Bowling Green, Ohio: Bowling Green University Popular Press, 1983).

5. A vivid description of the problems with and importance of water in early Orange County can be found in Jessamyn West's *South of the Angels* (New York: Harcourt, Brace, 1960), especially chap. 16. West's family, like that of her cousin Richard M. Nixon, was among the original settlers of Yorba Linda.

6. Garland W. Coltrane, interview with Milan Pavlovich, 2 Sept. 1970, transcript 15, Oral History Program, California State University, Fullerton.

7. Quotes from *Anaheim Gazette,* 8 July 1871; Lucana Isch, interview with Karen Wilson Turnbull, 20 Aug. 1975, transcript 3–4, Oral History Program, California State University, Fullerton; Otto Evans, interview with C. Dean McComber, 22 Dec. 1977, transcript 2, Fullerton Public Library.

8. *Anaheim Gazette,* 29 June 1905.

9. *Fullerton News Tribune,* 2 July 1960.

10. Robert J. Myers, *Celebrations: The Complete Book of American Holidays* (Garden City, N.Y.: Doubleday, 1972).

11. T. B. Talbert, *My Sixty Years in California* (Huntington Beach, Calif.: Huntington Beach News Press, 1952), 52.

12. Frances Wright Bowen, *The Franklin: Orange Co. and So. Cal. Twenties* (n.p.: Kumquat Press, ca. 1977), 31.

13. Paul Arbiso, interview with Karen Wilson Turnbull, 30 Dec. 1975, transcript 11, Oral History Program, California State University, Fullerton.

14. *Anaheim Gazette,* 13 May 1871; 3 July 1880.

15. *Anaheim Gazette,* 6 July 1876. *Santa Ana Register,* 16 Sept. 1935; 17 Sept. 1930; 5 May 1925; 16 Sept. 1930. There is much historical work to be done on ethnic communities and culture in Orange County. See Mary Lisbeth Haas, "The Barrios of Santa Ana: Community, Class, and Urbanization, 1850–1947" (Ph.D. diss., University of California, Irvine, 1985).

16. Raymond R. Thompson, interview with Gerald M. Welt, 23 May 1968, transcript 21, Oral History Program, California State University, Fullerton.

17. George F. Kohlenberger, interview with Vivian Allen, 19 Mar. 1974, transcript 4, Oral History Program, California State University, Fullerton.

18. *Huntington Beach News,* 9 July 1915; Tonia Morales, "The Fourth of July

Parade in Huntington Beach" (Huntington Beach Public Library, 1976, typescript).

19. *Anaheim Gazette,* 3 June 1876.

20. Quoted in F. A. Henderson and W. W. Wieman, "W.P.A. Research Project #3105, Sponsored by the Board of Education, Santa Ana" (Anaheim Public Library, n.d., typescript), 45.

21. *Anaheim Gazette,* 27 June 1885; see also Henderson and Wieman, "W.P.A. Research Project #3105."

22. *Anaheim Gazette,* 27 June 1885.

23. *Huntington Beach News,* 4 Apr. 1935; 28 June 1973.

24. The Huntington Beach Company, founded in 1903 as an oil and real estate development company, is currently a subsidiary of Chevron Corporation and derives most of its income from rental and commercial properties (including the Huntington Center Shopping Mall and various residential developments) and, to a lesser degree, oil production. See *Walker's Manual of Western Corporations,* 78th ed. (Garden Grove, Calif.: Walker's Manual, 1986), 881–82. For a history of oil industry in Huntington Beach, see Barbara Ann Milkovich, "A Study of the Oil Industry on the Development of Huntington Beach, California, Prior to 1930" (master's thesis, California State University, Long Beach, 1988).

25. *Huntington Beach News,* 9 July 1915; 9 July 1920; 7 July 1960; 7 July 1905.

26. *Orange Daily News,* 3 July 1930; *Huntington Beach News,* 9 July 1920; *Fullerton News Tribune,* 2 July 1925.

27. *Anaheim Gazette,* 29 June 1905; *Yorba Linda Star,* 2 July 1920.

28. *Fullerton News Tribune,* 3 July 1940; 1 July 1955; *Santa Ana Register,* 3 July 1960; *Fullerton News Tribune,* 1 July 1960; 3 July 1980; 5 July 1975. See also *Irvine World News,* 25 Sept. 1975.

29. *Huntington Beach News,* 22 June 1978.

30. Quoted in Robyn Maltby and Renee Schulte, eds., *Huntington Beach: An Oral History of the Early Development of a Southern California Beach Community* (Fullerton: Oral History Program, California State University, 1980), 90–91.

31. Quoted in Jim Sleeper, *Turn the Rascals Out! The Life and Times of Orange County's Fighting Editor Dan M. Baker* (Trabuco Canyon, Calif.: California Classics, 1973), 292.

32. For a sample of the extensive effort involved in putting on a Huntington Beach Fourth of July, see C. E. Bauer, "4th of July Report" (Huntington Beach Public Library, 25 Sept. 1973, typescript).

33. Anaheim Parks, Recreation, and Community Services Department, "Anaheim July 4, 1982 Committee" (Anaheim Public Library, 12 Apr. 1982, typescript).

34. *Orange Daily News,* 4 July 1955.

35. Quoted in *Huntington Beach News,* 2 July 1964.

36. The role of fireworks in Orange County's economy and politics as well as in its patriotic celebrations invites further investigation. See *Los Angeles Times,* 20 June 1984, for an article describing the refusal of Orange County supervisors to ban the sale of fireworks in unincorporated areas and the controversial political donations made by Anaheim fireworks manufacturer W. Patrick Moriarty.

37. *Huntington Beach News,* 26 June 1930; 9 July 1953; 1 July 1965.

38. *Huntington Beach News,* 9 July 1920; 11 July 1935.

39. In 1957, for example, over ninety trophies were awarded to equestrian participants.

40. For more information on the participation of the Japanese American community in early Orange County public life, see Clarence Nishizu, interview with Arthur A. Hansen, 14 June 1982, transcript, Oral History Program, California State University, Fullerton.

41. Preliminary research suggests other cross-cultural celebrations in early-twentieth-century Orange County, with Anglos taking part in local ethnic celebrations like Mexican Independence Day and Cinco de Mayo. See, for example, *Santa Ana Register,* 20 Sept. 1900. The authors wish to thank Beth Haas for sharing her research and insights regarding public life in Orange County's Mexican American community.

42. Sleeper, *Turn the Rascals Out!,* 289; Maltby and Schulte, *Huntington Beach,* 171–72.

43. *Huntington Beach News,* 27 June 1935.

44. *Huntington Beach News,* 9 July 1953; 30 June 1955; 4 July 1955; 7 July 1960.

45. *Huntington Beach News,* 2 July 1953.

46. Bauer, "4th of July Report," 5; *Huntington Beach News,* 8 July 1965.

47. Bauer, "4th of July Report," 19; *Huntington Beach News,* 30 June 1955.

48. *Huntington Beach News,* 2 July 1964.

49. *Huntington Beach News,* 14 July 1957.

50. *Huntington Beach News,* 26 June 1930; 27 June 1935.

51. *Huntington Beach News,* 28 June 1978.

52. *Huntington Beach News,* 8 July 1910; *Fullerton News Tribune,* 15 July 1917; 3 July 1925.

53. *Anaheim Gazette,* 1 July 1915.

54. *Orange County Register,* 17 Oct. 1984.

55. *Los Angeles Times,* 29 Jan. 1989.

56. *Orange County Register,* 24 May 1987; 30 May 1987. In a 1987 court decision, a nineteen-year-old Joshua Tree, California, youth was sentenced to one year in jail for his part in the Labor Day riot.

57. *Orange County Register,* 9 May 1987.

58. *Orange County Register,* 24 May 1987.

REFERENCES

Anaheim Parks, Recreation, and Community Services Department. "Anaheim, July 4, 1982 Committee." 12 Apr. 1982. Anaheim Public Library. Typescript.

Arbiso, Paul. Interview with Karen Wilson Turnbull. 30 Dec. 1975. Oral History Program, California State University, Fullerton.

Bakhtin, Mikhail. *Rabelais and His World.* Trans. Helene Iswolsky. Bloomington: Indiana University Press, 1984.

Bauer, C. E. "4th of July Report." 25 Sept. 1973. Huntington Beach Public Library. Typescript.

Bowen, Frances. *The Franklin: Orange Co. and So. Cal. Twenties.* N.p.: Kumquat Press, ca. 1977.

Coltrane, Garland W. Interview with Milan Pavlovich. 2 Sept. 1970. Oral History Program, California State University, Fullerton.

Davis, Susan. *Parades and Power: Street Theatre in Nineteenth-Century Philadelphia.* Philadelphia: Temple University Press, 1986.

Evans, Otto. Interview with C. Dean McComber. 22 Dec. 1977. Fullerton Public Library.

Haas, Mary Lisbeth. "The Barrios of Santa Ana: Community, Class, and Urbanization, 1850–1947." Ph.D. diss., University of California, Irvine, 1985.

Henderson, F. A., and W. W. Wieman. "W.P.A. Research Project #3105, Sponsored by the Board of Education, Santa Ana." n.d. Anaheim Public Library. Typescript.

Isch, Lucana. Interview with Karen Wilson Turnbull. 20 Aug. 1975. Oral History Program, California State University, Fullerton.

Kohlenberger, George F. Interview with Vivian Allen. 19 Mar. 1974. Oral History Program, California State University, Fullerton.

Maltby, Robyn, and Renee K. Schulte, eds. *Huntington Beach: An Oral History of the Early Development of a Southern California Beach Community.* Fullerton: Oral History Program, California State University, 1980.

Manning, Frank E. *The Celebration of Society: Perspectives on Contemporary Cultural Performance.* Bowling Green, Ohio: Bowling Green University Popular Press, 1983.

Milkovich, Barbara Ann. "A Study of the Oil Industry on the Development of Huntington Beach, California, Prior to 1930." Master's thesis, California State University, Long Beach, 1988.

Morales, Tonia. "The Fourth of July Parade in Huntington Beach." 1976. Huntington Beach Public Library. Typescript.

Myers, Robert J. *Celebrations: The Complete Book of American Holidays.* Garden City, N.Y.: Doubleday, 1972.

Nishizu, Clarence. Interview with Arthur A. Hansen. 14 June 1982. Oral History Program, California State University, Fullerton.

Ryan, Mary P. "The American Parade: The Representation of the Nineteenth-Century Social Order." In *The New Cultural History,* ed. Lynn Hunt, 131–75. Berkeley: University of California Press, 1989.

Skorupski, John. *Symbol and Theory: A Philosophical Study of Theories of Religion in Social Anthropology.* Cambridge: Cambridge University Press, 1976.

Sleeper, Jim. *Turn the Rascals Out! The Life and Times of Orange County's Fighting Editor Dan M. Baker.* Trabuco Canyon, Calif.: California Classics, 1973.

Talbert, T. B. *My Sixty Years in California.* Huntington Beach, Calif.: Huntington Beach News Press, 1952.

Thompson, Raymond R. Interview with Gerald M. Welt. 23 May 1968. Oral History Program, California State University, Fullerton.

Trexler, Richard C. *Public Life in Renaissance Florence*. New York: Academic Press, 1980.

Turner, Victor. "Liminality and the Performative Genres." In *Rite, Drama, Festival, Spectacle: Rehearsals toward a Theory of Cultural Performance*, ed. John J. MacAloon, 19–42. Philadelphia: Institute for the Study of Human Issues, 1984.

Walker's Manual of Western Corporations. 78th ed. Garden Grove, Calif.: Walker's Manual, 1986.

West, Jessamyn. *South of the Angels*. New York: Harcourt, Brace, 1960.

SEVEN

Narcissism or Liberation?
The Affluent Middle-Class Family

Mark Poster

In the United States, the family is currently under intense scrutiny. Government and church officials, social scientists and publicists have all voiced concern over its fate. Statistical indexes of family troubles are indeed rising at alarming rates. The growing incidence of divorce, teenage pregnancy, child abuse, alcoholism, drug abuse, familial rape, and wife beating are crude indications of the contemporary situation.[1] In addition certain historic values of family life are seriously challenged by feminists, gay activists, communitarians, ecologists, and others. These groups, each for its own reasons, resist the traditional ideal of the nuclear family, finding it in some ways repressive or uncomfortable. Thus the family both in practice and as an idea is increasingly open to question.

In this context family life has been changing rapidly. Dual-career families, stepfamilies, blended families, binuclear families, gay and lesbian families, single-parent families, single-person households, and communes all have established themselves in American society. And yet the ideal of the nuclear family persists because permanent monogamy and domestic privacy remain strong values.

I propose to test the persistence of the nuclear family and to chart the extent and character of alternatives to it by focusing on a structural feature of family life that goes beyond demographics and behavioral features of the family to what I regard as its core: the pattern of age and sex hierarchies and the pattern of authority and love in the relations between adults and children during their early developmental stages.

A POINT OF VIEW

The literature concerned with families for the most part focuses on the methodological problem of obtaining objective information about family

190

life or, when it deals with substantive issues, tends to focus on the problem of quantifying complex social relationships, such as the distribution of power between husbands and wives.[2] There is now interest in a historical perspective, one that would assess long-term changes in family life to gain a sense of where it is going.[3] My work is a contribution to this new direction.

In addition to these trends in family research, it usually has a "policy" orientation. Many of the most distinguished family researchers assume as part of their task determining how children should be raised and, more broadly, how the family should be structured to provide the healthiest environment for the child as well as for the adults. Although on the surface these aims appear laudatory, in practice they result in a narrow, pragmatic perspective. The researcher takes the position of a middle-class family member in the present and assumes that the social system surrounding the family is fixed, along with many features of the family that are tied closely to the social system. Boldly put, the researcher takes as his or her question, How can the family produce successful, well-adapted children?[4]

Although this question is indeed on the minds of many parents, it does not provide a research strategy that can go far in assisting us to comprehend the dynamics of family life because it takes for granted what it should be putting into question, the structure or the structures of the family. In addition to this difficulty, the pragmatic approach assumes that the researcher knows the best way to rear children or, more basically, that there is an absolute best way to raise children regardless of time or place. Although every researcher is entitled to his or her values and, as you will see, I certainly have my own, the problem I am raising is the scientific status given to the researcher's norms or values when in fact they are political positions. What I object to in the pragmatists' perspective, however valuable their work may be in other respects, is that their norms about child rearing and about family life in general unintentionally attain scientific status in their writing.

In contrast to these tendencies in family studies I attempt to treat the family historically and critically. I am interested in long-term trends that point to basic structural features of the families under study. By putting aside the question of what parents should do now with their children to make them successful in society as it is, I raise what I think is a more profound issue. My research question is, Can the classical nuclear family survive the broad changes that have taken place in society since the industrial revolution began two centuries ago? And I am interested also in the critical question, Should it survive? or, in other words, Does the nuclear family today provide the best possible framework for those social experiences we normally associate with family life?

This question, which is the heart of my study, presumes both that all types of families contain structures of domination and that domination is undesirable. This is a political, not a scientific, judgment, one that the reader is free to reject. I do not claim to know what is the best family form, the one that best realizes a democratic structure. I take it as my task to point out, at a level that may not be obvious, the structures of domination that do exist or have existed.[5] The question of domination in the family is complex because (1) the family is profoundly affected by forms of domination in the surrounding society, (2) social ideology puts great pressure on the family to reproduce those forms of domination in children, and (3) in addition to a child's biological dependence there is an apparently ineradicable residue of domination in the mere fact that children are born into a world not of their own making but already structured, a world that is presented to them as both good and unalterable.

THE OEDIPAL FAMILY

Considerable light is shed on the situation of the contemporary family when it is contrasted with the family of a century ago. Before presenting the results of my research on the Orange County family in 1986, I present a description of the ideal type of the middle-class white family of 1880 as it existed in both Europe and the United States.

What we think of as the nuclear family is a relatively recent phenomenon. Historians of the family have since 1970 provided a reasonably coherent, if still debated, account of its emergence. The nuclear family began some two centuries ago, when middle-class members of Western societies began a deliberate effort to separate work from family life, to base the choice of a spouse on romantic love and to make it the personal decision of the prospective partners (as opposed to its being a parental decision based on political or economic strategy), to insist on monogamous sexual relations as the ideal between husband and wife, to commit the partners to lifelong association, to value the social respectability of the marriage above the individual needs of the partners, to separate sharply the roles of husband and wife with the husband as breadwinner outside the family and the wife as child raiser and domestic manager, to separate the personality traits of men and women with men defined as rational and women as emotional, and, above all else, to create the family residence as a world set apart from the rest of society, a private space for the sharing of intimate experience that, in principle, excluded even close relatives.[6]

This brief description is highly stereotyped and requires many qualifications. But for the purposes of this chapter it will have to stand as a rough indication of a complex social phenomenon. The important point is that each of the traits listed was at the time of its inception a radical innovation in family life. The nuclear family emerged in Europe in opposition to existing family forms, notably the aristocratic and the peasant.[7] The values associated with the nuclear family gained widespread though far from universal acceptance among the middle class, eventually being adopted by the working class as well.[8]

Such an understanding of the nuclear family leaves out perhaps its most important feature: the unique emotional structure that it originated. But before describing this feature, let me define what I mean by emotional structure. I compare family types on the basis of how the hierarchies of age and sex within them are the foundation for differing patterns of authority and love, patterns that constitute the emotional core of the family. These patterns are unconscious to the family members and must be constructed by the social scientist through an analysis of adult-to-adult and adult-to-child relationships. This perspective allows me to go beyond the study of child-rearing practices as they are normally understood because I can attempt to discover a pattern in the many actions and beliefs of families. This pattern, not any particular practice (such as scheduled feeding of the infant, feeding on demand, or hiring wet nurses), differentiates one family type from another, reducing the complex phenomena of everyday life to sets of coherent and defined emotions.

The emotional structure of the family is determined by (1) establishing the relationship of the family to the wider society; (2) determining how relations between age and sex groups within the family constitute hierarchies (for example, the old dominate the young, or men dominate women); (3) investigating how those hierarchies are manifested in child-rearing practices, specifically those concerning feeding, toilet training, and sexuality;[9] (4) determining how those practices form a pattern in relation to a particular mixture of authority and love. The emotional structure is thus not a family mood, nor is it the sum of the individual personality types within the family. It focuses specifically on the character and intensity of love expressed by adults when they exert their authority over children in practices concerned with feeding, toilet training, and sexuality. This analysis is similar to Freud's, but it attempts to make explicit the interactive, not simply the intrapsychic, nature of the emotions.[10]

From this standpoint the originality of the nuclear family is most clearly evident, for within its boundaries a most unique microsystem of emotional behaviors was established. First, the relations among family members, especially those between parents and children, were isolated from the rest of society to the greatest extent possible. This isolation allowed relations between members of the nuclear family to be maximally intensified, especially the bond between children and their parents. Second, mothers were understood to have major responsibility for the children's physical and moral development. Finally, a system of early child rearing was established in which the child relinquished as much as possible direct bodily gratification in exchange for parental affection and love. Mothers expressed a great deal of love toward their children, showering them with affection and care. When the young child failed to conform to rules established by the mother, she did not physically punish the child but withdrew her love. Authority was imposed by the removal of love.

During the child's early years the emotional structure worked as follows. These nuclear families established a highly valued regimen that intensified the love bond of children for parents by depriving children of banal forms of sensual pleasure. During the first year of life children were fed on a rigid schedule. Their bodies were satisfied not when they were hungry but when the schedule allowed. They enjoyed the breast only when the fixed routine prescribed it. Next, as early as possible children were toilet trained. Parents often attempted this feat well before the children had sphincter control. Recommended sanctions against inevitable failures in this task were not the Puritan whip but the withdrawal of love. Again bodily gratification in acts of elimination was sharply curtailed in exchange for parental love. Finally, a little later, when children discovered that touching the genitals produced pleasure, parents imposed the strictest rules against masturbation, in some cases resorting to alarm devices to extend their surveillance into the night. Boys were threatened routinely by their mothers with castration, the surgery to be accomplished, they were told, by fathers or doctors. I refer to these three areas of early child rearing—feeding, toilet training, and sexuality—as stages of development.

The consequence of these practices on the personality development of the child was the subject of Freud's work. The child's emotional attachment to parents was greatly intensified in the directions of both love and hate. Ambivalent feelings in the child were cultivated by the nuclear family, unintentionally but with significant results. Unable to tolerate strong conflicting feelings toward the same person and unable to express anger and rage against more powerful beings, the child was left with one alternative: to internalize the anger and direct it against himself or herself. Such internalization established within the child a watchdog (Freud called it the superego) by which the child unconsciously was able to deny bodily desires, exert self-control, defer gratification. This important personality trait, generated by what Freud called the Oedipus complex, was the basis of the child's later individualism, the ability to decide what to do in social institutions like the market—institutions that require autonomous action in a competitive context.

The application of my theory of the family to what we know about the nineteenth-century middle-class family yields the following conclusion.[11] The Oedipal family reproduced in the child structures of domination regarding age and sex. Parents imposed clear and strong authority on the child, authority that placed the position of the man higher than that of the woman and sharply segregated their roles. Unlike other family types, the Oedipal family introduced a unique combination of love and authority. Parents imposed authority (denying the child bodily pleasure) by tendering warm affection or threatening to withdraw that affection.[12] Authority and love were thus exercised at the same time, heightening the bond between parent and child. This bond was further augmented by the unprecedented degree of isolation of the child from other adults and children. The secret power of the Oedipal family is thus revealed as an emotional structure, unconscious to all participants, that achieved an extraordinary internalization of the parents by the child, an internalization that drew on the powerful feelings elicited in the child by the family structure, enabling the child to control her or his feelings, delay gratification, and autonomously marshal energies for the task of work, among other results. Most simply put, the work ethic was won at the cost of considerable emotional and sexual repression. Thus the nuclear family contributed to the development of industrial capitalism, producing people who acted not according to tradition but by autonomous choice and self-control. When the family system failed, it produced hysterics and neurasthenics, people who displaced bodily urges into physical symptoms of distress, symptoms that had no actual physical basis.[13]

The question now at hand may be posed with precision: Does the mechanism of the exchange of the child's bodily gratification for parental love during the first years of life still exist both as ideal and in practice? Is the transmission of hierarchies of age and sex still accomplished through the same pattern of authority and love as was the case in the nineteenth century? Do the general social characteristics of the nuclear family survive today? To what extent do the old characteristics survive? If they do not, what has taken their place in forming the general conditions of the family, the patterns of love and authority, and the mechanisms for reproducing age and sex hierarchies? Is there a single new pattern or are there many? How do these new patterns compare with the pattern of domination in classical nuclear families? These questions informed my research, and I shall now address them.[14]

A PROFILE OF THE PARTICIPATING FAMILIES

To obtain a sample I distributed invitations to participate in the study through preschools, day-care centers, and kindergarten classes in public schools in Irvine, Laguna Beach, Newport Beach, and El Toro, all cities in Orange County, California. I selected preschools randomly from the phone directory. The Irvine School District was selected (the only public

TABLE 7.1   Size of Households

Size	N	%
2	18	6.2
3	75	25.9
4	130	44.8
5	42	14.5
6	14	4.8
7	7	2.4
8 or more	4	1.4
Total	290	100

school system in the sample) because of its location in a largely middle-class community. Only families with at least one child age six or younger were invited, so that parents either were involved with feeding, toilet training, and sexuality or were relatively close in time to those stages of development of the children. Families that responded to the invitation were mailed questionnaires. These asked that mothers fill them out and return them by mail.[15] If after two weeks the questionnaires were not returned, mothers were contacted by phone and reminded about them.[16] I generated the questions in the research instrument from my knowledge of the Oedipal family. The questions, mostly closed-ended, had a response scale from 1 to 5, from strongly agree to strongly disagree.[17]

The respondents to my questionnaire (290 mothers) are by no means representative of the population of Orange County, much less the United States. I distributed the instrument in some of the wealthier communities in the southern part of the county because I wanted to compare an affluent group today with a similar group from the nineteenth century, the group that was most similar to the Oedipal or classical nuclear family. By this means I could measure the endurance of the nuclear family among the social class that was associated with its birth and early development. Possibly the Oedipal family remains characteristic of Orange County, even if it is not prevalent in the social group that I studied. We do know that for certain indicators, particularly attitudes concerning sexuality, the contemporary working class more closely resembles the classical nuclear family than does the contemporary middle class.[18]

Because I distributed the questionnaire only to households with children, it is not surprising to learn that they were somewhat larger in size than the average American household. The average household among the respondents contained four people, somewhat above the national figure (table 7.1).[19] The family income of the participants in the study was high (table 7.2). The income figures reflect the occupations of the respondents. Both the men and the women who worked were disproportionately

TABLE 7.2 Family Income

Income	N	%
Less than $20,000	20	7.0
$20,000 to $35,000	36	12.7
$35,000 to $50,000	68	24.0
$50,000 to $65,000	53	18.7
More than $65,000	106	37.6
Total	283	100

TABLE 7.3 Religious Preference

Religion	N	%
Catholic	49	18.6
Jewish	23	8.7
Mormon	13	4.9
Protestant	99	37.5
Other	30	11.4
No preference	50	18.9
Total	264	100

professionals, managers, and proprietors. Only a handful listed working-class, service, or white-collar occupations that are associated with lower salaries. A few were students, and this group accounts for most of the families with incomes under twenty thousand dollars. The respondents were also female, with only 5 of the 290 cases being male.

The respondents were also overwhelmingly white (92 percent). The next largest ethnic group was Asians, only 3.5 percent of the total, a distribution not uncommon in the cities surveyed.

The religious preference of the respondents was not atypical, given the class and the location of the sample (table 7.3).[20] Even though about 10 percent of the invitations to participate in the study were distributed to families with children in denominational preschools, the respondents were disproportionately nonreligious. One-third never attended a worship center; another 28 percent attended only a few times a year. Only 27 percent attended church at least once a week.

The group was older than might be expected. Because I was most interested in the early years of child rearing, I wanted families with young children. Yet 70 percent of the respondents were between thirty and thirty-nine (table 7.4). Only 23 percent were twenty-nine or less, the youngest being twenty. These figures support the national trend of women bearing children late in the life cycle.[21]

TABLE 7.4   Age of Respondents

Age	N	%
20 to 29 years	66	22.9
30 to 39 years	201	70.0
Over 39 years	21	7.2
Total	288	100.1

With regard to marital status, an index that is important to my study, the group was highly uncharacteristic both of Orange County and of the nation. Eighty-six percent of the respondents were married, two-thirds of these for the first time. Less than 3 percent were never married. These figures indicate that the group under study is much like the classical nuclear family regarding marital status. The ideal of the Oedipal family was lifelong association, and there were few divorces in the nineteenth century; marriages were broken mainly by the death of one partner. In addition the respondents are unusual for Orange County in that they have been together for a long time (table 7.5). Fifty percent were with their current spouse/partner for more than ten years. Over 86 percent were together more than five years. The families under review are thus unusually committed to their marriages. In this respect as well they are similar to their nineteenth-century counterparts. The only reason for the unrepresentative marital stability of the participants that I can offer is that participation is somehow related to the conformity of the family to the dominant ideal of "good" families.

On many important criteria, then, I have a group that closely resembles the nineteenth-century nuclear family: They are white; they have a small number of children; they are married, largely for the first time; and they have been together for a long time. If these families' emotional structure varies considerably from the Oedipal family, it would be strong evidence that the classical nuclear family has disappeared from the group in which it originated and therefore may in general be on the wane.

One other important variable needs to be discussed concerning the profile of the families studied: the respondents' occupation. One-quarter of the respondents listed their occupation as housewife. In the nineteenth century this figure would have been over 99 percent. In contrast to women in the nuclear family of the past, many women today work outside the home, and in this respect the designation *nuclear family,* as sociologists have shown, applies to only 10 percent of the population in the United States.[22] This change in women's job status is one of the most profound social trends affecting the family and is no doubt an important condition for many of the other changes in the family that I have observed.

TABLE 7.5   Years Living
with Spouse/Partner

Number of Years	N	%
Fewer than 3	7	2.9
3 to 5	26	10.7
6 to 10	88	36.4
More than 10	121	50.0
Total	242	100

PATTERNS IN CHILD REARING

One of the main findings of my study is that the child-rearing patterns of the classical nuclear family have been almost completely abandoned. The structure of authority and love confronting the contemporary Orange County child in the sample is simply different from that confronting his or her nineteenth-century counterpart. If the nuclear family may be understood in part as one in which the child, during the early years, receives parental affection in exchange for relinquishing bodily gratification, then the nuclear family no longer exists. I document these changes here and then present portraits of the new family structures, such as my sample permits.

In the nineteenth century scheduled breastfeeding was the norm for the middle class. In my study, only 5 percent of mothers breastfed, and of these only two, or 15 percent, scheduled the feeding. The alternative adopted by the majority of mothers, bottle feeding, offers advantages that are apparently highly valued in today's families. Bottle feeding enables spouses/partners to share in the feeding activity. More than 77 percent of those using bottle feeding stated that their spouse/partner shares the activity to some extent. In this regard, middle-class families in Orange County have overwhelmingly rejected the strict sex-role segregation of their nineteenth-century counterparts. However, a mere 16 percent shared the feeding activity equally. Already something of a pattern in child rearing is emerging: Although the strict division of tasks between man and woman has been rejected, the redistribution of child-rearing tasks has been moderate. This pattern may indicate that although the man's privileged role in the family has been rejected in principle, the practice of sex-defined tasks has not been radically altered.

Again rejecting the nineteenth-century pattern, the few schedule feeders preferred flexibility to rigid adherence to the clock. The nineteenth-century ideal of machinelike regularity in feeding has been abandoned. The child's bodily needs now take priority over a regimen that valued punctuality in feeding children as much as in industry. In addition only 10 percent (of the 5 percent who were nursing) nursed longer than one year, whereas in the classical nuclear family, in part under the influence of Jean-Jacques Rousseau and the Romantic movement, extended breast-feeding by mothers was the norm.

Among breastfeeders a potential fear is insufficient milk. Less than a fourth of the breastfeeding mothers reported they experienced such anxiety, an indication that the mothers are well nourished, but also a sign that the feeding process is accomplished with confidence. Almost 90 percent said that feeding was a happy, relaxed experience for them. There is some evidence that in the nineteenth century middle-class mothers were insecure about breastfeeding, burdened as the activity was with high moral and spiritual purposes.[23] Such insecurity corresponds with their imposition of a rigid schedule. It bespeaks a circumstance in which mothers were breaking with the tradition of employing wet nurses as well as of being in contact with older women's networks.[24] The relative absence of such anxiety today suggests an emotionally fuller experience for the infant and parent, whether the infant is being fed by the mother or her spouse/partner. It might be mentioned that the perception of feeding as sometimes being a chore was proportionally distributed among sampled Orange County mothers between the housewives and mothers who work outside the home (about one-third for each group), a finding that contradicts the view that working mothers are less able to enjoy child rearing than housewives.

These observations lead to the issue of the degree of isolation of the family both from relatives and from the community. More than 40 percent of the mothers never got advice from a relative about feeding, and almost 60 percent never got advice from a friend. Of those who did get advice on feeding from a relative, three-quarters did so from their mothers. Mothers in the sample turned more frequently to doctors and to literature than to family and friends. Of the 80 percent who received advice on feeding from doctors, one-half thought it important. Only one-fourth of the mothers consulted other health-care professionals on the subject. But the vast majority read books and magazines on feeding: Of these, two-thirds named *Parents Magazine* as the periodical of choice, and Dr. Benjamin Spock was the author most frequently mentioned. It is worth noting that the mothers' attitudes about child rearing resembled closely those of Dr. Spock, just as those of nineteenth-century middle-class mothers were similar to contemporary medical opinion.

These results imply that parents today are considerably isolated from kin and community. Because Orange County is a rapidly growing area (with a population of one million in 1965, which doubled by 1980), many residents have immigrated from elsewhere, leaving relatives and friends behind. The design of Orange County discourages the formation of new ties, with its centralized shopping malls and few places for casual congregation. Little evidence allows us to compare with any accuracy the degree of isolation of Orange County mothers with that of nineteenth-century mothers. No doubt the circumstances of the two groups are similar, and today's family continues the trend of isolation from neighborhood and kin established by the classical nuclear family. The chief difference today is that most mothers work outside the home, making contacts on a daily basis that were not available to their nineteenth-century counterparts.

If the exchange of parental affection for bodily gratification on the child's part no longer characterizes the feeding period, that conclusion also applies even more clearly to the next developmental phase, toilet training. Mothers in the Oedipal family were obsessively concerned with the child's cleanliness. Historians have noted the similarity of this trait to the values of cleanliness, punctuality, and orderliness in industrial society.[25] No doubt these middle-class mothers were also reacting against what they regarded as the unhealthy slovenliness of working-class (and, in Europe, peasant and aristocratic) children whose parents were casual if not negligent about separating children from their wastes. Nineteenth-century physicians and writers on child care strongly insisted on early, strict toilet training as a key to the child's moral well-being. The standard sanction against the child's resistance was not corporal punishment but the withdrawal of love.

In Orange County today, judging by the evidence of my sample, toilet training is considerably different. Only half the children were toilet trained by two years of age. Girls were trained earlier than boys, with 60 percent of the girls and only 34 percent of the boys trained by the age of two. I should mention that this is the only significant difference in child rearing by sex of child in my study, a difference that is probably due to the more rapid development of girls rather than to any variation in their treatment during this stage.[26] These findings indicate that middle-class children are being trained significantly later than in earlier times. People tend to assume that their own child-rearing practices are normal or natural. But that is far from the case. For example, an eminent American doctor stated as late as 1931 that "there is general agreement that training to use a vessel for bowel-movements should begin very young, as young as six weeks or two months of age."[27] Such early training was an example of parental intrusion on the child's bodily functions, with parents insisting on control even before it was physically possible for the child to do so. The practice of late training today signifies that parents permit children to enjoy their bodies and that parents have thus abandoned the practice of the Oedipal family.

The mothers in the study also abandoned the sanctions previously imposed when the child failed to comply. Only 2 mothers out of 290 said they tell children they will not love them if they do not use the potty. This finding may reflect the mothers' attitude about toilet training more than it does their practice. Even so it represents a drastic shift in attitude from that of the Oedipal family. A similarly small number of mothers admitted that they spank the child to achieve toilet training. Some 10 percent use scolding and getting angry as a sanction, instances that should be added to the number of those who withdraw their love because these methods imply such a withdrawal. The typical response to the child's refusal to use the potty is to encourage the child to do better the next time.

In addition to dropping sanctions, the Orange County mothers deviate from the Oedipal mothers by sharing the task of toilet training with spouses/partners. More than half the spouses/partners (57 percent) helped with toilet training often or regularly, which is another indication that the rigid role distinctions of the classical nuclear family are disappearing. However, middle-class parents today receive little assistance from kin and friends in this child-rearing task. They are probably as isolated from support systems as their earlier counterparts. In sum, data about the toilet-training phase, like those on the feeding phase, indicate that the sampled parents no longer follow the patterns of the past.

Children's mastery over their bodies is more sorely tested over the issue of touching the genitals, or what is known as childhood masturbation. Such activity was the bête noire of the Oedipal family, a sign of serious moral degeneration. Doctors in the nineteenth century warned parents of the dire consequences of masturbation among five-year-olds: Pimples, headaches, deformities, and fatal diseases were the sure result.[28] Even in the 1930s experts encouraged parents to be sure their children were physically exhausted when they went to bed so that the problem would be avoided, although by then the hyperbole was gone.[29] Reacting against Christian notions of original sin, the middle classes of the past regarded children as *innocent* and defined that term as meaning without sexuality. Parents reserved their sternest sanctions for trespasses below the waist.

Today the child's little pleasures are treated differently, or at least such is the claim of the respondents. The general attitude in the home about sexuality is different from that in the Oedipal family, with its Victorian reserve about these matters. Two-thirds of the mothers allowed their small children to roam the house in the nude, presenting the child with a neutral attitude toward his or her *déshabillé*. Also, more than 85 percent of the parents allowed the child to see them in the nude, an indication to the child that the body is not a forbidden object. Almost all mothers noted that their child is aware of sexual difference and is interested in human reproduction. In this environment the child tends to accept the body as a natural fact rather than developing Victorian fears of the flesh.[30] Mothers reported that they are aware that their children touch their genitals and that they tend to ignore the behavior. Two families never punished their child for touching genitals or warned that someone else would do so. A few parents (5 percent) encouraged the activity, and a few (2 percent) strongly discouraged it. Most (62 percent) did neither.

In the Oedipal family there is little evidence of masturbation among girls, although since grown women were regarded as asexual, it is likely that masturbation by girls presented such cognitive dissonance that it could not be recognized as such. For boys the habitual sanction against childhood masturbation was the infamous threat of castration. Such threats were a matter of course. For example, in the case of "little Hans," Freud reported a conversation between Hans and his mother. When Hans was three-and-a-half "his mother found him with his hand to his penis. She threatened him in these words: 'If you do that, I shall send for Dr. A. to cut off your widdler. And then what'll you widdle with?'"[31] Freud reports these words without any indication that they are unusual.

Among those in my Orange County sample who discouraged masturbation, none, I am bound to report, uttered such threats. Only two mothers told their child that touching the genitals is dangerous to their health. Fewer said they "angrily" discourage masturbation than said they are "angry" with their child for not using the potty. Many (23 percent) said they "calmly told the child not to do it." Only 2 percent of those who discourage the activity did so strongly. In this third stage of child development, as in the previous two, the contemporary middle-class family avoids the Oedipal strategy of intensifying the child's ambivalent feelings by coercing an exchange of parental love for bodily gratification.

Part of the effectiveness of the Oedipal strategy in the nineteenth century derived from the isolation of the child from adults and from children outside the nuclear family. Parents, and perhaps a servant or two, were thought to be the only salutary influences for the child. The urban street was considered a dangerous, dirty place. During the early years the child was sequestered in the apartment or town house as much as possible. With severely restricted contacts, the child's emotional ties to the immediate family were intensified. Such "explosive intimacy" multiplied the effect of the child's ambivalent feelings toward the parents.[32] Perhaps this isolation helps explain why Freud discovered strong love feelings in the child for the parent of the opposite sex.

Although the middle-class Orange County family is likewise isolated from the external world, the child is not sequestered in the home. Mothers reported that their children play with other children frequently (77 percent), visit their homes (56 percent), and are sent to preschools (81 percent) and day-care centers (34 percent). A significant minority of the children spend considerable periods with relatives. Consequently these

children have more contact with adults outside the family than their
nineteenth-century counterparts did, establishing bonds with a variety of
adults. More important, from an early age they encounter children outside the family, also finding in them objects for their feelings. In this
context their parents remain the most important people in their lives, but
for them the intensity of intrafamilial relations is less than for the children
in Oedipal families.

This comparison of the emotional structure of Oedipal and contemporary families during the early stages of the child's development reveals
dramatic changes. Parents abandoned the Oedipal strategy over a period
of a century, although the precise pace of the change at any time is
difficult to determine. We can, however, compare the situation today with
that in the mid-1950s because Robert Sears studied 379 mothers in the
Boston area at that time, asking questions that are similar to those in the
present study.[33] In general, Sears's findings fall mid-way between those
for the Oedipal family and those for the Orange County family of the
mid-1980s.[34] Only 29 percent of Sears's families fed children on demand,
and more of the schedule feeders did so rigidly than in my study.[35] Far
more of Sears's families toilet trained their children before two years than
did mine: A full 80 percent completed training by two years.[36] Another
great difference in the studies concerns the child's sexuality. Sears's mothers tended not to permit nudity in the home: Sixty percent allowed no
nudity at all or at most allowed it only on the way to and from the
bathroom.[37] Half of Sears's families did not allow their children to touch
their genitals, and another 25 percent discouraged it. Forty percent of his
mothers said they never noticed the child masturbating, compared with 7
percent in my study, an astonishing index of the effects of the "sexual
revolution" of the 1960s and 1970s.[38] Although Sears's findings suggest
considerable change from the Oedipal family to the family of the 1950s,
they also indicate an even more rapid period of transition from the 1950s
to the 1980s.

NEW PATTERNS OF AUTHORITY AND LOVE

Sociologists have observed since the 1970s that the classical nuclear family
is a waning institution. Based on the criteria of one partner for life and
strict sex-role segregation with only the husband working outside the
home, the nuclear family constitutes less than 10 percent of the whole, as
we have seen. I have shown that for the middle-class family in Orange
County, the emotional heart of the nuclear family—its mechanism of
personality formation by intensifying ambivalence in the child, its pattern
of exchanging parental love for bodily gratification in the early phases of
development—has also disappeared. Instead, today's families allow the

child considerable exploration and enjoyment of his or her body. By being flexible with feeding schedules or feeding on demand, by toilet training relatively late, by allowing children to touch their genitals, by allowing them to roam the house in the nude and see nude adults, by encouraging questions about human reproduction, middle-class Orange County parents place positive value on children's bodily impulses. By exposing children to adults and children outside the home, parents defuse to some extent the emotional intensity of the children's bonding with them. By giving children considerable leeway in making their own rules, parents encourage autonomous ego development.

The pattern of age and sex hierarchies in the sampled Orange County family is also considerably at variance with that of the Oedipal family. The imposition of authority by parents on children has lessened dramatically. Mothers were asked whether they direct children's play or permit the children to determine their own activities. One-third of the sample reported that they rarely or never direct play. Only 2 percent said they always direct play, which is the tendency of the Oedipal family. Parents are also reluctant to impose strict rules on the child: Only 24 percent noted that they do so often or always, while 35 percent reported that they do so rarely or never. If one is to judge by what mothers report in the questionnaire—and let me remind the reader at this point that my study tests attitudes only, not behavior—children are encouraged to take responsibility for themselves, to learn self-direction not by a forced internalization of parental demands, as was the case in the Oedipal family, but by exploration of their desires and needs. The parenting style in Orange County is far less authoritarian than was the case in the Oedipal family.

One may argue the merits of such a relaxation of authoritarian child-rearing styles, an issue of staggering complexity and great controversy. To some extent the optimum degree of structure varies from child to child. Some children thrive on tight adult regulation of their behavior, while others furiously resist it. Even so, evidence of children's response to authority is not an adequate criterion by which to evaluate this issue. Parents' views must be considered. The influence of other adults (relatives, teachers, and friends of the family) and the media must be added into the equation, both factually (what is their authority) and normatively (what ought to be their authority). As we will see, relaxation of parental authority has been accompanied, among my sample families, by the increased "authority" of figures from the child's subculture, as they are presented to the child through the media, as well as of adults outside the family, like preschool teachers. It is difficult to judge whether the overall mix of authority on Orange County children is in sum greater or less than that on children of the Oedipal family. Yet the diffusion of authority to many rule-making social agents means that the child confronts conflicting values, styles, and role models. This situation is different from that of the child in the Oedipal family.

My study indicates that the division of roles between parents is infinitely more flexible today than in the nineteenth century, an indication of the waning of patriarchy, at least in the attitudes reflected in the questionnaire. In 81 percent of the sample, parents reported that they share the decision on major purchases; 60 percent share financial decisions; two-thirds share child-rearing decisions; 50 percent share child-rearing tasks. Responses are egalitarian concerning other household chores: Twenty-three percent share house cleaning, and 16 percent share cooking, while spouses/partners do most of the yardwork and home repairs. The picture that emerges is that of the fading of sharp gender separation in decision making and doing chores, a vast change from the nineteenth century. Parents are no longer legally and morally stereotyped by gender to the same degree as in earlier times. Patriarchy, or the general authority of husbands over wives, men over women, however, is not yet dead. Most women work outside the home and at the same time do a disproportionate share of the work within the home. Because hired child care is neither plentiful nor cheap, contemporary women pay a heavy price for the degree of emancipation they have won from earlier restrictions. Even so, the rigid gender roles of the Oedipal family are discredited and slowly disappearing.

The middle-class Orange County family of the 1980s presents an emotional structure that is far more open than that of the Oedipal family. Children can be heard as well as seen; their desires count for something. The child's body and feelings are validated by parents and given expression outside the home.

Family members want more from life than the nineteenth-century goals of social respectability and economic success. Organized in the pursuit of these goals, nineteenth-century families single-mindedly calculated and planned daily life for their attainment. The Oedipal family was a shrine of instrumental rationality. By contrast, the Orange County family seeks a wider range of accomplishments. In addition to social and economic success, which requires calculating rationality, today's family pursues emotional and sexual fulfillment. Mothers report that their families engage in a wide range of leisure activities, suggesting a life-style that balances immediate enjoyment with long-term security. The vaunted ability of the Oedipal family to accumulate wealth by savings is a forgotten ideal. In the contemporary family context the child is no doubt both bewildered and enthralled by what life has to offer.

Given these new trends in child rearing, children will likely grow up with a greater sense of the need for sensual gratification and give a greater value as adults to their emotional fulfillment than did children in Oedipal families. They will be less driven by superego demands, less prone to defer gratification for success, and have less rigid egos because they are not burdened by having to systematically repress bodily impulses. Because they live in dual-career families or families with working single parents, and because their parents tend to divide household work, children will have role models and images of adults (or ego ideals) that are less gender based than those of Oedipal children. It is possible as well that as adults the Orange County children will bring new demands to the political arena, demands based less on the work ethic of the past than on a rounded vision of a fulfilling life.

However, in other aspects of life the Orange County family continues to promote the Oedipal family pattern. Today's family remains an isolated unit, with a clear sense of the privacy of domestic interactions. Perhaps even more than the Oedipal family, the contemporary family is remote from relatives and, as a unit, is not actively involved in the daily life of the surrounding community. My sample was taken from cities that are essentially bedroom communities, very different from the urban settings of the nineteenth-century middle class. Isolated from networks of sociability, the middle-class Orange County family is open to the influence of the wider society, especially to the consumer culture, having even fewer resources than the Oedipal family to resist outside incursions. New technologies, like TV, the VCR, and the computer, bring that outer world into family life with awesome realism and power. These technologies work to divide family members from one another, encouraging isolated activities within the home, and they deflect the attention of family members away from one another toward individual subcultures.[39] Cartoons and MTV for children, soap operas for women, and sports for men, to use the case of television, constitute miniworlds within the home that are neither like traditional communities with their face-to-face interactions nor like single-person activities such as reading a novel, which was so popular in the nineteenth century. In these respects the new family pattern promotes a deterioration of public life, at least in the traditional sense.[40]

A NARCISSISTIC FAMILY?

The ambiguities of current family patterns have led some observers to highly negative conclusions. One hypothesis, offered by Christopher Lasch, has received considerable recognition and deserves our attention. In a series of highly regarded though controversial books,[41] Lasch argues that the nuclear family is disappearing, although he does so without investigating families empirically. Instead he studies a variety of cultural phenomena to test for the moral stature of Americans. He contends that the nuclear family nurtured strong egos and superegos as a consequence of unambiguous paternal domination. With fathers clearly in charge of the family and mothers specializing in the care of their young, children confronted firm and repressive discipline, a pattern that I have called the exchange of parental love for bodily gratification.

Lasch warns that today's family no longer inculcates strong egos, one of the bases for democracy, or strong superegos, the basis for personal self-restraint. He recites a litany of modern family trends responsible for narcissism in our culture:

> the emergence of the egalitarian family, so-called; the child's increasing exposure to other socializing agencies besides the family; and the general effect of modern mass culture in breaking down distinctions between illusions and reality. . . . The modern family is the product of egalitarian ideology, consumer capitalism and therapeutic intervention.[42]
>
> [Child care outside the family] exposed children to new forms of manipulation, sexual seduction, and outright sexual exploitation.[43]
>
> [Children watch too much television, attend too many child-care centers, eat junk food,] listen to junk music, read junk comics and spend endless hours playing video games, because their parents are too busy or too harried to offer them proper nourishment for their minds and bodies. They attend third-rate schools and get third-rate advice from their elders.[44]
>
> Many children today encounter less and less cultural opposition to fantasies of sexual and generational interchangeability, [which are strengthened by] early exposure to sexual images, [by sex education, and by the idea of children's equality with adults].[45]

The pivot of Lasch's argument is taken from psychoanalysis. The hysterical patients of Freud's time have been replaced today by narcissists,[46] individuals who are unable to define the boundaries of their own egos, merging self and other, thereby confusing their own gratification with their relations with others. Heinz Kohut, an analyst relied upon heavily by Lasch, describes the change this way:

> During the era preceding our own, the overstimulating closeness with the adults to which the child was exposed led later in adult life to the hostilities and inhibitions which . . . Freud's explanations may have ultimately helped us to overcome to a degree. Now we may see the results of a deadening distance to which children are exposed, leading in adulthood to a different kind of psychopathology, the disorders of the self.[47]

If nineteenth-century hysterics were symptomatic of the Oedipal family in that they were incapable of repressing their urges as the family trained them to do, contemporary narcissists bespeak a different family pattern, one where parents do not care about their children, where no effort is made by parents to define limits to the child's experience, where in the absence of parental attention children are left at the mercy of dangerous nonfamily institutions—child-care centers, commercial television, the helping professions. Instead of having bodily gratification clearly re-pressed, the child is indulged so as not to require attention. Lasch con-tends that the child's fantasies run wild, stimulated by urges the child neither controls nor comprehends. The child's ego remains weak because it has little sense of achieving control over the body, and the superego indistinct because it has not internalized clearly defined parental images.

In therapy sessions, Lasch reports, narcissistic patients "regularly de-scribe their fathers as 'ciphers' while characterizing their mothers as both seductive and 'mortally' dangerous.'"[48] The father's emotional absence removes, for these individuals, "an important obstacle to the child's illu-sion of omnipotence." Today the threat of nuclear destruction heightens these tendencies within the family. People want to take their pleasures without thinking of tomorrow. In the family, the fear of imminent de-struction intensifies the fear of separation and "weakens the psychological resources that make it possible to confront this fear realistically." In addi-tion, society contributes to narcissism by substituting a consumerist fan-tasy world of objects for a real world that can be controlled and mastered. In the haze of electronically transmitted images, individuals merge their dreams with the fantasies aimed at them, further confounding the border between self and other.

Lasch's denunciation of the practices of the contemporary family is powerful and coherent. Although it may apply to a minority of families, my research indicates that it is largely mistaken. It is too sweeping in its claims, generalizing too easily from psychoanalytic diagnoses of narcis-sism to sociological facts; it overlooks many of the advances made in contemporary families over the limitations of the Oedipal family (limita-tions that Lasch fails to acknowledge); and it fails to distinguish excesses in cultural patterns, which are harmful to individuals, from those cultural patterns themselves, which may offer new possibilities for genuine grati-fication.

To test the thesis of narcissism I asked the mothers how they reacted to the terrible-twos phase of their child's development. Parents with nar-cissistic tendencies confuse their own feelings with their child's, being unclear about the boundary of their egos.[49] About one-third responded in ways indicating that narcissism might be a problem: They believed that their children, during this period, are testing their parents' wills or chal-lenging their authority. Half the mothers thought their children are attempting to define their own boundaries by the behavior, a clear indica-tion of a sense of the separateness of parent and child. The remaining group was divided between those who think the child is asking for disci-pline and those who have a somewhat conventional attitude, stating simply that the child is going through a phase.

Another question attempted to detect the parent's sense of anxiety at being separate from the child, a sign of a desire for merger with the child or a need for total control of the child. Mothers were asked whether they fear that children will break things if they are not constantly watched. About 7 percent indicated that they are beset by this fear often. Another 28 percent said "sometimes." Those in the first group may tend to hover over the child, restricting his or her ability to achieve autonomy and perhaps developing narcissistic tendencies in the child. Overall, however, few mothers demonstrate narcissogenic tendencies either by confusing self-boundaries or by evincing a lack of concern for their children.[50] Additional work needs to be done to reach firm conclusions about this question, work that examines families more intensively than is possible using survey research methods.

Although clear indications of parental boundary confusion are not present in my findings, they do confirm Lasch's intuition of a new pattern in family life. Three-quarters of the mothers work outside the home. More than 85 percent send their children to day-care centers or preschools. Almost all have TVs, with one-quarter having three or more; three-quarters own VCRs. Most spouses/partners participate to some extent in child care, house cleaning, and cooking, domains that nineteenth-century patriarchs scrupulously avoided. Orange County families are, in Lasch's terms, "egalitarian," prey to "consumer capitalism," and they freely subject their children to the "dangers" of child-care centers. Yet if Lasch's diagnosis of narcissism is largely incorrect, what are the new family patterns that have emerged to replace those of the Oedipal family? To answer this question the findings about child rearing during the first three stages must be correlated with data about parenting style, relations between adults in the family, the family's use of new technologies, and its general social characteristics.

A LIBERATED FAMILY?

Comparisons between child-rearing variables and general family traits, to begin with the last index, yielded surprisingly little variance. Because almost all the families were white, ethnic or racial difference is eliminated. There was also no significant difference in child-rearing methods when cross-tabulated with family income, except that the wealthier families, as one might expect, hire more help for child rearing than the less wealthy. Discrepancies in wealth are explained in part by the fact that the wealthier families are also the older families. The younger families are simply at earlier stages of their careers than the older families, hence they have lower incomes. In all likelihood the sample is highly homogeneous in social class. Differences within the sample, one may deduce, are due to life-style choices, not income.

Nor do religious differences account for much of the variation in child-rearing methods. Jews and Protestants are somewhat more flexible in scheduling the feeding of their children than are Mormons and Catholics. Jews wean their children later than Catholics and Protestants. Catholics begin toilet training earlier than the rest, especially than those with no religious preference. Spouses/partners of Jews and Protestants help with toilet training more than others do. Mormons and Catholics rank highest in discouraging nudity among their children and in forbidding their children to see adult family members nude. Mormons especially discourage children from touching their genitals.[51] These differences do begin to divide the sample into those who are closer to the Oedipal family (Mormons and Catholics) and those who are most divergent from it (Jews and nonreligionists), with Protestants falling somewhere in between. Although these are interesting and perhaps anticipated results, the variance in child-rearing method because of religious preference does not account for much of the overall variance.

I divided the sample by traditional and nontraditional marital status, traditional status applying to those married for the first time (188) and nontraditional status reserved for those never married (8) and those divorced at least once even if currently remarried (94). Because in the Oedipal family divorce was rare and unmarried mothers unheard of, marital status provides another criterion by which to array the families on degree of deviation from that norm. Again this criterion yielded few significant results. There were a few differences in child-rearing method, but no consistent pattern. Mothers married for the first time are not closer to the Oedipal family than the rest of the sample. I then divided the sample by mothers' occupations, comparing housewives (70) to mothers with careers (220). Once again the results showed little variation: Housewives were not closer to the Oedipal family than career mothers, even though they are similar to ninteenth-century middle-class mothers in their daily occupations. The only difference between housewives and career mothers is that housewives rate higher on the narcissism scale: They are more worried about the children breaking things and are less aware than career mothers that children in the terrible-twos phase are defining their own boundaries. It may be that people restricted to domesticity are more likely to manifest these traits. Yet overall the differences are not great.[52]

From these analyses we reach the important conclusion that differences in the emotional structure of the family, within a white middle-class sample, are the consequence of parenting styles, not the result of income, religion, marital status, or mother's occupation. No doubt some variable, one not tested in this study, may correlate with differences in parenting style. But my finding seems to suggest that family relationships have

TABLE 7.6   Adults Direct Child's Play, Percentage

Family Type	Always	Sometimes	Never
Conservative	23	54	23
Democratic	15	52	33
Experimental	10	46	44

become the object of intentional social practices, that partners define their family type as part of their deliberate choice of life-style. In other words, once the classical nuclear family has been rejected in the white middle class, which, as I have shown is the case with the families I studied in contemporary Orange County, the major social determinants may no longer fully account for family structure. Because the Oedipal family is gone, family patterns are in flux, and partners have a degree of freedom in choosing a type of authority and love relation with their children. The question remains: What are those types and how great is the variety among them?

To answer this question, I created models of three family types. To distinguish the types, I use political terms, but these are not meant to reflect political allegiances, which often do not correlate directly with family type. Instead they designate only the degree of difference from the Oedipal family. In the conservative family parents still exert considerable authority over their child's daily life, and adult roles conform to some extent to the gender divisions of the nineteenth century. In the democratic family parents grant a degree of autonomy to their children, and a serious effort is made to share family decisions and tasks between adults. In the experimental family the child is encouraged to define some of the rules, and adults attempt to divide decisions and tasks equally. I then selected those variables that were good indicators of the extent of the difference between the Oedipal and Orange County families, selecting further those values for each variable that best fit each family type.[53] The distribution of family types is 19 percent conservative, 36 percent democratic, and 45 percent experimental, a somewhat arbitrary but nonetheless interesting result. Some 80 percent of the sample are families in which participants reported that the hierarchies of age and sex as well as the pattern of authority and love during the child's early years vary considerably from the Oedipal family.

There are also clear differences among the Orange County families according to their degree of difference from the Oedipal family. Like the Oedipal family, the conservative families feed their children more on a schedule and the spouses/partners help with feeding less than in the democratic and experimental families. But during the toilet-training and

TABLE 7.7 Age at Which Child
Sets Own Rules, Percentage

Family Type	Over 8	6 to 8	Under 6
Conservative	70	17	13
Democratic	25	22	53
Experimental	8	5	87

sexuality stages the conservative families were not closer than the other types to the Oedipal family. Regarding the tasks of cooking and cleaning the house and the decisions about how to raise the child, the experimental family was farthest from nineteenth-century gender roles; the democratic family was next farthest; and the conservative family was closest.

Family types are confirmed when they are cross-tabulated against both the variables for adult direction of children's play and for the age at which children are permitted to set their own rules (tables 7.6 and 7.7). Mothers read the following paragraph:

> There are many activities in a child's life which parents may regulate or allow the child to regulate himself or herself. Parents differ greatly in the way they impose limits on these activities. Examples of activities which may or may not be strictly regulated are the child's bedtime, the child's choice of friends, the number of hours a day the child watches television. The following questions ask about the manner and the extent to which you regulate these and similar activities of your child.

Mothers were then asked (see table 7.6) whether they or their spouse/partner or other adults in their family direct the child's play or permit the child to decide on his or her own activities. Conservative families reported most often that they always direct the child's play and least often that they rarely direct the child's play. Experimental families reported least often that they always direct the child's play and most often that they rarely did so. Parents were also asked (see table 7.7) at what age they permitted their children to set their own rules. The conservative families permitted rule setting latest and experimental families permitted it earliest. On both questions there were serious differences among the family types, differences that form a line of increasing divergence from the Oedipal family pattern. These findings indicate that the statistical construction of the three family types is valid and that Orange County families, while rejecting the Oedipal model, may be arrayed by their degree of difference from that model.

More plainly put, among middle-class white Orange County families with at least one child six or younger there is serious disagreement about what the age and sex hierarchies should be like. In the conservative group, the smallest of the three in my sample (19 percent), adults maintain to some extent the traditional gender-role divisions and sustain a relatively high degree of adult authority over children. In the experimental group, the largest in my sample (45 percent), adults report that they have completely abandoned gender-defined roles, equally sharing tasks and decisions, and report that they have abandoned parental domination of children to considerable extent, refusing to impose strict rules on them. In the democratic group, constituting 36 percent of the sample, family arrangements fall in between the other groups.

If Lasch's thesis about narcissistic families were correct, then the experimental family would show the highest correlation with variables for narcissism and the conservative family the lowest because the experimental families appear to be the least involved with their children and the conservative families the most involved. However, exactly the opposite is the case: The conservative families rated highest on the narcissism questions, and the experimental families the lowest. This result indicates that egalitarian relations between adults and children are not a sign of indifference on the adults' part, as Lasch would have us believe. On the contrary, the experimental families are as concerned as the other types about their children, but the parents in the experimental group are more aware of the border between their own egos and that of their children than are the parents in the other families. The results suggest that Lasch and others who bemoan contemporary family trends make a hasty and faulty equivalence between authoritarian families with gender-differentiated roles and patriarchical domination structures, on the one hand, and the child's maximal development as an independent, capable adult, on the other hand.

If the families of the 1980s disagree about the pattern of age and sex hierarchies, they are fundamentally uncertain about how to structure parental authority and love during the early stages of child development. The findings of the study indicate no clear distinctions in this regard among the conservative, democratic, and experimental family types, perhaps because of the limitations of the questionnaire in providing a detailed picture of such subtle issues. Or it may be that rapid social changes, along with the new pattern of age and sex hierarchies revealed here, have not yet resulted in definable emotional structures.

There is a third possibility, one that constitutes the conclusion of this study. It may be that a coherent structure of authority and love (such as the insistence on trading off bodily gratification for parental love) is characteristic of families that are emotionally isolated from the wider society (such as the Oedipal family). The middle-class Orange County family of the 1980s is decidedly not so isolated. In my sample children are in preschools and most mothers work outside the home. Both adults and children experience significant relationships outside the family. In the questionnaire, mothers disclosed that leisure activities, even watching TV, were engaged in by the family as a whole only sporadically. Visiting amusement parks or public parks, camping, going to the movies, visiting relatives or friends, going shopping—all these activities that could be done as a family unit were only rarely the occasion of family solidarity. The activity most often engaged in by the family as a unit was dining in restaurants, an indication of the wealth of the families sampled but also a sign of the complexity of their lives because restaurants relieve the pressure to prepare meals.

The family then is a segmented group, dividing its time between family and nonfamily relations, just as other chapters in this book suggest that Orange County as a whole is a segmented metropolis. With the family as a segmented group, each individual following in part a course separate from the others, the love/authority structure may no longer constitute the crucial determinant of the child's experience and personality development.

The segmentation of family life goes beyond individuated activities outside the home. The penetration of the home by electronically mediated communication systems provides continuous contact for each family member with its subculture.[54] Through TV, telephones, and VCRs, the child, for example, receives communications from nonfamily members while being physically in the home. The widespread use of TVs, VCRs, and computers by Orange County families, as demonstrated by the high proportion of families who own these devices and use them frequently, mollifies the intensity of family interactions, permitting a diffusion of emotional bonding.[55]

Middle-class families in Orange County are at a crossroads. Surrounded by an emerging new social formation, which I call *the mode of information* and others refer to as *postindustrial society*, families have rejected the classical nuclear-family pattern. They are testing new family structures, some of which eliminate to a considerable degree earlier forms of domination in the family. One senses a tremendous burden on these microunits of society and accordingly a deep contradiction in the emerging social formation. These Orange County families have great ambitions: They want to remove restrictions on women's choices; the adults want to achieve emotional and sexual gratification; they want to develop in their children an ability for self-directed personal growth; they want to enjoy the sophisticated technologies available to them. These goals suggest a new type of integration between the family and the community, placing new demands on the society, such as high-quality, plentiful day care, even in workplaces; richer community life; extensive sharing of information and activities concerning new technologies. Yet society resists the changes implied in these demands. The modern family thus constitutes itself as a segmented unit, adapting its goals to a recalcitrant environment and bearing the great stress of experimentation without adequate support.

NOTES

Acknowledgments: This study simply would not have been possible without the assistance of Alladi Venkatesh of the University of California at Irvine Graduate School of Management, who gave freely of his time at every stage of the investigation. Wendy Goldberg of the University of California at Irvine Program in Social Ecology also was generous with her time. Also helpful at the University of California at Irvine were Rob Kling, Spencer Olin, Jonathan Wiener, Marianne Poster, Lynton Freeman, Michael Johnson, and Francesca Cancian. The University of California at Irvine Graduate Division provided me with funds for summer work, as did the Research Committee of the Humanities School at the University of California at Irvine. Robert Sieber, Dennis Bryson, and David Romagnolo helped with statistical analysis. A different version of this chapter appears in Mark Poster, *Critical Theory and Poststructuralism* (Ithaca, N.Y.: Cornell University Press, 1989).

1. Good statistical evidence of rising incidence in these categories exists only for divorce. For the rest, reported incidences are rising, but there is also reason to expect, in each case, much nonreported incidence.

2. For a good critique and proposed alternative to this tendency, see Joan Aldous, "Family Interaction Patterns," *Annual Review of Sociology* 3 (1977): 105–35.

3. See, for example, Albert Davis in his review of the current literature on the family, "Parent-Child Interaction in the Socialization Process: A Critical Analysis of the Research," *Contemporary Education* 50 (Winter 1979): 86–92.

4. The important work of Diana Baumrind displays this tendency. See, for example, "The Development of Instrumental Competence through Socialization," in *Minnesota Symposia on Child Development,* ed. A. Pick (Minneapolis: University of Minnesota Press, 1973), 3–46.

5. The term *domination* has many definitions. I use it as in the tradition of critical social theory to denote asymmetrical social relations, those in which the subordinate position is not able legitimately to question the authority of the dominant position. The question of the "necessary" subordination of children to adults is dealt with in Mark Poster, *Critical Theory of the Family* (New York: Continuum, 1978), 147ff.

6. See Philippe Ariès, *Centuries of Childhood: A Social History of Family Life,* trans. R. Baldick (New York: Vintage Books, 1965); Edward Shorter, *The Making of the Modern Family* (New York: Basic Books, 1975); Jacques Donzelot, *The Policing of Families,* trans. R. Hurley (New York: Pantheon, 1979). For the United States, see Michael Gordon, *The American Family: Past, Present and Future* (New York: Random House, 1978); Michael Gordon, ed., *The American Family in Social-Historical Perspective* (New York: St. Martin's Press, 1973); Donald Scott and Bernard Wishy, eds., *America's Families: A Documentary History* (New York: Harper & Row, 1982);

and Carl Degler, *At Odds: Women and the Family in America from the Revolution to the Present* (New York: Oxford University Press, 1980).

7. See Lawrence Stone, *The Family, Sex and Marriage in England: 1500–1800* (New York: Harper & Row, 1977), and Mark Poster, *Critical Theory of the Family* (New York: Continuum, 1978).

8. See Michael Young and Peter Willmott, *Family and Kinship in East London* (London: Penguin Books, 1957).

9. In this study I have not explored the relation between sex hierarchies and child-rearing practices as they affect gender differences in children. My data do not provide insight into gender differences, a failing that derives from the instrument I used in the survey.

10. One may question the value or the relevance of the Freudian aspects of child rearing that I focus on. My reply is that attention to these stages of development in the present permits a comparison with the earlier nuclear family and leads to an assessment of the extent to which child rearing has changed since that benchmark.

11. For a more complete discussion of the theory, see Poster, *Critical Theory of the Family*.

12. Mary Ryan in *Womanhood in America* (New York: Watts, 1983) writes, "The favored punishment of the nineteenth century child-rearing manual was the withdrawal of love, exercised by the curtailment of a mother's smiles and kisses or ostracism from the warmth of the family circle" (p. 145).

13. See Jean Strouse, *Alice James* (New York: Bantam, 1980), for a compelling example.

14. Most of the data analysis, especially the frequencies, was done using the Statistical Package for the Social Sciences. Many of the cross-tabulations were done on Systat.

15. I requested that "mothers" complete the questionnaire to avoid inconsistency of informants. By designating the "mother" rather than, say, the "female adult," I allowed for male adults who consider themselves mothers to participate in the study. If a family contained two partners and both considered themselves mothers, both would answer the questionnaire.

16. Approximately 3,000 invitations were distributed. These elicited responses from 318 people, of whom 290 returned completed questionnaires.

17. Open-ended questions that were coded and included in the study concerned the occupation of the respondent and spouse/partner, and books and magazines consulted by the respondent on child-care issues. A copy of the questionnaire may be obtained by writing to Professor Mark Poster, History Department, University of California, Irvine, Calif. 92717.

18. See Jeffrey Weeks, *Sex, Politics and Society: The Regulation of Sexuality since 1800* (London: Longman, 1981).

19. The national figure for 1984 was an astonishing 2.71. This figure was down from 4.76 in 1900 and 5.79 in 1790, the earliest record. See Bureau of the Census, *Household and Family Characteristics: March 1984* (Washington, 1985), 9.

20. See Bureau of the Census, *Statistical Abstracts of the U.S.* (Washington, 1986).

21. See Prithwis Das Gupta, *Future Fertility of Women by Present Age and Parity: Analysis of American Historical Data, 1917–80* (Washington: Bureau of the Census, 1985), 3.

22. Marvin Harris, "Growing Conservatism? Not in Family Patterns," *Los Angeles Times*, 23 Dec. 1981, pt. II, 9.

23. Ryan, *Womanhood in America*, 144.

24. See Carroll Smith-Rosenberg, "The Female World of Love and Ritual: Relations between Women in Nineteenth-Century America," in *Disorderly Conduct: Visions of Gender in Victorian America*, ed. Carroll Smith-Rosenberg (New York: Oxford University Press, 1985), 53–76, who shows how some women's networks survived the privatization of the nuclear family.

25. Peter Cominos, "Late Victorian Sexual Respectability and the Social System," *International Review of Social History* 8 (1963): 18–48, 216–50.

26. Chi-square = 5.297, with 1 degree of freedom; p = 0.021. Contingency coefficient = .1395. Lambda = .1154, with sex of child as the dependent variable. Uncertainty coefficient = .0144, with sex of child as the dependent variable.

27. Helen T. Woolley, "Eating, Sleeping and Elimination," in *Handbook of Child Psychology*, ed. Carl Murchison (Worcester, Mass.: Clark University Press, 1931), 52.

28. See Mary S. Hartman, "Child-Abuse as Self-Abuse: Two Victorian Cases," *History of Childhood Quarterly* 2 (Fall 1974): 221–48.

29. Woolley, "Eating, Sleeping, and Elimination," 67.

30. One historian, Peter Gay, has attempted to revise our attitude about Victorian antisexuality. See *The Bourgeois Experience: Victoria to Freud*, vol. 1, *The Education of the Senses* (New York: Oxford University Press, 1984). Yet even he is hard put to prove his case in the matter of childhood masturbation.

31. Sigmund Freud, "Analysis of a Phobia in a Five-Year-Old Boy," trans. in *The Sexual Enlightenment of Children*, ed. Philip Rieff (New York: Macmillan, 1966), 49.

32. Stephen Kern, "Explosive Intimacy: Psychodynamics of the Victorian Family," *History of Childhood Quarterly* 1 (Winter 1974): 437–62.

33. These results were published as Robert Sears et al., *Patterns of Child Rearing* (Evanston, Ill.: Row, Peterson, 1957). Working at Harvard University, Sears interviewed mothers in a laboratory setting, whereas my study has been limited to having mothers respond to a questionnaire.

34. Sears's sample was significantly different from mine. His work was done in Boston and in a laboratory, as already noted. More important, about half his respondents were working class (174), and it is well documented that the twentieth-century working-class family resembles the nineteenth-century middle-class family in child-rearing patterns. Because Sears did not report the results for each class separately, his findings are weighted toward the Oedipal pattern by the inclusion of working-class mothers in the sample. Nonetheless, his results differ from mine to such an extent that it is unlikely that the variable of class accounts for all the variance. Sears's respondents, like mine, were primarily white, but he had more Catholics and Jews than were in my sample, no doubt because of the difference in the location of the studies.

35. Sears, *Patterns of Child Rearing*, 78.

36. Ibid., 109.

37. Ibid., 193.

38. Ibid., 200.

39. For the isolating effect of the computer, see the following informative studies: Alladi Venkatesh, "A Conceptualization of the Household/Technology Interaction," in *Advances in Consumer Research*, ed. E. C. Hirschman and M. Holbrook, vol. XII, 189–95 (Provo, Utah: Association for Consumer Research, 1985); and Nicholas Vitalari, Alladi Venkatesh, and Kjell Gronhaug, "Computing in the Home: Shifts in the Time Allocation Patterns of Households," *Communications of the ACM* 28 (May 1985): 512–22.

40. Richard Sennett, *The Fall of Public Man* (New York: Knopf, 1977).

41. *Haven in a Heartless World: The Family Besieged* (New York: Basic Books, 1977); *The Culture of Narcissism: American Life in an Age of Diminishing Expectations* (New York: Norton, 1979); and *The Minimal Self: Psychic Survival in Troubled Times* (New York: Norton, 1984).

42. *The Minimal Self*, 185.

43. Ibid., 186.

44. Ibid., 188–89.

45. Ibid., 191.

46. Lasch uses the term *narcissism* in several ways, somewhat diminishing its analytic power in his text. For an excellent critique of his use of the term, see Jesse Battan, "The 'New Narcissism' in 20th-Century America: The Shadow and Substance of Social Change," *Journal of Social History* 17, no. 2 (1978): 199–220. Battan concludes that "the concept of narcissism merely clouds our understanding of . . . complex social and cultural issues" (p. 221).

47. "Thoughts on Narcissism and Narcissistic Rage (1972)," in *Self Psychology and the Humanities: Reflections on a New Psychoanalytic Approach*, ed. Charles Strozier (New York: Norton, 1985), 168.

48. *The Minimal Self*, 191.

49. For an excellent article on the question of the historical roots of narcissism, see Michael Bader and Ilene Philipson, "Narcissism and Family Structure: A Social-Historical Perspective," *Psychoanalysis and Contemporary Thought* 3, no. 3 (1980): 299–328. They define narcissism as "the incapacity to hold oneself in esteem as an autonomous being and to wholly love and be intimate with another, [which derives from] the difficulty in an earlier period of self-other differentiation vis-à-vis the mother" (p. 311).

50. One would not expect people who fill out questionnaires on the family to be indifferent to their children. On this count no conclusion can be reached about narcissism based on a self-selecting sample.

51. Religious affiliation plays a role as follows: follow flexible feeding schedule: Jews 74 percent, Protestants 73 percent, Mormons 58 percent, Catholics 60 percent; wean one year or later: Jews 48 percent, Catholics 27 percent, Protestants 24 percent; begin toilet training earlier than two years: Catholics 58 percent, next closest are Jews 48 percent, nonreligionists 38 percent; have help from spouse/partner with toilet training: Jews 76 percent, Protestants 61 percent,

Catholics 46 percent, nonreligionists 53 percent; discourage child's nudity: Mormons 86 percent, Catholics 22 percent, Jews 12 percent, Protestants 8 percent; discourage child from touching genitals: Mormons 100 percent, Jews 35 percent, Catholics 32 percent, Protestants 31 percent.

52. On fear of the child's breaking things: housewives 12 percent, career mothers 6 percent. On thinking that terrible twos are defining their own boundary: housewives 60 percent, career mothers 70 percent. On all other child-rearing variables, the differences between housewives and career mothers were less than 5 percent.

53. Here is the precise way I divided the variables and values into the family types:

	Conservative	Democratic	Experimental
Feeding	on schedule	both	on demand
Spouse helps	rarely	sometimes	half or more
Toilet training	before 2 years		later than 2 years
Spouse helps	once or less	often	regularly
Allows child to see nude adults	rarely/never	sometimes	often/always
Ignores masturbation	rarely/never	sometimes	often/always
Makes rearing decisions	mother	mostly mother	adults and child
Does cooking	mother	mostly mother	adults equally
Does cleaning	mother	mostly mother	adults equally
Imposes strict rules	always/often	sometimes	rarely/never
Makes rules	always mother	mostly mother	adults and child

Although the relationship between the values and the family types is somewhat arbitrary, I consistently used the criterion of degree of difference from the Oedipal family pattern as the guide.

54. I have analyzed these communication systems under the concept of the mode of information. See Mark Poster, *The Mode of Information* (London: Polity, 1990).

55. It must be noted that few of the respondents admitted that they or anyone in their family watched TV more than three or four hours a week, considerably below the national average. It must be concluded that their responses on this question were less than accurate, itself an interesting indication of ambivalence about new communication media.

REFERENCES

Aldous, Joan. "Family Interaction Patterns." *Annual Review of Sociology* 3 (1977): 105–35.

Ariès, Philippe. *Centuries of Childhood: A Social History of Family Life.* Trans. R. Baldick. New York: Vintage Books, 1965.

Bader, Michael, and Ilene Philipson. "Narcissism and Family Structure: A Social-Historical Perspective." *Psychoanalysis and Contemporary Thought* 3, no. 3 (1980): 299–328.

Battan, Jesse. "The 'New Narcissism' in 20th-Century America: The Shadow and Substance of Social Change." *Journal of Social History* 17, no. 2 (1978): 199–220.

Baumrind, Diana. "The Development of Instrumental Competence through Socialization." In *Minnesota Symposia on Child Development*, ed. A. Pick, 3–46. Minneapolis: University of Minnesota Press, 1973.

Bureau of the Census. *Household and Family Characteristics: March 1984*. Washington, 1985.

Bureau of the Census. *Statistical Abstracts of the U.S.* Washington, 1986.

Cominos, Peter. "Late Victorian Sexual Respectability and the Social System." *International Review of Social History* 8 (1963): 18–48, 216–50.

Das Gupta, Prithwis. *Future Fertility of Women by Present Age and Parity: Analysis of American Historical Data, 1917–80*. Washington: Bureau of the Census, 1985.

Davis, Albert. "Parent-Child Interaction in the Socialization Process: A Critical Analysis of the Research." *Contemporary Education* 50 (Winter 1979): 86–92.

Degler, Carl. *At Odds: Women and the Family in America from the Revolution to the Present*. New York: Oxford University Press, 1980.

Donzelot, Jacques. *The Policing of Families*. Trans. R. Hurley. New York: Pantheon, 1979.

Freud, Sigmund. "Analysis of a Phobia in a Five-Year Old Boy." Trans. in *The Sexual Enlightenment of Children*, ed. Philip Rieff, 47–184. New York: Macmillan, 1966.

Gay, Peter. *The Bourgeois Experience: Victoria to Freud*. Vol. 1: *The Education of the Senses*. New York: Oxford University Press, 1984.

Gordon, Michael. *The American Family: Past, Present and Future*. New York: Random House, 1978.

———, ed. *The American Family in Social-Historical Perspective*. New York: St. Martin's Press, 1973.

Harris, Marvin. "Growing Conservatism? Not in Family Patterns." *Los Angeles Times*, 23 Dec. 1981, pt. II, 9.

Hartman, Mary S. "Child-Abuse as Self-Abuse: Two Victorian Cases." *History of Childhood Quarterly* 2 (Fall 1974): 221–48.

Kern, Stephen. "Explosive Intimacy: Psychodynamics of the Victorian Family." *History of Childhood Quarterly* 1 (Winter 1974): 437–62.

Kohut, Heinz. "Thoughts on Narcissism and Narcissistic Rage (1972)." In *Self Psychology and the Humanities: Reflections on a New Psychoanalytic Approach*, ed. Charles Strozier. New York: Norton, 1985.

Lasch, Christopher. *The Culture of Narcissism: American Life in an Age of Diminishing Expectations*. New York: Norton, 1979.

———. *Haven in a Heartless World: The Family Besieged*. New York: Basic Books, 1977.

———. *The Minimal Self: Psychic Survival in Troubled Times*. New York: Norton, 1984.

Poster, Mark. *Critical Theory of the Family*. New York: Continuum, 1978.

———. *The Mode of Information*. London: Polity Press, 1990.

Ryan, Mary. *Womanhood in America*. New York: Watts, 1983.

Scott, Donald, and Bernard Wishy, eds. *America's Families: A Documentary History.* New York: Harper & Row, 1982.

Sears, Robert, et al. *Patterns of Child Rearing.* Evanston, Ill.: Row, Peterson, 1957.

Sennett, Richard. *The Fall of Public Man.* New York: Knopf, 1977.

Shorter, Edward. *The Making of the Modern Family.* New York: Basic Books, 1975.

Smith-Rosenberg, Carroll. "The Female World of Love and Ritual: Relations between Women in Nineteenth-Century America." In *Disorderly Conduct: Visions of Gender in Victorian America,* ed. Carroll Smith-Rosenberg, 53–76. New York: Oxford University Press, 1985.

Stone, Lawrence. *The Family, Sex and Marriage in England: 1500–1800.* New York: Harper & Row, 1977.

Strouse, Jean. *Alice James.* New York: Bantam, 1980.

Venkatesh, Alladi. "A Conceptualization of the Household/Technology Interaction." In *Advances in Consumer Research,* ed. E. C. Hirschman and M. Holbrook, vol. XII, 189–95. Provo, Utah: Association for Consumer Research, 1985.

Vitalari, Nicholas, Alladi Venkatesh, and Kjell Gronhaug. "Computing in the Home: Shifts in the Time Allocation Patterns of Households." *Communications of the ACM* 28 (May 1985): 512–22.

Weeks, Jeffrey. *Sex, Politics and Society: The Regulation of Sexuality since 1800.* London: Longman, 1981.

Woolley, Helen T. "Eating, Sleeping and Elimination." In *Handbook of Child Psychology,* ed. Carl Murchison, 28–70. Worcester, Mass.: Clark University Press, 1931.

Young, Michael, and Peter Willmott. *Family and Kinship in East London.* London: Penguin Books, 1957.

EIGHT

Intraclass Conflict and the Politics of a Fragmented Region

Spencer Olin

A newly arrived national and international business class in Orange County has persistently displaced the small-scale farmers, local merchants, and manufacturers who previously wielded economic and political power in the region. These larger corporate interests, representing the forces of information capitalism, have pushed for rapid growth and for rationalized, metropolitanwide government. The smaller commercial and manufacturing entrepreneurs and their political allies have pursued their own redevelopment plans and have fought to preserve local governmental autonomy.

This continuing and often volatile contest over the structure of the political system, land use, and the allocation of space contains all the classical elements of similar struggles elsewhere, including uneven regional development with its attendant social polarization and spatial inequalities. Because Orange County has emerged as a center for global capital and as a key component of the larger Los Angeles region, this contest increasingly has been won by those favoring growth and regional integration. A heavy stream of foreign investment and global economic ventures by banking, financial, and multinational corporations has thus helped to shape the information economy and postsuburban landscape of Orange County, and its political character as well.[1]

How has the increasing maturation of Orange County's economy affected county and municipal politics? The many conflicts over metropolitan growth that have characterized interactions among segments of Orange County's business class since World War II and the ways in which those conflicts have been reflected in the political system are the primary concerns of this chapter. An inquiry of this kind is difficult, especially so in a region as politically fragmented as Orange County. With twenty-eight muncipalities in a sprawling, deconcentrated postsuburban metropolis lacking a central urban core, Orange County poses special problems for those seeking to understand how economic growth has affected political institutions and behavior.

The region's special characteristics require careful analytical strategies designed to reveal the nature of economic and political change since World War II. The theoretical perspective adopted here for this purpose insists on the significance of class and on the explicit relationship between the process of suburban development and the structures of capitalism. Within suburbs, as within the larger state, the distribution and exercise of political power are determined by capitalist class relations. The control of the workplace resulting from the ownership of capital, in other words, is duplicated in urban, suburban, and postsuburban space.[2] My analysis thus proceeds from the assumption that social class is an indispensable concept for understanding the relationships among economic development, social structure, and politics. Many of the most significant political conflicts are rooted in class antagonisms, not merely between an owning and a working class but also (and in Orange County most especially) within the owning class itself.[3]

Reliance on class analysis in attempting to understand the complex interaction between economics and politics in a rapidly growing region should not blind us to those forces and pressures that may at times cut across both class lines and the private and public sectors. Public officials, after all, are often significant owners of property. I refer here to what M. Gottdiener identifies as "growth networks." "Much of the development which has occurred in our large cities," Gottdiener argues, "is a result of the actions of growth networks rather than the decisions of individual corporations, banks, and the like. Their popularity has been sustained by a general belief in the virtues of growth, especially its beneficial effects on employment levels."[4] Such growth networks certainly include the real estate sector and representatives of finance and corporate capital, but they can also incorporate politicians, lawyers, local booster groups, speculators, and construction and building unions. Thus, we may even find elements of the working class coalescing into networks that actively promote growth. As we shall see at the conclusion of this chapter, opponents of these growth networks mobilize around the ideology of slow (or no) growth and local control. "In short," insists Gottdiener, "the clash between growth and no growth represents a basic cleavage in society, involving economic, political, and ideological practices. . . . Indeed, the clash of pro growth versus no growth is as fundamental to the production of space as is the struggle between capital and labor."[5]

The political process as envisioned here, therefore, consists of far more than such formal and observable activities as joining parties, registering voters, and holding elections. In addition, it reflects deeper, though less obvious, economic and social forces in a given region. For one thing, the political life of cities in suburban and postsuburban areas is shaped by the need to stimulate and maintain their economic vitality. This requirement results in close interactions between muncipal and county governments, on the one hand, and private business, on the other, to protect what is called the process of capital accumulation.[6]

It is important to note in this regard, however, that just as growth networks can cut across class lines, so too can government officials (or state managers) maintain some autonomy; they are not simply the agents of capital. Nevertheless, they are obliged to induce economic performance from those who own and control productive assets in the region in which they exercise political power. The challenge for historians analyzing metropolitan development, then, is to understand the complex relationships among accumulation, space, and political practice.[7]

Furthermore, from the point of view of the capitalist class, the role of municipal and county governments in the capital-accumulation process must be insulated as much as possible from popular political challenge. Institutional arrangements must be designed to reduce the chances for land-use decisions, among others, to become a matter for public dispute. The role of the public is reduced, for example, by structuring agencies so as to favor access by economically powerful groups and by ensuring that agencies responsible for economic growth are relatively autonomous from elected officials.[8] Helpful in this regard is the notion of technical expertise and professionalism, which serves to legitimate the insulation of certain government agencies and to discourage popular involvement in their activities. There is, therefore, a persistent upward shift in political decision making and a concomitant depoliticization that accompanies the economic maturation of a region such as Orange County.[9]

Moreover, the challenge of gaining (or retaining) control of suburban and postsuburban space creates conflicts between various class segments of the business community.[10] In Orange County, such conflicts have continually occurred between representatives of regional capital and those of national and international capital. Unlike owners of national and multinational corporations, who can relocate elsewhere if local conditions become a liability, regional capitalists own geographically concentrated and physically immobile firms. They are thereby, in effect, trapped in space because their economic well-being remains tied to the growth of the particular region in which they are located. Because they are also more vulnerable than national and multinational corporations to changes in municipal governments that threaten their interests, they often resist efforts by those groups to acquire dominant economic and political power in the local area. Yet, as a segment of capital, self-employed regional entrepreneurs and proprietors have continually declined in significance throughout the twentieth century, as their power and influence have been undermined by the increasing consolidation and concentration of capital in large corporations. In these struggles, the forces of cosmopolitanism and regional integration mobilized by national and international capital have gradually overcome the resistance of regional capital and its local political representatives.[11] In general, this has been the experience of Orange County.

It is important to point out, however, that politics in a postsuburban region such as Orange County is more than an intraclass (or even inter-class) feud between clashing social factions. It is also an effort to provide municipal services for citizens insistent on increasing levels of comfort and convenience. The property tax is a major source of revenue for these services and is also the one over which local governments have the most control (see Chapter 10). Because property-tax yields are closely related to land-use patterns, local and regional governments faced with the need to increase the tax base promote the most lucrative development. Such types of development, however, are generally not the major consumers of public services. Low-yield residential properties consume far in excess of what they return in taxes. This lack of spatial correspondence between resources and needs has had important political implications in Orange County, as I will attempt to demonstrate.[12]

With these concepts and analytical strategies in mind, I will seek to ex-plain sociospatial confrontations among class segments in Orange County since World War II. Such confrontations have constituted the bulk of local and regional politics, especially as they have increasingly taken the form of growth-control clashes. My empirical inquiries include studies of sev-eral developments of historical significance in the region: the incorpora-tion and city-manager movements of the 1950s and early 1960s; a typical conflict over land use in the 1960s; and the arrival during the 1970s and 1980s of global capitalists and their continuing quest for regional integra-tion as a response to the perceived negative consequences of metropolitan fragmentation.

THE INCORPORATION AND CITY-MANAGER MOVEMENTS

Historians of suburban development in the United States generally have not delved deeply into the ways municipalities are formed. In particular, they have not examined how class relations help determine the political allocation of space at the municipal level or how class organizations (such as chambers of commerce and industrial leagues) influence the formation of suburban municipalities. Nor have historians often evaluated the polit-ical efforts for incorporation on the basis of the class composition of the city councils elected in these newly formed cities. In short, they have not explained how the formation of local governments reflects class relations.

In California, for example, the Municipal Incorporation Law of 1933 requires three separate phases for municipal formation: petition, hearing, and implementation (or election). In the petition phase, at least twelve property owners must receive permission from the county clerk to incorporate a new municipality. The proposed city must include a minimum of five hundred residents. Having been granted permission by the county clerk to proceed, the initial petitioners have fifty days in which to obtain signatures of approval from owners of at least 25 percent of the total assessed value of land within the proposed boundaries. Therefore, class bias is evident within the rules for incorporation. The possession of land, it is clear, dictates who can initiate the process.

To be successful during the hearing phase, the original petitioners must have drawn boundaries to incorporate land owned by more supporters than opponents of their effort. Such boundaries are often manipulated by petitioning landowners so as to include proponents (and to exclude opponents) of the incorporation attempt. In addition, they must receive approval from the county board of supervisors.

Although both the petition and hearing phases are characterized by structural advantages for the owners of valuable land, there are no such obvious advantages in the final (or implementation) phase, when incorporation must be approved by a majority of the registered voters living within the proposed city. Residence, not ownership, then becomes the prerequisite for participation. The implementation referendum is accompanied by the selection of a particular form of government—mayor-council, commission, or council-manager—and the election of municipal officials.

Considering the fact that the state legislature endorsed criteria of ownership and control in the laws regarding incorporation, it is not at all surprising that local landowners and possessors of development capital dominated the formation of new municipalities in Orange County during the 1950s. As we examine this process, therefore, we must determine the contours of class underlying the politics of incorporation. This analysis clearly shows that the success of incorporation efforts depended largely on the advantages of class.[13]

Nearly half of Orange County's twenty-eight municipalities were formed prior to the 1930s and were therefore not covered under the 1933 law (table 8.1). These included four of what became its largest cities: Anaheim (1876), Santa Ana (1886), Fullerton (1904), and Huntington Beach (1909). During the 1930s and 1940s, because of slow population growth, there were no successful incorporation efforts. In the 1950s and early 1960s, however, as the county began to experience rapid industrial

TABLE 8.1 Incorporation Dates for Orange County Municipalities

City	Date	City	Date
Anaheim	1876	Costa Mesa	1953
Santa Ana	1886	La Palma	1955
Orange	1888	Stanton	1956
Fullerton	1904	Garden Grove	1956
Newport Beach	1906	Cypress	1956
Huntington Beach	1909	Westminster	1957
Seal Beach	1915	Fountain Valley	1957
Brea	1917	Los Alamitos	1960
La Habra	1925	San Juan Capistrano	1961
Placentia	1926	Villa Park	1962
Laguna Beach	1927	Yorba Linda	1967
Tustin	1927	Irvine	1971
San Clemente	1928	Mission Viejo	1988
Buena Park	1953	Dana Point	1988

growth, eleven new cities were established, with the incorporation attempt of one town stimulating similar attempts in neighboring towns. Careful investigation of these incorporation movements confirms the central roles played by commercial capitalists, service professionals, and local chambers of commerce in successful efforts at municipal formation. Furthermore, those who were initial petitioners and those ultimately elected to city councils were often the same people.

Consider, for example, Garden Grove. Today a major center for Korean and Vietnamese immigrants, it was in the early 1950s rapidly transformed from a minor trading center of four thousand people into a fully incorporated city; it soon became Orange County's third most populous municipality. Of crucial importance to the incorporation campaign was a civic committee organized by the Garden Grove Chamber of Commerce. The four recipients of the largest number of votes for city council in the implementation election of April 1956 were prominent members of that civic committee and also signatories of the initial incorporation petition. In Stanton, an adjoining municipality also incorporated in 1956, three of the original petitioners were elected to the city council in May of that year, as were the leaders of the incorporation committees in Fountain Valley and Los Alamitos, which are also neighboring cities incorporated in 1956.[14]

In the main, the individuals who mobilized support for incorporation were regional commercial capitalists. The chambers of commerce, as the organizations most actively promoting the formation of these municipalities, also drew their members and leaders from that same segment of capital. Members of that class, it would appear, had sufficient class consciousness to mobilize on behalf of their perceived self-interest and to use the organizational clout of the chambers of commerce in their area to achieve predetermined political ends.[15]

These chambers of commerce, as has been suggested, were organized by representatives of regional capital—essentially small employers and service professionals—to pursue the seemingly limitless opportunities for small-scale investment and industrialization made possible by suburban growth. In some instances, such as in Santa Ana in the early 1950s, the chambers of commerce received substantial funds from the city treasury to promote local growth and development, as the economic and political interests of commercial capitalists became closely identified with the public interest.[16] Lacking sufficient capital to create large corporations capable of carving out profitable sectors of the national market, such small employers and self-employed entrepreneurs sought instead to secure a monopoly of trade in their local communities. These regional capitalists sought, as well, to achieve political cohesion for their own social class. As Paul D. Dutton, then an owner of local tire and appliance companies in Santa Ana and candidate for a city council seat, declared in March 1951: "I think the city should be operated like a business and that its governing body should be comprised of business men."[17] Further, the working-class residents of these communities did not resist this establishment of political control.

As we have seen, the implementation phase of an incorporation movement includes selection of the form of city government: mayor-council, commission, or council-manager. In the council-manager form, which predominated in Orange County by the late 1950s, a city council is the elected body and makes policy decisions that are then carried out by an appointed city manager. Although the council members work part-time for small salaries and modest stipends, the city manager is a full-time employee hired by the council and, in Orange County at least, is well paid.[18]

Not only did every municipality created in the 1950s and 1960s adopt the council-manager form of government, but so also did all the cities that had been incorporated prior to 1930. The selection of this new form of government generated a good deal of political heat in the 1950s, as many citizens were highly skeptical of claims about the superiority of the council-manager system over the prevailing mayor-council one. If all that was at stake in the decision to change forms of government was the promise of "the highest degree of efficiency" (to use the language of a 1951 Santa Ana ordinance), then such intense conflict seems unwarranted.

Developments in the county's largest city, Santa Ana, typify the struggles that characterized this selection process throughout the county. In the 1930s and 1940s that city's leadership was composed of landed ranchers, small bankers, and independent merchants. This governing class resisted pressures for increased industrialization. In the immediate postwar years, they were challenged by an activist group of businesspeople who urged city leaders to attract additional industry to the area. During late 1949 and 1950 this group mobilized to gain control of Santa Ana's political system and, indeed, to transform it. In subsequent years its efforts were aided by a "little Hoover Commission" composed of eleven local businessmen (three of whom were recommended by the chamber of commerce and another three by a business association). Patterned after the national Hoover Commission of the early 1950s, which had investigated the operations of the federal government, the Santa Ana version made a similar inquiry into municipal affairs. Drawing on the findings of consultants who were hired to make a complete study of administrative policies, procedures, and practices, the commission ultimately recommended the divorce of municipal legislative functions (to be vested in a city council) from executive authority (to be the province of a strong city manager).[19]

By 1951 the group of businesspeople favoring industrialization and political change managed to take over the Santa Ana City Council on a platform calling for "a sound business-like administration of city affairs" and a reactivation of a former city-manager ordinance. Within a month of taking office, the new council members created the position of city administrator (as a prelude to a more powerful city manager); the administrator was to be the "undisputed boss of city business" and was "to crack the whip over all municipal departments."[20]

Members of the old guard resisted this effort, partially on the ground that a council-manager form of government would drastically alter prevailing power structures. One dismayed member, recalling those events in an interview after more than thirty years, expressed concern about the "dictatorial, unrepresentative" nature of the new form of government adopted by Santa Ana in the early 1950s.[21] The resistance of such people to these changes, and to their displacement by a new class segment, proved unsuccessful however; in 1952 a new charter was passed.

This new Santa Ana leadership group was challenged, in turn, in the mid-1960s by another segment composed of recently arrived corporate executives, who were even more strongly committed than the previous group to the application of managerial techniques in both private corporations and public administration. Unlike their predecessors—the ranchers and local businesspeople who had for years dominated the city council—this newly ascendant corporate class employed by such Santa Ana–based companies as AMF-Voit Rubber, Collins Radio, and Coleman Electronic Systems usually lived outside the city, and its members therefore could not

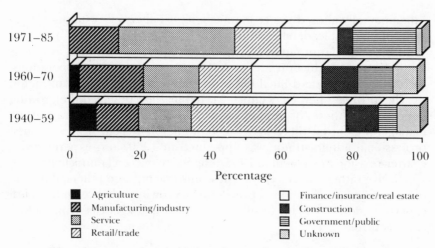

SOURCE: These data were gathered with the assistance of two graduate research assistants in the University of California at Irvine Department of History, William Billingsley and Will Swaim. The statistical graphics were prepared by Timlynn Babitsky of JFS Consulting in Tustin, California.

Fig. 8.1. Occupations of members of Orange County city councils, 1940–85

themselves hold office. Instead, they gave their backing to candidates sympathetic to their views.[22]

Similar struggles among ruling segments composed, on the one hand, of landowners and small entrepreneurs and, on the other, of corporate businesspeople and professionals occurred in other Orange County cities as well during the 1950s and 1960s. Figure 8.1 reveals occupational characteristics and trends for Orange County city councils in the post–World War II era. (Statistical graphics for twenty selected city councils during the same period are also available on request; they have been omitted here for reasons of space.) The occupational categories are those used by the California State Department of Employment. These data demonstrate that occupations of the political leaders of Orange County changed in direct correspondence with changes in the economic base of the region. That is to say, as Orange County was transformed from a predominantly agricultural area to one that was increasingly industrial and, in the 1970s and 1980s, increasingly service- and information-oriented, the occupations of those elected to city councils reflected these underlying economic shifts. In Fullerton, for example, a few large landholding families exercised consistent leadership throughout the 1950s. These families, which had become wealthy from agriculture and oil, invested their capital in Los Angeles enterprises rather than in local ones. By 1965, however, the arrival of Hunt Foods and new aerospace/defense firms fundamentally altered the economic base of Fullerton, resulting also in shifts of political leadership.

In Brea and Huntington Beach, however, most of the land as well as the industrial production was under the control of large corporations, such as Union Oil and Shell Oil in Brea and Signal Oil in Huntington Beach. In Brea a new city council elected in 1962 reflected the growing importance of these corporations, and the first professionally trained city manager was hired there in 1964. Huntington Beach, where the first professional administrator was appointed in 1960, also experienced a charter-revision movement in 1966 designed to make all municipal offices appointive rather than elective. These movements, and others, illustrate the general trend mentioned previously: a growing reliance on technical expertise and a resultant insulation of municipal agencies from democratic control.

CONFLICT OVER LAND USE

Equally revealing of the struggles among contending segments of capital in Orange County are continuing controversies over land use throughout the region. In Fountain Valley in the mid-1950s and thereafter, to cite just one example, large owners of potential industrial land and owners of local industries became concerned that incorporated land being held for industrial development would be developed instead as residential suburbs. They were joined in their concern by homeowners who also favored increased industrial zoning as a means to reduce taxes. This goal brought those groups into open conflict with ranchers, who feared that neighboring cities would annex agricultural property and then zone it for industrial use, which would force farmers to sell their land in a depressed industrial land market. "We were like anyone else," one of those early ranchers reminisced three decades later. "We wanted a good price for our dirt."[23]

This intraclass conflict—between ranch owners and local industrialists joined with homeowners—was eventually played out in the mid-1960s in an effort to recall several members of the city council who resisted industrial zoning. The *Orange Coast Daily Pilot* addressed the matter in a lead editorial: "At this moment in its young life, Fountain Valley as a corporate entity is walking a thin line. A nudge from industrial and commercial developers, and the city would evolve into a healthy, well-rounded community. A nudge in the other direction and Fountain Valley will be just one big bedroom."[24] Finally, convinced that the city council was controlled by real estate interests that were damaging the city's chances for "balanced" economic growth, voters in September 1969 recalled three council members and replaced them with members favoring commercial and industrial development.[25]

In Fountain Valley, as in other areas of Orange County, political conflict arose because property-tax yields are closely related to land-use patterns, and because residential properties consume more than they return in taxes. In the absence of a spatial correspondence between high tax yields and residential land use, there was certain to be intense disagreement among various segments of capital and their respective allies over the allocation and use of space.

POLITICAL RESULTS

By the mid-1960s, then, several marked changes in political structures and practices had occurred that clearly favored the interests of a certain class segment, first of regional capitalists and next of owners of national and international corporations. These changes appear to have been the response to an underlying transformation of the region's economic base and to discernible shifts in the attitudes of decision makers. First, one class segment had replaced another, with ranchers and small independent entrepreneurs slowly giving way to the owners of large corporations and their professional managers. Second, an increased depoliticization of municipal administration had taken place through the imposition of the council-manager system and the move away from elected officials toward appointed ones. Third, an increased centralization of both business organizations and public administration may be observed in the creation of the Orange County Chamber of Commerce, the Orange County League of Cities, the Citizens' Committee on Industrial Development, and, in 1967, the new position of county administrative officer.[26] Finally, the countless disputes over land use and zoning clearly reveal the clashes of class interests, as typified in the case of Fountain Valley.

These important changes in the distribution and exercise of political power in Orange County during the 1950s and 1960s concentrated decision making in the hands of a small number of public officials who could be expected to represent the interests of the new industrial and corporate segments. The new city managers (such as Carl J. Thornton, former city manager of Bakersfield, hired by Santa Ana in 1951) were less and less members of the old-boy networks of local chambers of commerce and service clubs and were more and more tied into the networks of large businesses and county, state, and federal governments. The standard explanation for these changes—in Orange County and elsewhere in the United States throughout the twentieth century—is that they were made for the purpose of efficiency. Allegedly, the goal was to improve urban services by shifting power to nonpartisan, public-minded officials and away from formerly powerful special interests and "self-serving" politicians.

If we carefully analyze the political forces behind such changes in municipal government, while at the same time paying attention to underlying economic developments, we can uncover the antidemocratic implications of suburban politics in those years. We can see, for example, that important areas of public authority were removed from the control of locally elected officials and were taken over by relatively autonomous and distant governmental agencies largely insulated from the political process. The council-manager form of government, to be sure, stresses professional quality in public administration but does not require the city manager to be answerable directly to the electorate. At the time the shift to the council-manager system was being debated in Santa Ana, for example, one knowledgeable observer expressed concern about the political consequences: "The chief of police, city clerk, city judge, and city attorney are elected officials and are responsible to the people, . . . but the administrator [or the city manager] will be privileged to go into offices headed by officials and to do just about as he pleases."[27]

It appears, therefore, that appointing a city manager was one way sharply to centralize the process of decision making. Such centralization enabled corporate business groups favoring certain kinds of growth to nudge aside an agrarian and commercial segment, to move directly into the inner circles of government, and once there to dominate more effectively than before municipal affairs. In this effort, they encountered little effective opposition from the older ruling groups, which had lost their vitality and cohesiveness. Nor was there resistance from the organized labor movement, which historically has been less potent in Los Angeles and Orange counties than in the more centralized urban areas of the nation and which has typically directed its demands to the workplace and not to municipal politics.[28]

REGIONAL INTEGRATION

As industrialization advanced in the 1960s and 1970s, and as the region increasingly acquired a high-technology economic base, Orange County's big business leaders grew in influence. It was in their understandable self-interest to expand the means by which they could exercise power in governmental affairs commensurate with what they exercised in the economic arena. Not surprisingly, members of this new corporate class were highly dissatisfied with the existing system of municipal government and its characteristic fragmentation. They would undoubtedly have agreed with the assessment of historian Jon Teaford, who concluded that the result of such fragmentation has been "inefficiency, confusion of authority, and disparity in shouldering the burdens of the metropolis." As countless city councils enact ordinances for their particular locales, according to Teaford, regional planning is stymied.[29]

Municipal home rule, in short, with its proliferation of semiautonomous local units of government, was seen by representatives of global information capital to impede the economic and political integration of the larger Orange County region. The prevailing political system, according to this perspective, simply enabled local, particularistic interests to dominate, thereby stunting the region's economic potential. City council members, after all, were local leaders with local followings whose local interests they sought to advance. They spoke for their local constituencies rather than addressing the general concerns of a geographically larger region. From the perspective of the new corporate class, such political leaders and their business allies had performed their tasks well, building cities to serve the needs of a former era. But new problems of growth had arisen—pollution, traffic congestion, increased international air transportation, rising housing costs, overburdened municipal services—which an older style of politics was simply ill-suited to confront effectively.

The aspirations and shared ideology (indeed, the class consciousness) of owners and managers of these newly ascendant international corporations were of necessity different from those of the previous group, being much more cosmopolitan in scope. By the late 1970s and 1980s, after all, it was no longer possible to overlook the importance of international trade to the Orange County business community. Nearly 25 percent of county-based firms were by then involved in overseas commerce, and one in seven jobs depended on international trade. By the end of 1987 three local banks—Citizens Bank of Costa Mesa, Commerce Bank in Newport Beach, and a branch of the National Bank of Long Beach in Santa Ana—were offering international financial services to the growing number of Orange County companies engaged in world trade.[30] "People don't think of Orange County as being an export center," noted James Lacy, director of the United States Office of Export Trading Company Affairs in mid-1986, "but more and more new companies are being formed, especially biotech and medical supply companies, and other countries want their products."[31] Interviewed in the summer of 1987, attorney Richard Schwarzstein, a founding member of the World Trade Center Association of Orange County and then chair of its board, noted that world trade "is becoming an important component of our future economic welfare."[32]

The concerns of such owners and professional managers were certainly not bound by geography or based on territorial prerogatives. Their broad, comprehensive perspective on governmental affairs and suburban and postsuburban politics fully acknowledged the manner in which many interrelated factors throughout the entire county, the nation, and the world affected business growth in individual Orange County cities. During the 1970s and 1980s, therefore, the economic limitations of Orange County's fragmented metropolis prompted representatives of national and international capital to assert their own ambitious aspirations for the region. Many corporate leaders began to complain about the lack of regional planning and spoke out vociferously in favor of a regionalized political structure so as to establish, in the words of one leading scholar of the urban process, "a coherent geopolitical presence in the face of the fragmentations."[33]

Such concerns about the consequences of political fragmentation were by no means first expressed in the 1970s and 1980s, nor were they limited to Orange County. Across the country steps had been taken much earlier to curb the creation of new governmental units. In 1959, for example, Minnesota lawmakers made incorporations subject to the review of a state municipal commission. In that same year, Wisconsin created the position of state director of regional planning. Also in 1959 California's governor, Edmund G. Brown, appointed a Commission on Metropolitan Area Problems and charged it with taking "a new look at the structure of local government." The commission's report, issued in December 1960, concluded that local governments in the state could not "plan, budget, and program ahead for the entire metropolitan region" because of the lack of unified control. What was badly needed, in the commission's view, was an "area-wide framework" to achieve regional or metropolitan planning.[34] Although these various efforts may have limited further fragmentation, they did little to erase the divisions that already characterized the nation's metropolises, including Orange County. Political fragmentation continued, therefore, along with disturbing patterns of social, economic, and residential segregation.

Indeed, the 1985 Orange County Annual Survey conducted by Mark Baldassare of the University of California at Irvine revealed clearly that south Orange County had become quite distinct from central and north Orange County in income, attitudes, and social and political agendas. Wealthier South County residents were most concerned about transportation and the environment, while lower-income residents in the central and northern parts of the county worried about problems with drug and alcohol abuse, the public schools, and refugees. Baldassare anticipated that such marked divisions—such zones of privilege and zones of deprivation—would become increasingly sharp and produce friction and conflict over resources and public policies. "The growing divisions in the county mean that it is inaccurate to consider Orange County as a homogeneous entity," concluded Baldassare, "and that it will be more difficult in the future to reach consensus on countywide policies."[35] Moreover, the segregation of wealth noted in the 1985 study had become even more pronounced by 1987, when the South County median household income jumped to forty-eight thousand dollars compared with forty thousand dollars for the rest of the county.[36]

One response by lawmakers to the administrative and political (although not the economic and social) consequences of this fragmented situation in Orange County and elsewhere was the creation of special-purpose metropolitan districts intended to encourage intermunicipal cooperation. By the 1960s the number of water districts, library districts, park districts, sewer districts, and cemetery districts had dramatically increased. By the mid-1980s, there were forty-nine independent special districts in Orange County.[37] These districts, however, simply augmented the number of governmental agencies, thus adding to the confusion and further separating municipal bureaucracy from citizen control. If city council members failed to perform their duties, they could be voted out of office. The electorate had no such recourse when confronted with an incompetent metropolitan water commissioner. The resort to special districts, in short, confused rather than clarified metropolitan governmental structure.[38]

Big business leaders and other Orange County residents who sought clear lines of authority and increased coordination among government agencies felt that other alternatives were urgently needed. Responses to persistently rapid regional growth and the perceived limitations of metropolitan fragmentation occurred in both the public and private sectors during the 1970s. In May 1971, for example, the Board of Supervisors directed its general planning staff to launch a top-priority study of "population growth policy and development strategy." Its major objective was to identify "the real choices which local government may make which can guide and influence the growth and development of the county."[39] One consequence of this study (and of a thorough review of it during the year after its completion by a group of twenty-five top county administrators) was a directive from the Board of Supervisors to the county administrative officer, Robert Thomas, to examine various options for changes in county governmental structure.

In early 1974 Thomas recommended, and in April 1974 the Board of Supervisors adopted, a specific solution in the form of the Environmental Management Agency, which was designed to increase coordination among thirty-three separate departmental units and to reduce fragmentation of planning. This agency was to be responsible for all land-use planning under the jurisdiction of the county and was set up to centralize under the command of an appointed agency director hitherto independent planning divisions.[40]

On the private side, in 1970 sixteen corporate executives formed the

Greater Irvine Industrial League (GIIL). The league's membership region was a circular area twenty miles in diameter, with the Orange County airport at its center. This organization of major corporations was designed to promote coordination among representatives of national and international capital (as opposed to chambers of commerce, which were composed primarily of regional capitalists) and to present a unified position in regard to such growth-related issues as transportation, water, and waste disposal. Among other projects on which the league initially concentrated were the completion of the long-delayed Corona del Mar freeway and of the Von Karman overpass of the San Diego freeway. As Robert Clifford, a charter GIIL director and president of Air California, declared in 1976: "[The organization] gives us the opportunity to cross-check our ideas, identify mutual problems, and form a course of action."[41]

This new group's focus was decidedly divergent from that of chambers of commerce at both the local and county levels. While chambers usually comprised the owners and middle-level managers of small firms, the GIIL was controlled by senior-level executives and chief executive officers of major corporations. Because the organzation's member firms had interests beyond the Irvine area, the GIIL went countywide and in 1982 was renamed the Industrial League of Orange County (ILOC) to reflect the scope of its activities. Within five years its membership had grown to eight hundred companies employing more than 130,000 people. Unlike chambers of commerce, the ILOC did not accept public funds to run its operations (it was supported by corporate donations), nor did political officeholders sit on its board of directors. It directed its lobbying efforts at the county Board of Supervisors, the state legislature, and various state agencies rather than at local city councils, bringing to bear the power and prestige of the large firms that constituted its core (such as the Irvine Company, Fluor Corporation, Rockwell International, Northrop Corporation, Hughes Aircraft Company, and First Interstate Bank).[42]

THE SLOW-GROWTH MOVEMENT

The different membership bases, ideological orientations, and lobbying strategies of the ILOC, on the one hand, and of local and county chambers of commerce, on the other, were indications of a continuing intraclass struggle between larger corporate interests and smaller commercial entrepreneurs. However, local businesspeople and local governments were not impotent in the face of these new and powerful economic forces. "Because local government requires political legitimation," Gottdiener reminds us, "it is sensitive to citizen demands. If by chance opposition to growth should aggregate to a sufficient level, it can fundamentally affect the ability of growth networks to carry out their objectives."[43] It is apparent, therefore, that under certain circumstances growth networks can be constrained by the political process.

In fact, in the mid-1980s, grass-roots efforts at the municipal level designed to slow development and to assert local autonomy began to flourish, as those forces came to realize the threat that regionalism under corporate auspices posed to their power. In Irvine, for example, a new slow-growth majority on the city council elected in mid-1986 quickly proposed changes in the city's general plan so as to rezone hundreds of acres of land as permanent open space. Council members there, respond-ing to the expressed wishes of ten thousand petitioning residents, voted not to participate in the countywide joint-powers authorities created to help finance and design two controversial freeways until after residents had a chance to vote on participation. In Seal Beach a group of local residents, fearing development "of every square inch of open space," pushed for a slow-growth initiative, thereby bypassing a reluctant city council. So also in affluent Newport Beach a slow-growth movement called Gridlock emerged to do battle with the Irvine Company.[44] Even in several unincorporated areas in southern Orange County—Mission Viejo and Dana Point (both of which incorporated in 1988), Laguna Niguel, El Toro, Laguna Hills, Lake Forest, and Capistrano Beach—efforts to incor-porate were linked with control of growth.[45]

In early 1987 local slow-growth groups banded together to push for a growth-control initiative that would be put to a countywide vote. It had become painfully apparent to many that if regional limits on growth were not promoted and constructed from the bottom up, then such growth would most certainly be imposed by powerful interests from the top down. Leading slow-growth activists who were aware of this fact included city council members Larry Agran, Grace Winchell, Robert Gentry, and Tom Lorch, representing Irvine, Huntington Beach, Laguna Beach, and San Clemente, respectively. Organizers of the countywide movement were especially critical of the Board of Supervisors for allegedly allowing too much development without first putting in place the necessary infra-structure. This charge was later repeated by another Irvine council mem-ber (and a University of California at Irvine professor of urban planning), Ray Catalano, who asserted that "a reasonable person could infer from recent history that the political institutions of Orange County have be-come extensions of the development community."[46]

The most radical grass-roots movement arose in the mid-1980s in Santa Ana, the county's second largest city. Calling itself Santa Ana Merged So-ciety of Neighbors (SAMSON), this unprecedented coalition was formed after a decade of urban movements in Santa Ana and thus brought together diverse racial, ethnic, and political factions.[47] Unlike previous coalitions in Santa Ana, SAMSON sought to revamp city government

along former lines by replacing the appointed city manager with an
elected mayor. It sought as well to elect council members from wards
rather than by citywide vote and to elect the then-appointive planning
commission. Many of SAMSON's concerns were informed by a desire to
increase democratic participation and could be traced directly to Santa
Ana's redevelopment programs. Although the group's plans to restructure municipal government failed to be adopted by one percentage point
in a June 1986 election, there was every reason to expect those issues to
surface again.[48]

Making such resistance difficult was the impressive power mobilized by
the new global capitalists of the region's information economy (bankers,
financiers, and owners and managers of Orange County's largest corporations) when joined by the handful of individuals, families, and corporations that owned nearly all the remaining developable land in the southern portion of the county.

Compared with the boom of the 1950s in the North County, in which
many builders and buyers participated, future growth would be determined largely by this development oligopoly composed of big builders,
big banks, and big real estate companies, which had come to advocate
"good planning" rather than the unrestrained growth that had by then
become so unpopular.[49] They had the financial backing, the organization, and the staying power that the grass roots lacked, despite mounting
evidence in the late 1980s of surging sentiment throughout the county in
favor of slow growth.[50]

Such slow-growth sentiment could be found even among many business leaders, which was perhaps not surprising considering the sharp
divisions among Orange County's business class that had long characterized the region's history. A survey conducted in late 1987 by University of
California at Irvine Professor Jone Pearce revealed that 46 percent of the
corporate leaders questioned favored a proposed countywide slow-growth
initiative that would require developers to widen roads and make other
improvements linked to traffic flow before they could build in unincorporated areas, while 54 percent opposed it. This split, according to Pearce,
was evident in all business sectors.[51]

To counteract the slow-growth forces, which obviously included many
from their own ranks (who were at least willing to express their genuine
views in private), Orange County builders by late 1987 had amassed a
$250,000 legal-defense fund to pay for legal challenges to Measure A,
known as the Citizens' Sensible Growth and Traffic Control Initiative.
Declaring the need to become proactive, such large landholders as Anthony Moiso, president of the Rancho Santa Margarita Company, Donald
Bren of the Irvine Company, and Harvey Stearns of the Mission Viejo

Company closed ranks with other developers and with the Southern California Building Industry Association to design a less restrictive initiative measure.[52]

In the bitter political struggle that occupied most of Orange County's attention for the next six months, opponents of Measure A mounted an extremely well-financed attack (California's most expensive progrowth/ slow-growth campaign to date), spending more than $2.5 million as against $106,000 by its supporters. The ultimate defeat of the initiative in June 1988 was due in large measure to an intensive five-week campaign conducted by paid political consultant Lynn Wessell. Wessell effectively used some of the techniques of information capitalism (computerized demographic analyses and well-funded telephone banks in four No on A offices around the county) as well as traditional methods (such as thirty-one-hundred door-to-door campaigners, many of them paid). Also important was the marked division between central and north Orange County, on the one hand, and south Orange County, on the other, strikingly revealed in the 1985 Orange County Annual Survey. Targeting five large central and north cities—Anaheim, Fullerton, Garden Grove, Orange, and Santa Ana—Wessell's organization was instrumental in converting public opinion that was once four to one in favor of the initiative into a 56 percent to 44 percent defeat.[53] In this instance, clearly, the Orange County growth network—including the real estate sector, representatives of information capital, many politicians and lawyers, as well as owners and parts of the working class in the construction and building industries—had not been constrained by the political process.

With the initiative defeated, the battle shifted to a committee appointed by the Board of Supervisors that was charged with devising tighter controls on growth. As Supervisor Roth was quoted as saying, "I think there's a signal out there that the natives are restless and we have to do a good job of controlling growth and providing transportation." Another supervisor, Gaddi H. Vasquez, declared, "One clear message coming out of this whole scenario is that it is never going to be business as usual again."[54] Slow-growth leaders such as Belinda Blacketer, Norm Grossman, Gregory Hile, and Tom Rogers were highly skeptical of these declarations, believing that the Board of Supervisors was largely responsible for overdevelopment and traffic problems. Nonetheless, they vowed to continue their fight and to build a strong statewide coalition.

SUMMARY

In this chapter we have seen how the nature of political conflict in Orange County since World War II has been conditioned by that region's most

distinguishing characteristics. These include its decentralized spatial organization, its metropolitan fragmentation, its highly diversified information-oriented economy, the growing importance to that economy of international trade and finance (with accompanying changes in its class
structure), and its weak labor movement.

In this social setting, the major struggles over the structure of the
political system, land use, and the built environment have been waged by
competing segments of the business class. The heterogeneity of that class
is somewhat difficult to perceive. The historical record, however, provides
abundant evidence of its longstanding internal cleavages and clashes of
interest. The goals and activities of local chambers of commerce, for
example, often have been in sharp contrast to those of the more cosmopolitan ILOC. Although it is possible to oversimplify a complicated
situation, clearly those whom I have called regional capitalists, whose
economic and political influence was predominant in the years immediately following World War II, slowly and perhaps inexorably have given
way to global capitalists. Members of this internationally oriented business class have persistently and effectively pushed for rapid growth, as
well as regional economic and political integration, so as to thrust Orange
County prominently into the international marketplace.

The apparent triumph of global capital in Orange County has not
gone unchallenged. Those regional capitalists who wished to retain some
degree of local autonomy and control over growth joined an interesting,
even unlikely, amalgam of political forces composed of conservative Republicans and liberal Democrats that emerged in the mid- to late 1980s to
wage a struggle for the future of the region. Coalescing around the
ideology of slow growth, these political activists initially conducted various grass-roots campaigns in the affluent municipalities on or near the
coast, such as San Clemente, Laguna Beach, Irvine, Newport Beach, and
Huntington Beach. In the late 1980s, these local slow-growth efforts
merged in a countywide initiative campaign. This Citizens' Sensible
Growth and Traffic Control Initiative provoked a powerful, and ultimately successful, response from Orange County's growth network,
composed of representatives of global capital aligned with large landholders, developers, financiers, and owners and workers from the construction industry.

By the end of the 1980s, then, growth clearly had become Orange
County's major political issue. The defeat of the countywide initiative in
mid-1988 had by no means resolved the fractious disputes among contending classes and groups competing for dominance and control. Moreover, the issue of growth was inextricably linked with other pressing social
problems sufficiently complex to ensure contention for years to come.

NOTES

1. In this regard, Orange County reflects similar patterns in other sunbelt regions, where younger representatives of national and international corporations have challenged older, established elites. See William Issel, *Social Change in the United States, 1945–1983* (New York: Schocken, 1985), 134, and Carl Abbott, "The Suburban Sunbelt," *Journal of Urban History* 13 (May 1987):295. For an important analysis of the larger Los Angeles region, see Edward Soja, Rebecca Morales, and Goetz Wolff, "Urban Restructuring: An Analysis of Social and Spatial Change in Los Angeles," *Economic Geography* 59 (April 1983):195–230.

2. See Patrick Ashton, "Urbanization and the Dynamics of Suburban Development under Capitalism," in *Marxism and the Metropolis: New Perspectives in Urban Political Economy,* ed. William K. Tabb and Larry Sawers (New York: Oxford University Press, 1984), 54–81. Also see Richard A. Walker, "A Theory of Suburbanization: Capitalism and the Construction of Urban Space in the United States," in *Urbanization and Urban Planning in Capitalist Society,* ed. Michael Dear and Allen J. Scott (New York: Methuen, 1981), 383–429. For the general process of suburbanization in the United States, see Jon C. Teaford, *City and Suburb: The Political Fragmentation of Metropolitan America, 1850–1970* (Baltimore: Johns Hopkins University Press, 1975); Jon C. Teaford, *The Twentieth-Century American City* (Baltimore: Johns Hopkins University Press, 1986); and Kenneth Jackson, *Crabgrass Frontier: The Suburbanization of America* (New York: Oxford University Press, 1985). For a discussion of competing theoretical approaches to the use of space, see Martin Cadwallader, "Urban Geography and Social Theory," *Urban Geography* 9 (May-June 1988):227–268, and especially the several comments regarding his contentions (pp. 252–68).

3. The term *class* is used often in both Marxist and non-Marxist analyses of society. For this reason, the meanings assigned to the term vary widely. Because there is so much disagreement over what class means, and because it is conceptually central to this chapter, it is important briefly to identify how the term is used here. Stated most simply, a class is a group of people who share a common position in the economy with respect to the means and the process of production. This concept of class differs substantially from the common social science usage, which defines classes as various strata based on levels of income (thus, upper, middle, and lower classes). Instead, class is properly related to the production, appropriation, and distribution of surplus labor. In this sense, a class is defined as a group of people who share a common social position of producing surplus labor (workers) or of appropriating it from the producers (owners) or of receiving shares of it from the appropriators (those professionals, administrators, managers, and engineers who manage the production process). See Richard Wolff and Stephen Resnick, "Power, Property, and Class," *Socialist Review* 86 (March-April 1986):97–124, as well as Jon Elster, *An Introduction to Karl Marx* (New York: Cambridge University Press, 1986), and Jeffrey Isaac, *Power and Marxist Theory: A Realist View* (Ithaca, N.Y.: Cornell University Press, 1987).

4. M. Gottdiener, *The Social Production of Urban Space* (Austin: University of Texas Press, 1985), 221. An alternative concept—progrowth coalitions—is used

by John H. Mollenkopf, *The Contested City* (Princeton, N.J.: Princeton University Press, 1983), 3–5, 155–69, 242–50. In my opinion, Mollenkopf incorrectly elevates the role of public actors ("political entrepreneurs") over that of private economic interests. For yet another approach, which emphasizes "growth machines," see John R. Logan and Harvey L. Molotch, *Urban Fortunes: The Political Economy of Urban Space* (Berkeley: University of California Press, 1987).

5. Gottdiener, *Social Production of Urban Space*, 222.

6. Capital accumulation refers to the means whereby the capitalist class reproduces both itself and its domination of labor. Helpful in understanding the basic logic of the accumulation process and its relation to the urban process under capitalism (or the spatial dynamics of accumulation) is David Harvey, *The Urbanization of Capital: Studies in the History and Theory of Capitalist Urbanization* (Baltimore: Johns Hopkins University Press, 1985), 3–27. For a criticism of Harvey's theory of accumulation, especially its alleged deficiencies in explaining why overinvestment occurs in the "secondary circuit of capital" (investment in the built environment for production or fixed assets and consumption goods), see Gottdiener, *Social Production of Urban Space*, 97–100. Also see, among others, Roger Friedland, Frances Fox Piven, and Robert R. Alford, "Political Conflict, Urban Structure, and the Fiscal Crisis," in Tabb and Sawers, eds., *Marxism and the Metropolis*, 273–97, and Stephen L. Elkin, "Twentieth Century Urban Regimes," *Journal of Urban Affairs* 7 (1985):11–27.

7. See, for example, Arnold Fleischman and Joe Feagin, "The Politics of Growth-Oriented Urban Alliances: Comparing Old Industrial and New Sunbelt Cities," *Urban Affairs Quarterly* 23 (December 1987):209–10.

8. See Friedland, Piven, and Alford, "Political Conflict, Urban Structure, and the Fiscal Crisis," 282.

9. On depoliticization, see Gottdiener, *Social Production of Urban Space*, 270–274: "The present is witness to the progressive marginalization and spatial confinement of those social groups least able to play an active role in the political economy. . . . Local political cultures in the United States, for example, are presently dying out, as manifested by low voter turnouts, low participation rates in other political activities, and an increasing social apathy." For a more complete elaboration, see M. Gottdiener, *The Decline of Urban Politics: Political Theory and the Crisis of the Local State* (Beverly Hills, Calif.: Sage, 1987). As Lisbeth Haas indicates in Chapter 9, however, Santa Ana's Hispanic population has had some success resisting its depoliticization and political marginalization.

10. The concept of class segment is most helpful in understanding the increasingly complex social structure of the contemporary United States. It is customarily used to describe how the modern capitalist labor market is segmented or fragmented along several dimensions, including race, ethnicity, and gender. But such class segmentation is not restricted to the working class (such as agricultural, blue-collar, white-collar, and service workers). It also characterizes the capitalist class (the agricultural, industrial, and service employers of workers) and the "middle" class (small farmers, small businesspeople, lower- and middle-level managers and supervisors, professionals, and technicians). *Middle* may not be the most appropriate adjective to describe this group because it suggests a location

equidistant from the other two. In doing so, it may obscure the fact that a lack of control over the workplace under information capitalism characterizes the work both of members of the new middle class of technicians, managers, and bureaucrats, and of their industrial, working-class predecessors. See, for example, Dale L. Johnson, *Class and Social Development: A New Theory of the Middle Class* (Beverly Hills, Calif.: Sage, 1982). The primary focus of this chapter, it should be stressed, is on segments of the capitalist class of Orange County, a class that is by no means homogeneous or harmonious.

11. See Charles Hoch, "Municipal Contracting in California: Privatizing with Class," *Urban Affairs Quarterly* 20 (March 1985): 312–18.

12. For general discussions, see I. M. Barlow, *Spatial Dimensions of Urban Government* (New York: Research Studies Press, 1981), especially chap. 3 ("City Government Expenditures"), 27–48, and Ann R. Markusen, "Class and Urban Social Expenditures: A Marxist Theory of Metropolitan Government," in Tabb and Sawers, eds., *Marxism and the Metropolis*, 82–100.

13. A useful discussion of this process is Hoch, "Municipal Contracting in California," 303–12. For a general analysis of the formation of local governments, see Charles Hoch, "City Limits: Municipal Boundary Formation and Class Segregation," in Tabb and Sawers, eds., *Marxism and the Metropolis*, 101–19.

14. I thank Michael Williams for his assistance in gathering copies of original petitions for incorporation efforts in several Orange County cities during the 1950s. These conclusions are based on those petitions and related materials. The four Garden Grove members were Harry Blades, Kenneth Dugan, George Honold, and Harry Lake. The three original petitioners elected to the Stanton City Council were Herbert Cook, Henry Mendez, and Jesse Phillips. Robert Wardlow and James Bell led the incorporation movements in Fountain Valley and Los Alamitos, respectively.

15. On the one hand, class is a descriptive category—the way in which people are organized in society and participate in production. On the other hand, classes are not solely economic phenomena; they are also composed of political and ideological forces. Another use of the term, then, is in reference to a formation—a class as self-conscious and in acknowledged conflict with other classes. When members of a class recognize that they share ambitions, beliefs, life-styles, and political values with others who occupy the same social position, they may be said to have acquired class consciousness. This perception of common class interests fosters the creation of organizations designed to advance such interests. I am therefore modifying the conventional use of the concept, for I am interested here in the consciousness of class segments, not consciousness across an entire class. In Orange County, several organizations, such as local chambers of commerce and countywide leagues, have been established to serve the interests of competing business segments.

16. See the *Santa Ana Register*, 3 July 1951, reporting a grant of fifty-one hundred dollars to the chamber of commerce "to disseminate knowledge to the people of the county regarding the friendliness and desirability of Santa Ana as a place for home and business." Stewart McPherson, president of the Santa Ana Chamber of Commerce in 1951–52, also stressed the chamber's role in backing

the new city charter and in selecting the five-man slate that took over the city council in 1951. Oral history interview by author, 3 Aug. 1984. Similarly, in Costa Mesa, which incorporated in 1953, the chamber of commerce contributed $750 toward the $1,500 filing fee and, under the organizational umbrella of Costa Mesa United, conducted public meetings in favor of incorporation, while many chamber members were active in the incorporation movement. See *Costa Mesa Historical Society Quarterly*, July 1978.

17. "Operation of City as Business, Goal of City Council Candidates," *Santa Ana Register*, 1 Mar. 1951.

18. See "City Managers' Pay Here Outstrips U.S. Averages," *Los Angeles Times*, 4 Mar. 1984. On the role of the city manager, see Richard J. Stillman, *The Rise of the City Manager: A Public Professional in Local Government* (Albuquerque: University of New Mexico Press, 1974), and LeRoy F. Harlow, ed., *Servants of All: Professional Management of City Government* (Provo, Utah: Brigham Young University Press, 1981).

19. See the *Santa Ana Register*, 13 Jan., 7 Feb., 28 Sept. 1950.

20. The new city council was composed of Courtney Chandler (a Standard Oil Company chemist), Milford Dahl (past president of the Santa Ana Chamber of Commerce), Orson Hunter (past commander of the American Legion and a member of the Santa Ana Chamber of Commerce), William Jerome (a service station owner), and John McBride (former city engineer). See the *Santa Ana Register*, 18 Apr. and 18 May 1951. Chandler later expressed his belief in the virtues of "expert government" and praised the support given his group's efforts by the Santa Ana Chamber of Commerce (oral history interview conducted on 16 July 1984).

21. Oral history interview conducted with Virgil Reed of Newport Beach, California, on 21 July 1984. From the first time he was elected to the Santa Ana City Council in 1955, Ogden Markel also opposed "that certain clique" who sought to transform the city into a modern urban center. See Steve Emmons, "Santa Ana Gadfly Retains His Sting," *Los Angeles Times*, 6 Nov. 1983.

22. See Leonard C. Moffitt, "Community and Urbanization: Orange County, California" (Main Library, University of California at Irvine, 1967), 139.

23. Oral history interview with Henry Boer of Fountain Valley, 25 July 1986.

24. *Orange Coast Daily Pilot*, 6 Apr. 1966. I greatly appreciate the discovery of this recall election by my graduate research assistants Will Swaim and William Billingsley.

25. For a description of the new city council members, see the *Santa Ana Register*, 5 Oct. 1969. The *Daily Pilot* contains good coverage of the recall campaign (see, for example, 26 Mar., 23 July, 25 July, 3 Aug. 1969). For a general discussion, see Bill D. Holder, "The Urban Development of Fountain Valley, California" (master's thesis, California State University, Fullerton, 1974).

26. Robert E. Thomas, a retired Navy captain, became the first county administrative officer and immediately pledged himself to install "a coherent and rational management system." *Orange County Business*, fourth quarter 1967, 6. William J. Phillips, who became a supervisor in 1957, was the first to call for the creation of a county administrative officer to coordinate county functions, administrative procedures, and agency budgets. His efforts were vigorously resisted by a

long-time supervisor, Willis Warner, who believed that such authority should be retained at the elective level. The opposition of Warner and other groups forestalled the creation of the position until 1967. See Moffitt, "Community and Urbanization," 296, and the Willis Warner Papers, Special Collections, University of California at Irvine.

27. Fletcher Robertson, "'Wonder Boy' Administrator Is Needed by City If Requirements of Council's Big 3 to Be Met," *Santa Ana Register*, 19 Oct. 1949.

28. For a perceptive analysis of this process earlier in this century, see Samuel P. Hays, "The Politics of Reform in Municipal Government in the Progressive Era," *Pacific Northwest Quarterly* 55 (1964): 157–69. Also see William Issel, "'Citizens Outside the Government': Business and Urban Policy in San Francisco and Los Angeles, 1890–1932," *Pacific Historical Review* 57 (May 1988): 117–45. It is important to note that unionized workers have persistently declined as a percentage of Orange County's increasingly white-collar labor force. By the mid-1980s the county's unionization rate was the lowest of any metropolitan area in the state. See John O'Dell, "County's Unions Register 12% Gain over Two Years," *Los Angeles Times*, 23 Dec. 1986.

29. Teaford, *City and Suburb*, 1–2. Similar conclusions are reached by urban sociologist Mark Baldassare in his study *Trouble in Paradise: The Suburban Transformation in America* (New York: Columbia University Press, 1986), based on information gathered for his 1982 and 1983 Orange County Annual Surveys, published under the auspices of the Public Policy Research Organization of the University of California at Irvine. As he notes there (p. 22): "There is little evidence of collaboration [among local governments] on issues of mutual interest."

30. See Michelle Vranizan, "Independent Banks Go Global with International Divisions," *Orange County Businessweek*, 9 Nov. 1987.

31. As quoted in James S. Granelli, "U.S. to Sponsor Irvine Seminar on Export Act of '82," *Los Angeles Times*, 24 Apr. 1986. Also see *Business to Business*, March 1985, 3. On the increasing flow of foreign capital into Orange County, see Leslie Berkman, "The Japanese in Orange County," *Los Angeles Times*, 9 Apr. 1987.

32. "Richard Schwarzstein: Chairman of World Trade Center Association Tries to Make Orange County a Major Player in World Trade," *South County/ Spectrum*, August 1987.

33. Harvey, *Urbanization of Capital*, 160. Also see Philip J. Trounstine and Terry Christensen, *Movers and Shakers: The Study of Community Power* (New York: St. Martin's Press, 1982), 191: "By attempting to shift the decision-making arena to a regional rather than local scale, [the corporate elite] could enhance their power and weaken the grassroots accordingly." This corporate elite, it should be pointed out, has not acted in unison with respect to the issue of a regional airport. See Mark P. Petracca, "Community Power and Airport Politics: A Perspective on Representative Government in Orange County," *Journal of Orange County Studies* 2 (Spring 1989): 5–15.

34. Commission on Metropolitan Area Problems, *Meeting Metropolitan Problems: A Report of the Governor's Commission on Metropolitan Area Problems* (Sacramento, Calif., 1960), 10, 12. Also see Teaford, *City and Suburb*, 172, for similar efforts elsewhere in the country.

35. As quoted in Dawn Bonker, "Orange County: A Neighborhood Patch-

work," *Irvine World News*, 26 Sept. 1985. Also see Lanie Jones, "Survey Finds a Polarization in County's Neighborhoods," *Los Angeles Times*, 25 Sept. 1985.

36. See Steve Hawk, "South County Richer, Happier Than North," *Orange County Register*, 12 Dec. 1987.

37. See Kim Murphy, "49 Fiefdoms: Special Districts Called Archaic by Some, Real Democracy by Others," *Los Angeles Times*, 1 Apr. 1984.

38. On the limitations of the metropolitan special district, see John C. Bollens, *Special District Governments in the United States* (Berkeley: University of California Press, 1961).

39. Forest Dickason, *Orange County Progress Report* (Orange County, Calif.: Orange County Planning Department, 1972), 43. This move to create an inter-governmental council, which never got much beyond the conversation stage in the early 1970s, was resuscitated in 1987 by Supervisor Harriet M. Wieder. It was not until 1976, in fact, with the formation of the Orange County Transportation Commission, that any regional agency existed above the level of local munici-palities to deal with such issues as transportation and traffic congestion. See Pete Johnson, "Dead End: The Future Shock of Orange County's Roadways," *Orange Coast Magazine*, January 1987, 99–109. An informative account of increased friction within the Board of Supervisors as county issues became regional in scope is Kim Murphy and Jeffrey Perlman, "Urban Headaches Plague One-Time Pot-hole Fillers," *Los Angeles Times*, 9 Sept. 1984. Ray Watson, who in 1987 was vice-chairman of the Irvine Company, was highly skeptical of efforts on behalf of regional integration that relied for implementation on the Board of Supervisors; he argued that since the passage of Proposition 13 in 1979, the board's power has been greatly diminished. (Oral history interview by author, 16 July 1987.)

40. See Orange County Board of Supervisors, Staff of General Planning Pro-gram, *Orange County's Top Management Views Growth, Policies, and the Future of Orange County* (Orange County, Calif., 1972); Orange County Administrative Office, *Orange County Proposal for Reorganization* (Orange County, Calif., 1974); and Orange County Environmental Management Agency, *Biennial Report—July 1, 1975–June 30, 1977* (Orange County, Calif., 1977). In August 1974 the Board of Supervisors appointed H. George Osborne, formerly chief engineer of the Or-ange County Flood Control District, as the first director, and by 1975 the agency was in operation.

41. As quoted in Richard Jenks, "It's No Little League: Three Hundred Firms Team Up to Get Things Done," *New Worlds*, April/May 1976, 57.

42. Much of the information in this section was derived from interviews with Todd Nicholson, president of the ILOC (8 July 1986, and 13 July 1987), and Anson McArthur, vice-president of corporate relations for the Orange County Chamber of Commerce (30 June 1986).

43. Gottdiener, *Social Production of Urban Space*, 223.

44. Ted Appel, "Slow-Growth Group Swings into Action," *Los Angeles Times*, 26 Sept. 1986. For more on slow-growth movements, see Chapter 3.

45. For representative coverage of various slow-growth movements, see the following (all from the *Los Angeles Times*): Heidi Evans, "Development Dominates Race for 2 Costa Mesa Council Seats," 28 Oct. 1986; David Reyes, "Growth Seen

as Key Issue in Orange's Council Race," 29 Oct. 1986; Bill Billiter, "Development Hotly Argued in Newport Council Race," 30 Oct. 1986; Heidi Evans, "'Slow Growth' Emerges as Key Issue in Local Politics," 2 Nov. 1986; Heidi Evans, "Newport Beach Voters Reject Center Expansion," 26 Nov. 1986. See also Jane Glenn Haas, "Frustration: Orange County Voters Are Saying They've Had Enough," *Orange County Register,* 2 Dec. 1986. A general discussion appears in Christopher B. Leinberger and Charles Lockwood, "How Business Is Reshaping America," *Atlantic Monthly,* October 1986, 43–52.

46. "New Cities to Face Old Problems," *Los Angeles Times,* 17 May 1987. Also see Donald E. Skinner, "Slow-Growth Advocates Study County Referendum," *Orange County Register,* 24 Jan. 1987, and Lisa Mahoney, "Slow-Growth Push Starts County-wide," *Orange Coast Daily Pilot,* 24 Jan. 1987.

47. See Chapter 9 by Lisbeth Haas for an analysis of the previous decade of urban movements in Santa Ana.

48. For accounts of SAMSON, see the following (all from the *Los Angeles Times*): Andy Rose, "Group Proposes Shake-Up in Santa Ana, Urges Vote," 28 Dec. 1985; Mark Landsbaum and Andy Rose, "Diverse Allies Join Forces to Fight City Hall in Santa Ana," 12 Jan. 1986; and Andy Rose, "SAMSON Sees Return of Ward Elections Issue," 5 June 1986. Indeed, in early 1987, a similar effort was launched in Newport Beach by a new city council member, Phil Sansone, who sought to curb the power of progrowth forces in that wealthy city. See *Orange County Register,* 23 Jan. 1987.

49. For an informed discussion of large landowners in Orange County, see Michael A. Hiltzik, "Orange County's Vast Ranches Spawned Vast Fortunes," *Los Angeles Times,* 4 July 1982, and John O'Dell, "Orange County's Future in Hands of a Few Developers," *Los Angeles Times,* 29 Jan. 1984. See also "Tomorrow: The New Corporate Elites versus the Grassroots" in Trounstine and Christensen, *Movers and Shakers,* 189–92.

50. In the 1987 Orange County Annual Survey, 78 percent of those questioned favored a slow-growth measure tied to traffic standards in cities where they lived, while 74 percent favored such a measure for the county as a whole. This poll prompted an astonished Orange County Supervisor Don R. Roth to declare, "It's hard for me to believe that people will vote to lose their jobs." Jeffrey A. Perlman, "Slow Growth Is Favored in Orange County Study," *Los Angeles Times,* 11 Dec. 1987.

51. I am grateful to Pearce for sharing her data analyses with me. For a report of her survey, see John O'Dell, "Orange County Executives Split on Growth Initiative," *Los Angeles Times,* 23 Jan. 1988.

52. See Jane Glenn Haas, "Builders Ready to Counterattack," *Orange County Register,* 7 Nov. 1987, and Michael Flagg, "Home Builders May Sue If Orange County Passes Slow-Growth Initiative," *Los Angeles Times,* 31 Dec. 1987.

53. See Jane Glenn Haas, "Making Slow Growth a No-Go," *Orange County Register,* 9 June 1988. The initiative carried in only the five South County cities— Irvine, Laguna Beach, Mission Viejo, San Clemente, and San Juan Capistrano— and in the unincorporated areas. See Ray Perez, "Totals Show North, West County Cities Scuttled Measure A," *Los Angeles Times,* 22 June 1988.

54. Jeffrey A. Perlman and Michael Flagg, "Money Beat Measure A, Foes, Supporters Agree," *Los Angeles Times*, 9 June 1988, and Bill Boyarsky, "Slow-Growth Campaigners Learn Some Hard Lessons," *Los Angeles Times*, 10 June 1988. Also see Mark Baldassare and Cheryl Katz, "Measure A Defeat Came after Questions Arose and Went Unanswered," *Los Angeles Times*, 12 June 1988.

REFERENCES

Abbott, Carl. "The Suburban Sunbelt." *Journal of Urban History* 13 (May 1987): 275–301.

Ashton, Patrick. "Urbanization and the Dynamics of Suburban Development under Capitalism." In *Marxism and the Metropolis: New Perspectives in Urban Political Economy,* ed. William K. Tabb and Larry Sawers, 54–81. New York: Oxford University Press, 1984.

Baldassare, Mark. *Trouble in Paradise: The Suburban Transformation in America.* New York: Columbia University Press, 1986.

Baldassare, Mark, and Cheryl Katz. "Measure A Defeat Came after Questions Arose and Went Unanswered." *Los Angeles Times,* 12 June 1988.

Barlow, I. M. *Spatial Dimensions of Urban Government.* New York: Research Studies Press, 1981.

Berkman, Leslie. "The Japanese in Orange County." *Los Angeles Times,* 19 Apr. 1987.

Billiter, Bill. "Development Hotly Argued in Newport Council Race." *Los Angeles Times,* 30 Oct. 1986.

Bollens, John C. *Special District Governments in the United States.* Berkeley: University of California Press, 1961.

Bonker, Dawn. "Orange County: A Neighborhood Patchwork." *Irvine World News,* 26 Sept. 1985.

Boyarsky, Bill. "Slow-Growth Campaigners Learn Some Hard Lessons." *Los Angeles Times,* 10 June 1988.

Cadwallader, Martin. "Urban Geography and Social Theory." *Urban Geography* 9 (May-June 1988):227–68.

Catalano, Ray. "New Cities to Face Old Problems." *Los Angeles Times,* 17 May 1987.

Commission on Metropolitan Area Problems. *Meeting Metropolitan Problems: A Report of the Governor's Commission on Metropolitan Area Problems.* Sacramento, Calif., 1960.

Dickason, Forest. *Orange County Progress Report.* Orange County, Calif.: Orange County Planning Department, 1972.

Elkin, Stephen L. "Twentieth Century Urban Regimes." *Journal of Urban Affairs* 7 (1985):11–27.

Elster, Jon. *An Introduction to Karl Marx.* New York: Cambridge University Press, 1986.

Emmons, Steve. "Santa Ana Gadfly Retains His Sting." *Los Angeles Times,* 6 Nov. 1983.

Evans, Heidi. "Development Dominates Race for 2 Costa Mesa Council Seats." *Los Angeles Times,* 28 Oct. 1986.

———. "Newport Beach Voters Reject Center Expansion." *Los Angeles Times,* 26 Nov. 1986.

———. "'Slow Growth' Emerges as Key Issue in Local Politics." *Los Angeles Times,* 2 Nov. 1986.

Flagg, Michael. "Home Builders May Sue If Orange County Passes Slow-Growth Initiative." *Los Angeles Times,* 31 Dec. 1987.

Fleischman, Arnold, and Joe Feagin. "The Politics of Growth-Oriented Urban Alliances: Comparing Old Industrial and New Sunbelt Cities." *Urban Affairs Quarterly* 23 (December 1987):207–32.

Friedland, Roger, Frances Fox Piven, and Robert R. Alford. "Political Conflict, Urban Structure, and the Fiscal Crisis." In *Marxism and the Metropolis: New Perspectives in Urban Political Economy,* ed. William K. Tabb and Larry Sawers, 273–97. New York: Oxford University Press, 1984.

Gottdiener, M. *The Decline of Urban Politics: Political Theory and the Crisis of the Local State.* Beverly Hills, Calif.: Sage, 1987.

———. *The Social Production of Urban Space.* Austin: University of Texas Press, 1985.

Granelli, James S. "U.S. to Sponsor Irvine Seminar on Export Act of '82." *Los Angeles Times,* 24 Apr. 1986.

Haas, Jane Glenn. "Builders Ready to Counterattack." *Orange County Register,* 7 Nov. 1987.

———. "Frustration: Orange County Voters Are Saying They've Had Enough." *Orange County Register,* 2 Dec. 1986.

———. "Making Slow Growth a No-Go." *Orange County Register,* 9 June 1988.

Harlow, LeRoy F., ed. *Servants of All: Professional Management of City Government.* Provo, Utah: Brigham Young University Press, 1981.

Harvey, David. *The Urbanization of Capital: Studies in the History and Theory of Capitalist Urbanization.* Baltimore: Johns Hopkins University Press, 1985.

Hawk, Steve. "South County Richer, Happier Than North." *Orange County Register,* 12 Dec. 1987.

Hays, Samuel P. "The Politics of Reform in Municipal Government in the Progressive Era." *Pacific Northwest Quarterly* 55 (1964):157–69.

Hiltzik, Michael A. "Orange County's Vast Ranches Spawned Vast Fortunes." *Los Angeles Times,* 4 July 1982.

Hoch, Charles, "City Limits: Municipal Boundary Formation and Class Segregation." In *Marxism and the Metropolis: New Perspectives in Urban Political Economy,* ed. William K. Tabb and Larry Sawers, 101–19. New York: Oxford University Press, 1984.

———. "Municipal Contracting in California: Privatizing with Class." *Urban Affairs Quarterly* 20 (March 1985):303–23.

Holder, Bill D. "The Urban Development of Fountain Valley, California." Master's thesis, California State University, Fullerton, 1974.

Issac, Jeffrey. *Power and Marxist Theory: A Realist View.* Ithaca, N.Y.: Cornell University Press, 1987.

Issel, William. "'Citizens Outside the Government': Business and Urban Policy in

San Francisco and Los Angeles, 1890–1932." *Pacific Historical Review* 57 (May 1988):117–45.

———. *Social Change in the United States, 1945–1983.* New York: Shocken, 1985.

Jackson, Kenneth. *Crabgrass Frontier: The Suburbanization of America.* New York: Oxford University Press, 1985.

Jenks, Richard. "It's No Little League: Three Hundred Firms Team Up to Get Things Done." *New Worlds,* April/May 1976, 55–58.

Johnson, Dale L. *Class and Social Development: A New Theory of the Middle Class.* Beverly Hills, Calif.: Sage, 1982.

Johnson, Pete. "Dead End: The Future Shock of Orange County's Roadways." *Orange Coast Magazine,* January 1987, 99–109.

Jones, Lanie. "Survey Finds a Polarization in County's Neighborhoods." *Los Angeles Times,* 25 Sept. 1985.

Landsbaum, Mark, and Andy Rose. "Diverse Allies Join Forces to Fight City Hall in Santa Ana." *Los Angeles Times,* 12 Jan. 1986.

Leinberger, Christopher B., and Charles Lockwood. "How Business Is Reshaping America." *Atlantic Monthly,* October 1986, 43–52.

Logan, John R., and Harvey L. Molotch. *Urban Fortunes: The Political Economy of Urban Space.* Berkeley: University of California Press, 1987.

Mahoney, Lisa. "Slow-Growth Push Starts County-wide." *Orange Coast Daily Pilot,* 24 Jan. 1987.

Markusen, Ann R. "Class and Urban Social Expenditures: A Marxist Theory of Metropolitan Government." In *Marxism and the Metropolis: New Perspectives in Urban Political Economy,* ed. William K. Tabb and Larry Sawers, 82–100. New York: Oxford University Press, 1984.

Moffitt, Leonard C. "Community and Urbanization: Orange County, California." 1967. Main Library, University of California at Irvine.

Mollenkopf, John H. *The Contested City.* Princeton, N.J.: Princeton University Press, 1983.

Murphy, Kim. "49 Fiefdoms: Special Districts Called Archaic by Some, Real Democracy by Others." *Los Angeles Times,* 1 Apr. 1984.

Murphy, Kim, and Jeffrey Perlman. "Urban Headaches Plague One-Time Pothole Fillers." *Los Angeles Times,* 9 Sept. 1984.

O'Dell, John. "County's Unions Register 12% Gain over Two Years." *Los Angeles Times,* 23 Dec. 1986.

———. "Orange County Executives Split on Growth Initiative." *Los Angeles Times,* 23 Jan. 1988.

———. "Orange County's Future in Hands of a Few Developers." *Los Angeles Times,* 29 Jan. 1984.

Orange County Administrative Office. *Orange County Proposal for Reorganization.* Orange County, Calif., 1974.

Orange County Board of Supervisors, Staff of General Planning Program. *Orange County's Top Management Views Growth, Policies, and the Future of Orange County.* Orange County, Calif., 1972.

Orange County Environmental Management Agency. *Biennial Report—July 1, 1975–June 30, 1977.* Orange County, Calif., 1977.

Perez, Ray. "Totals Show North, West County Cities Scuttled Measure A." *Los Angeles Times,* 22 June 1988.

Perlman, Jeffrey A. "Slow Growth Is Favored in Orange County Study." *Los Angeles Times,* 11 Dec. 1987.

Perlman, Jeffrey A., and Michael Flagg. "Money Beat Measure A, Foes, Supporters Agree." *Los Angeles Times,* 9 June 1988.

Petracca, Mark P. "Community Power and Airport Politics: A Perspective on Representative Government in Orange County." *Journal of Orange County Studies* 2 (Spring 1989):5–15.

Reyes, David. "Growth Seen as Key Issue in Orange's Council Race." *Los Angeles Times,* 29 Oct. 1986.

Robertson, Fletcher. "'Wonder Boy' Administrator Is Needed by City If Requirements of Council's Big 3 to Be Met." *Santa Ana Register,* 19 Oct. 1949.

Rose, Andy. "Group Proposes Shake-Up in Santa Ana, Urges Vote." *Los Angeles Times,* 28 Dec. 1985.

———. "SAMSON Sees Return of Ward Elections Issue." *Los Angeles Times,* 5 June 1986.

Skinner, Donald E. "Slow-Growth Advocates Study County Referendum." *Orange County Register,* 24 Jan. 1987.

Soja, Edward, Rebecca Morales, and Goetz Wolff. "Urban Restructuring: An Analysis of Social and Spatial Change in Los Angeles." *Economic Geography* 59 (April 1983):195–230.

Stillman, Richard J. *The Rise of the City Manager: A Public Professional in Local Government.* Albuquerque: University of New Mexico Press, 1974.

Teaford, Jon C. *City and Suburb: The Political Fragmentation of Metropolitan America, 1850–1970.* Baltimore: Johns Hopkins University Press, 1975.

———. *The Twentieth-Century American City.* Baltimore: Johns Hopkins University Press, 1986.

Trounstine, Philip J., and Terry Christensen. *Movers and Shakers: The Study of Community Power.* New York: St. Martin's Press, 1982.

Vranizan, Michelle. "Independent Banks Go Global with International Divisions." *Orange County Businessweek,* 9 Nov. 1987.

Walker, Richard A. "A Theory of Suburbanization: Capitalism and the Construction of Urban Space in the United States." In *Urbanization and Urban Planning in Capitalist Society,* ed. Michael Dear and Allen J. Scott, 383–429. New York: Methuen, 1981.

Warner, Willis. Papers. Special Collections, University of California at Irvine.

Wolff, Richard, and Stephen Resnick. "Power, Property, and Class." *Socialist Review* 86 (March-April 1986):97–124.

NINE

Grass-Roots Protest and the Politics of Planning: Santa Ana, 1976–88

Lisbeth Haas

Between 1976 and 1987 tens of thousands of Latinos in Santa Ana, the former urban center of Orange County, organized to oppose the policies of city government that threatened to destroy their neighborhoods and homes. This urban movement developed in three phases. During the early years working-class residents organized neighborhood associations to demand changes in city development plans and enact municipal reform. Undocumented Latino immigrants took the lead in the second phase of grass-roots mobilization. In 1984 tenants organized a rent strike that involved over five thousand immigrants in a struggle to establish and protect their rights as renters. At the height of the strike the third phase of the movement began with the formation of a coalition of tenants, former leaders of the neighborhood associations, and middle-class residents, all of whom united to democratize municipal politics. This coalition was the most radical of similar organizations that had formed in the county by 1986 (discussed by Spencer Olin in Chapter 8) because it grew out of a decade-long urban mobilization and responded to the acute racial and class tensions that characterize politics in this older city.

This chapter examines this history of protest and provides a view of the social world of long-established Latino residents and recent, predominantly Mexican, immigrants, whose community ties provided the foundation for the close-knit neighborhood and block-level organizations that sustained grass-roots political action. The examination of the community basis of grass-roots politics illustrates the conceptual limitations of the postsuburban construct to define the social world of the nonwhite working class in Orange County. Although previous chapters have characterized postsuburbia by its racial heterogeneity, its privatized residential and commercial space, the location of commercial activity in decentralized

multipurpose malls, and the prevalence of new middle-class family practices, this sociospatial organization does not adequately describe Santa
Ana. The concept is useful, however, to explain the loss of the city's
traditional urban function and to analyze the intent and vision of planners and politicians who introduced elements of postsuburban spatial
organization into Santa Ana after 1982. Perhaps most important, the
contours of postsuburban society that have been examined elsewhere in
this book illustrate the contradiction between larger developments within
the county and the experience of most Santa Ana residents. This contradiction fostered the unprecedented mobilization of the city's working
poor and undocumented immigrants, heretofore highly marginal groups
in urban politics.[1]

The chapter also examines the significance of racial and class prejudices in the planning and politics of postsuburbia. It argues that at each
stage the urban movement has acknowledged these biases and that its
internal momentum has been gained by the infusion of this political
consciousness in different sectors of the population. The particular strategies for this infusion were based on shifts in urban policy and on the
rapidly changing demographic structure of Santa Ana. To examine these
changes in urban policy and demography in relation to the various phases
of the movement reveals the political environment out of which urban
protest grew.

In the 1960s and 1970s Santa Ana's urban plans were conceived in
traditional ways and focused on expanding or rebuilding the city's existing industrial, administrative, and commercial zones. Redevelopment of
the city's urban core fortified the single centralized urban function the city
had retained—that of being the county's administrative center.[2] In 1982
Santa Ana began to implement a new redevelopment plan that incorporated 20 percent of the city's territory and that included designs to build
multiuse industrial corridors parallel to the freeways, as well as modern
corporate convention and hotel centers, and to "revitalize" more aggressively than before the downtown and civic-center area for use by a
middle-income residential and commercial population. These plans were
introduced well after the formerly small towns of Anaheim, Fullerton,
and Newport Beach, and major new cities such as Irvine, had built decentralized spaces for industrial, corporate, commercial, and leisure activity, and had surpassed Santa Ana as growth centers within the region.

Santa Ana's urban planning responded slowly to the county's economic, political, and social reorientation; plans were formulated after
Santa Ana had lost its diverse and centralized urban functions and while
the city was rapidly losing its socially heterogeneous population. Whereas
36 percent of the county's urban residents, or nearly a quarter of Orange
County's population, resided in Santa Ana in 1950, by 1970 only 12

TABLE 9.1   Population of Santa Ana
and Orange County, 1930–80

	Santa Ana	Orange County	Santa Ana as % of County
1930	30,322	118,674	25
1940	31,921	130,760	24
1950	45,533	216,224	21
1960	100,530	703,925	14
1970	156,601	1,420,386	11
1980	203,713	1,931,570	10

percent of the county's urban residents lived in the city. Santa Ana contained 11 percent of the county's total population and 26 percent of its
Latino population in 1970. After 1970 the rise in Santa Ana's population
was due primarily to Latino migration into the city; by 1980, 41 percent of
all the Latino immigrants in Orange County resided in Santa Ana. In
1986 the city's population was 62 percent Latino.[3] Contrary to the intent
of planners and city politicians, by the 1980s Santa Ana had become the
Latino center of the county (tables 9.1 and 9.2).

Because the city's redevelopment plans prior to 1982 focused on the
old urban core, they threatened to destroy three well-established barrios.
Neighborhood associations organized to contest this demolition. This
first phase of the movement (1976–82) also built a political consciousness among the city's established Latino residents, who organized within
the neighborhood associations to secure federal funds from the Economic Development Block Grant program for the improvement of services
and conditions in neighborhoods and the larger urban area.[4] The 1982
redevelopment plans, which introduced postsuburban design, encom-
passed primarily unbuilt and commercial space at the city's periphery.
Protest against this new phase of urban planning focused on securing an
increased share of the tax revenue generated from redevelopment projects for low- and moderate-income housing and on protecting small
businesses from removal.[5]

Although the formal 1982 redevelopment plans did not include further demolition of neighborhoods, the city council established a far-
reaching code-enforcement program in 1984 intended to change the
central city's demography by forcing the largely undocumented immigrant population out of substandard rental units. Opposition to code
enforcement was organized by thousands of immigrant tenants. Through
a rent strike and litigation, renters sought to make the code-enforcement
program work to their advantage by refusing to move from or pay for
substandard housing and by demanding that their units be brought up to

TABLE 9.2 Spanish-Surname Population of Santa Ana and Orange County, 1930, 1960–86

	Santa Ana	% of City Population	Orange County	% of County Population
1930	3,633	12	16,536	14
1960	15,372	15	52,576	7
1970	40,421	26	160,168	9
1980	90,646	44	286,331	15
1986	161,129	62	n.a.	n.a.

NOTE: "n.a." means not available.

code. At the height of the rent strike two new groups joined the protest. Latino merchants initiated individual lawsuits and built an organization to contest their removal from the "revitalized" downtown. Middle-class residents organized to fight various adverse effects of city plans that would transform their neighborhoods. By December 1985 a large coalition against city government formed with the objectives of restructuring municipal government and making the city council, planning commission, and mayor more directly responsible to the electorate than they had been. This coalition represented the final phase of the movement. Unlike previous movements, this coalition considered the reorganization of city government a precondition for democratic urban politics and planning.

Grass-roots mobilization, initially fostered by professional organizers using well-tried models, succeeded in gaining tangible victories for immediate objectives and successively brought politically unorganized sectors of the population into the political process, but the movement faced long-term constraints. As a result, victory was commonly followed by the implementation of city plans that undermined the movement's long-range objectives.[6] These constraints were imposed by the political economy of urban growth. The redevelopment agency grew from a relative handful of people in 1973 to being the city's second largest agency a decade later. Taking off in the early 1980s, it incorporated other departments, added personnel and functions, and consolidated its power by 1986.[7] The expansion of the redevelopment agency and its fiscal power is explained by the fact that the redevelopment process became the single most important source of revenue for California cities after passage of Proposition 13 in 1978. (See Chapter 10 for a discussion of the California tax revolt.) Tax-increment revenue from redevelopment areas goes directly to the city and is not used for the city's traditional responsibilities of providing social services. Instead, the revenue backs bonds for infrastructural development and subsidizes a large array of projects for the private sector. Critics argue that redevelopment projects are often fiscally unsound.[8] Although they provide the city with a promised tax increment, no guidelines exist to balance the city's outlay of capital and its recovery of that money. In response to urban protest, the State of California increased the amount of tax-increment funds redevelopment agencies must spend on low- and moderate-income housing, but the state has not created the personnel to enforce those regulations.[9] Hence, even while the urban movement in Santa Ana has focused on the need for family housing, the city has met most of its obligation to replace or construct low- and moderate-income housing by building units for senior citizens. And, following the county pattern, Santa Ana has produced more high-income than low-income housing in its redevelopment areas.

The power of the redevelopment agency over the city's fiscal and administrative life has posed an increasingly complex problem for the urban movement. The entrenched racial prejudice of the city's voting population has posed a second problem and thwarted significant political change within muncipal government in both 1985 and 1986, when the reaction to grass-roots political activity was directed solely against Latino tenants and undocumented immigrants despite the broad representation of diverse ethnic and social groups in the movement by these dates. Although the momentum of the movement has built in the years subsequent to 1986, the complex obstacles to a democratic urban politics have progressed apace. The following pages thus examine a yet inconclusive chapter in the contemporary urban process.

THE SOCIAL BASIS OF THE URBAN MOVEMENT

The high concentration of Latinos in Santa Ana by 1970 is part of a regional social geography that replicates an ethnic segmentation of the working class. Within this class Latinos hold a significant number of the blue-collar manufacturing jobs. The total rise in the county's Latino population after 1960 corresponds to an expansion of the blue-collar work force, which doubled between 1970 and 1980.[10] Table 9.2 suggests the geographical and historical dimensions of this segmentation. The proportion of Latinos in the county by 1980, when Latino blue-collar workers had become one of the fastest-growing segments of the work force, corresponds most closely to the proportion in 1930, when Latinos constituted the principal labor force for agriculture. The ethnic division of the work force that is reflected in the region's geography produced a consistently low level of income for Latino families. In 1966, 50 percent of all Anglos in Santa Ana earned more than seven thousand dollars, while only 26 percent of Latinos, the majority of whom came from families that had resided in the United States for generations, earned that amount.[11] The immigrants' position in the economy has reinforced these trends. By

1977, 88 percent of Orange County's Latino population earned below the median income.[12] Santa Ana has become the primary area of residence for these working poor; it contained eight of the county's ten poorest census tracts in 1980.

The history of this ethnic segmentation helps to explain the social basis of the urban movement. Work-force segmentation has been part of a system of social segregation fought against by Latinos in various social movements dating from the 1920s. Mitigating the adverse effects of this segregation, a web of relationships has developed within the barrios that helps sustain daily life and that spans generations. These ties have been used to build the urban struggle. The first phase of the movement was organized among Latino residents who had lived or continued to live in barrios formed at the turn of the century, when the city's geography was strongly polarized by ethnicity.[13] Between 1910 and 1940 segregation in housing formed part of the systematic segregation of Latinos in the workplace, in "Mexican" elementary schools, and in public life. Postwar economic growth and civil rights action significantly improved most Latinos' economic situations, yet the effect of persistent racism was evident in the virtually unaltered ethnic geography of Santa Ana in 1960, when Latinos resided primarily in or near the long-established barrios and inhabited the old neighborhoods in the city center. During the 1960s this ethnic residential concentration was reinforced (map 9.1). By 1970 eight elementary schools, all located in or near the older barrios and in the city center, had student bodies between 60 and 90 percent Latino.[14] As a new social differentiation of space emerged within the region, Latinos moved into neighborhoods throughout central Santa Ana. By 1975 most of the elementary schools were over 50 percent Latino, and by 1986 only five of the city's twenty-four elementary schools were less than 50 percent Latino, while Latinos constituted 85 to 95 percent of the students in eleven elementary schools.[15] Santa Ana also has the largest black and Asian populations in the county, but Latinos are the numerically dominant ethnic group.

Santa Ana's role as the Latino urban center of the county is further illustrated by comparing its ethnic organization with that of other cities in the county. In 1970 Santa Ana's pattern of ethnic residence and ethnic distribution was similar to those of older Orange County cities and towns. Twenty-six percent of Santa Ana's population was Latino, and other places had comparative distributions: In Placentia 19 percent of the population was Latino, in San Juan Capistrano 18 percent, in Stanton 16 percent, and in La Habra 15 percent. Latinos were everywhere concentrated near the old town centers in well-established barrios. By 1980, however, Santa Ana's Latino population had expanded throughout most of the city, while that in the older towns of the citrus belt remained more

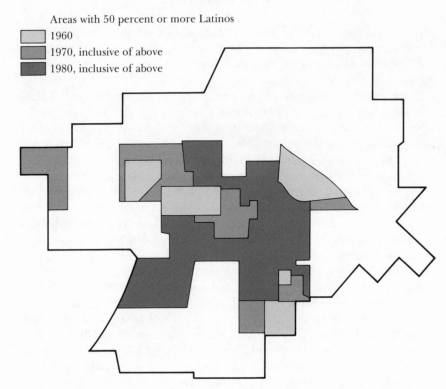

Map 9.1. The geographic concentration of the Latino population in Santa Ana, 1960–80

highly concentrated in ethnic enclaves and grew in relatively smaller proportion to the total population. The proportion of Latinos declined in San Juan Capistrano after 1970, where an expansion of suburban housing for middle- and higher-income residents allowed them rapidly to dwarf the predominantly lower-income Latino population of the small city.[16]

Latinos are drawn to Santa Ana because of the relatively low rents and the established immigrant neighborhoods. The structure of immigration influenced this demographic shift and contributed to the social basis of protest in the 1980s. Immigrants migrate through kinship/friendship networks that determine largely where they settle and that link particular communities in Mexico to settlement cores in the United States.[17] Through these networks immigrants are introduced to potential employers, aided in finding housing and in making medical and educational arrangements for their families, and provided with an emotional and material support system. These networks are present in the older barrios of Santa Ana as well as in the newer immigrant neighborhoods. In Santa Ana's Delhi Barrio, for example, marriage patterns between 1947 and 1979 demonstrated "network endogamy"; 40 percent of the immigrants who married in Our Lady of Guadalupe church had married people from their own or nearby communities in Mexico.[18] Strong links have also been forged between Latinos from the United States and Mexican nationals through marriage.[19]

Immigration to Santa Ana has contributed to the coherence of Latino neighborhoods. Although the rapid expansion of the immigrant population after 1970 and the low wages they are paid produced a scarcity of housing and encouraged the proliferation of slumlords, family life is supported by well-established and interconnected social networks. Moreover, many areas of the city have been restructured by immigrants, and city life has generally been transformed. Between 1970 and 1980 Latino merchants purchased or rented space in neighborhood shopping centers. Latino street vendors selling clothing, fruit, vegetables, and other goods regularly frequented neighborhoods.[20] The downtown area, long cited by city officials and administrators as an example of the city's decline, was revived in 1970 as a commercial and cultural center by Latino merchants. Some of these merchants had first established themselves on East Fourth Street much earlier. The Olivos family presents an exemplary case of how these businesses expanded simultaneously with the growth of the Latino population. In 1938 the family opened a Spanish-language cinema downtown. In the early 1950s they bought one of the city's largest theaters, and by the early 1980s they had purchased all the downtown theaters to show Spanish-language films. Two Spanish-language newspapers were published and widely distributed in Santa Ana by 1980.[21] The important place of Latinos in Santa Ana's contemporary urban life is underlined by the policies of Police Chief Ralph Davis, who in 1983 announced the unprecedented policy that the Santa Ana police force would not cooperate with the Immigration and Naturalization Service in their raids and roundups of undocumented immigrants.[22]

THE NEIGHBORHOODS ORGANIZE

Latino residents acted to organize urban life in Santa Ana but until the mid-1970s did so outside the political arena. Latinos began to mobilize in force when city planning threatened the existence of their homes and neighborhoods, a process dating from 1976, with the implementation of the first phase of redevelopment. Early redevelopment had three objectives that required the demolition of a number of central-city neighborhoods. The primary objective was to "revitalize" the downtown and expand the civic-center complex. City council members and planners envisioned a downtown oriented toward persons working in government, finance, and professional activities. The second objective was to sustain economic growth by building high-density apartments and condominiums for middle-income residents. A third planning objective, to eradicate "incompatible land uses" or the coexistence of homes and industry, also threatened older barrios. Toward these ends, planning documents invariably cited substandard housing in the barrios and city center, and recommended the demolition of homes and apartment units or else strict code enforcement to eradicate what planners defined as blight.

The Orange County Sponsoring Committee, formed by twenty Latino community activists, brought a group of professional organizers to Santa Ana to establish a stable grass-roots organization that could respond to the threats posed to the neighborhoods by redevelopment. The committee secured a two-year budget from the Catholic Church, local businesses, and other churches, and contracted with Jesuit organizers from the Oakland Training Institute.[23] Three Jesuit priests and four young-adult lay organizers constituted the team, which began organizing in the fall of 1976. Using the Alinsky model of community organizing, they aimed at empowering the working poor by training them in confrontational politics at the municipal level. The organizers proceeded by canvassing neighborhoods to discover the issues most troubling to their residents, to locate potential leaders, and, in particular areas, to spread news about the city's plans. Through this process they established the foundations for neighborhood associations, the basic units for grass-roots participation in the urban movement between 1977 and 1982. These associations were the core of the pluralistic model of urban politics envisioned by Saul Alinsky; they promoted local autonomy and widespread citizen participation and thereby fostered the democratization of municipal politics.[24] The organizers considered the issue-oriented agendas of the neighborhood associations tactical, a means through which small victories would bring members into the association and promote the growth of militancy.

During the early months the organizers began systematically to train neighborhood residents in community organizing. Jenny Casamina described her first meeting with organizer Meg Gaff. Gaff knocked at her door and asked,"Do you speak English? Do you know the city is going to knock these places down and get rid of you guys?" Casamina answered, "They didn't notify me. . . . They're crazy if they think I'm going to move." That evening she went to a meeting with other soon-to-be leaders from diverse barrios, the priests, and lay organizers. These training sessions were long and difficult. Numerous neighborhood leaders recall tears and agony as the organizers prepared them to confront the hostility and the race and class prejudices of city officials. Out of the process, however, Casamina argues that the priests taught them "to fight for our rights without hurting others." Everyone learned "discipline, solidarity and cooperation," lessons that remained a foundation for a grass-roots politics through 1987.[25] Grass-roots leaders were placed in important positions as neighborhood organizers, and by May 1977 eight neighborhood associations joined together to form Santa Ana Neighborhood Organizations (SANO).

SANO was a highly democratic organization whose leadership included women and members of ethnic groups in virtually exact proportion to the distribution of these ethnic groups in each neighborhood. This democratic structure was embedded in the organization's neighborhood base and drew on neighborhood networks to recruit members and sustain major battles with the city over urban issues. Women, the center of these networks, constituted a majority of SANO's neighborhood organizers and spokespersons.[26] SANO's leadership, argued a former president, was representative of "truly grassroots people, the people that never set foot in city hall, the people that never knew they could be potential leaders." Some of the top leaders were "your everyday farmworker. . . . I myself am a cabinet maker, for instance, and the vice-president is a beautician."[27] Although ethnic tensions caused many other community organizations to decline in membership, SANO was successful in bringing ethnic groups together because it promoted ethnic consciousness. Well over half the membership and a corresponding proportion of the leadership was Latino, but black, Anglo, and a few Asian residents also played an important role in building the neighborhood associations. SANO was also successful in building a multiethnic, democratic structure because it developed a culture of protest. Celebrations and festive fundraisers were an important part of the organization's agenda. The street demonstrations, rallies, candlelight vigils, and actions at City Hall often drew on popular religious

and cultural activities and infused these with a new political consciousness. At its height in 1982 SANO had a membership of approximately
ten thousand households and thirteen neighborhood associations. Each
neighborhood organization formulated wide-ranging demands such as
paving streets, replacing sidewalks, improving parks, monitoring neighborhood industry for safety standards, improving street lighting, and
eradicating cockroaches. SANO monitored the city's Community Economic Development Block Grant budget (federal funds for urban improvement) and requested those funds after having determined collectively how to pool them to meet each neighborhood's needs. SANO also
formed a housing committee that monitored city housing programs and a
crime committee that monitored police activity and mediated between
residents and the police in cases involving conflict. An education and
health committee took up a series of issues that affected SANO neighborhoods and the city's working poor.

THE TACTICS AND SCOPE OF PROTEST: THREE CASES

SANO's agenda, organized around the neighborhood so as to make municipal government responsible to its citizens, did not change the city's
political structure or alter the goals of urban policy. Nonetheless, it did
produce major victories that affected all SANO's thirteen neighborhoods
and promoted the development of a new political life and consciousness.
Only months after the first neighborhood associations had formed, their
presentations before the city council were, in the words of one council
member, "as neat and well-organized as anything I've seen come before
the council. They click off five or six or seven points, . . . and they are
finished in maybe twenty minutes." The city manager lamented the effectiveness of these tactics, arguing that the activists "egg others into similar
actions by taking pictures at the council meetings that later appear in
Spanish newspapers indicating what organizing can achieve."[28] By late
April 1977 neighborhoods had begun inviting city council members and
the planning staff to their community meetings, thus turning around the
power relationships embedded in territorial control and encouraging
ever larger numbers of community residents to act. Three neighborhood
associations conducted fairly prolonged battles with the city beginning in
early 1977. Consideration of them shows the nature and scope of urban
struggle during these years.

   In the Civic Center Barrio, formed as a Latino neighborhood between
1945 and the mid-1960s, four hundred families were forcibly removed
when the barrio was demolished in 1977 for middle-income and senior-
citizen apartments and condominiums on the downtown's west side. They
remained organized after their displacement and formed a community

housing corporation by 1980. The neighborhood, in its early stages of organizing when the evictions began, first negotiated with the city in late November 1976 to secure relocation allowances for displaced residents. In early January over two hundred neighbors, including the elderly and parents with young children, attended a city council meeting. The neighborhood's well-coordinated agenda was translated, and neighbors, such as an elderly tailor, spoke in Spanish before the council, making known the hardships residents experienced when evicted. Their appearance was dramatic, an unprecedented intervention by long-established Latino residents and recent immigrants into the political life of the city. Emphasizing the degree to which this early organizing had increased the residents' expectations of government, one council member complained, "The people began to perceive this as the way . . . the city ought to be, [but it goes] far beyond what is technically required in the relocation process."[29]

Many of their proposals for relocation were accepted by the city, and in March 1977 the neighborhood association negotiated an agreement with the Redevelopment Agency and the developer to secure 58 of the 318 planned rental units for displaced renters; but in 1979 the developer changed the rental units into condominiums, with city approval.[30] A battle ensued during the course of which the neighborhood formed the Civic Center Barrio Housing Corporation (CCBHC), entitled to produce, own, operate, and manage housing. The corporation's board of directors was made up of former barrio residents and professionals in housing, government, and banking. The residents retained a slight majority. Thus, the barrio association, with its residents dispersed throughout the city and county, not only remained alive but also had reconstituted itself as a corporate entity responsible for the multiple tasks of producing and managing housing. In 1981 the association entered litigation to recover the amount still owed by the developer from the May 1980 settlement of $1.4 million to build low- and moderate-income housing in Santa Ana.

Although the participation of the original barrio residents gradually declined, 150 of those residents joined for a victory party to celebrate the establishment of the corporation in 1980, and many continued to envision the reconstitution of the community in a single neighborhood. Juvenal Capistrano echoed these intentions: "Since the moment we left the barrio my dream has always been to come back."[31] Those who remained active in the neighborhood battle were represented in the administration of a $1.5 million housing budget, and the board of directors continued to be composed of the most active grass-roots leaders. Between 1982 and 1987 the CCBHC became the owner of an increasing number of rental units organized along the principles of cooperation that residents learned during the neighborhood struggle. An elected committee organized the maintenance of the buildings and enforced agreed-upon rules, and neighbors cooperated in watching the children, aiding in crises, and organizing parties and other events. The CCBHC also directed the construction of owner-built homes cooperatively organized along the principles developed in the neighborhood battles.

Logan Barrio's fight to halt its destruction presents a different case of urban protest. In 1976 city planners recommended that Logan Barrio be brought into the redevelopment project as the first phase of a project to construct a modern industrial park near the downtown.[32] Logan was zoned industrial in 1929, but the small firms that had located in the barrio since 1945 coexisted well with the barrio's approximately 507 residents. Because a substantial number of the firms also faced removal, they joined in a coalition with the residents between 1977 and 1979 to fight the barrio's incorporation into the redevelopment zone and to rezone it from industrial to residential usage with appropriate guarantees to protect existing industry.[33]

The tactics used in the Logan struggle were some of the most innovative in Santa Ana. For the first time, a Latino neighborhood defined itself to the public and press, making its history and the organization of community life the grounds on which the neighborhood should be saved. As Josefa Andrade argued to the press and city government: "People like me were born and raised here, and raised our own kids here, and some of their kids." Helen Moraga pointed out that her family had lived in Logan for five generations: "It's still the kind of neighborhood where people watch out for one another's children and elderly parents."[34] Residents had lived in the barrio an average of twenty-three years; in 1979 fully one-quarter of the population had lived there for forty years or more. Thirty percent of the dwellings were owner-occupied. In many instances these people owned one or more additional homes on their own lot or next door, which they rented out, bringing the owners who lived in the area to 50 percent. Often these properties were rented to family relations. Fifty-four percent of Logan residents had relatives living in another home within the barrio.[35]

These close networks of family and friends had sustained urban protest in the early 1970s, when city plans to extend Civic Center Drive East through the neighborhood were successfully defeated and the thoroughfare was rerouted.[36] They were again successful after a two-year battle in City Hall. In 1979 the neighborhood was rezoned for residential use through a specially designed (R2x) zoning ordinance that allowed industry to coexist with or to replace or be replaced by housing. Logan residents continue to be organized as a neighborhood and have avoided further demolition.[37] Like many other neighborhoods, they are now formally incorporated into a city neighborhood program.

The barrio of Artesia-Pilar, which defended its opposition to the destruction of forty dwellings to make way for a new police station on the grounds that the poor had a right to their homes and community, presents a third case of a successful neighborhood association's battle against urban renewal in the late 1970s. The tactics used by the neighborhood also demonstrate the importance of a shared political culture of protest. When informed of the city plans, the residents organized as a SANO neighborhood and met in homes, patios, and the local Catholic Church to organize against removal. The police station was never built, and the city promised to spend more than $200,000 to rehabilitate or rebuild 110 homes in the barrio. Ninety were supposed to be done by 1980, but work had not begun on even one when a second protest erupted. The city was considering incorporating the neighborhood into its redevelopment area. The city gave a consortium of three developers the right to negotiate for a redevelopment project to extend middle-class housing near the civic-center condominium project. Residents again responded, with protest made into a festive act; neighborhood residents, young and old, drew a huge line in red crepe paper over a large number of city blocks to symbolically mark the limits of redevelopment.[38] These events took place with high-profile news coverage. After SANO's demise (which we discuss later in this chapter) and as late as 1986, Jovita Hernandez, the principal spokeswoman for the Artesia-Pilar neighborhood, noted the existence of a network whereby neighbors kept each other abreast of city plans.[39]

In all three cases, these urban struggles produced grass-roots leaders and formal and informal neighborhood organizations that continued to influence the political life of the city even after a decline in SANO's activity and influence beginning in 1983. SANO declined because it lost most of its professional staff. The Jesuits departed from Santa Ana in 1983, leaving only two paid organizers as full-time staff. Neighborhood leaders, already burdened by long working days and family responsibilities, could not undertake the consuming work of organizing a multifaceted protest without sufficient personnel. Simultaneously, the umbrella organization that trained SANO's leaders and sponsored its staff shifted its organizing strategy to church-based community action and withdrew its support for neighborhood-based groups. By the spring of 1984 few neighborhood associations met. One year later the General Board of Directors merged SANO with a countywide, church-based group. Some of the SANO neighborhoods have retained their identity, but they work separately with the city's much expanded planning department.

TENANTS' STRIKE

Grass-roots organizing again gained momentum in 1984, when Santa Ana launched the most aggressive code-enforcement policy in California.

Tenants whose landlords refused to bring their buildings up to code were evicted. Code enforcement was a strategy, previously used sparingly, through which the city attempted to gain some control over demographic change by forcing tenants from their homes and pressuring landlords to upgrade housing to attract a higher-income and, presumably, largely Anglo population. Neighborhoods near the central city were the target areas for code enforcement. Unlike previous city planning policies, this one was focused on neighborhoods that had rapidly become Latino after 1970. Hence, it affected primarily the undocumented immigrant population and did not encroach on long-established barrios. This produced a major shift in the strategy of urban struggle, and for the first time the primarily undocumented immigrant population took the lead. The strike activity of tenants was a sharp departure from the neighborhood-based protest of SANO, and it publicized the rights of undocumented immigrants to adequate housing. The strikes eventually formed part of a larger political mobilization that worked against redevelopment and for reforming the structure of city government and the planning commission.

In 1984, during the early implementation of code enforcement, tenants mobilized to protest the eviction notices they received. Although the city ordered the evictions, the city council voted three times against making relocation funds available to displaced tenants. A coalition of civic and religious groups was formed to organize and represent the tenants; it pressed the city council to make available ample relocation benefits and to establish a moratorium on evictions.[40] After hundreds of undocumented immigrants organized, the city finally approved a tenant relocation program.[41] Relocation was not the answer to the problems of substandard housing and displacement. Because the enforcement policies focused on eight of the ten most impoverished census tracts in the county, evicted tenants could not find affordable replacement housing in the city or county. In fact, six months after the establishment of the relocation program, only ten families, out of hundreds evicted, had been assisted in finding new homes.[42] The dearth of housing, the relatively large size of families, and the fact that many tenants were well established in their neighborhoods made many unwilling and unable to move.

The rent strike that began in January 1985 grew out of this resistance to relocation and constituted the second phase of the tenants' movement. Hermandad Mexicana Nacional, an immigrants' rights group that established a chapter in Santa Ana in the early 1980s, coordinated the strike activity and took the lead in subsequent litigation and organizing. Hermandad's strategy was influenced by three models: the Alinsky model of community organizing, labor organizing, and the Mexican mutual-aid societies of the Southwest and Mexico.[43] The influence of labor organizing and mutual-aid societies made Hermandad's objectives and organizational form distinct from those of SANO. The organization addressed a larger range of issues, such as the legal status and employment conditions of immigrants. While SANO's emphasis was on building autonomous neighborhood associations for participation in municipal politics, Hermandad's concern was to eradicate the general conditions of exploitation experienced by the immigrant. Its goal was to build organizations at the workplace as well as in the community. The rent strike and extensive court litigation that characterized the tenants' movement further distinguish this urban movement from the neighborhood-based struggle.

Hermandad grew from a small group of approximately ten families in 1982 to encompass close to three thousand families by 1987. A budding grass-roots leadership emerged from the strikes, and a second influx of members became active by 1987, often drawn into the organization by Hermandad's work in processing immigration papers. Some of the grass-roots leaders had been activists in land and labor struggles in Mexico and the United States, but many had gained their experience in the course of the urban struggle in Santa Ana. As in SANO, community women were some of the most militant and outspoken strike leaders. Maria Rosa Ibarra, instrumental in forming Hermandad in Santa Ana, consciously built on the female consciousness that has encouraged women to act when housing and subsistence are the issues, and sought to promote the development of this feminist consciousness and female leadership in the organization.[44]

Many of the Catholic churches in Santa Ana supported the rent strike. By 1987 organizers were able to go to any parish in Santa Ana to make announcements during the mass, pass out literature, and collect letters of support outside the church door. The strong familial and kinship networks among immigrants sustained Hermandad's growth by bringing an ever larger number of people into the strike.

On New Year's Day, 1985, twenty families on Minnie Street vowed to withhold their rent; in early February the strike spread to seventy-five other families.[45] The strikers were subject to eviction if their dwellings were not brought up to code and for failure to pay their rent; hence litigation was essential to the success of the strike. In February tenants began proceedings to obtain court protection against harassment and eviction. By late February they won a court-approved plan to make the Orange County Legal Aid Society the temporary landlord for nearly four hundred apartments. The judge also placed a restraining order on seven landlords, restricting them from harassing their tenants by cutting off utilities or by calling the Immigration and Naturalization Service.

This protection allowed the tenants to take the offensive in defining the code-enforcement program; they immediately began to stage public demonstrations to protest their living conditions and to demand city inspection of units they declared unfit for habitation. More than three hundred tenants appeared before the city council after having waited many months for the inspection of their dwellings.[46] By April 1985 the renters began to seek court orders to reduce the rents on their dwellings until repairs were made. In 1985 and 1986 tenants sustained and joined the strike and were active in street processions and demonstrations, while court victories and out-of-court settlements favoring tenants encouraged an ever-increasing number of renters in substandard dwellings to strike, independent of the direct pressure exerted through code-enforcement evictions.[47] The number of persons involved fluctuated; for example, when families from 130 units joined the strike in June 1987, they joined others who had already been on strike for more than eighteen months.

Why did tenants strike? One tenant leader echoed the vast majority of women leaders when she argued, "For the good of ourselves and our children; because it's very ugly there."[48] In court proceedings tenants testified that they went on strike because their ceilings were falling, walls were caving in or had large holes, plumbing leaked, the windows were unsafe, cockroaches and rats infested their buildings. They argued that their low incomes, large families, and well-established neighborhood life made it impossible to find sufficient replacement housing.[49] One tenant faced with eviction from a large unit argued: "We are poor families that cannot move."[50] In other complexes the unfair practices of the landlords were enough to bring people into the strike.[51]

The city council initially established the code-enforcement program so that it was grossly unfavorable to the tenants. Owners who violated codes were fined a $150 administrative fee when the city issued a notice of violation for renting out an unsafe dwelling; tenants who refused to vacate an unsafe housing unit, however, faced fines up to $500 per day. The Rental Relocation Fund established by the city council in December 1984 represented a compromise with the tenants and housing activists, and increased slightly the burden of responsibility on the landlords. The pressure tenants had exerted on the city by that date also resulted in city lawsuits against particular landlords for their failure to comply with codes. But the city refused to place a moratorium on evictions, and in the first year of the program an estimated 1,240 to 3,000 persons were evicted. After three years of the program, hundreds of people had faced multiple displacements as they moved from residence to residence within Santa Ana's pockets of poverty. The city government stepped up pressure against tenants in 1986.

This new offensive developed when the city council voted to interpret the Uniform Housing Code conservatively and established an overcrowding ordinance that drastically reduced the number of people who could legally inhabit a home.[52] Overcrowding citations brought a new wave of eviction notices. Not accidentally, and because of the pressure exerted by landlords, the bulk of these notices went to three hundred of the four hundred units successfully defended in court. Units with the same or a similar number of inhabitants that had not either won their cases or taken the landlords to court did not receive the notices.[53] Despite over ten thousand letters of protest the city council upheld its interpretation of the occupancy code. *Overcrowding* became a major political issue and a code word for expressing anti-immigrant and anti-Mexican sentiment in city council meetings and during municipal elections.

A BROAD COALITION AND POLITICAL REACTION

In July 1985 fifteen hundred rent strikers and other Latinos met at Madison Park in Santa Ana for a celebration dinner and fundraiser; the event was sponsored by tenants and housing advocates, and included a host of speakers from organizations long involved in the nearly decade-old urban movement. At this celebration the tenants announced their decision to join the coalition of forces against redevelopment.[54] They made this decision in a crucial moment, when the protest against re-development was firmly fixed on the question of affordable housing. Between 1982 and 1985 housing advocates sought to extend the amount of tax-increment funds to be used for low- and moderate-income housing beyond the state-mandated 20 percent. In 1984 housing advocates won an out-of-court settlement of lawsuits filed immediately after the new redevelopment plans were announced in 1982; in this settlement the city committed 30 percent of the revenue from two new redevelopment proj-ect areas and 60 percent from a third for such housing.[55] However, in the wake of this settlement, the city began to accelerate its downtown re-development project and announced the strict code-enforcement pro-gram discussed previously. As in all redevelopment projects, the city subsidized the acquisition and improvement of downtown sites for private developers. For example, the city's total costs to acquire and prepare the land for a condominium project amounted to $3.45 million; the de-veloper bought the property from the city for only $250,000. The Al-liance for Fair Redevelopment formed to block a hotel/office complex and an apartment project downtown, arguing that the city should develop affordable rental units for the low-income families displaced through code enforcement.[56]

As housing activists mobilized to demand an increased share of re-development funds and housing for tenants and other working-class residents, downtown Latino merchants began to fight their removal in a separate battle. City planners considered most of the Latino merchants economically and socially marginal to the new downtown. As the director of the Downtown Development Commission stated, "New businesses, which cater to tourists, young urban professionals, and the upper-middle class will take the place of many existing Latino businesses."[57] The deputy city manager also argued that new residential construction would appeal to "yuppies . . . who will make downtown exciting, who will bring all kinds of demands to the area."[58] In 1984 the city stepped up its enforcement of building codes downtown and, in a contradictory move that would bring the destruction of those same buildings, sent out offers to two hundred corporate developers to buy and restructure the area as a shopping and entertainment center. As a result José Ceballos, who owned three buildings on East Fourth Street, had to bring them up to the city's seismic code at great cost, but in the projected plans for "revitalization" Ceballos's buildings faced probable demolition within two years.[59] In late June 1984 the downtown Latino merchants put forth their own plans for the 4.31-acre site in partnership with a local development firm. These merchants organized at a time when other Latino businesses were forming the Hispanic Chamber of Commerce in Santa Ana and when middle-class Latino residents were beginning to take an active role in municipal politics.

In December 1985 a new political coalition joined together previous SANO members, Hermandad, the Alliance for Fair Redevelopment, and middle-class neighborhood organizations.[60] The Santa Ana Merged Society of Neighbors (SAMSON) wanted to replace the partial ward system, in which voters elected all city council members including those from within and outside their ward, with a direct ward vote for that district's city council representative. (See Olin's discussion of SAMSON in Chapter 8.) The coalition also sought to replace the appointed planning commission with elected commissioners and to replace the appointed city manager with an elected, executive mayor.[61] The city council refused to put these proposed city-charter amendments on a special June 1986 election ballot. In response, SAMSON organized a voter-registration drive and collected enough signatures to place the initiative on the ballot. They succeeded, but Measure C, which proposed the creation of an executive mayor's position and a ward vote for city council members, lost by a narrow margin. SAMSON members claim that a series of mailers sent by the anonymous Good Government Committee distorted the measure, were deceptive and misleading, and led to its defeat. "Prior to the 'hit pieces,' " the SAMSON chairman argued, "the polls indicated a 2 to 1 support for Measure C." Absentee ballots (reflecting decisions made prior to the mailing) gave Measure C a 2-to-1 edge.[62]

The attacks on Measure C were directed against the tenants' movement and Latino immigrants, and generally argued that a conspiratorial group in the city had introduced the initiative to do away with code-enforcement policies. One mailer argued, "If they win, their first action will be to strike down code enforcement laws." A second argued that Measure C's proponents "would use their City Hall takeover to strike down code enforcement and open our neighborhoods up to rundown, overcrowded boarding houses."[63] SAMSON's membership was not composed primarily of Latinos, and yet its initative was contested wholly on the basis of attacks against the organized Latino population, suggesting that the grass-roots Latino activists were the most effective target to use to mobilize the predominantly Anglo, middle-class voting public (fully 77 percent of the registered voters in Santa Ana).[64] SAMSON placed a similar measure on the November 1986 ballot. Misleading anti-immigrant and antitenant brochures, now written by the anonymous Santa Ana Neighbors for Excellence, argued that proponents of the measure wanted to make Santa Ana into a slum. After the failed election, Latino grass-roots activists and lawyers began to plan for a major voter-registration drive among Latinos and for new challenges to the municipal government's policies on urban development and political representation.

CONCLUSION

The history of grass-roots protest illustrates the political process that began as Latinos became a majority of Santa Ana's population. This protest has a strong civil rights focus and, as elsewhere, has brought the struggle for civil rights into the sphere of municipal politics by addressing the economic and political implications of urban development for the city's Latino working class. Although race is not a singular indicator of social-class standing in postsuburban society, a majority of Latinos in Orange County remain residentially concentrated and poorer than the Anglo majority; in 1977 fully 88 percent of Latinos in the county earned below the median income. The politicization of this population during the decade-long struggle considered in this chapter remains one of the most important long-term consequences of urban protest in Santa Ana.

The political mobilization of Santa Ana's Latino residents was furthered by the tangible results of grass-roots action. Neighborhoods were saved from destruction and funds were secured for neighborhood improvements determined by the residents. A grass-roots housing corporation was successfully established. In its units and cooperative housing projects, as in other neighborhoods, residents have maintained informal structures through which they make democratic decisions regarding neighborhood life and check the actions of city government. Another important legacy of the once-powerful neighborhood associations is the political consciousness and continued activism of a significant sector of the city's long-established Latino population. After 1982, redevelopment efforts shifted to focus on previously unbuilt land adjacent to the freeways, and suits brought against the redevelopment plan to secure an increased portion of redevelopment tax-increment funds for low- and moderate-income housing initiated an era when urban conflicts were frequently taken to court. During this period immigrant tenants organized to fight their displacement from eight of the county's ten poorest census tracts. The rent strike secured increased protection of tenants' rights and improvements in many of their living conditions. Downtown Latino merchants organized at the same time as the strike and increased their representation in the city's commercial, urban, and political affairs. The urban movement gained full force in the coalition formed to restructure municipal government in 1985. Although the coalition's goals were not attained, its defeat at the polls was followed by a voter-registration drive among Latinos that promises to produce a new majority in future elections.

The logic of Santa Ana's urban planning was described by Mayor Daniel Griset, who declared in 1986, "This city council is not advancing the politics of poverty. . . . Our politics are the politics of progress."[65] The meaning of progress was widely debated between 1976 and 1986. The grass-roots movement fought for a vision of progress that included the right to maintain well-established neighborhoods, to secure a substantial quantity of standard low-rent housing, and to build a quality neighborhood and urban life for the majority of the city's residents. The attempt to reform local government and the planning process, which became a focus of the movement after 1985, directly challenged the power of the county's new corporate elite to define alone the nature of urban change. By that date the fiscal importance and bureaucratic strength of the redevelopment agency had committed the city to continued urban reorganization, and the ballot had become pivotal to influence the direction of this process. At the conclusion of a decade of urban protest the political innovation introduced by the previously most marginal sectors of the city's population remains salient; this arm of grass-roots protest remains essential to bring about a fundamental democratization of municipal government.

NOTES

1. For a discussion of urban movements and historical case studies of urban struggles, see Manuel Castells, *The City and the Grassroots: A Cross-Cultural Theory of Urban Social Movements* (Berkeley: University of California Press, 1983).

2. According to City Manager Carl Thornton (1951–73) the city was in serious jeopardy of losing its county administrative functions to the rapidly developing cities elsewhere in the county. The city and private citizens donated "a lot of property outright, free of charge" so the civic-center complex could be con-

structed. *Los Angeles Times*, 21 Sept. 1975, XI:12. Nancy Kleniewski notes that when cities did not have resources (such as the administrative complex) to facilitate a shift to a corporate (as opposed to an industrial) city, their urban-renewal projects failed. "From Industrial to Corporate City: The Role of Urban Renewal," in *Marxism and the Metropolis*, ed. William Tabb and Larry Sawers (New York: Oxford University Press, 1984), 212.

3. Antonio Delgado, "An Analysis of Hispanic Youth in Santa Ana: Recommended Public Policy Direction," May 1986 (report available at City Manager's Office). (Fifty percent of these Latino residents were foreign-born; 91 percent were of Mexican ancestry.)

4. For a discussion of the history of federal urban-renewal and redevelopment policy, see John Mollenkopf, *The Contested City* (Princeton, N.J.: Princeton University Press, 1983).

5. Consistent with the history of federal urban policy, Santa Ana's redevelopment and planning projects were not intended primarily to benefit the city's predominantly working-class population, although housing advocates since the 1930s have attempted to shape a federal policy that is favorable to the urban poor. For a concise history of this problem, see Marc Weiss, "The Origins and Legacy of Urban Renewal," in *Urban and Regional Planning in an Age of Austerity*, ed. Pierre Clavel, John Forester, and William Goldsmith (New York: Pergamon Press, 1980), 53–80.

6. For studies concerning the political economy of urban change and the course of urban protest elsewhere, see Clarence Stone and Heywood Sanders, eds., *The Politics of Urban Development* (Lawrence: University Press of Kansas, 1987); Susan Fainstein et al., eds., *Restructuring the City* (New York: Longman, 1983); and Sidney Plotkin, "Democratic Change in the Urban Political Economy," in *The Politics of San Antonio*, ed. David Johnson et al. (Lincoln: University of Nebraska Press, 1983).

7. Interview by author with Rob Balen, former senior planner for the City of Santa Ana, 2 Oct. 1987.

8. Interview by author with Gordon Bricken, former Santa Ana mayor, 5 Oct. 1987.

9. Denise Arend, from the California Department of Housing and Community Development, argued that "vocal activists do more to ensure agencies comply with the law than the state housing agency." *Orange County Register*, 11 Sept. 1985, B6.

10. See Allen Scott, "High Technology Industry and Territorial Development: The Rise of the Orange County Complex, 1955–1984," *Urban Geography* 7 (January–February 1986): 3–45, and Alfred Serrato, "The State of Hispanics in Orange County—1980," 1981 (report available at County Administrative Building Library). Serrato argues that Latinos also constitute a significant segment of the construction work force in the county, which rose from 15,900 workers in 1958 to 62,500 in 1980, while manufacturing workers increased from 85,000 to 164,500 between 1970 and 1980.

11. City of Santa Ana, *Santa Ana Special Census* (available at Santa Ana City Library).

12. Serrato, "The State of Hispanics," 15.

13. For a discussion of the early formation of the barrios in Southern California, see Albert Camarillo, *Chicanos in a Changing Society* (Cambridge, Mass.: Harvard University Press, 1979); Ricardo Romo, *East Los Angeles* (Austin: University of Texas Press, 1982); and Richard Griswold del Castillo, *The Los Angeles Barrio* (Berkeley: University of California Press, 1979).

14. Santa Ana Unified School District, *Ethnic Distribution by Percentages* (Santa Ana, Calif., 15 Oct. 1970). The schools and percentages of Spanish-surname students were: Edison 75 percent, Franklin 69 percent, Fremont 72 percent, Lowell 64 percent, McKinley 83 percent, Monroe 90 percent, Muir 65 percent, and Roosevelt 70 percent.

15. Santa Ana Unified School District, *Racial and Ethnic Characteristics* (Santa Ana, Calif., October 1975 and October 1986). A 1982 map divided Santa Ana into sixteen barrios that covered the whole of the city south of Seventeenth Street. This map hung on the wall of the office of the Santa Ana police department's Barrio Program, directed by Theresa Bradley.

16. According to the 1980 census, the comparative figures are: Placentia 20.3 percent, Stanton 21.4 percent, La Habra 22.2 percent, Orange 12.4 percent, Anaheim 17.1 percent, and 11 percent in San Juan Capistrano. (Santa Ana, 44.5 percent.)

17. See, for example, the study by Richard Mines on the nature of these migration networks. *Developing a Community Tradition of Migration to the U.S.* Monograph #3. La Jolla: Program in U.S.–Mexican Studies, University of California at San Diego, 1981.

18. Ina Rosenthal-Urey, "Church Records as a Source of Data on Mexican Migrant Workers: A Methodological Note," unpublished manuscript, ca. 1983, 13–15 (in possession of author).

19. An increasing number of single women and female heads of households have characterized the immigrant stream since the late 1960s. For an informative study on the relationship between border industrialization, female labor-force participation, and the increase in female immigration to the United States, see María Patricia Fernández-Kelly, *For We Are Sold, I and My People: Women and Industry in Mexico's Frontier* (Albany: State University of New York Press, 1983).

20. Interview by author with Pedro Vasquez, August 12, 1987. He and other vendors (who work largely in Anaheim's Latino community) formed the Unión de Comerciantes Latinos del Sur de California in 1975. They changed their name to the Southern California Latino's Small Business Association in 1986. They formed the organization because of city and police harassment against them in Anaheim. Vasquez noted that Santa Ana was, to date, a refuge from harassment for vendors.

21. *Miniondas* began as a bilingual paper in 1975 and since 1980 has been published in Spanish only. *Semanario Azteca* was founded in 1980 and provides excellent professional coverage of local and Latin American news. A number of small Spanish-language papers have come and gone since the late 1970s.

22. Jerome Skolnick and David Bayley, *The New Blue Line: Police Innovation in Six American Cities* (London: Collier Macmillan, 1987), 35. The Legal Aid Society

of Orange County has brought a number of class-action suits to stop raids and the harassment of individuals by the Immigration and Naturalization Service in Santa Ana and elsewhere in Southern California since 1979. They have won restraining orders against the agency that have kept it off the street for varying lengths of time.

23. The Institute was established in 1972 by two Jesuit priests who had been trained in organizing at the Alinsky Industrial Areas Foundation in Chicago.

24. See Saul Alinsky, *Rules for Radicals* (New York: Random House, 1969); also see Castells, *The City and the Grassroots*, 61. Castells argues that the Alinsky model represented the major cultural heritage of the neighborhood-based protest of the 1960s.

25. Interview with Jenny Casamina by author, 7 Aug. 1987.

26. See, for example, *Neighborhood News*, 10 Sept. 1980.

27. Interview with Sam Romero by author, 8 June 1982.

28. *Los Angeles Times*, 3 Apr. 1977, X:7–8.

29. Santa Ana City Council minutes, 7 Feb. 1977.

30. Santa Ana City Council minutes, 29 Mar. 1977. The Redevelopment Agency entered these negotiations with the barrio association and its Western Center on Law and Poverty and the Legal Aid Society of Orange County. The agreement also stipulated the conditions under which a handful of former residents could buy or rent rehabilitated homes moved from the project site, and it established a fund to help provide rent-subsidized housing for low-income residents who would not move into the fifty-eight units. All residents who applied for relocation allowances received those funds for a four-year period, longer than the state mandated, as a result of the neighborhood's politicization.

31. Quoted in *El Quetzal*, 4 (May 1980), 1.

32. Santa Ana Planning Department, *Central Santa Ana: Community Plan— Final Report* (Santa Ana, Calif., 1977), 2–3. Approximately half the city's 3,080 acres in industrially zoned land was vacant at the time the plans were devised.

33. Businesses backed out of the coalition in early 1979 and hired their own lawyer to represent them to the city. They feared that residential zoning would threaten their property values and chances for future expansion. The zoning ordinance finally passed by the city was a compromise between businesses and residents.

34. *Los Angeles Times*, 26 June 1977, X:2, and 3 April 1977, X:9.

35. Advanced Planning and Research Associates, *Environmental Impact Report: Logan Neighborhood* (Santa Ana, Calif., January 1979), 31–32, 58–60.

36. *Orange County Register*, 16 Dec. 1970, F6.

37. In 1986 Logan residents won rezoning as R2, new residential construction only.

38. *Orange County Register*, 11 Dec. 1980, B1.

39. Interview by author with Jovita Hernandez, 22 July 1986.

40. The coalition included the League of Latin American Citizens, SANO, public housing and social agencies, the Legal Aid Society, various church and union organizations, and Hermandad Mexicana Nacional. In July 1984 the coalition took the name Concerned Citizens of Santa Ana and began, with Herman-

dad, to organize families directly affected by code-enforcement programs. On November 25 it adopted the name David Coalition for Housing.

41. *Los Angeles Times*, 11 Dec. 1984, 1.

42. LeDale Dunbar, then head of the Feedback Foundation, which administered the relocation funds, reported in the *Orange County Register* on June 1985 that of the one hundred eligible families who had applied for housing, more than 75 percent were working for the minimum wage, with average gross incomes of about ninety-six hundred dollars a year.

43. Interview by author with Nativo Lopez, director of Hermandad Mexicana Nacional, in Santa Ana, 6 Aug. 1987.

44. Interview by author with Maria Rosa Ibarra, 15 Aug. 1987.

45. Minnie Street is an immigrant neighborhood approximately one-quarter of a mile long. The one- and two-bedroom units house from six to sixteen people.

46. *Orange County Register*, 21 May 1985.

47. In 1985 alone thirty jury trials were held on an apartment-complex basis. Interview by author with Richard Spix, attorney for Hermandad Mexicana Nacional, 29 July 1987.

48. Interview by author with tenant-strike leader, 15 Aug. 1987.

49. Superior Court of the State of California, County of Orange. Mario Gonzalez et al. *v.* Carmine Esposito et al. Case 451577.

50. Interview by author with tenant-strike leader and inspection of a unit on strike, 15 Aug. 1987.

51. Interview by author with tenant-strike leaders, 12 Aug. 1987.

52. The Uniform Housing Code mandates seventy square feet of sleeping area for the first two occupants of a dwelling and an additional fifty square feet for each additional occupant. Unlike other California cities and counties that included the dining room and living room in their calculation of sleeping space, allowing a family of five to inhabit a one-bedroom unit, Santa Ana included only bedrooms when calculating sleeping space.

53. Interview by author with Spix, 29 Aug. 1987.

54. *Orange County Register*, 6 Sept. 1985, and 8 Sept. 1985.

55. *Los Angeles Times*, 24 Sept. 1984, local section, 1, 5–6, and *Santa Ana Business Journal*, Mar. 1984, 1, 7. In addition, the city agreed to find a new site for a number of businesses before displacing them; it promised no retaliation against the property of those who filed suit and agreed not to use its power of eminent domain over other businesses and homes until 1989.

56. *Orange County Register*, 22 July 1985, B1.

57. *Orange County Register*, 5 Sept. 1984, 5.

58. *Los Angeles Times*, 24 Sept. 1984, local section, 5.

59. *Orange County Register*, 24 July 1984.

60. These middle-class organizations consisted of a group of north Santa Ana residents (primarily Anglo American) that had joined together to oppose the diversion of traffic through their street; a second group formed to oppose the establishment of a domed basketball stadium at the location of the Santa Ana Stadium; and a third established to fight the construction of a replacement football stadium in their neighborhood.

61. SANO had long criticized Santa Ana's partial ward system. In 1977 Sadie Reed, a black candidate from Ward 5, lost the election and took her case to court, arguing that the system effectively disenfranchised the city's black and Chicano residents. SANO backed her case, but she lost.

62. Letter to Parker Kennedy, chairman, Santa Ana Chamber of Commerce, from Jim Lowman, chairman, SAMSON, dated 5 June 1986.

63. Four mailers sent by the Santa Ana Good Government Committee.

64. *Orange County Register,* 31 July 1988 (contrasting to an estimated 60 percent of the population who were Latino).

65. *Los Angeles Times,* 12 Jan. 1986, 7.

REFERENCES

Advanced Planning and Research Associates. *Environmental Impact Report: Logan Neighborhood.* Santa Ana, Calif., January 1979.

Alinsky, Saul. *Rules for Radicals.* New York: Random House, 1969.

Camarillo, Albert. *Chicanos in a Changing Society.* Cambridge, Mass.: Harvard University Press, 1979.

Castells, Manuel. *The City and the Grassroots: A Cross-Cultural Theory of Urban Social Movements.* Berkeley: University of California Press, 1983.

Delgado, Antonio. "An Analysis of Hispanic Youth in Santa Ana: Recommended Public Policy Direction." May 1986. (Report available at City Manager's Office.)

Fainstein, Susan, Norman Fainstein, Richard Child Hill, Dennis Judd, Michael Peter Smith, eds. *Restructuring the City.* New York: Longman, 1983.

Fernández-Kelly, María Patricia. *For We Are Sold, I and My People: Women and Industry in Mexico's Frontier.* Albany: State University of New York Press, 1983.

Griswold del Castillo, Richard. *The Los Angeles Barrio.* Berkeley: University of California Press, 1979.

Kleniewski, Nancy. "From Industrial to Corporate City: The Role of Urban Renewal." In *Marxism and the Metropolis,* ed. William Tabb and Larry Sawers, 205–22. New York: Oxford University Press, 1984.

Mines, Richard. *Developing a Community Tradition of Migration to the U.S.* Monograph 3. La Jolla: Program in U.S.–Mexican Studies, University of California at San Diego, 1981.

Mollenkopf, John. *The Contested City.* Princeton, N.J.: Princeton University Press, 1983.

Plotkin, Sidney. "Democratic Change in the Urban Political Economy." In *The Politics of San Antonio,* ed. David Johnson, John A. Booth, Richard J. Harris, 157–74. Lincoln: University of Nebraska Press, 1983.

Romo, Ricardo. *East Los Angeles.* Austin: University of Texas Press, 1982.

Rosenthal-Urey, Ina. "Church Records as a Source of Data on Mexican Migrant Networks: A Methodological Note." Unpublished manuscript, ca. 1983 (in possession of author).

Santa Ana Planning Department. *Central Santa Ana: Community Plan—Final Report.* Santa Ana, Calif., 1977.

Santa Ana Unified School District. *Ethnic Distribution by Percentages.* Santa Ana, Calif., 15 Oct. 1970.

————. *Racial and Ethnic Characteristics.* Santa Ana, Calif., October 1975 and October 1986.

Scott, Allen. "High Technology Industry and Territorial Development: The Rise of the Orange County Complex, 1955–1984." *Urban Geography* 7 (January–February 1986):3–45.

Serrato, Alfred. "The State of Hispanics in Orange County—1980." 1981. (Report available at County Administrative Building Library.)

Skolnick, Jerome, and David Bayley. *The New Blue Line: Police Innovation in Six American Cities.* London: Collier Macmillan, 1987.

Stone, Clarence, and Heywood Sanders, eds. *The Politics of Urban Development.* Lawrence: University Press of Kansas, 1987.

Weiss, Marc, "The Origins and Legacy of Urban Renewal." In *Urban and Regional Planning in an Age of Austerity,* ed. Pierre Clavel, John Forester, and William Goldsmith, 53–80. New York: Pergamon Press, 1980.

TEN

The Taxpayers' Revolt

William F. Gayk

The rise of suburban metropolitan regions since the 1950s marks a major departure from the centralization of population, industry, and commerce that was integral to the industrialization of the United States.[1] The spatial features of this contemporary urban form are apparent to even the most casual observer who has witnessed this transformation: The woods, fields, farms, dairies, orchards, groves, and grazing lands of bygone years, which were dotted with a town or village, are now blanketed with a quilt of population and employment centers. From a demographic perspective, there was a massive migration of the nation's population from central cities to suburbs and from the frostbelt to the sunbelt. The deconcentration of population was so sweeping that by 1970 more people resided in suburban areas than in major central cities.

We also became a nation of homeowners during this same period. The concurrence of decentralization and increased homeownership was not a mere coincidence because the prospect of owning one's own home was an indispensable ingredient in the blossoming of suburbia. Single-family, owner-occupied housing is virtually synonymous with the suburban community. Through various government subsidy programs and the investment of private capital in residential development, millions of people have become homeowners. Statistics on owner occupancy speak to the extent of this change. Prior to World War II less than half of the nation's homes were owner-occupied; by 1960 owner occupancy reached 60 percent (Downs 1970). Although not sustaining the levels of growth experienced in the two decades following the war, owner occupancy reached 64 percent nationally in 1980 (Department of Commerce 1983). It is uncertain whether the rate of owner occupancy will increase much more be-

281

cause of continued rising housing costs. It is certain, however, that owning one's home is a dominant value of our society.

A set of distinctive issues affiliated with homeownership has surfaced,
and these issues play a central role in defining suburban politics (Dunleavy 1979, Gottdiener 1985, Saunders 1978).[2] These issues are rooted in
both the social and the economic factors connected with housing and
homeownership. One's house conveys social meaning, as does one's car,
jewelry, and clothing. Consumption of these commodities by themselves
is evidence of the way that one has achieved success in life as well as of the
degree of one's success (see Chapter 5). In a culture of consumerism such
as ours, we all realize that gradations of success come to be associated with
different commodities, brands, and spatial locations. Thus, a house conveys information about the owners' social standing in a community, the
type of people they associate with, and their style of life. This information
serves as a basis on which family, friends, and acquaintances evaluate the
owners and is also used by the owners to evaluate themselves (Agnew
1981).

Thus, a house is a symbol of status. Traditionally, status is based on the
prestige and honor accorded to different strata or groups of people
(Weber 1946). Status differences are related to differential patterns of
consumption, and a home, because it is for most people the single most
important purchase, conveys status differences. Beyond the physical
structure itself, the prestige of a home is integrally tied to the neighborhood and community in which it is located. Certainly the land-development and real estate industries recognize and exploit this fact.[3] Protecting
and maintaining the social value of one's home, neighborhood, and community result in specific interests that in turn can serve as a catalyst for
political action (Agnew 1981).

In addition, unlike most other commodities, a house allows its owners
to accumulate considerable wealth. Take, for example, some of the other
major commodities that are valued and consumed in our society: A new
car typically depreciates to scrap value over its useful life; clothing loses all
but a small portion of its original price almost immediately after purchase
and certainly as soon as new fashions arrive; fine jewelry keeps pace with
inflation at best. In contrast to these commodities, a house in our free-
market economy produces real income for its owners (Saunders 1978,
Thorns 1981). Housing values have been rising at a rate greater than the
rate of inflation. In addition, the real interest rates on home mortgages
are almost negligible because, first, they are lower than interest rates on
other forms of loans and, second, they are subsidized by government
through income-tax deductions. Homeowners form a social class because
of these income-producing features of their property.[4] Most individuals
recognize these income-producing features[5] and are willing to sacrifice

considerably in order to purchase a home. In today's market, having dual incomes and using a large share of a household's income are common practical strategies often required for homeownership.

The protection and promotion of both the status value and the economic value of housing are rallying points around which homeowners take political action (Agnew 1981; Cox 1973, 1978, 1981; Danielson 1976; Saunders 1979; Wirt et al. 1972; Wood 1958). In addition, strong evidence indicates that protecting the quality of life in communities is closely related to political issues associated with housing (Gottdiener 1985, 1987). Thus along with the suburban transformation, we have witnessed the emergence of a political agenda in the suburban metropolitan region conspicuously different from the agenda that prevailed during the first half of the century. In this earlier period, bread-and-butter issues tied to the conflict between labor and capital dominated national politics. The local political agenda mirrored these concerns because of strong party organizations.

In contrast, the contemporary political agenda embedded in the suburban metropolitan region embraces such focused issues and concerns as low-cost and high-density housing (Agnew 1978, Cox 1973, Danielson 1976), exclusionary zoning (Gottdiener 1977, Nieman 1980, Shlay and Rossi 1981), growth control (Gottdiener and Nieman 1981), and property taxation (Saunders 1978). In short, many of our contemporary political issues flow from the building and ownership of single-family homes. Certainly, these issues sometimes surface in central cities, but what distinguishes them in the suburban setting is that they are the major concerns and the important political issues.

These particular issues are not the only concerns of residents of the suburban community. Obviously, issues that are regional and national in scope concern suburbanites. Residents' positions on these issues, not surprisingly, are based on social and economic differences between urban and suburban dwellers.[6] But these issues are not indigenous to the suburban community. The unique issues generated because of the nature of the suburban community are tied to homeownership and its attendant social and economic interests, which place an emphasis on the quality of life. Thus, the suburban community both generates its unique issues and is a setting in which broad issues are aired.

THE FISCAL-LIMITATION INITIATIVES

Although there had been rumblings, rhetoric, and some previous ballot measures, the taxpayers' revolt is commonly understood to involve three fiscal-limitation measures that appeared on the California state ballot between 1978 and 1980.[7] The first of these issues, the Jarvis-Gann initiative, appeared as Proposition 13 on the June 1978 California primary ballot. In response to unprecedented increases in property taxes, the primary provision of this measure limited property-tax assessment to 1 percent of the market value of property and restricted increases to no more than 2 percent annually thereafter. Two-thirds of the California voters supported this measure, radically altering local-government financing and seemingly setting off a continuous string of other tax- and spending-reform measures in the state and nation. The second California measure appeared as Proposition 4 on the ballot of a special election held in November 1979. This measure was sponsored by Paul Gann, the lesser known member of the Jarvis-Gann alliance. Proposition 4 was a rather technical measure consisting of eight major provisions and several sub-provisions. The primary objective was to limit increases in state- and local-government spending to a rate not exceeding the combined total of the annual rate of inflation and the annual rate of population growth. This measure was promoted as the "Spirit of 13" initiative. Support for this measure came from more than 74 percent of California voters, an increase of nearly ten percentage points over the support for Proposition 13. The third measure was sponsored by Howard Jarvis. Its major provision limited state income taxes and eliminated the business inventory tax. It qualified as Proposition 9 on the June 1980 ballot.[8] This measure was defeated at the polls, with 54 percent of the voters opposing it statewide, thus marking the end of the taxpayers' revolt in California.

The prevailing view of the public, professional politicians, and many social scientists is that these three initiatives were all part of a single social or political movement (Sears and Citrin 1985). Admittedly, the use of the label *taxpayers' revolt* sustains this perspective. It follows from such a perspective that each of the fiscal-limitation initiatives expressed the same fundamental concerns and needs. Although different explanations of the taxpayers' revolt have been put forth (Danzinger and Ring 1980, Lowery and Sigelman 1981, Sears and Citrin 1985), almost all assume a single cause for the measures. The self-interest explanation (Citrin 1979, Courant, Gramlich, and Rubinfeld 1979, Levy 1979) regards support and nonsupport of tax and spending measures as a function of the benefits that categories of people or groups would secure through passage or failure of the measures. The social-movement explanation (DeCanio 1979, Lowery and Sigelman 1981) treats the tax revolt as a symbolic expression of deep-seated problems, such as inflation and unemployment, that affect social strata differentially. A third perspective, the political-ideology perspective (Lipset and Raab 1978, Musgrave 1979, Wolfe 1979), attributes both the emergence of and the subsequent support for these initiatives to the shift of the electorate to the right.

Each of these perspectives assumes that the measures individually and in the aggregate have the same common, albeit simple, explanation. Putting the need for parsimony in scientific explanation aside, we can criticize these explanations for ignoring the complexity of the three initiatives, involving as they did many different economic, social, and life-style changes. To start with Proposition 13, passage of this initiative resulted in direct monetary savings to homeowners, landlords, and land-owning businesses in the form of reduced property taxes. There was even the possibility that these savings could have been passed on to renters.[9] Passage of Proposition 13 should have also benefited homeowners with marginal resources, such as retirees with fixed incomes.

Social and economic costs were associated with the passage of Proposition 13 as well. Receiving the most attention were the anticipated severe cuts in funding for public education, police protection, fire protection, road construction and maintenance, public sanitation, public health services, library services, and park acquisition and maintenance. Cuts in these services would affect some segments of a community more than others, but together they would reduce the overall quality of community life. Local control was also at stake because passage of Proposition 13 was expected to shift program funding and consequently program control to the state.[10] Local concerns about maintaining property values and preserving neighborhoods were expected to give way to state policies that would translate into programmatic requirements.[11]

Many of the costs and benefits of Propositions 4 and 9 were similar to those of Proposition 13, although some were more indirect. Both of these measures were expected to result in the reduction of various government programs and services. Proposition 4 limited any program growth by capping both state- and local-government spending. Additionally, bailouts by the state of local programs affected by Proposition 13 were tempered by the state's spending limitations. Proposition 9, like Proposition 13, was expected to result in some direct service cuts because it would severely limit the state's revenues. Proposition 4 would also provide indirect economic benefits by placing a limit on government spending and thus the need to increase taxes. Wage earners would have paid less in taxes under Proposition 9, but this was a graduated benefit that would have increased with income.

In sum, there were several and often cross-cutting social, economic, and life-style concerns attached to each of these measures. This combination of issues associated with the taxpayers' revolt contrasts with single-factor explanations. But, more important, it reveals some of the complexity of political behavior in the suburban setting. Proposition 13, as a property-tax measure, is an issue whose origin we would expect to find in the suburban community and in the pervasiveness of homeownership. All three measures, however, can be attributed to basic social and economic problems that originate beyond but are still found in the suburban environment. This is to say, the taxpayers' revolt was not necessarily a cohesive set of initiatives that can be accounted for by a single cause. We are left with the tasks of both offering an account that recognizes this complexity and substituting an explanation or explanations for the three previously noted.

THE TAXPAYERS' REVOLT IN ORANGE COUNTY

The features that define a suburban metropolitan region are exaggerated in Orange County. Taking growth first, Orange County has been a major national growth center since the 1950s. Its population has increased over tenfold from 1955, when it had slightly over two hundred thousand people, to the present, when it has more than 2.2 million. Similarly, the number of jobs in the county has grown from under one hundred thousand in 1950 to over one million today. This growth is due to both demographic and economic deconcentration. Second, nearly 70 percent of the housing in the county is owner-occupied. Even in its larger, older, and so-called urban cities, most of the housing is owner-occupied. Third, all but a scant portion of Orange County's housing has been built since 1960. Thus the housing is relatively new, typically single-family and low-density, and it was built during a period of rapid suburbanization, both locally and nationally. Correspondingly, property values have been increasing since the 1960s. Today the cost of housing in Orange County is among the highest in the state and the nation.[12] Owning a home in Orange County in itself conveys a certain amount of prestige, and visions of achievement are evoked by residence in many cities and communities throughout the county such as Corona del Mar, Lido Isle, Turtle Rock, Sunny Hills, Anaheim Hills, Huntington Harbor, Cowan Heights, Mission Viejo, Laguna Niguel, and Villa Park.

Fourth, Orange County is made up of twenty-eight municipalities, none of which is the focal point for county political issues. The developed portion of the county encompasses competing population and employment centers, which are blended together to form a polynucleated metropolitan region. In addition, Orange County is for the most part socially, culturally, and economically autonomous from Los Angeles, for which it not long ago served as a bedroom community. Fifth, there is considerable socioeconomic differentiation between and within the cities and communities in Orange County. Finally, the issues that constitute the political agenda in the suburban environment nationally have all been key issues in the county.

Orange County was also a hotbed of the taxpayers' revolt. Voting patterns in Orange County followed statewide voting patterns on the three fiscal-limitation issues. Thus, like their counterparts in other parts of the state, Orange County voters supported the first two initiatives and rejected the third. However, Orange County voters supported Propositions 13 and 4 more enthusiastically than statewide voters, while their support for Proposition 9 was less enthusiastic than that statewide. Prior to these three initiatives, Orange County was one of the few counties in which the appropriation-limitation measure sponsored by Governor Reagan was supported in 1973. Finally, Orange County voters did not approve a sales-tax increase for transportation improvement, although similar measures have been approved in neighboring counties.

We have in Orange County an ideal territory in which to explore the nature of suburban politics. By associating support for the three fiscal-limitation measures with differential characteristics of neighborhoods, we can reveal the social and economic basis of Orange County and therefore provide some understanding of suburban politics in general and politics in Orange County specifically.

PATTERNS OF SUPPORT FOR PROPOSITIONS 13, 4, AND 9

We begin our analysis by asking what types of neighborhoods did and did not support the three measures. *Support* here is operationally defined as voting yes on Propositions 13, 4, and 9, and *neighborhood* is defined as a federal census tract.[13]

We begin by using discriminant analysis to identify characteristics that differentiate those census tracts that did and did not support the three initiatives. Seventeen variables measuring different social, economic, political, and environmental characteristics of the census tracts were entered into analysis, of which thirteen variables were associated with support and nonsupport of these measures.[14] These thirteen variables were the percentage of the population that is black, the percentage of the population that is Hispanic, the percentage of the population that is five to nineteen years old, the percentage of the population that is sixty-five and above, the percentage of the housing that is owner-occupied, the percentage of the housing that is multiple-family, median years of education, median family income, the welfare rate, the percentage of the labor force that is in clerical and sales jobs; the ratio of 1970 to 1979 median housing value, the percentage of the voters who are Republican, and the ratio of median housing value to median family income.

Individually these variables differentiate groups who would benefit from passage or defeat of these initiatives. Areas with high concentrations of blacks, Hispanics, welfare recipients, and school-age children all are more dependent on government services than those with low concentrations of these groups. We would thus expect these areas to be less support-

TABLE 10.1   Factors in Taxpayers' Revolt

Variable	Factor 1	Factor 2	Factor 3
Welfare rate	.892	−.092	.066
Percentage of voters Republican	−.826	.046	.270
Percentage of population Hispanic	.822	−.068	.155
Median years of education	−.798	.231	.238
Median family income	−.643	.684	.221
Percentage of population black	.516	.049	.070
Percentage of population ages 5 to 19	.102	.906	−.121
Percentage of housing owner-occupied	−.267	.808	−.005
Percentage of housing multiple-family	.092	−.784	−.025
Ratio of median housing value to median family income	.235	−.609	−.751
Percentage of population ages 65 and over	−.033	−.586	.189
Ratio of 1970 to 1979 median housing value	.033	−.197	.568
Percentage of labor force in clerical and sales jobs	.154	−.134	−.444
Eigenvalue	4.66	2.62	1.10

ive of fiscal-limitation initiatives. We would also expect the more urban areas of the county to be less supportive of fiscal-limitation initiatives because blacks, Hispanics, and welfare recipients are more likely to reside in these areas. However, neighborhoods characterized by high concentrations of owner-occupied housing units, upper-income families, higher occupational statuses, and Republicans would be more likely to support fiscal limitation because they would obtain the greatest monetary benefits from tax and spending cuts and would support such cuts ideologically. Finally, we would expect areas with an above-average concentration of senior citizens and generally lower-middle-class persons to have supported some but not all of these measures. As homeowners with marginal economic resources, these people would have benefited from the property-tax cut from Proposition 13 but would suffer the service cuts that were anticipated in Proposition 9, particularly cuts in health and educational services. The ratio of 1970 to 1979 median housing value is an indicator of the differential effects of inflation on housing value and thus taxation. Following a rational economic model, we would expect greater support for these measures, especially Proposition 13, in areas where this ratio is high than in areas where it is low. The ratio of median housing value to median family income as a measure of the relative economic burden of homeownership would be inversely related with support for Proposition 13.

Looking at these thirteen variables collectively, we have no clear indica-

TABLE 10.2   Regression of Propositions 13, 4, and 9 on
Factors

	Proposition 13	Proposition 4	Proposition 9
Factor 1	−.32	−.39	−.59
Factor 2	.41	.14	.41
Factor 3	−.14	.07	.10

NOTE: Standardized regression coefficients ($n = 317$)

tion of the types of basic social, economic, or life-style concerns influencing the support and nonsupport of the fiscal-limitation measures. However, by using factor analysis, we find that three dimensions appear to underlie the thirteen variables (table 10.1).[15] Although the factors are not totally independent of one another, the combination of the variables associated with them suggests definable theoretical dimensions. Factor 1 reveals an inverse socioeconomic-status dimension; the welfare rate, the percentage of the population that is Hispanic, the percentage of the population that is black, the percentage of Republican voters, median years of education, and median family income are all strongly associated with it. Factor 2 is associated with features that characterize, in the typical sense, suburban communities, or suburbanism. These variables include the percentage of the population that is five to nineteen years old, the percentage of the housing that is owner-occupied, median family income, the percentage of the housing that is multiple-family, the ratio of median housing value to median family income, and the percentage of the population that is sixty-five and over. Homeownership is an important element in defining this factor and cuts across traditionally defined class lines. Factor 3 seems to tap some of the economic dimensions of homeownership, and in particular housing-value inflation. The ratio of median housing value to median family income and the ratio of 1970 to 1979 median housing value load the highest on this factor.

Looking at the relationship between these factors and support for the three initiatives exposes some important features of the taxpayers' revolt in Orange County. As can be seen in table 10.2, the explanatory relevance of the individual factors was different for Proposition 13 than it was for Propositions 4 and 9. The suburbanism-homeownership factor (factor 2) accounts for more of the support for Proposition 13 than do the other two factors. In the case of Propositions 4 and 9, the socioeconomic-status factor (factor 1) accounts for more of the variation than do the other two factors. Although the housing-value-inflation factor (factor 3) does not account for much variation in the levels of support for the three fiscal-limitation initiatives, a subtle change does take place: Its relationship with

Proposition 13 is negative, while its relationship with Propositions 4 and 9 is positive.

These results suggest that the alignment that prevailed for Proposition 13 was based primarily on concerns and issues involving the suburban community and homeownership. However, traditionally defined socioeconomic status was also operative to some extent. In the case of Propositions 4 and 9, voters were aligned on the dimension of socioeconomic status. That is to say, socioeconomic status was more important in determining the outcome of Propositions 4 and 9 than it was in determining the outcome of Proposition 13. However, suburbanism and homeownership also had some influence on the support for Proposition 9. In fact, the strength of the relationship was as great for Proposition 9 as it was for Proposition 13. The fact that both factor 1 and factor 2 were related to support for Proposition 9 may indicate the interactive effect of socioeconomic status and residing in suburban communities. Nevertheless, socioeconomic status was more important than homeownership in accounting for the support for Proposition 9.

Thus, the taxpayers' revolt cannot be explained by any one single cause but rather by a complex matrix of factors interacting with and crosscutting one another. Class and status along with suburbanism and homeownership all played a part in the revolt. Consistent with Citrin's (1979) finding that homeowners were more likely than nonhomeowners to support Proposition 13, we saw that the level of support for this measure can be explained more by suburbanism and homeownership than by socioeconomic status. However, Propositions 4 and 9 were explained more by socioeconomic status than by suburbanism and homeownership. This result does not surprise us because voter preferences for initiatives and referenda have tended to follow socioeconomic differences (Bowman, Ippolito, and Levin 1972; Hahn 1968, 1970; Levy 1975). More than anything else, these results reveal the complexity of the social basis of support for political issues in the suburban environment.

From a methodological standpoint, it is nearly impossible to separate the social and life-style effects from the economic ones. All the traditional indicators of socioeconomic status have both a social component and an economic component. To take education as an example, it is directly related to lifetime income, but it also carries with it social esteem and certainly influences one's consumption patterns, tastes, and choice of associates. Income is part of the economic component, but it is also a measure of purchasing power, which brings it into the realm of consumption and thus also status. In summary, complexity arises from both the multiplicity of social, economic, and life-style factors influencing suburban politics and the interrelationships of these factors.

Likewise, from a theoretical standpoint we have a much more difficult issue—namely, the relationship between the economic and social factors. Median family income loaded high on both the socioeconomic-status and the suburbanism-homeownership factors, suggesting that homeownership is not independent of social class and social status. We can argue that homeownership is an important element in suburban politics, but it is difficult to separate it from socioeconomic status because access to housing is tied to social class and housing certainly is a major object of consumption.[16] Putting this debate aside, we see that suburban politics is influenced by an intricate web of overlapping and interacting social and economic factors.

HOMEOWNERSHIP AND SUBURBAN POLITICS

We conclude this chapter by refocusing our attention on homeownership and suburban politics.[17] On the surface, it is self-evident that homeowners would support a measure that reduces their property taxes. This expected relationship follows from an unadulterated self-interest explanation. But a self-interest explanation by itself is pedestrian and lacks explanatory power. We are hoping here to move beyond that. To this end, we argue not only that homeowners are likely to oppose property taxes or to support a measure reducing them, but also that the social, life-style, and economic features of home ownership all act together to make property taxes a political issue.

These connections come about in the following way. Property taxes are perceived to threaten homeowners both economically and socially. As they rise, the cost of owning a home increases. Unlike other costs associated with owning a home, such as improvements, upgrades, or repairs, property taxes neither maintain nor enhance the value of a home. In the extreme, they are perceived as a direct threat to homeownership.[18] This fear is tied, in part, to a fear of losing one's social standing (Edel 1982). In addition, homeowners and property taxpayers in general both are the majority in suburban communities and are also more likely to be registered voters and to participate in elections. Homeowners and property taxpayers are therefore more likely than nonhomeowners to influence the outcome of issues that arise in the community or are addressed in the community. From this analysis we see two crucial paths we need to take. The first directs us to the constitution of significant issues in the suburban community. The second directs us to participation in the political process.

Single-family, owner-occupied housing is a dominant feature of the suburban community. Historically, the desire to own a home was a major reason for moving to the suburbs (Gans 1967). The value placed on owning a home is maintained even when owning a home requires living a great distance from work and spending hours commuting in congested traffic. In an economy where escalating prices are excluding many people from the housing market, homeownership is still a prevailing value (Baldassare 1986). Although high land and housing costs result in the increased availability of high-density, attached housing, most people desire a single-family, detached unit. A survey conducted in Orange County found that 81 percent of the respondents preferred to live in a single-family, detached home (Baldassare and Katz 1987). Condominiums and townhouses, which are appearing increasingly on the suburban landscape, are for the most part perceived as a preliminary step to obtaining a single-family, detached unit, a perception that also applied to rental units.

In this consumer culture, a house is the consummate commodity. Cost is not the only factor (although a house normally costs several years' income). The current meaning of a house also makes it the consummate commodity. Traditionally, a house was purchased to serve as and symbolize home. In that era one's home was a rather permanent shelter that provided its occupants both physical and emotional security. Today, a house is a commodity that is bought and sold regularly, and a home is consequently fluid and transitory, changing periodically if not on a regular timetable. Houses are bought and sold regularly to transfer equity to a better style, more quality, larger size, more amenities and upgrades, better location, and more desirable style of life.

Unlike other major commodities in our culture of consumption, this bundle of features is convertible into both social and economic value. Socially, these features signal one's achievements and accomplishments as well as the life-style that one leads. The locational attributes of a house—that is, the neighborhood and community in which it is located—weigh much more heavily in determining the social value of a house than do the product attributes. The very same house in different areas commands different prices. Thus, we can see that there is a strong and definite symbiotic relationship between a house, a neighborhood, and a community. When one buys a house, he or she is buying into the society and life-style of the neighborhood and community. There is an underlying assumption and expectation on the part of the homeowner that these attributes will endure. Like its social value, the economic value of a house is also tied strongly to its attributes and to the neighborhood and community. Homeowners perceive many threats to the social and economic value of their homes, neighborhoods, and community. The list of threats is varied and extensive; it includes residential and commercial development, vanishing open space, low-cost housing projects, inclusionary zoning, property taxation, noise, group homes, halfway homes, mental hospitals, jails, and roads and highways.

Orange County's political agenda in the 1980s has been replete with many of the issues mentioned here. Citizen groups are suing over the location of proposed jails. The operation and expansion of John Wayne Airport, the county's commercial airport, were litigated because of residents' complaints about noise levels. Citizen groups have fought vigorously against the approval of affordable housing projects. Angry citizens have packed city halls protesting the issuance of permits for halfway homes or other facilities serving "undesirables." Voters have qualified, and in some cities have passed, measures that limit or control both residental and commercial development. The litany of homeowner protestations echoes a variety of social, economic, and life-style concerns: "My property value will be lowered"; "we moved here to get away from traffic and congestion and noise"; "this is incompatible with a residential neighborhood like ours"; "we moved to this community because of all the open space, so we could feel like we were living in the country"; "I don't want to look out my window and down on those homes and see clothes hanging on lines"; "it will not be safe for my children to walk to school"; and "this is a quaint residential community."[19]

Local government is expected actively to protect and promote the interests of homeowners (Gottdiener and Nieman 1981) and to manage the quality of life for its citizens (Gottdiener 1987). It does so in two ways. First, local government is seen as the representative or voice of the assumed public interest. The political agenda in the suburban community is a seemingly endless potpourri of single-problem and often conflicting issues. Residents want solutions to these narrowly defined, practical problems and issues. Within a suburban metropolitan region such as Orange County, the potential to generate specific issues is unlimited because of the conflict between the social and economic interests of homeowners, the interests of business, and the demands on local government to provide unpopular services and facilities. When confronted with issues that pose a threat to homeowners or with opportunities to foster the interests of homeowners, local government is expected to voice the will of the people. Thus, demands are placed on government to implement exclusionary housing policies, relocate the homeless, down-zone housing projects or disapproved development plans, and ensure that "undesirable" facilities, such as jails, airports, and low-cost housing projects, are not located within or near one's neighborhood.

Second, local government is expected to provide a package of municipal services, such as police, fire, parks, street maintenance, sanitation, and code enforcement, that together make a community a desirable place to live. Not only must the services be available, but they must be provided at an adequate level. Providing services at an adequate level limits the services local government can provide. Olin, in Chapter 8, notes that politics in a region such as Orange County is an effort to provide the services that guarantee the citizens' comfort and convenience.

Having seen how homeownership determines the significant political issues in the suburban community, we can now look at how it affects participation in the formal political process. In most suburban areas, homeowners are the numerical majority. In addition, as we have seen, they are more likely to be registered voters and are more likely to participate in elections than nonhomeowners. With stronger ties to the community than more mobile renters, homeowners are more likely to participate in grass-roots political activities (Cox 1982). Some of the more common forms of grass-roots political actions are organizing and attending neighborhood meetings, attending and speaking at public hearings, writing and circulating petitions, and working to qualify initiatives and recalls. Homeowners' stronger political commitment to the community can be attributed in part to their firsthand experience with residential property taxes. Most homeowners receive an annual property-tax bill, which they pay personally. Although renters pay their landlords' property taxes, their awareness is clouded because property taxes are a hidden cost in their rent or lease payments. The common perception if not the assumption of homeowning taxpayers is that they have more vested interests in their community than do "nontaxpayers." The result is an expectation that local government should attend particularly to their needs and concerns. This combination of mobilization potential, political commitment, and a sense of vested interests contributes to homeowners' tremendous influence in shaping the themes of the local political agenda.

The taxpayers' revolt was ignited because of homeowners' growing frustration with rapidly rising property taxes and the lack of an immediate response from local and state government. As a result we were launched into an era of ballot-box government financing. We may likewise be at the brink of an era of ballot-box planning because citizens are using the initiative process more frequently than before to set policies in the area of growth control, facility location, and land-use planning. The prospects for a continuing and increasing number of citizen-initiated ballot measures in this area depend on some current, but often contradictory, trends and patterns that are influencing the social, economic, and political environment within the suburban metropolitan region.

One of these trends is that local governments' ability to fund and provide municipal services through property taxes has been constrained. Residents want more and better services but are unwilling to spend more. Although transportation improvements were sorely needed in Orange County, the voters overwhelmingly rejected a sales tax to fund transportation projects. Other land uses, especially commercial and industrial uses, are a means to increase local government revenues. These uses can generate more sales taxes, as well as property taxes, than can low-density housing. But these higher-yield projects are seen by homeowners as threats to the residential or suburban nature of their communities.

The rising cost of housing is another key issue. At present, the lines between homeowners and renters are not clear because renting is seen as a temporary stage while one saves money to purchase a home. However, these lines may crystallize as rising housing costs exclude potential buyers permanently from the housing market. Each group, owners and renters, may place different demands on local government, especially in the area of housing. Renters will want to see local government do more to provide affordable and low-cost housing and control rents, while homeowners will want local government to protect them from the perceived threats of low-cost projects.

Housing is also becoming a factor in environmental regulations. The connection between housing and environmental quality is based on the relationship between workers and jobs. People desiring a single-family, detached home are continually being forced to move beyond the boundaries of the suburban metropolitan area. Riverside and San Bernardino counties are now serving as new markets for people unable to afford a home in Orange County. However, the movement of jobs has not kept pace with the movement of people. For the most part, these former Orange County residents still work in the county. The result is that the volume of vehicle miles traveled surges upward, the transportation system is taxed beyond its limits, and air quality deteriorates. Environmental regulations now include provisions to reduce this imbalance between worker location and job location by encouraging additional housing near employment centers. These policies are being tied into state policies directed toward providing low-cost and affordable housing, especially in areas where there is a limited supply.

There is a growing awareness that many of the major problems facing the suburban metropolitan area, such as air quality, transportation, and growth, are regional. A solution is for local governments to work in concert to solve some of these problems (Baldassare 1986). Some critics even attribute many of these problems to the way that local governments act independently if not in a vacuum and thereby promote their own parochial interests. Despite the growing interest in regionalism, no consensus has emerged on what constitutes a viable, effective regional approach. Existing regional governments are not structured to represent or respond to constituents directly. Officials on regional governing boards and committees are appointed and thus are not directly accountable to the people. There is considerable potential for conflict if the bodies imposing rules and regulations are not sensitive to the interests and expectations of homeowners.

Whether Orange County enters an era of ballot-box planning is uncertain. Many of the ingredients that could lead to such actions—trends and patterns that pose threats and challenges to homeowners' interests and expectations—are appearing. Homeowners have dominated the political agenda because of sheer numbers and a strong political commitment. Their grip on the local political agenda may weaken as their numbers decline and as growing numbers of racial and ethnic minorities settle in Orange County. The agenda may then move beyond some of the narrowly defined problems that revolve around homeownership in the community.

NOTES

1. Different terms are used to describe this social-spatial form. Rob Kling, Spencer Olin, Mark Poster, and Martin Schiesl use *postsuburban* in this book. The term *polynucleated metropolitan region* has been used by M. Gottdiener (1985). Each of these terms reflects various spatial, functional, and temporal features of this form. These terms were chosen to highlight perceptions by residents as well as to emphasize that we are no longer dealing with bedroom communities. In this chapter I use the term *suburban* to characterize Orange County because it fits residents' perceptions.

2. The political significance of home ownership has been recognized by a growing number of scholars. Among them are John Agnew (1981), Kevin Cox (1973, 1978, 1981, 1982), Patrick Dunleavy (1979), Jozsef Hegedus and Ivan Tosics (1983), John Rex and Robert Moore (1967), Rex (1968), and Peter Saunders (1978, 1982). According to Saunders (1978, 234), "Domestic property ownership is the basis for the formation of a distinct political force."

3. The marketing of new housing developments in Orange County, as elsewhere, is based on creating visions of the "good life," the "California dream," and "living in the splendor of. . . ." Schiesl (Chapter 3) notes that the Irvine Company chose such a strategy by marketing Irvine as a high-income, homogeneous place to live.

4. The notion of social class follows from Max Weber's (1946) definition of class. Like Marx, he defined classes as social objects with an economic base, but, unlike Marx, Weber proposed that classes can arise in both labor and property markets. Property classes are based on the ownership of property, which can be used to generate income.

5. The real estate industry heightens owners' awareness of property value by having agents go door to door to seek possible listings, by providing free market appraisals, and by publicizing the price of homes recently sold in the neighborhood.

6. There has been considerable discussion of the alignment of suburban dwellers on state and national issues (Berger 1960, Campbell et al. 1960, Walter and Wirt 1972, Wirt et al. 1972, Wood 1958). Suburbanites are more likely to be economic and political conservatives and more likely to be members of and supporters of the Republican Party than urbanites are. However, there is consid-

erable differentiation in this support. Bennett Berger (1960) found that residents of a working-class suburb maintained their allegiance to the Democratic Party. Benjamin Walter and Frederick Wirt (1972) and Wirt et al. (1972) found that the Republican vote in suburbs increased as the affluence of the community increased. The association of conservatism and suburbanization is not inherent but rather results from the fact that suburban areas and their residents in general have higher socioeconomic status than do their central-city counterparts (Guest and Nelson 1978, Schnore 1957).

7. Prior to the taxpayers' revolt of the 1970s, fiscal-limitation measures appeared on the California ballot in 1968, 1972, and 1973. Two were sponsored by Philip Watson, the Los Angeles County assessor, and the other by Governor Ronald Reagan. These three measures failed, but many of the provisions limiting property taxes and government spending reappeared in the later measures.

8. Information capitalism played a role in the qualification of this measure for the ballot. Although the Proposition 13 campaign was grass roots and populist in character, Butcher-Forde (a political-consultant firm specializing in direct-mail campaigns using computerized address listings) was retained by Jarvis and his new organization, the California Tax Reduction Movement, to manage the Proposition 9 campaign. To qualify the initiative, over six million pieces of mail containing both a petition for Proposition 9 and a request for a donation were sent to registered voters. More than 800,000 signatures were obtained through this process.

9. Jarvis, allegedly speaking for the Apartment Owners Association, promised that the property-tax savings from Proposition 13 would be passed on to renters. There is no evidence that this promise was kept. Rents continued to climb even immediately after the passage of Proposition 13. The turnover rate of rental properties for speculative purposes may have kept the property-tax assessment high even with the benefits of Proposition 13.

10. Ironically, passage of Proposition 13 provided the state with additional income to help fund these services because the deduction for property tax in calculating the state income tax was collectively less. In the same vein, it should be noted, increased federal income-tax revenues were not passed back to local government in California.

11. An example of the loss of local control is in new school construction. School districts with year-round classes receive higher priority in obtaining state aid for new school construction than do districts without year-round classes. Many local school districts strapped for funds but needing additional space feel they are being forced to implement year-round classes.

12. An article in the *Los Angeles Times* reported a California Association of Realtors survey that found that the median price of resale single-family houses in Orange County was the highest in the major metropolitan areas of California.

13. The 1970 federal census tract was used for this study because of the availability of a rich data base, although inferences cannot be made from it about individual voters.

14. Discriminant analysis was used to differentiate between the supporting and nonsupporting census tracts.

298   WILLIAM F. GAYK

15. Each factor has an eigenvalue above 1, the commonly accepted standard of a significant factor.

16. This issue of the relationship between homeownership and social class and social status has been debated in the literature (Dunleavy 1979, Edel 1982, Harloe 1984, Saunders 1978, 1979, 1981).

17. This is not to dismiss the importance of socioeconomic status. However, much literature already explores the relationship between socioeconomic status and political behavior.

18. This is certainly an issue raised by Jarvis. In his 1979 book, *I'm Mad as Hell*, he noted that his motivation for fighting taxes was the tens of thousands of people who were being forced out of their homes because of high property taxes. According to Jarvis, the extreme threat was to one's life. He began the book by relating the story of a middle-aged woman who died in front of him while describing to government officials the prohibitive level of property taxes on her home.

19. Each of these is a paraphrase of a statement made at different public hearings dealing with such topics as affordable housing, highways, jails, airports, and facility location.

REFERENCES

Agnew, John A. 1978. "Market Relations and Locational Conflict in Cross-National Perspective." In *Urbanization and Conflict in Market Societies,* ed. Kevin R. Cox, 128–43. Chicago: Maaroufa Press.

———. 1981. "Homeownership and the Capitalist Social Order." In *Urbanization and Urban Planning in Capitalist Society,* ed. Michael Dear and Allen J. Scott, 457–80. New York: Methuen.

Baldassare, Mark. 1986. *Trouble in Paradise: The Suburban Transformation in America.* New York: Columbia University Press.

Baldassare, Mark, and Cheryl Katz. 1987. *1987 Orange County Annual Survey.* Irvine: Public Policy Research Organization, University of California.

Berger, Bennett M. 1960. *Working-Class Suburb.* Berkeley and Los Angeles: University of California Press.

Bowman, Lewis, Dennis S. Ippolito, and Martin L. Levin. 1972. "Self-Interest and Referendum Support: The Case of Rapid Transit Vote in Atlanta." In *People and Politics in Urban Society,* ed. Harlan Hahn, 119–36. Beverly Hills, Calif.: Sage.

Campbell, Angus, Philip E. Converse, Warren E. Miller, and Donald E. Stokes. 1960. *The American Voter.* New York: Wiley.

Citrin, Jack. 1979. "Do People Want Something for Nothing? Public Opinion on Taxes and Government Spending." *National Tax Journal* 32:113–29.

———. 1982. "California Voting Behavior: The Influence of Information, Self-Interest and Broad Political Trends." Paper presented at conference, Proposition 9 (Jarvis II): Information, Credibility and the California Voter, sponsored by UCLA Extension.

Courant, Paul N., Edward M. Gramlich, and David L. Rubinfeld. 1979. "Why

Voters Support Tax Limitation Amendments: The Michigan Case." *National Tax Journal* 32:1–20.

Cox, Kevin R. 1973. *Conflict, Power and Politics in the City: A Geographic View.* New York: McGraw-Hill.

———. 1978. "Local Interests and Urban Political Processes in Market Societies." In *Urbanization and Conflict in Market Societies,* ed. Kevin R. Cox, 94–108. Chicago: Maaraufa Press.

———. 1981. "Capitalism and Conflict around the Communal Living Space." In *Urbanization and Urban Planning in Capitalist Society,* ed. Michael Dear and Allen J. Scott, 431–55. New York: Methuen.

———. 1982. "Housing Tenure and Neighborhood Activism." *Urban Affairs Quarterly* 18:107–29.

Danielson, Michael N. 1976. *The Politics of Exclusion.* New York: Columbia University Press.

Danzinger, James N., and Peter Smith Ring. 1980. *Recent Research on Fiscal Limitation Measures: A Selective Survey.* Irvine: Public Policy Research Organization, University of California.

DeCanio, Stephen J. 1979. "Proposition 13 and the Failure of Economic Politics." *National Tax Journal* 32:55–66.

Department of Commerce. 1983. *County and City Data Book.* Washington.

Downs, Anthony. 1970. *Urban Problems and Prospects.* Chicago: Rand McNally.

Dunleavy, Patrick. 1979. "The Urban Basis of Political Alignment: Social Class, Domestic Property Ownership, and State Intervention in Consumption Processes." *British Journal of Political Science* 9:409–43.

Edel, Matthew. 1982. "Home Ownership and Working Class Unity." *International Journal of Urban and Regional Research* 16:205–21.

Gans, Herbert. 1967. *The Levittowners: Ways of Life and Politics in a New Suburban Community.* New York: Vintage Books.

Gottdiener, M. 1977. *Planned Sprawl: Private and Public Interests in Suburbia.* Beverly Hills, Calif.: Sage.

———. 1985. *The Social Production of Urban Space.* Austin: University of Texas Press.

———. 1987. *The Decline of Urban Politics.* Beverly Hills, Calif.: Sage.

Gottdiener, M., and Max Nieman. 1981. "Characteristics of Support for Local Growth Control." *Urban Affairs Quarterly* 117:55–73.

Guest, Avery M., and George H. Nelson. 1978. "Central City/Suburban Differences: Fifty Years of Change." *Sociological Quarterly* 19:7–23.

Hahn, Harlan. 1968. "Northern Referenda on Fair Housing: The Response of White Voters." *Western Political Quarterly* 21:483–95.

———. 1970. "Ethos and Social Class: Referenda in Canadian Cities." *Polity* 1:295–315.

Harloe, Michael. 1984. "Sector and Class: A Critical Comment." *International Journal of Urban and Regional Research* 8:228–37.

Hegedus, Jozsef, and Ivan Tosics. 1983. "Housing Classes and Housing Policy: Some Changes in the Budapest Housing Market." *International Journal of Urban and Regional Research* 7:467–94.

Jarvis, Howard. 1979. *I'm Mad as Hell.* New York: Times Books.

Kasarda, John D. 1983. "Urbanization, Community, and the Metropolitan Problem." In *Cities and Urban Living,* ed. Mark Baldassare, 43–69. New York: Columbia University Press.

Levy, Frank. 1979. "Understanding Proposition 13." *Public Interest* 56:66–89.

Levy, Mickey. 1975. "Voting on California's Tax and Expenditure Initiative." *National Tax Journal* 28:426–35.

Lipset, Seymour Martin, and Earl Raab. 1978. "The Message of Proposition 13." *Commentary* 66:42–46.

Lowery, David, and Lee Sigelman. 1981. "Understanding the Tax Revolt: Eight Explanations." *American Political Science Review* 75:963–74.

Musgrave, Richard A. 1979. "The Tax Revolt: Causes and Cures." *Social Science Quarterly* 59:697–703.

Nieman, Max. 1980. "Zoning Policy, Income Clustering and Suburban Change." *Social Science Quarterly* 61:666–75.

Rex, John A. 1968. "The Sociology of a Zone of Transition." In *Readings in Urban Sociology,* ed. R. E. Pahl, 211–31. Oxford: Pergamon Press.

Rex, John A., and Robert Moore. 1967. *Race, Community, and Conflict.* London: Oxford University Press.

Saunders, Peter. 1978. "Domestic Property and Social Class." *International Journal of Urban and Regional Research* 2:233–51.

———. 1979. *Urban Politics.* London: Hutchinson.

———. 1981. *Social Theory and the Urban Question.* London: Hutchinson.

———. 1982. "Beyond Housing Classes: The Sociological Significance of Private Property Rights in Means of Consumption." *International Journal of Urban and Regional Research* 8:202–27.

Schnore, Leo F. 1957. "The Socioeconomic Status of Cities and Suburbs." *American Sociological Review* 28:76–85.

Sears, David O., and Jack Citrin. 1985. *Tax Revolt.* Cambridge, Mass.: Harvard University Press.

Shlay, Anne B., and Peter H. Rossi. 1981. "Keeping Up the Neighborhood." *American Sociological Review* 46:703–19.

Thorns, David C. 1981. "The Implication of Differential Rates of Capital Gain from Owner Occupation for the Formation and Development of Housing Classes." *International Journal of Urban and Regional Research* 5:205–16.

Walter, Benjamin, and Frederick M. Wirt. 1972. "Social and Political Dimensions of American Suburbs." In *City Classification Handbook: Methods and Applications,* ed. Brian J. L. Berry, 97–123. New York: Wiley.

Weber, Max. 1946. "Class, Status, Party." In *From Max Weber: Essays in Sociology,* ed. H. H. Gerth and C. Wright Mills, 180–95. New York: Oxford University Press.

Wirt, Frederick M., Benjamin Walter, Francine F. Rabinovitz, and Deborah R. Hensler. 1972. *On the City's Rim: Politics and Policy in Suburbia.* Lexington, Mass.: Heath.

Wolfe, Alan. 1979. "2 Views on Proposition 13—Defense of the State." *Social Policy* 10:16–18.

Wood, Robert C. 1958. *Suburbia: Its People and Their Politics.* Boston: Houghton.

CONTRIBUTORS

William F. Gayk is the county demographer of Orange County and an instructor with the Graduate Center for Public Policy and Administration at California State University, Long Beach. He received his Ph.D. from the University of California, Riverside, and in his dissertation analyzed voting patterns for Propositions 4, 9, and 13. He has coauthored articles on political sociology that have appeared in such journals as the *Western Political Quarterly* and the *Pacific Sociological Review* and is currently serving on the advisory board for the *Journal of Orange County Studies* and the research advisory committee of the Orange County Annual Survey.

M. Gottdiener is professor of sociology and chair of the urban studies program at the University of California, Riverside. He is the author or editor of six books, including *The Social Production of Urban Space* (1985), *The City and the Sign: An Introduction to Urban Semiotics* (1986), and *The Decline of Urban Politics: Political Theory and the Crisis of the Local State* (1987). His main research interests are in theories of social organization, urban public policy, urban theory, and semiotics.

Lisbeth Haas is assistant professor of history at the University of California, Santa Cruz. Her work includes a published master's thesis on the bracero program in Orange County and an unpublished dissertation, "The Barrios of Santa Ana: Community, Class, and Urbanization, 1850–1946." She is writing a book concerning class, race, and gender relationships in Orange County from the Spanish colonial period to 1940.

Debra Gold Hansen has a Ph.D. in history from the University of California, Irvine, with a specialty in American women's history. From 1981 to 1987 she served as the associate editor of the *Oral History Review* and is currently adjunct professor of library and information science at San Jose State University.

George Kephart completed his Ph.D. in sociology and demographics at the University of Wisconsin, Madison, and is assistant professor of sociology at Pennsylvania State University. He has published in *Demography* and is writing a book on the relationship between spatial and economic changes in the United States.

Rob Kling holds professorial appointments in the Program in Information and Computer Science, the Graduate School of Management, and the Public Policy Research Organization at the University of California, Irvine. Since the early 1970s, he has studied the social opportunities and dilemmas that computerization presents for managers, professionals, workers, and the public. His research has been reported in more than sixty journal articles and book chapters, as well as in such coauthored and coedited books as *Computers and Politics: High Technology in American Local Governments* (1982) and *Computerization and Controversy: Value Conflicts and Social Choice* (1991).

Spencer Olin is professor of history at the University of California, Irvine, specializing in modern American and California history. The author or editor of four books—*California's Prodigal Sons: Hiram Johnson and the Progressives, 1911–1917* (1968); *Racism in California: A Reader in the History of Oppression* (1972) with Roger Daniels; *Why War? Ideology, Theory, and History* (1980) with Keith Nelson; and *California Politics: The Emerging Corporate State* (1981)—he is also coeditor of the *Journal of Orange County Studies.*

Mark Poster is professor of history at the University of California, Irvine, where he teaches and writes in the areas of European intellectual history and critical theory. He is the author of numerous books and articles, including *Existential Marxism in Postwar France* (1976), *Critical Theory of the Family* (1978), *Foucault, Marxism & History* (1985), *Critical Theory and Post-structuralism* (1989), and *The Mode of Information* (1990).

Mary P. Ryan is professor of history and women's studies at the University of California, Berkeley. Her publications include *Cradle of the Middle Class: The Family in Oneida County, New York, 1790 to 1865* (1981) and, most recently, *Women in Public: Between Banners and Ballots, 1825 to 1880* (1990).

Martin J. Schiesl is professor of history at California State University, Los Angeles. His specialties are American urban history and the historical development of Los Angeles and California. The author of *The Politics of Efficiency: Municipal Administration and Reform in America, 1880–1920*

(1977), he has also written a chapter on Los Angeles politics and government in the early twentieth century for *The Age of Urban Reform: New Perspectives on the Progressive Era* (1977), edited by Michael Ebner and Eugene Tobin. In addition, he has contributed a chapter on the defense industry in Los Angeles from 1945 to 1960 to *The Martial Metropolis: U.S. Cities in War and Peace* (1984), edited by Roger Lotchin. He has coedited with Norman M. Klein a volume of original essays on cultural and social developments in Los Angeles since 1900; the book is entitled *20th Century Los Angeles: Power, Promotion, and Social Conflict* (1990).

Clark Turner is a practicing attorney who holds an M.A. in mathematics and is pursuing his Ph.D. in information and computer science at the University of California, Irvine. He is interested in the social impacts of advanced computer technology.

Alladi Venkatesh is a member of the faculty at the Graduate School of Management, University of California, Irvine. He has a law degree from the University of Madras, India, and a Ph.D. in management from Syracuse University. His research interests include the study of macro consumption phenomena, the social impacts of information technologies, and the changing household structure and its impact on work and home life. His publications have appeared in *Telecommunications Policy*, the *Journal of Economic Psychology*, the *Journal of Consumer Research*, and the *Journal of Macromarketing*.

INDEX OF NAMES AND PLACES

Compositor: Keystone Typesetting, Inc.
Text: 10/12 Baskerville
Display: Baskerville
Printer: Edwards Brothers, Inc.
Binder: Edwards Brothers, Inc.